1. The principle of quantificational equivalence (QE):

   (a) $\sim(x)Fx \equiv (\exists x)\sim Fx$

   (b) $\sim(\exists x)Fx \equiv (x)\sim Fx$

   (c) $[(x)Fx \cdot (x)Gx] \equiv (x)(Fx \cdot Gx)$

   (d) $[(\exists x)Fx \lor (\exists x)Gx] \equiv (\exists x)(Fx \lor Gx)$

2. The principles of instantiation and of generalization:

   (a) Universal instantiation (UI):

   (b) Ex

      Th

   (c) Ex

      Th   r by a form

      de

   (d) Ur

      Th   El and the *u*

      in   or *reductio*)

      pr

3. Princip

   (a) [($Fx \lor P)$

   (b) [($\supset Fx)$

   (c) [$P \supset Fx)$

                              variable or

                              $y)$ or $(\exists y)$

4. Quan   ases of dis-

   juncti

   (a)

   (b)

   (c)

An Introductory Logic

An Introductory Logic

WILLIAM J. KILGORE
Baylor University

HOLT, RINEHART AND WINSTON, INC.
New York   Chicago   San Francisco   Atlanta   Dallas
Montreal   Toronto   London

To Mr. and Mrs. J. Newton Rayzor

Copyright © 1968 by Holt, Rinehart and Winston, Inc.
All rights reserved
Library of Congress Catalog Card Number: 68-30722

2713758

Printed in the United States of America

1   2   3   4   5   6   7   8   9

Preface

The general purpose of this book is to set forth in an elementary way principles and procedures essential for sound reasoning. The work is designed for individuals interested in studying the basic principles of logic. It is specifically intended for use as an undergraduate text in that the difficulties of students in learning deductive logic have been kept in view.

The text does not presuppose any previous study of logic, and it is designed to meet the interests of students who will not have additional courses in logic. It is basically sound in regard to the logical procedures set forth so that with a minimum of adaptation, primarily in the section on quantificational logic, the student will be able to progress to more advanced treatments of the subject.

In presenting this subject over a period of twenty years to more than fifty classes, I have formed several conclusions about teaching this material. Flexibility and adaptability of the material of the course are highly desirable. Different teachers as well as the same teacher with different classes will vary the order of presentation, and some classes learn the material more quickly than others. If attention is given only to students who are able to grasp deductive logic readily, the others can become confused. Progress in the study of deductive logic appears to occur more by large jumps than by constant small gradations; it is more like climbing stairs than like walking up an inclining ramp. A careful review of the text after classroom discussion can strengthen the student's understanding of the material. Occasional coaching sessions can also be quite useful. The amount of material a teacher of introductory logic might prefer to cover is usually greater than the amount he actually can cover if his teaching is thorough. I have made an effort to relate these conclusions to the manner of presentation of material in this work.

Some discussions, particularly in the deductive sections, are more detailed than certain students may need, but these students will find sufficient challenge in the terminal chapters in deductive logic, where a degree of rigor is approached that is usually found in more formalistic treatments of the subject.

The flexibility and adaptability of the material is evident in the different ways in which a course can be organized. In a comprehensive one-semester course with about 50 class hours, 10 hours can be spent on the first section, 12 hours on the third section, and 28 hours on the second section. If cross references are occasionally used, many different orders of presentation are possible. The first, third, or portions of the second section can be omitted. If a more rigorous approach is followed, Chapters 12 and 13 can be omitted, and Chapters 7, 8, 9, and 10 can be omitted, or studied in part after the section on quantificational logic has been begun. If a more relaxed approach is desired, then Chapters 14 and 15 and portions of 13 can be omitted. It is possible to present traditional logic, including analysis of arguments using compound statements, without symbolic logic. On the other hand, an introductory course directed primarily toward symbolic logic in the deductive section can be taught with only an occasional reference to the chapters on traditional logic.

There is more material here than can reasonably be taught in a 3-hour, one-semester course. If the complete chapter on quantificational logic is taught, then several other chapters will have to be omitted or assigned for supplementary reading.

All standard subject areas for introductory classes are included in the text, and a number of topics are treated at greater length than is usual in elementary texts. These include distinctions in linguistic expressions (such as mention and use of words, general and proper names), relational terms, sorites, the use of compound statements in arguments with an optional form of proof for extended arguments before studying the truth table, the degree of development of quantificational logic, and statistical generalizations. The final chapter, "Controverting Objectionable Arguments," can serve as a summary and review of some of the material presented.

This book is primarily a pedagogical instrument for the teaching of logic. There may be some innovations, but the book is not designed as an original, creative contribution to the subject matter.

I have attempted to relate logic to ordinary situations. Although I do not use a formalistic approach, I do not take issue with those who prefer a highly formalistic and more rigorous course in elementary logic. I have tried to show the relevance of logical analysis to situations encountered in everyday experiences and in research and to point to the dependence of such analysis upon a rigorous development of logical theory.

I am particularly indebted to former colleagues and teachers whose discussion of some of these topics have contributed to my own understanding of logic. Included among these are Professor David L. Miller of The University of Texas, Dean Leonard A. Duce of Trinity University, Professor A. C. Benjamin (retired) of the University of Missouri, Professor Haywood R. Shuford of the University of Houston, and my present colleagues, Professors William G. Toland, Elmer H. Duncan, William F. Cooper, and Robert M. Baird. Professor Cooper has used portions of the manuscript in class and has made helpful suggestions for its improvement. I also am indebted to my students, who have made suggestions regarding the content and clarity of the manuscript as they have used the material in class. My sister-in-law, Mrs. Carol Isensee Kilgore, read the manuscript and made helpful suggestions.

My colleague, Professor Robert G. Packard of the Department of Physics, has made valuable suggestions regarding illustrative material found in the section on inquiry in the sciences. Professor Glenn Capp has made helpful suggestions regarding the chapter on "Controverting Objectionable Arguments." Editor-in-Chief Harry Provence of Newspapers Inc. and the Waco Tribune-Herald has been most helpful in sending me copies of printed materials circulated by various interest groups. Some of this material has been adapted for use in the exercises.

I am indebted to Mr. and Mrs. J. Newton Rayzor whose financial and moral support of the Philosophy Department of Baylor University has assisted in making possible the preparation of this manuscript.

I also wish to express appreciation to the publishers for their editorial assistance and to their reviewers, whose valuable suggestions have improved the manuscript. Like other writers of logic texts, I am highly indebted to the contributions others have made in the classical and current literature.

I want to thank the student assistants who assisted in typing the manuscript and to acknowledge the continuing support and encouragement of my wife in the preparation of the manuscript.

Appreciation is also expressed to the editors of *New Scientist* and *Editor and Publisher* for permission to quote material from their publications.

Any errors in the content of this material are my own responsibility and are not to be attributed to the many people who have made suggestions regarding the content of this work.

WILLIAM J. KILGORE

June 15, 1968

Contents

Part III   Logic and Scientific Inquiry

An Introductory Logic

Part I
Logic and
Language

Chapter 1
Introduction

1.1 Logic as the Analysis and Development of the Structure of Reliable Inference

Logic is both a rigorous discipline and an art. As a rigorous discipline it analyzes and develops the structure of reliable inference. As an art it brings order and rationality to inferences or judgments drawn from evidence accepted as trustworthy. As a rigorous discipline logic justifies the forms of valid inference. As an art it uses these forms to draw conclusions relevant to specific beliefs, ideas, and claims of knowledge.

The technical use of the term *logic* is far more restricted than the popular use. In ordinary language one may refer to a "logical plan," a "logical step," a "logical idea," or a "logical person" in contrast to "a poorly conceived plan," "a rash step," an "inadequately supported idea," or "an irrational person." In such uses *logical* means roughly "rational," "well supported," "satisfactorily thought through," or "reasonable."

In a technical sense *logic* means a critical analysis and development of the structure of reliable inference. Conclusions are claimed to follow from propositions by virtue of their meaning and interrelationship. Consider the relation between the following propositions:

> If LSD is taken, the chromosomes of the white blood cells are damaged.
> LSD is taken.

The meanings and the interrelation of these propositions logically justify the inference:

3

Therefore, the chromosomes of the white blood cells are damaged.

The facts of a situation are not the strict object of the logician's inquiry. The facts are determinable by types of inquiry appropriate to the subject matter. Mascara may not be as dangerous as LSD, but it is the medical researcher and not the logician who determines such facts. However, the meaning of the proposition, "If women wearing evening clothes use mascara, they are more attractive," allows the logician to derive justifiable inferences from it. Affirmation of the original proposition and of the statement, "Women wearing evening clothes use mascara," justifies the conclusion, "They are more attractive." The logician in this case is concerned with the statements' *structure*. Given the form in which the propositions are stated, the truth of the original statements requires the truth of the conclusion.

The logician, then, is not the arbiter of facts but of the form in which inferences are made. He is crucially concerned with whether the interrelatedness of propositions presented as evidence has a structure that permits a valid conclusion to follow.

It is a mistake to regard logic merely as the analysis of reasoning. The physiological processes in reasoning are not the logician's concern, nor does he seek to analyze the social or psychological conditions underlying various points of view. If an adult expresses fears of an attack by foreign powers, the development of his anxieties may be analyzed by specialists such as anthropologists, sociologists, and psychologists—but not by logicians. The logician is concerned, not with a social or psychological study of how beliefs come to be accepted in a social group or how ideas are transmitted in a community, but with the structure by which propositions (that is, beliefs or ideas) are related and with the inferences that are rationally justifiable on the basis of this structure.

Although the logician is not concerned technically with insight into the character, social background, or economic interest of persons who make statements, such considerations nonetheless may help explain personal choices of evidence and preferences in conclusions. The emphasis on the structure of arguments in logic is not intended to minimize the significance of their content, but to point to the technical area with which logic is concerned. The rigorous examination of personal views includes, but is not limited to, the material developed in the study of logic.

The study of logic is concerned with the identification and use of structures of reliable reasoning. Sound reasoning uses valid logical procedures to advance arguments based upon reliable evidence. In a valid argument the evidence always is sufficient to justify the conclusion derived from it. In an invalid argument or logical fallacy, the structure of the evidence is insufficient to justify the conclusion.

An *argument* in logic is a set of propositions, in which a *conclusion* is inferred, or is claimed to be inferred, on the basis of evidence offered as *premises*. Consider the following three propositions:

EVIDENCE:

If the first phase of the Cosmos testing program is over, the Soviets have developed elements of space vehicle design. The first phase of the Cosmos testing program is over.

CONCLUSION:

Therefore, the Soviets have developed elements of space vehicle design.

The conclusion is inferred from the meaning and interrelation of the propositions (premises) offered as evidence. The structure of the argument is valid; any argument having this structure also would be valid. In this structure, whenever the premises are true, the conclusion also is true.

1.2 Traditional Divisions of Logic

The traditional approach to elementary logic takes into account three major areas of study: (1) an elementary logical analysis of language, (2) deductive logic, and (3) the logic of scientific inquiry. The *logical analysis of language* is concerned with the meaning and use of symbols. *Deductive logic* is an analysis and development of procedures of necessary inference. The *logic of scientific inquiry* analyzes and develops the structure of probable inference.

Semiotics is the logical analysis of the interrelation, meaning, and use of symbols. Semiotics traditionally is divided into syntactics, semantics, and pragmatics. *Syntactics* analyzes the manner in which words or symbols can express meaning by their relation to each other. *Semantics* in its narrow sense is the analysis of the meaning of symbols or of the relation of symbols to their referents in an expression. *Pragmatics* analyzes the application or the use of words or symbols to achieve some form of communication or response. Consider the expression:

The orbit of the satellite ranged from 109 miles to 572 miles from the Earth.

Syntactics analyzes the manner in which different symbols, such as "orbit," "satellite," "ranged," and "from," are related to each other to express some meaning. Semantics in its restricted sense analyzes the manner in which the symbols taken in such a context refer to some object or signify some state of affairs. Pragmatics analyzes the manner in which such symbols function in a practical manner to achieve some task or purpose in a linguistic context.

Deductive logic analyzes the structure of necessary inference. Consider the following Aristotelian syllogism:

All circadian rhythm patterns are established in early life.

Temperature, heart rate, and blood pressure are circadian rhythm patterns.

Therefore, temperature, heart rate, and blood pressure are established in early life.

The structure and relation of the propositions stating the evidence justify logically the inference stated in the conclusion. Given the meaning of the language in this context and the logical structure relating these propositions, the conclusion cannot be false if the evidence presented in the premises is true.

Deductive logic determines the structure of valid argument forms. A *valid* argument form yields a true conclusion whenever the premises are true; its validity depends on its form or structure. A *sound* argument requires both a valid argument form and true premises. The argument may be valid, but it cannot be sound, if any premise is false. To assert that an argument is valid is to point out that *if* the premises are true, *then* the conclusion is necessarily true. The truth of propositions offered as premises is not determined by deductive logic.

The logic of scientific inquiry analyzes and develops procedures for appraising the reliability of propositions related to experience or experimentation. Consider the statements:

> Sharks have sense organs known as Lorenzini's ampullae, which are identifiable by deep pores in the skin found near the snout.

> LAW III: Reaction is always equal and opposite to action; that is to say, the actions of two bodies upon each other are always equal and directly opposite. (Newton)

Inquiry following careful procedures appropriate to the subject can determine the evidence available to support such statements. The logic of scientific inquiry is particularly directed to the justification of explanatory hypotheses, and it seeks to justify probable inferences based upon experience and experimentation.

The distinction between semiotics, deductive logic, and the logic of scientific inquiry is analytically useful. In practical problems of inference the principles of each are usually relevant in evaluating different parts of the argument. The major parts of this text are divided among these areas of logic. The remainder of Part I develops elementary notions in the analysis of language and of informal fallacies. Part II analyzes the elementary structure of deductive reasoning. Part III analyzes basic procedures in the logic of scientific inquiry.

1.3 EXERCISES

1. Propose eight or ten sentences in ordinary discourse using the term *logic* or *logical*. Analyze the meaning of the term in each use. Are any of these uses equivalent to the meaning given to *logic* in this text?

2. Write several arguments that have the same structure as the valid arguments referred to in this chapter.

3. Does irrelevance of the character of the person advancing an argument prejudice the logician's analysis?

4. State two arguments and indicate parts relevant to syntactics, semantics, and pragmatics.

The following problems are adapted from traditional problems in reasoning.

5. A bucket is placed under a leak. The amount of water in the bucket doubles each hour. In twelve hours the bucket is full. How long does it require for the bucket to be half full of water?

6. Three men who are either lawyers or crooks meet on the street. The lawyers tell only the truth. The crooks tell only lies. The first man identifies himself to the second and the second tells the third that the first man said he was a lawyer. The third replies that the first man was not a lawyer but a crook. How many lawyers are there in the group?

7. A mother is on a picnic with three children. She has 30 ounces of punch in one jar, and she has three empty jars that hold 16 ounces, 14 ounces, and 4 ounces. How can she divide the punch equally for the children?

8. Smith, Brown, and Jones have numerals placed on their backs. Each is unable to see his own number. Smith and Brown are permitted to see the numbers the others are wearing, but Jones is not. They are told that at least two of the numbers are even. The person who first determines whether he has an odd or an even number and shows how he knows he is correct wins an expense-paid trip to the World Series. Smith and Brown say they cannot make such a determination but Jones says he can. Is Jones wearing an odd or an even number, and how does he know?

9. Three couples are skiing. There is only one lift, which carries only two persons. It is agreed that until all persons are at the top of the hill, at least one person must always ride in the ski lift. The men distrust each other and insist that no man can ride on the lift or be left at the base or the top of the hill with a girl that is not accompanied by her date. How can everyone get to the top of the lift in these circumstances?

10. An airline company flies a plane nonstop each hour from Rome to New York. Exactly eight hours are required from the time the plane leaves the terminal until it stops at the terminal of destination. How many planes of this company on this nonstop New York to Rome flight will a given pilot meet while he is making the flight?

11. Ann, Betty, Carol, and Dorothy are married to Frank, Earl, George, and Henry, but not necessarily in that order. George's sister-in-law has a new car, which she bought from Frank. Carol and her husband visit frequently with Earl and his wife. Ann is the only sister of Earl's wife. Henry is married to the sister of Earl's wife. Betty and George do not have any brothers or sisters. Who is Betty's husband?

12. Herbert, John, Kelly, Louis, and Marty are in the following professions but not necessarily in this order: physician, engineer, attorney, architect, and dentist. The engineer is a bachelor and he plays golf with Kelly. Louis is 5 feet 6 inches tall; he is shorter than Kelly and 6 inches shorter than Herbert. Herbert is taller than John but shorter than Marty. John is 3 inches taller than Kelly. The physician is the tallest member of the group; his nearest neighbor is the shortest of the group. Herbert's wife is a social worker. John swims frequently in Herbert's pool. The nearest neighbor of the physician is an attorney. The architect does not have a swimming pool. Who is the architect?

Chapter 2
Language Uses
and Disputes

2.1 Linguistic Analysis and Arguments

Logic appraises the validity of arguments by examining the correctness of their form. Correct form, in turn, requires correct, clear, and precise use of language.

Improper use of language in arguments becomes a source of erroneous inference. Consider the following example:

> Violation of equal justice for all citizens is contrary to our Constitution.
>
> Inequality of educational opportunities is a violation of equal justice for all citizens.
>
> Therefore, inequality of educational opportunities is contrary to our Constitution.

The words used in this argument require clarification and analysis. In one premise "justice" has only a legalistic meaning; in another it includes a non-legalistic sense. Likewise, "equal" has different meanings in these statements. In a legal sense "equal" refers to certain constitutional rights a citizen enjoys. He has redress in courts of law if he can establish that such rights have been violated. In a social sense "equal" can refer to comparable ability or opportunity to achieve certain tasks. No one affirms comparable abilities of persons in this sense. The members of a class in logic do not have equal abilities in mastering the basic techniques of logic, and in such a context they do not have equal opportunities to make the same grade in the class. "Inequality of educational opportunities" likewise is vague. If "inequality of educational opportunities" is based on discrimination in public institutions on considerations of national origin, race, or religion, there would be an obvious juridical ground for disapproval. If "inequality of educational opportunities" is based on greater intellectual stimulation in the homes of some students, then charges of violation of constitutional rights would be legally irrelevant.

Any satisfactory appraisal of an argument must make explicit what is being asserted by the argument. If the meanings of the words shift from one premise to another, then the argument fails to conform to minimum standards of clarity.

Clarity and precision of language in arguments is developed by an analysis of linguistic uses. The logician seeks to identify the principles of clear and precise meaning that apply in every linguistic community.

2.2 Disagreements and Verbal Disputes

Man is born into a linguistic community. He learns to adapt himself, to confront new problems, and to share experiences by the use of language. Language helps to solve some problems and becomes an obstacle to the solution of others.

Language plays a significant role in disagreements. Not only is it the means of expressing differences regarding the facts of a case, attitudes related to a situation, and interpretations regarding the future significance of a state of affairs, but it frequently becomes the source of a dispute.

Clarification of disputes requires a proper analysis of the factors involved. Consider the following case. Bill and Tom are discussing the decision to escalate the war in Vietnam in 1965. Bill remarks that this decision was entirely unjustified. Tom replies, "But there are many justifications for the escalation." This disagreement may concern differences in their beliefs about the *facts* leading to the conflict. Tom points out that the United States' pledge to SEATO includes a commitment to defend any allied nation if it is attacked. Bill states that the conditions were those of a civil war and that the United States government had no right to intervene. Tom insists that a steady infiltration of troops and supplies by one country into a neighboring country is an act of aggression and must be resisted. At this point a lengthy *verbal* dispute could arise about the meaning of the term "civil war."

Besides disagreeing about facts and about words, the disputants may differ in *feelings* and *attitudes*. Bill can be saying, "I am opposed to war under any conditions; no justification for escalating any war is rational." Tom can be saying, "War is an unfortunate consequence of modern relationships between states; under certain conditions participation in a limited war may be the only way to avoid war on a much broader scale."

They also could be disagreeing on the *significance* of the escalation of the war in Vietnam in 1965. Bill could be saying, "We have been trapped into tying down military personnel and resources in a cause that is bound to be lost unless we are willing to take over the political government of South Vietnam. The latter course overrules democratic processes and it becomes an act of outright imperialism." Tom could reply, "But the alternatives to the escalation of the war are infinitely worse for democratic institutions. We were confronted with the choice of supporting an ally or of abandoning him when the situation got rough. It was necessary to escalate the war to assure allies in Southeast Asia that we would resist Communistic aggression wherever it occurs. It prevents a domino technique of governments' being victimized by Communistic infiltration and taken over one by one."

In such a discussion, disputants could be differing in at least four different ways: about (1) facts, (2) the meaning of words, (3) attitudes, and (4) significance. Sixteen possible variations of agreement and disagreement are illustrated in Table 2.1.

Table 2.1

Facts	Words	Attitudes	Significance
Agree	Agree	Agree	Agree
Agree	Agree	Agree	Disagree
Agree	Agree	Disagree	Agree
Agree	Agree	Disagree	Disagree
Agree	Disagree	Agree	Agree
Agree	Disagree	Agree	Disagree
Agree	Disagree	Disagree	Agree
Agree	Disagree	Disagree	Disagree
Disagree	Agree	Agree	Agree
Disagree	Agree	Agree	Disagree
Disagree	Agree	Disagree	Agree
Disagree	Agree	Disagree	Disagree
Disagree	Disagree	Agree	Agree
Disagree	Disagree	Agree	Disagree
Disagree	Disagree	Disagree	Agree
Disagree	Disagree	Disagree	Disagree

The first row in the table indicates that the participants agree on the facts relevant to the argument, on the meaning of the words used in the argument, on attitudes reflected in the discussion, and on the significance of the matter discussed. The sixth row indicates that the participants agree about the relevant facts and in their attitudes, but they disagree on words used in the discussion (such as "civil war") and on the significance of the matter discussed (such as the effect of the escalation on the leadership role of the United States in its efforts for world peace). The eleventh row indicates an agreement on the words used in the argument and the significance of the escalation but a disagreement about the facts of the case (such as the degree of participation of the Vietnamese in the conflict) and in attitudes about the escalation (such as approval and disapproval).

This table may obscure other significant features of disputes. Differences about what constitutes the relevant facts of the situation may be limited or they may be wide. Several verbal disputes may be involved. Attitudes may range from deploring any military involvement to supporting an "all-out effort." Judgments of the significance of the escalation may range from the position that the consequences would be totally disastrous to the view that the escalation was the only tenable alternative, given the conditions at the time.

Another instance of a verbal dispute might arise as two students discuss the value of the study of logic. "A syllogism," according to James, "does not really provide you with any information you do not already have." Frank disagrees: "But it most certainly does." The key words in this dispute are "does not provide you with information you do not already have." James argues that the conclusion is implicit in some sense in the premises of a syllogism and that the conclusion does not provide any additional information. Frank recognizes that although the conclusion may have been implicit in the premises, it may not have been explicitly known. Furthermore, he holds that additional knowledge is gained by showing that a sound argument supports the conclusion.

Disputes in need of linguistic clarification and precision are a particular concern of the logician. In clarifying a verbal dispute, we can take the following steps:

1. Identify the specific words giving occasion for the dispute.

2. Restate the meanings of key words in the dispute in order to make explicit the interpretations given to them.

3. Apply restated meanings of key words to the original statements.

4. Render a decision on the basis of each explicit interpretation of the statement in question.

Consider, for example, the following discussion. George bets John a dollar that John cannot throw a rock across the river. John throws a flat-surfaced rock, which skips across the top of the water to the far bank. John declares himself winner. George claims that the rock was not thrown across the river but was skipped across. Who won the bet?

Let us clarify this verbal dispute by using the procedure recommended above.

1. Identify the key words in the dispute. The key words are "throw across."

2. Restate different meanings of key words.
    (a) "To throw across" means to cast a rock so that its first point of impact is the far bank of the river.
    (b) "To throw across" means to cast the rock so that it comes to

  rest on the far bank of the river on any one throw regardless of the manner in which it is accomplished.

3. Apply restated meanings of the key words in the context.

  (a) John cast a rock so that its first point of impact was on the far side of the river.

  (b) John cast the rock so that it came to rest on the far bank of the river on one throw with the rock skipping across the surface of the water.

4. Rendering a decision with regard to each restatement of the key words.

  (a) With the first meaning John did not throw the rock across the river.

  (b) With the second meaning John did throw the rock across the river.

This clarification does not determine who won the bet. It does focus attention on the need for clarification of language and on the possibility of disputes arising even though factual differences may not be present.

2.3 EXERCISES

1. Analyze the following examples to determine the different kinds of disputes that may be involved. In cases of verbal disputes propose a clarification according to the rules recommended.

(a) William James related an incident about a hunting trip. One hunter saw a squirrel dart behind a tree. As he walked to different positions about the tree the squirrel kept the tree between himself and the hunter. Later the hunter remarked that if he had been able to walk around the squirrel, he could have shot him. A companion argued that the hunter did walk around the squirrel, since he walked around the tree into which the squirrel had climbed. Did the hunter walk around the squirrel?

(b) Mary borrows Carol's logic book. She promises to return it to Carol's room before ten o'clock that evening. At ten-thirty Carol phones Mary and wants to know where her logic book is. Mary says, "But I returned it to your room at nine-thirty and put it on the dresser." Carol replies, "But it is not on the dresser now, and if you had returned the book, it would be there."

(c) Two newspapers, the *Houston Chronicle* and the *Houston Post,* entered into an agreement with the Houston Typographical Union No. 87 that local advertising would be reproduced by the members of the union in the composing rooms of the newspapers. National advertisements could be used without local reproduction. In a court case the newspapers claimed that advertising with the newspapers through local firms might constitute national advertising if the kind of advertising featured was on a national basis. The representatives of the union claimed that national advertising needed to be placed nationally by the advertisers and this was to be done either directly or through an agency.[1] To what extent was this dispute verbal?

---

[1] Source: *Editor & Publisher,* March 12, 1966, p. 18.

(d) Jones: "This is an unbearably hot summer." Smith: "The temperature is about normal for summers in this part of the country."

(e) White: "We are confronted with the possibility of the destruction of human life by nuclear explosions and fallout." Brown: "The probability of mass attacks by nuclear weapons is decreasing with the growing realization that their use would involve also the destruction of the populations of the countries who use them."

(f) Carl: "The Middle East crisis has provided a basis for a more durable peace in that area." David: "The Middle East crisis has sown the seeds for future armed conflicts."

(g) Jim: "The financial deals of congressmen, as exposed through investigations, destroy the confidence of the public in Congress." Tom: "There is nothing new in the kinds of financial deals made by members of Congress. We have survived public scandals in the past and we shall continue to do so."

(h) Mary: "The television industry provides the kinds of programs in which the majority of the viewing public are interested." Nan: "The television industry provides the kinds of programs that will assure their producers of the greatest profit in the long run."

(i) Susan: "We are having a delicious lunch but it will result in our gaining weight." Harry: "We are having a nourishing lunch that will provide the food value we need to compete in strenuous athletic contests."

2. Propose some statements in which the meaning of key words or phrases is in need of clarification. Show how shifts of the meaning of these words may affect an argument.

3. Propose some contrasting statements that illustrate different types of disagreement.

4. State two examples of verbal disagreement, and clarify each dispute by following the steps suggested in the text.

2.4 Emotive and Neutral Words

In ordinary discourse some words have essentially an emotive meaning and others essentially a neutral meaning. Persuasive discourse frequently uses emotive words. Consider the following examples:

> Smith is progressive in his political activities.

> Smith is a dangerous radical in his blundering political deals.

> Jones is restrained and conservative in his activities.

> Jones is a narrow reactionary in his fumbling political shenanigans.

The first and third statements consist of words that are essentially neutral in character, although "progressive" and "conservative" may have emotive connotations in some contexts. The second and fourth statements contain obvious emotive expressions. Such expressions are designed to express the attitude and feelings of the speaker and to influence or condition the attitudes and feelings of the hearer.

The essential difference between an emotive word and a neutral word is the appeal of the emotive word to feelings of approval or disapproval and the appeal of the neutral word to the rational recognition of content. Some emotive words, particularly profane ones, are strongly expressive of feelings; others express feelings with greater restraint. Likewise, some words that are essentially neutral in character may have emotive overtones in certain contexts. Some words that are emotive are *starry-eyed, bigoted, rascal, pigheaded, true-blooded, scalawags,* and *hokum.* Some words that are neutral are *book, ocean, microscope, atom, germ theory,* and *oxygen.* Words that may be emotive in some contexts but essentially neutral in others are *liberal, conservative, right, left, politician, utopian,* and *cynical.*

The use of emotive words to influence the attitudes, feelings, and actions of an informed audience frequently is more successful if it is done in a subtle or sophisticated manner. An enlightened audience may respond negatively to a speaker if he calls his opposition a liar. However, if he claims his opposition has stretched and misrepresented the truth, his view might find acceptance more readily.

The appeal to emotion through colorful uses of language, such as may occur in good rhetoric or poetry, does not justify a rejection of the advocated views. Such views must be appraised in the light of supporting evidence. If they stand up to critical examination, the appropriateness of the mode of expression should be appraised by literary standards rather than merely by a logician's concern with neutral language. The language of discourse would be impoverished greatly if emotive words were eliminated.

The logician, however, is concerned essentially with neutral words. If emotive words are used in an argument, we need to reduce them to a neutral content to analyze properly the structure of the argument. Emotive words tend to introduce vagueness and ambiguities into an argument, and in many contexts they serve to distract attention from the content of the argument and to condition an audience to accept a conclusion on the basis of insufficient evidence.

2.5 The Uses of Language

Appraisals of language require an analysis of the function of words in a given context. Consider the statement "A little learning is a dangerous thing." How is this statement to be interpreted? Is it conveying information? Is it expressing attitudes? Is it persuading a person to make a more extended investigation of a subject matter? Is it justifying an anti-intellectual point of view? Is it performing multiple functions? Answers to such questions require not only an examination of the context in which the statement occurs but an awareness of the different uses to which language may be put.

For purposes of analysis we divide the uses of language into such classes as directive, expressive, evaluative, cognitive, formalistic, ceremonial, and mixed uses. In ordinary discourse language usually serves multiple functions, and in determining its use we must consider its context and the purpose of the speaker or writer.

The *directive* use of language is concerned with influencing the behavior or action of a person or of a group. It is designed to get a particular job accomplished. It may take such forms as commands, requests, suggestions, questions, and reports. Consider the following examples:

"Put the book on the desk."

"Is the door locked?"

"The oven is too hot."

"Please give me the paper when you have finished."

The directive purpose in language may occur in conjunction with other purposes of discourse. A student may state to his roommate who is still in bed, "Your class meets in fifteen minutes." Such a statement not only is informative but is designed to influence the action of the roommate.

The *expressive* use of language employs words, phrases, or sentences to reflect the feelings, emotions, attitudes, and dispositions of the speaker or to condition the emotive responses of the hearer or reader. A player in a game of cards may exclaim to his opponent, "You lousy rascal! You trumped my ace!" He is at least expressing his feelings, and he may hope to influence the attitude of his opponent. The poet or the novelist, the politician and the advertiser frequently use language to evoke an emotional response from their audience. They may also be making other uses of language, such as the directive or informative uses. Consider the following examples:

"A thing of beauty is a joy forever."

"The shack was falling down and the pantry was bare."

"My opponent has made himself rich at the public expense."

"Everybody admires couples who have a jet-set sports car."

The *evaluative* function of language ascribes some value to objects, processes, or events. Evaluative terms such as *good, bad, right, wrong, worthy,* and *unworthy* exemplify this language function. The evaluative use of language often occurs together with expressive or directive uses. In some cases the primary purpose of a statement that appears to be evaluative is expressive and directive. Judgments about the linguistic use of such statements have to be based on the context, including the apparent purpose of the speaker and his evidence for supporting the statement. Some examples of the evaluative use of language are the following:

"Cheating is wrong."

"The novel has great literary merit."

"The sunset is beautiful."

"The play is great."

The *cognitive* use of language seeks to provide information, clarification, explanation, argument, or classification relative to beliefs or claims of knowledge. Cognitive use of language seeks to increase, support, modify, or change beliefs or claims of knowledge or the reasons for accepting or altering them. The cognitive use of language is complex and often is combined with other uses. A simplified classification of cognitive uses of language includes the following five cases:

1. The *informative* use of language conveys knowledge about a proposed state of affairs. It sets forth the facts about a situation. It asserts "what is the case." In its narrower sense it functions to set forth "what the facts are." Examples of the informative use of language are the following:

"Isaac Newton was a mathematician and a physicist."
"John Locke was a physician and a philosopher."
"New York is east of St. Louis."
"Lead is heavier than water."

2. The *interpretative* function of language seeks to clarify the meaning of language that interrelates notions or events to each other and to specify the range of applicability of general principles or rules to particular contexts. A witness in court may improperly seek to interpret an event. He may have seen the defendant pick up a bottle and hit the plaintiff on the head. If the witness states that the defendant was trying to kill the plaintiff, then he would be adding an interpretation of the events. A reader may find an ambiguous sentence stating, "All's well that ends well." He may provide an interpretation of the context and propose that the author intended the meaning "All things with satisfactory outcomes are to be accepted as things worthy of praise" rather than "All things accepted as worthy of praise are things that end well." The interpretative function of language makes more explicit the meaning of statements occurring in a particular context.

3. The *explanatory* function of language seeks to account for a particular event, idea, or principle by reference to a more general series of events, ideas, or principles. In scientific inquiry an explanation sets forth a proposed causal relationship between an event and other events or between a principle accounting for particular events and a more general principle. Such explanations require a statement of causes that purport to account for what takes place. Trustworthy explanations require considerable skill and knowledge; in ordinary language many explanations are poorly grounded. Consider the following examples of explanatory uses of language:

"The lights went out because lightning struck the generator."
"The team won the game because they were fired up."
"The ice formed on the windshield because the temperature dropped below 32° F."
"John failed the exam because he broke a mirror."

4. The *argumentative* use of language sets forth a point of view with a conclusion supported by evidence. This use of language is subject to evaluation on the basis of standards of reliable inference. If the statements counting as evidence are expressed in a logical form such that in all cases in which

the conclusion is false at least one premise is false, the argument is valid. Likewise, the argument is invalid if the form of the statements makes possible a single instance in which the premises are true and the conclusion is false. An example of the argumentative use of language is the following:

If the defendant is guilty, then he was not at work at the time of the robbery.

He was at work at the time of robbery.

Therefore, the defendant is not guilty.

5. The *systematizing* use of language concerns the development of a set of statements structured to present a consistent and comprehensive view of a subject area, related to beliefs or claims of knowledge. The systematizing use of language is exemplified in a generalized text in biology, in a specialized text on organic chemistry, or in a work seeking to provide a unified account of political theories. The systematizing use of language is to be distinguished from a formalized use of language—to be discussed in the next paragraph—by its effort to present an ordered system including beliefs or claims of knowledge about some aspect of human experience or the context in which such experience occurs or should occur. The systematic use of language includes statements having more than merely formal content. The systematic use of language is particularly dependent upon valid inferences, which depend in turn upon the formalistic use of language.

The *formalistic* use of language concerns the development of a rational order or system based upon primitive terms, postulates, and operational procedures. Formal logic and mathematics, such as the geometries of Euclid or of Riemann, exemplify the formalistic use of language. The development of a formal order or system provides the basis for developing principles of valid inference in logic. The use of language in the parts of this text dealing with modern logic are based upon a formalistic use of language. The truth or falsity of statements in a formalistic system is determined by an analysis of the meaning of the statements and by the establishment of a proof for such statements from other statements in the system rather than by reference to experience. An example of the formalistic use of language is the theorem attributed to Pythagoras, "The square of the hypotenuse of a triangle with a right angle is equal to the sum of the squares of the other two sides."

The *ceremonial* use of language is based upon conventions of social propriety and facilitates adjustment of social relationships. Ceremonial language is regarded, within limits, as socially proper. Consider such statements as the following:

"Your party was out of this world."

"It was a pleasure to meet you."

"This home-made pie is delicious."

Ceremonial use of language is evaluated on the basis of its appropriateness rather than on the basis of its truth or falsity. However, in borderline cases one must exercise judgment in evaluating the purpose of the speaker. Consider the case of the coed who states in declining a date, "I have other plans for that evening, but I hope you will ask me out some other time."

The *mixed* use of language is not a separate linguistic use; rather it is a recognition that a given expression may have multiple uses in a given context. The statement, "The house is on fire," may not only provide information but also direct action. Consider other examples:

"My opponent is a scoundrel."

"My dear little dog would not harm anyone."

"You have a bug on your coat."

Logic is concerned with the use of language in arguments. The formalistic, cognitive, and evaluative uses of language occur in arguments reduced to neutral meanings for logical analysis. The formalistic function of language is used in the development of formal logic systems; the cognitive function is exemplified in the making of specific inferences or the providing of proofs related to claims of knowledge, in the analysis and clarification of statements and arguments, in the justification of a theory or of a hypothesis, or in the establishment of a preferred goal or plan of action; the evaluative function is exemplified in the making of distinctions—such as better or worse, more preferred or less preferred, more trustworthy or less trustworthy.

The technical concern of the student of logic with the use of language is with linguistic meaning and structure. For example, the economist might be concerned with the truth of the following statements: "If the demand for a product increases and its supply remains constant, then the cost of the product increases" and "The cost of this product increases." The logician also becomes concerned if any inference is offered on the basis of these statements. The affirming of these statements would not justify the conclusion, "The demand for this product increases and its supply remains constant." Given the form in which the evidence is presented, the conclusion introduces a formal fallacy in reasoning. The premises of the argument could be true and the conclusion false.

The directive, expressive, and ceremonial uses of language in ordinary discourse are of concern to the student of logic as they become the source for errors or fallacies in inference. Apart from their relevance to rational justification of conclusions, such uses of language are of special interest to the literary critic, the student of persuasive speech, or the semanticist.

Analyses of language uses are developed more completely in a study of semiotics or semantics. The logician's primary interest is the development of sound argument forms, the analyses of arguments by use of these forms, and the detection and avoidance of errors in reasoning. An appraisal of language uses begins with an insight into the purposes of the speaker. Additional distinctions important to the logician in the analysis of language are discussed in the next chapter.

2.6 EXERCISES

1. Determine which of the following words or statements are usually emotive, which are usually neutral, and which are emotive only in some contexts.

(a) *Battered, puppy, underdeveloped, culturally deprived, moralizing, stupid, sturdy, hillbilly, illiterate, donkey, fair-haired boy*, and *emotive*.

(b) *Provincial, purloin, pusillanimous, scion, scrape, scroll, taxes, territorial integrity, vocal suggestion, youthful, crook, freckle*, and *cheese eater*.

(c) "Smoke the cigarette of the thinking man."

(d) "Your fee is exorbitant."

(e) "The expatriates are monarchists."

2. Analyze ten advertisements for emotive words. Analyze several paragraphs of a propaganda article for emotive words.

3. Compare the use of emotive and neutral words in a stylistically conservative newspaper (such as *The New York Times*) and in one that seeks to "sensationalize" the news.

4. Analyze several articles in a popular publication (such as *The Reader's Digest*) to determine the uses of language exemplified in each article.

5. Determine the purpose of discourse in each of the following examples.

(a) The door is locked.

(b) Turn in your papers.

(c) Your lunch was well prepared.

(d) Lying is wrong.

(e) I like orange juice.

(f) The Yankees will rise again.

(g) The conference is scheduled for 2:00 P.M.

(h) Do not waste your food.

(i) Your father is arriving.

(j) Demonstrators are self-seeking persons.

(k) The postman is late.

(l) My political opponent is a do-gooder.

(m) The blade on the gasoline lawn mower is sharp.

(n) The pie is very tasty.

(o) Old dogs do not readily learn new tricks.

(p) The movie is unsuitable for children.

(q) You were so considerate to telephone.

(r) Take a pill after each meal and before going to bed.

(s) Your ideas are for the birds.

(t) Your flight leaves in twenty minutes.

(u) We have had a wonderful time.

(v) Anyone who rejects my conclusion is stupid.

(w) All conservative members of the legislature are supporting the bill.

(x) There is a mouse under the cabinet in the kitchen.

(y) You will never regret having purchased a color television set.

(z) "Across the channel to the west, in Cuba, independence of thought is equally submerged. But freedom of expression is not drowned in silence, as in Haiti, but buried beneath the incessant, nosy double-think of the political delinquents who mismanage that island. Imprisoned there today are at least thirty of our colleagues merely because they exercised the right to speak out and write their convictions."[2]

(a′) Although it was stated that all graduating seniors are expected to attend the reception, it is not required that they attend.

(b′) The chess move was superb.

(c′) Either the strategy was poorly thought out or there were serious deficiencies in carrying out the plans. The strategy was not poorly thought out. Therefore, there were serious deficiencies in carrying out the plans.

(d′) The engine missed because there was a piece of thread in the carburetor.

(e′) Peano, the Italian mathematician and logician, axiomatized the arithmetic of natural numbers by using the primitive terms "number," "0," and "successor" in five axioms:

   (i) 0 is a number.
   (ii) The successor of any number is a number.
   (iii) No two numbers have the same successor.
   (iv) No number has 0 as a successor.
   (v) Every number has the property P if P is a property such that both it is the property of 0 and, if it is the property of a number n, then the successor of n has P.

(f′) The physical sciences are traditionally divided into the following subject areas: physics, astronomy, chemistry, biology, and geology.

(g′) "Disdainful of modern camera equipment, Goodspeed is especially critical of what he calls the 'mini-cameras.' He focuses his beatup old four-by-five by judging distances, never with a view finder, and boasts he can get better prints than any man alive who uses the smaller cameras.

"'You gotta work fast when you operate like me,' Goodspeed says. 'There's too much margin for error with those damn little bugs.'"[3]

(h′) "A last minute amendment to the postal rate bill before House approval provided for a surcharge on all publications that mail more than 500,000 copies. We cannot imagine the Senate permitting this bit of nonsense to become law and we find it difficult to understand how supposedly intelligent members of the House of Representatives could approve such inanity."[4]

(i′) "Thoughtful people have a responsibility to stir interest among the great many who haven't really thought about the relationship between our free-choice system and the abundance we enjoy. I have every confidence that when their attention is focused on how much each individual benefits from his freedom to choose, the American people will put a checkrein on the erosive process of surrendering our freedoms, one at a time."[5]

(j′) "His guide for recruiters includes: 'Don't hire a man who bores you.' 'A dull man can be one with too much polish.' 'Another man to avoid is the kind with dull, sleepy eyes.'"[6]

---

[2] John T. O'Rourke, quoted by Robert U. Brown, "Shop Talk at Thirty," *Editor & Publisher,* April 2, 1966, p. 72.

[3] *Editor & Publisher,* January 6, 1968, p. 24.

[4] *Editor & Publisher,* October 21, 1967, p. 6.

[5] C. W. Cook, *Editor & Publisher,* September 16, 1967, p. 61.

[6] *Editor & Publisher,* September 30, 1967, p. 38.

Chapter 3
Elementary Distinctions in
Linguistic Expressions

3.1 Need for Elementary Linguistic Distinctions

We must recognize elementary linguistic distinctions in order to achieve clarity and precision of language and to identify basic faults in the ordinary use of language. Consider the following statements:

> Some unicorns are creatures to be feared.

> We can be assured that John is conservative since he affirms his belief in the American way of life.

In the first example a general term "unicorns" is applied to a context in a way that suggests there are creatures roaming the earth with the common name of unicorn. It is erroneous to assume, however, that any common name necessarily denotes individual members of an existing class of objects. Unicorns can be discussed without granting their existence.

In the second example we find a vague term: "the American way of life." Whatever this may refer to, it does not entail either a conservative or a liberal philosophy. Vague expressions of this sort can be used equally well to support opposing points of view.

The arising of such errors from improper or imprecise use of language indicates the need for further analysis of linguistic uses in arguments.

3.2 Proper Names and General Names

In the analysis of language proper names are distinguished from general names. A *proper* name refers to a singular individual thing, entity, or idea.

The referent in such cases may be real or fictitious, actual or imaginary. Examples of proper names (which sometimes are called singular names) are the following:

> George Washington
> The Father of Our Country
> The author of *Macbeth*
> General Eisenhower
> The present king of France
> The Boston Trio

Proper names do not indicate characteristics of their object. Thus, to claim that John's niece will become an attractive woman since her name is Elizabeth Taylor is to attribute characteristics erroneously to a proper name. Some proper names become general names through usage. Thus, it is sometimes said, "He met his Waterloo," "He is an Einstein," or "He is a Nero."

Although any individual thing could be given a proper name, few non-human objects have such names. A ship may be called "Victory," a government program "Operation Head Start," a dog "Rover," or a car "Galloping George." However, an attempt to give each individual object a name would unduly tax our memories, and we would still need a common word to refer to similar cases. This indicates a need for general names.

A *general* name refers to a group of individuals having an identifiable common property or characteristic. Such individuals constitute a class or collectivity. Examples of general names are the following:

> Field officers
> Professors
> College students
> Secretary of State
> All numbers divisible by three
> Synonyms

General names allow us to refer to whole classes of objects by means of a common term. Rather than being limited to individuals such as Rover I, Rover II, and Rover III, we can refer to dogs in general—past, present, and future ones. General names focus attention on properties shared in common; they sometimes tend to overemphasize the similarities and obscure the differences. The fact that an officer is a general does not mean that he thinks like other generals.

A *definite description* makes use of a general name together with a qualifying word or phrase that singularizes it. "That house on the hill," "your watch," "the lawyer who made my will," and "this book" are definite descriptions. Such descriptions refer only to a single object. However, the object may consist of a collectivity such as "that team" or "this class." Definite descriptions in a given context indicate the range of applicability or extensional meaning of a proper name.

The use of a name does not provide any assurance that the proposed referent or thing has actual existence. Both proper names and general names may be empty or vacuous. To insist on the existence of a proposed object merely because it has a name is to *reify* the object. The *fallacy of reification* is an argument that attributes existence to an object proposed by a name on the basis of no evidence other than the name itself. To claim that ghosts must exist on the grounds that the general name "ghosts" must refer to an existent object involves the fallacy of reification. Likewise, the use of vacuous names such as "the President of the United States before Washington" or "the first men to explore the moon before 1950" does not justify inferences that the proposed referents of such names have had existence. If providing a name for a proposed object or a class of objects constituted evidence for its existence, new objects and classes of objects could begin to exist merely on the basis of our originating names for them.

3.3 Words

Words are linguistic signs. Proper names and general names are linguistic signs. A *sign* is an object signifying some meaning associated with a referent other than the sign itself.

Signs can be distinguished as natural signs and linguistic signs. *Natural signs* refer by the meaning associated with an object in its physical environment apart from specific linguistic developments in a given language community. A ripple in fast-moving water may be a natural sign indicating a rock or obstruction close to the surface. Smoke is a natural sign of fire. A particular marking in soft earth may signify the proximity of a deer. *Linguistic signs* refer to particular objects or to classes of objects by the meaning associated with them in a language community. The meaning of linguistic signs is based on social conventions and is characterized by an arbitrary element. Linguistic signs also are symbols. Any proper name such as "John," any class name such as "machine," and any other meaningful word is a linguistic sign. No necessary connection holds between a linguistic sign and its meaning.

The physical character or the physical behavior of a sign is a *token*. A *sign-token* may consist of marks on a piece of paper or the sounds expressed in the utterance of a word. Each word in this sentence is a sign-token. If this sentence is read aloud, the sound of each word is a sign-token. If the expression, "fox . . . fox," is written in a sentence, have one or two words been used? Only one word but two sign-tokens have been used in this case.

A *referent* is whatever is signified or intended as the meaning of a sign. The referent of the linguistic sign "Washington, D.C." is the city that has this name. The referent of the linguistic sign "green" is a color. It cannot be assumed that any linguistic sign has a referent in any given realm of discourse. A speaker may discuss what he calls "dialectical process of differentiation and integration" without having any referent for his symbols. In such cases he can be charged with making a meaningless statement. That is, he makes an assertion that has no referent. Some speakers or writers who are said to be "profound," "deep," or "obscure" are only uttering meaningless assertions if there is no referent and hence no meaning to their statements. To clarify a statement consists in making more obvious its intended referent or meaning.

Words may have referents at one level of discourse but not at others. At the level of children's literature words such as "fairies" and "elves" may have referents, but to insist that they have referents at another level is to push them beyond their range. Words may be meaningful at one level of discourse and meaningless at another. Thus, the confusion of a level of discourse using referents known to be imaginary or fanciful with a level of discourse using referents believed to have spatial and temporal dimensions leads directly to errors in reasoning.

People sometimes use words as if they had some special, nonlinguistic property—some magical power or some natural connection with their referents. If an announcer assumes that reference to a pitcher's having a "no-hit" game going has a relation to the pitcher's completing a "no-hit" game, he is deferring to a popular belief in the magical power of words. Likewise, knocking on wood to avoid a state of affairs referred to in a conversation is an instance of a superstition based, in part, on belief in the magical power of words.

An instance of *successful communication* occurs if the following conditions hold:

1. A speaker intends a given referent. (For example, he intends to refer to the running of a child across the street.)
2. Appropriate symbols are chosen to express this meaning and the sign-tokens are produced. "The child is running across the street."
3. An interpreter receives (hears, sees, touches) the sign-tokens.
4. The interpreter responds to the sign-tokens by referring to the referent signified by the symbol and intended by the speaker.

The effort at communication is unsuccessful if the referent referred to by the interpreter is different or partly different from the one intended by the speaker.

3.4 Terms

Sentences have elementary units of meaning. These elementary units of meaning within a statement are called *terms*. A term is simple or atomic in character, although it may consist of several words. A singular name such as "the president of Columbia University" is a singular term. A general name or a general name with qualifying phrases such as "some men in life jackets" is a general term. Some terms signify relations, such as "equal to" and "greater than." Other terms signify location, such as "in the top drawer."

Since a term is a unit of meaning, it is not to be confused with the words or symbols used to signify the term. Different words can refer to the same term. Consider the expressions "Mr. Smith," "Herr Smith," "Señor Smith." The same word can refer to different terms, as does the word *fly* in the following statements: "The fly is on the table." "He hit a long fly." "The trout hit a fly." Other terms are signified by expressions such as "board," "molecule," "exciting time," "under the automobile," "next month," "bitter herbs," "news editors," "Abraham Lincoln," "the president who gave the Gettysburg Address," "a friend of," and "the theory of relativity."

A *complementary* term refers to anything to which a given term is inapplicable. The complementary term of "house" is "anything that is not a house." The complementary term of "student" is "anything that is not a student." In formulating a complementary term, we must include everything that is not referred to in the original term. Many words with prefixes such as "in-," "ir-," "un-," may not exclude everything from the original term and are not full complementary terms. Consider these examples: "rational" and "irrational," "cooperative" and "uncooperative," "responsible" and "irresponsible," and "competent" and "incompetent." Some prefixes, such as "in-," may not significantly change the fundamental meaning of a term; consider the expressions "flammable" and "inflammable."

Terms denoting relations such as "included in the class of" or "is older than" make inferences possible. If all of A is included in the class of B and all of B is included in the class of $C,$ then all of A is included in the class of $C.$ If John is older than Mary and Mary is older than Joe, then John is older than Joe.

3.5 Mention and Use

What is wrong with the following sentences? "Logic is spelled with five letters and logic is the study of the principles of valid reasoning. Therefore, the study of the principles of valid reasoning is spelled with five letters."

What is wrong is that in its first occurrence the word "logic" refers to the word itself and in the second occurrence it refers to a subject matter. In the first instance the word is mentioned; in the second instance it is used. The scholastics referred to the occurrence of a word in *suppositio materialis* as the case of mentioning a word. They referred to the occurrence of a word in *suppositio formalis* as the case of using a word. If a word is mentioned, it should be italicized or placed in quotation marks.

If a word is mentioned, the referent of the word is the word itself. If a word is used, the referent is something other than the word itself. The word *red* (or "red") is mentioned in the sentence, "*Red* begins with an *r* and *red* has fewer letters than *blue*." The word "red" is used in the following sentence: "Red is a bright color and red is a warm color."

This distinction between the mention and use of words is essential to prevent confusion. However, the use of quotation marks or italics in the mention of a term should not be confused with other uses of quotation marks and italics, as to indicate citations, emphasis, or unusual meanings.

3.6 Connotation and Denotation—Extension and Intension

Logicians distinguish between the individuals to which a general name is applicable and the characteristics or properties such individuals have in common. This distinction is made possible by a term's denotation and its connotation. The *denotation* refers to the specific individuals included in the meaning of the word; the *connotation* refers to the common set of characteristics, qualities, or properties shared by the individuals referred to. The denotation of the word "automobile" is every particular object included in or comprising the class of automobiles; the connotation refers to the characteristics, qualities, or properties shared by all the particular objects comprising the class of automobiles. Such characteristics can include such properties as "self-propelled vehicle," "vehicles that are driven on roads," and "vehicles used for carrying passengers."

A term's *extension* refers to the range of its denotation or to the objects to which it is applicable; its *intension* refers to its connotation or to the common properties characterizing all objects to which it is applicable. A term may be extended or it may be unextended. It is *extended* if it refers to every individual denoted; it is *unextended* if it refers to less than all of the individuals denoted. The following terms are extended in their denotation: "all men," "all college students," "any civilian personnel," "all bears in the zoo," and "every businessman." Some terms that are unextended in their denotation are: "most logic students," "few disgruntled persons," and "some biochemists." The determination of the extension of a term is particularly important in the analysis of propositions comprising a categorical syllogism. The connotation or intension of a term is used in definitions by genus and difference.

The logical connotation of a word needs to be distinguished from its subjective or psychological connotation. *Logical connotation* refers to properties of objects determined by objective and public considerations. Qualified observers should be able to agree on the logical connotation of a particular term. The logical connotation of the term "man" includes such properties as "rational and tool-making animal." The *subjective connotation* of a term varies with the disposition, emotional tone, or attitude of a particular person. The subjective connotation of the word "cat" varies with the attitudes of persons toward cats. Some people may be reminded of a small, affectionate, cuddly animal, others of an annoying animal that carries diseases. The objective and public connotation of a term interests the logician. Subjective connotations are particularly relevant in the persuasive use of speech.

3.7 Univocal and Equivocal Uses of Words

A word is used *univocally* if it has the identical meaning or connotation throughout a given context. A word is used *equivocally* if its meaning or connotation changes within a context. Consider the use of the word "star" in the following examples:

(1) All stars are in the heavens.
All stars are millions of miles from the earth.

(2) Any star is in the heavens.
John Celebrity is a star.
Therefore, John Celebrity is in the heavens.

In the first example the term "stars" has the same meaning and has a univocal use. In the second example the term "star" is used in two different ways, equivocally. In a unit of informative discourse, terms are expected to be used in a univocal sense in a given context. If a key word in an argument has different meanings, the *fallacy of equivocation* occurs. Many four-term fallacies to be considered in the study of the syllogism are the result of the equivocal use of the language.

In some cases equivocation may occur in a context that does not involve an argument. It may become a basis for humor: the jokes of some comedians turn essentially on the equivocal use of language.

3.8 Ambiguity and Vagueness

A word, phrase, or sentence is *ambiguous* if it can be interpreted as having two or more meanings in a given context. Consider the statement "All freshmen are not required to take math courses." At least two interpretations of the sentence are possible. The statement could mean "No freshmen are required to take courses in math" or it could mean "Some freshmen are not required to take courses in math."

Ambiguity is a frequent source of confusion and error in arguments. A speaker may intend one meaning and his interpreter understand a second meaning. If a speaker becomes pressed in a discussion, he may seek a way out by resorting to an ambiguity. An employer might claim, "The government should not establish minimum standards regarding wages and hours of work of employees, since such regulations violate the freedom of the employer to run his own affairs." After an initial interchange of arguments the employer might admit that under certain conditions, such as those involving the working conditions of women, regulations regarding health and sanitation, and performance of contractual obligations, there was not complete "freedom of the employer" in the sense of "absence of any government restraint" in relation to employment practices. He then might shift his meaning of "freedom of the employer to run his own affairs" to "opportunity to make decisions relative to the conduct of his business." This expression could be analyzed further to determine whether it included practices that were "contrary to law," such as violation of laws against unfair competition. A further revision in the meaning of "freedom of the employer to run his own affairs" might follow. In the end the employer may insist on the correctness of his position, but he would have to make further distinctions and refinements in his argument. A basic difficulty in the discussion is the introduction of the ambiguous phrase "freedom of the employer" without careful discrimination of its meaning. In discussions involving such ambiguities the meaning frequently shifts from one possibility to another, and equivocation occurs also.

In some cases ambiguity permits evasion of issues. Consider the letter of recommendation that states, "When you come to know this person as well as I know him, you will have the same regard for him that I do."

Amphiboly is a special case of ambiguity. In an amphibolous statement the ambiguity is due to the grammatical construction. For example: "Slain officer shoots bandit." Dangling participles also yield amphibolous statements. For example: "Seeking to collect more athletic equipment for the boys' club, the car stopped in front of John's fraternity house."

An expression is *vague* if the range of its applicability is left undetermined. The precise point at which the expression no longer remains applicable is fuzzy. In many contexts such phrases as "the democratic way of life," "a republican form of government," "the heritage bequeathed to us by our fathers," and "natural and inalienable rights" are vague. Occasions arise in persuasive speech in which a speaker deliberately chooses to be vague. If he appeals to "the American way of life," a politician is not likely to divide his followers. On the other hand, if he makes more precise the range of applicability of "the American way of life" to include the "great experiment" in government as proposed by Thomas Jefferson, some followers might think him too liberal. If he restricted "the American way of life" to the economic system championed by the great nineteenth-century entrepreneurs, he might alienate other followers.

The use of vague terms may make hedging possible on crucial issues, and their use can vary so widely in range of applicability as to become ambiguous. However useful they may be in evasive techniques, they are regarded as a logical fault. The logician stresses the need for clarity in the applicability of a term. A term's meaning is clear only if those situations in which it is applicable are distinguishable from those in which it is not.

3.9 EXERCISES

1. Determine the proper names and the general names in each of the following examples:

(a) The president of Jefferson College.

(b) College athletes.

(c) All plays on Broadway.

(d) The present Tzar of Russia.

(e) All taxpayers.

(f) All nuclear physicists.

(g) The book with the green cover on that shelf.

(h) The leprechaun with the red beard.

(i) All students with at least a "B" average.

2. Suggest some words that may become the occasion of the fallacy of reification.

3. Name some natural signs that are not referred to in the text.

4. Give some illustrations of possible use of words without referents.

5. Assume that an instance of successful communication and one of unsuccessful communication occur with each of the following statements. Describe the symbolic situation involved in each case.

(a) The bird flew the coop.

(b) The die is cast.

(c) The physician is highly ethical.

(d) The teacher does not cooperate.

(e) John made a good play.

6. Determine which of the following pairs are complementary terms:

(a) Tangible and intangible considerations.

(b) Animate and inanimate things.

(c) Professional and amateur golfers.

(d) Veterans and all things not veterans.

(e) Theists and atheists.

(f) Jurists and nonjurists.

(g) Repairable and irreparable losses.

(h) Separable and inseparable conditions.

(i) Dent and indent.

(j) Payable and nonpayable accounts.

7. Determine which words are mentioned and should have quotation marks in the following examples:

(a) War is evil and war begins with a "w," so some things beginning with a "w" are evil.

(b) Poliomyelitis is more difficult to spell than polio.

(c) Mary had written had had where Tom had had had; had had had had the approval of the instructor.

(d) Thirteen is unlucky.

(e) Words of commendation are good, excellent, splendid, and bravo.

8. Determine the extension of the italicized words in the following statements:

(a) Some exceptional *students* are industrious *persons*.

(b) Every *dog* has his day.

(c) Many *prizes* are not worthy *goals* of endeavor.

(d) All *roses* are *shrubs* and most *varieties* have prickly *stems*.

(e) Most *rules* of syntax are not difficult *things* to master.

9. Provide examples of the denotation and connotation of the following terms:

desk, chair, window, blackboard, student, democratic institution, constitutional government, airplane, bureaucracy, physicist, and *custom.*

10. Arrange each of the following series in order of increasing intension. Identify the added property or characteristic that distinguishes one degree of intension from others.

(a) Teacher, man, logic teacher at State College, human being, logic teacher.

(b) Symbolic logic textbook, book, logic textbook, textbook.

(c) Plane figure, quadrilateral, square, figure.

(d) Constitutional monarchy, political system, constitutional government, social organization, British constitutional monarchy.

(e) Philosophy of science, philosophy of natural science, philosophy, philosophy of physics.

11. Does the intension of an expression usually increase if the extension of the expression decreases? Does it always increase in such cases? Consider the following series of expressions: number and whole numbers; tools, hand tools, hand tools for turning screws; centaurs, healthy centaurs, centaurs over ten feet tall; presidents of the United States, presidents of the United States who were or are citizens, presidents of the United States over 34 years old at the time of their election.

12. Identify any equivocal use of words and expressions in the following statements:

(a) Any free man is free to do as he pleases.

(b) Not all is well that ends well.

(c) It is right that all rights should be protected by law.

(d) Anything that is according to nature is right. "An eye for an eye and a tooth for a tooth" is according to nature. Therefore, "an eye for an eye and a tooth for a tooth" is right.

(e) Honesty is the best policy. This is the best policy. Therefore, it is honest.

(f) The best things come to those who wait. Death comes to those who wait. Therefore, death is the best thing.

(g) Business is business.

(h) Any profitable undertaking increases income. Studying logic is profitable. Therefore, studying logic increases income.

13. Name eight or ten expressions that can be used in an equivocal manner and show how they could occur in a proposed argument.

14. Analyze the following expressions for vagueness and ambiguity. What different interpretations might be made in each case?

(a) Man is a political animal.

(b) Free enterprise encourages business growth.

(c) You should follow the right procedure.

(d) Business is better.

(e) You should recognize the merits of the opposition.

(f) We should support democratic processes.

(g) Popular education is the best assurance of an informed electorate.

(h) We support the rights of the oppressed.

(i) We need to have better employment opportunities.

(j) All students are not interested in doing their best in classes.

(k) Professor Smith is a good teacher.

(l) Democratic institutions are not applicable to situations where the masses are illiterate.

(m) Jones is not a religious person.

(n) Blank is a politician who supports liberal political traditions.

(o) Nothing is too good for you.

(p) "Hagan ran his finger through his hair and took out a cigar."[1]

15. Analyze ten advertisements, an article in a propagandizing publication, and an article on a contemporary situation in a reputable newspaper for ambiguous and vague expressions.

---

[1] *Indianapolis* (Ind.) *Star,* quoted in *Editor & Publisher,* February 3, 1968, p. 7.

Chapter 4
Definitions

4.1 The Purpose of Definitions

Satisfactory communication requires that we understand the range of applicability of words used in discussions. To determine the truth or falsity of a statement or its appropriateness we must understand the kinds of objects, ideas, or processes to which the words in a sentence apply. To answer such questions as "Does Greece have democratic processes of government?" or "Are some nonhuman animals rational?" we must determine the meaning in such contexts of expressions such as "democratic processes" and "rational." Definitions are designed to clarify the meaning of terms.

Some proposed definitions are unsatisfactory. Consider the following:

Social security is a racket of securing money from the employed to pay those who don't work or who failed to save for their old age.

A compromise is the sacrifice of a basic principle in order to get along with people.

Each of these proposed definitions fails to include all of the usual referents intended by the defined word and excludes some of its usual referents. Each of the definitions uses evaluative and emotive terms designed to affect the attitude of the hearer about the referent of the word. Neither definition states the essential qualities of the word defined.

A child does not usually learn the meaning of a word by a formal definition. He confronts an object such as a chair or a table. Its name may be repeated to him several times. Sooner or later he may repeat the expression and then begin to point to the object and say "chair." He may point to another object and say "chair," and he may be told the name of this other object is "stool." He also learns the meaning of words by observing actions— either his own or those of others. He may learn the meaning of "walk" and "run," "lie down," and "go to sleep." He learns to identify some common characteristic of an object or activity and to apply the word to objects or activities having these characteristics. By trial and error he learns to use simple words in a satisfactory manner.

The use of concrete cases as examples of meaning of words continues to have a useful function in many instances. If, for example, one is discussing the meaning of "due process," especially with visitors from a culture entirely different from our own, pointing to specific known cases helps in the clarification of the term.

We learn many words by hearing or seeing them used or applied in a context, and the meaning of some words— particularly slang words—appears to be picked up primarily in this manner. Likewise, we learn different meanings of the same word by interaction with a linguistic community. Many words in ordinary usage are not subject to clear-cut and precise definitions, since their use is subject to greatly varying ranges of application and meaning. It can be easier to give instances to which such words are applicable than to define them. For example, it is quite difficult to propose satisfactory definitions for nouns in some cases of ordinary language if a requirement of a satisfactory definition is the ability to interchange the defining part for the defined word in any context in which the latter occurs. Such cases would include the following examples:

Old fogies are squares.

Games are important for renewing the human spirit.

Definitions can be offered for such terms in ordinary usage, but the criteria applicable to good definitions usually indicate flaws in such cases.

Criteria for appraising definitions are particularly applicable in subject areas in which critical inquiry is undertaken. Such inquiry advances, in part, only as clarity and precision in terminology is attained. Thus, in the physical sciences, the social sciences, literary and art criticism, mathematics and symbolic logic, statistics, philosophy, law, and administration, terms can be rigorously appraised on the basis of definitions that are offered for them. Basic in such appraisals is the determination of the degree to which the definition clarifies and makes explicit the meaning and range of applicability of a linguistic sign.

In the evaluation of definitions, the occasion and purpose for their formulation as well as their intended audience are relevant considerations.

4.2 Real and Nominal Definitions

Are definitions descriptions of the essences of objects to which reference is made? Do they state simply a meaning ascribed to a linguistic sign and in this sense refer to the word being defined rather than to the essence of the object referred to by the word? To explain these questions would involve a lengthy discussion of "real" and "nominal" definitions. Adding to the difficulty is the highly varied manner in which different writers conceptualize "real" and "nominal" definitions.

One distinction proposes that real definitions describe the actual nature or essence of the thing being described. Thus, if a definition were asked for words such as "house" or "good," a real definition would state the "actual nature" of a house or of good—that is, of the referents of such words. Advocates of this view of real definitions have difficulty in showing how a verbal definition actually sets forth the essence of a nonverbal object merely by the use of words. Some writers question the usefulness of the notion of real definitions. The position taken in this discussion presupposes that definitions are nominal in the sense that they refer primarily to words rather than to things. A definition of "house" proposes to state how this term is used. A definition of "good," if such is possible, states the meaning of this term in a given context (such as "worthy of praise") rather than describing the "essence of good."

4.3 Kinds of Definitions

There are many different kinds of definitions. Their appropriate use depends upon the occasion and the needed degree of precision or technicality. The following list of ten kinds of definitions is not exhaustive, but it does include the kinds most often encountered.

1. *Synonymous* definitions use a word with the same or similar meaning as the word being defined. Found frequently in abridged or bilingual dictionaries, they state the meaning of words by using comparable expressions whose meanings are known. Examples of synonymous definitions are the following: *"Vagrant* means *vagabond." "Logic* means the same thing as the Spanish word *lógica."* This method of definition is helpful primarily in learning a new vocabulary. Synonymous definitions often are not equivalent, and they do not state the essential characteristics of the word defined.

2. *Denotative* or *ostensive* definitions point to specific objects, examples, or occasions to which a word is applicable. Their limitations are that they provide only a restricted number of examples of the referent of a word, and that the cases they point out may have a confusing variety of characteristics. Examples of denotative definitions are the following: "A mockingbird is the kind of bird you see sitting on that fence post." "A dictatorship is the kind of government Germany, Italy, and Russia had immediately prior to World War II." "A university is the kind of school of higher education that you find at Princeton, Harvard, Yale, Brown, and Columbia."

3. *Operational* definitions perform or state a series of operations that

exemplify the meaning of a word as it is applicable to a particular object or occasion. Operational definitions seek to specify the meaning of words by the use of actions rather than in terms of words, qualities, or characteristics. P. W. Bridgman, the physicist who formulated the operational point of view, states, "The concept is synonymous with the corresponding set of operations."[1] An operational definition of "acid" would state and carry out the procedures for determining whether a solution is an acid. Thus, the first part of this definition would be "An acid is a solution in which litmus paper turns red." The second step would be the specific act of putting the litmus paper in a solution in which the paper turns red. An operational definition is highly useful where it is relevant. It is applicable primarily to behavioral and laboratory situations.

4. *Genetic* definitions state the initial circumstances that account for the meaning given a word, explaining it by reference to the originating process or occasion giving rise to the use of the word. "A stalactite is an icicle-shaped formation found in the roof or on the sides of caverns and formed by deposits of calcium carbonate." "Islam is the religion whose founder was Mohammed." Limitations of a genetic definition are found in its failure to take account of changes occurring after an object or movement begins.

5. *Functional* definitions state the meaning of a word by reference to the word's use or function. A functional definition attempts to clarify a word by describing an activity that the referent of the word is significantly instrumental in carrying out. "A wrench is a tool used for tightening and loosening bolts." Functional definitions frequently are not equivalent to the word being defined. Other instrumentalities may be able to achieve the same end, and the referent may have other significant functions.

6. *Persuasive* definitions seek to state the meaning of a word so as to condition the attitudes or dispositions of audiences. They are offered to motivate the development of points of view or interests shared by the speaker through the manner in which terms are defined rather than through evidence. Persuasive definitions are frequently used in propaganda as a means of predisposing an audience to accept the perspectives, goals, and plans of action of the propagandist. Consider the following examples: "A conservative is a person who wishes to preserve the best of the past for future generations." "A liberal is a person who seeks to change the defects of the past to maximize the enjoyment of the good life in the future."

7. *Theoretical* definitions state a formal or technical meaning of a word for use by specialists in a given field. In physics such words as "mass," "force," "field," "stress," and "strain" are defined within the terminology usually known only to serious students in this subject area. Theoretical definitions provide for rigorous conceptualization stated in a context of precisely defined related notions. They help to develop a technical vocabulary that

---

[1] *The Logic of Modern Physics* (New York: The Macmillan Company, 1927), p. 32.

can be used with precision and consistency in a given field. An example of a theoretical definition is "Enzymes are special kinds of protein that control the different steps in the synthesis or breakdown of an organic molecule." Theoretical definitions are highly useful to specialists, but usually one must be technically proficient in a subject area to understand them.

8. *Lexical* definitions state the traditional or conventional meaning of a word as it has been established in different contexts. This kind of definition is found in the better dictionaries, which report the different meanings an expression has had and illustrate them by quotations from primary sources. Lexical definitions may be regarded as elliptical expressions that omit at the beginning of the sentence such a phrase as "A traditional usage of the word *X* is. . . ." If they are understood to include such expressions, lexical definitions can be appraised by such terms as "true," "reliable," "accurate," and "trustworthy."

9. A *stipulative* definition represents a speaker's decision to use a word in a specific way without being bound by its conventional or traditional usage. However, traditional uses may be relevant to the meaning that is stipulated. Since the formulation of a stipulative definition represents a decision, it has the form "Let us use the word *X* to mean. . . ."

Stipulative definitions frequently introduce new words into the vocabulary. They also may be used in a given context to give precision to a word with a wide range of meaning. The philosopher Whitehead gave many stipulative definitions in an effort to avoid misleading connotations of words in ordinary speech. Common usage may change a stipulative definition into a lexical or conventional one.

Stipulative definitions are appraised as useful or misleading, clear or obscure, but not as true or false.

In the use of stipulative definitions several rules are applicable:

(a) A speaker or writer has the privilege of determining the meaning he chooses to give to a word.
(b) The meaning given should facilitate the communication of his ideas and should not be designed to confuse his readers or hearers.
(c) A word should be used consistently with its stipulated meaning in any context for which it is designated.

10. Definitions by genus and difference, or *connotative* definitions, state a general class and a specific difference in determining the meaning of a word. The general class identifies a broad group to which the referent of the word belongs. The specific difference distinguishes the referent of the defined word from others of its general class. To the degree that a definition by genus and difference is offered as a conventional one, it can be appraised as being true or false as well as useful or misleading. Examples of connotative definitions are the following:

Man is a political animal.

A circle is a plane figure each point of which is equidistant from a common point.

Section 4.4 discusses in greater detail definitions by genus and difference.

Some definitions may be instances of more than one kind of definition. The functional definition of "wrench" as "a tool used for tightening or loosening bolts or nuts" could be considered also as a definition by genus and difference. If a definition of "French bread" consists of a set of instructions for its preparation along with the actual operations of preparation and baking, it contains elements both of genetic and operational definitions.

4.4 Connotative Definitions, or Definitions by Genus and Difference

Connotative definitions, or definitions by genus and difference, state the essential meaning or characteristics of the word being defined. Definitions are traditionally divided into the definiens and the definiendum. The *definiendum* is the word for which a definition is to be given. The *definiens* states the meaning of the word being defined. In the definition "Man is a rational animal," "man" is the definiendum and "rational animal" is the definiens. In a connotative definition the definiens is divided into the genus and the differentia. The *genus* refers to the general class to which the definiendum belongs. The *differentia* distinguishes the definiendum from the members of the larger class stated in the genus. In the definition above, the genus of the definiens is "animal" and the differentia is "rational."

Definitions by genus and difference may be evaluated in terms of the following seven rules:

1. A satisfactory connotative definition includes in its definiens a meaningful statement of the essential characteristics of the definiendum. A definition of "man" as "the animal that laughs" fails to state the essential characteristics of the usual meaning of the word "man." In a discussion regarding the importance of humor, such a definition might be appropriate at least for illustrative purposes. However, this notion is usually regarded as other than an essential characteristic of man. A definition of "habit" as "a practice that is hard to break" also illustrates the failure to state the essential characteristics of the definiendum.

2. A satisfactory connotative definition includes in the definiens all instances to which the definiendum refers and only those instances. It is too broad if it includes cases to which it should not refer and too narrow if it excludes cases to which it should refer. Some definitions are too broad in one sense and too narrow in another. The definition "A novel is a narrative story" is too broad in the sense that some narrative stories are not novels.

It is too narrow because some novels are not adequately characterized as "a narrative story." Other examples of the violation of this rule of connotative definition are the following:

> Pornography is printed matter that is offensive to the moral tastes of the majority of the public.

> A square is a plane figure with four sides.

3. A satisfactory connotative definition is stated in clear, precise, and neutral language. It should not be vague, obscure, poetical, figurative, facetious, sarcastic, or cynical. Examples of this fault are the following:

> Time is the moving image of eternity. (Plato)

> A fanatic is a person who intensifies his efforts after he has lost his bearings.

> An expert is an ordinary "pert" that is away from home.

Persuasive definitions also violate this rule.

4. A satisfactory connotative definition is stated in an affirmative manner. It should avoid different types of negative statements. Usually connotative definitions that violate this rule violate other rules as well. If a definition is negative, it will not state the essential characteristics of the definiendum. It likely will be too broad. Some examples of the violation of this rule are the following:

> A simple substance is a substance that is not compound.

> A vice is a habit that is not good.

> Barter is how you exchange goods when you don't have any money.

5. A satisfactory connotative definition avoids circularity. It should not be circular with other terms in the definition or with other definitions in the same context in which it is used. Repetition of the same word or a synonym of the word or the use of correlative terms tends to violate this rule. For example:

> A cat is a feline creature.

> A scientist is one who engages in scientific activity.

> A rat is a rodent.

> An effect is something that is produced by a cause and a cause is something that produces an effect.

6. A connotative definition is consistent with other definitions appearing in the same context. To avoid both inconsistency and equivocation in a given

context, the meaning of a given definition should not be incompatible with other definitions. Violations of this rule are found in the following examples:

> A simple substance is the essence of a body that has no parts, *and*
> A body is a substance that has parts.

> A straight line is a path of minimal distance between two points, *and*
> The minimal distance between two points is the path of a curved line.

7. A connotative definition should be helpful in furthering communication with an intended audience. A highly technical definition is appropriate for a group technically trained in the relevant subject area. A highly technical definition given to a predominantly lay audience does not facilitate the communication of ideas unless the meaning of the definition is broken down into terms they understand. This rule also is violated if a word whose meaning is fairly clear to an intended audience is defined by words whose meanings are more obscure than the definiendum. For example:

> A kiss is an osculatory activity usually consisting in the touching of the labial surfaces by people of different sex.

Definitions are to be appraised on the basis of their use in clarifying the meaning of expressions for an intended audience. The purpose for which they are given also has to be considered. They need to facilitate the attainment of precision in language use. What counts as a referent of the definiendum and what is excluded need to be made definite. Definitions should provide meanings that make communication simpler, that make understanding of ideas or points of view more readily attainable, and that illuminate rather than obscure the meaning of a definiendum.

4.5 EXERCISES

1. Distinguish between a denotative definition and an operational definition.
2. Ostensive definitions are sometimes distinguished from denotative definitions. The former demonstrate the meaning of a word by a physical gesture, such as pointing toward an object that exemplifies the word. The latter indicate an example merely by the use of words. Give examples of the use of such a distinction.
3. Give denotative definitions of the following:

(a) Logic book	(b) Mountain
(c) College teacher	(d) Congressman
(e) Experiment	(f) Dictatorship
(g) Constitution	(h) Sign-token
(i) Monopolistic practice	(j) Demonstration

4. Give connotative definitions of the following:

(a) Rectangle
(b) Logic
(c) Science
(d) Freedom
(e) Island
(f) Argument
(g) Socialism
(h) Justice
(i) Temperance
(j) Architect
(k) Civil rights
(l) Human nature

5. Give connotative definitions of five terms used frequently in your major area of study.

6. It is often stated that a speaker has the freedom to define his own terms. Do you agree?

7. Analyze the adequacy of the following examples by applying the rules of connotative definitions.

(a)   Duty is what one has an obligation to do.

(b)   A contract is an agreement that is illegal to break.

(c)   A dog is man's most faithful friend.

(d)   A judge is a lawyer who serves on the bench.

(e)   A clock is an instrument for keeping time.

(f)   A square is a plane figure with four right angles.

(g)   A good person is one who does the right thing.

(h)   Altruism is the virtue talked about the most and practiced the least.

(i)   Man is a biped that has lost its feathers.

(j)   A star is any stellar object.

(k)   A child is a youngster with parents.

(l)   Alimony is what happens when two people make a mistake and only one has to pay the consequences.

(m)   A tyrant is a man who bullies his own way about.

(n)   A disciple is one who learns from others.

(o)   A college is an institution of higher education.

(p)   Money is something that we can't keep.

(q)   A vice is a habit that is not good.

(r)   A car is an automobile.

(s)   A conservative is a man who wants to live in the past.

(t)   A liberal is a man who wants to sacrifice the best of the past for the uncertainties of impractical experiments in the future.

(u)   A Democrat is a man who wants to exploit the miseries of the poor to gain political power.

(v)   A Republican is a person who wants to have the rich get richer and the poor get poorer.

(w)   Politics by consensus is the policy of substituting mediocrity in leadership for initiative in decision-making.

(x)   Darkness is the opposite of light.

(y)   A bricklayer is a mason who lays brick.

(z)   A postman is the government employee that comes most frequently to residences.

(a')   Democracy is the form of government where the governed have some form of participation in forming the policies of government.

(b') Communism is a form of government that is in control of the Communist party.

(c') Man is the animal that plots the destruction of his own species.

(d') An airplane is a flying machine.

(e') A fink is a person who has an opinion about everything without knowing how to do anything.

Chapter 5
Informal Fallacies

5.1 Formal and Informal Fallacies

Logic is concerned with the structure of valid arguments. The conclusion of a valid argument is justifiable by the formal relation holding between the premises. A fallacy in reasoning occurs if an argument fails to provide adequate evidence for its conclusion. In a *formal fallacy* the structure of an argument allows an instance in which the premises could be true and the conclusion false. A formal fallacy is exemplified in the following argument:

> If clichés are used in a work of historical writing, then history is oversimplified in this work.
> History is oversimplified in this work.
> Therefore, clichés are used in it.

The formal fallacy of *affirming the consequent* occurs in the logical structure of this argument. Even though the premises are true, the conclusion may be false.

In an *informal fallacy* the proposed evidence is deficient on such grounds as irrelevance, circularity, oversimplification, or ambiguity. That is, the proposed evidence fails to justify the conclusion for reasons other than a formal error in the structure of the argument itself.

This and the following chapter discuss various informal fallacies. Such fallacies are inherently nonrational in character, and classification schemes for them tend to overlap. The major divisions under which these fallacies are discussed are oversimplification, misuse of appeal to emotion, involved assumptions, imprecision in the use of language, and appeals to irrelevance. A given example may be representative of more than one fallacy. In identifying a particular fallacy, one should give its specific type (such as a genetic fallacy) rather than merely the general heading under which it is classified.

5.2 Fallacies of Oversimplification

In fallacies of oversimplification the evidence presented to justify a proposed conclusion is too limited or one-sided. Sweeping assertions tend to be made, and statements are made without the necessary qualifications. The evidence needed to establish the proposed conclusion is more elaborate or complex than what is given. Additional facts or premises are required. In analyzing such fallacies we must consider the emphasis, thrust, or context of the argument.

Special Pleading or Card-Stacking.   In special pleading the presentation of evidence is highly selective. The pleader presents only evidence favorable to the proposed conclusion, ignoring opposing evidence or considering only those elements of it that are easily discredited. The deck is stacked to facilitate a desired outcome. An example of special pleading is the proposed argument: "During a period of war sales increase, prices rise, and greater profits are made. Therefore wars are brought about by persons who profit financially from them."

Special pleading occurs with great frequency in many arguments of partisans for a particular cause. Although it is expected on some occasions, counterbalancing factors usually operate in such contexts. A political candidate tends to emphasize the virtues of his platform and the shortcomings of the platform of his opposition. A lawyer is expected to present the most favorable case possible for his client. An advertiser is expected to play up the merit of his product. However, the electorate is expected to hear the case as presented by the opposing political candidate, the jury hears the argument for the attorney representing the other party in the case, and the consumer—if he is prudent—will consider the claims of advertisers of other competitive products.

Genetic Fallacies.   Genetic fallacies attempt to reduce the significance of a movement or a state of affairs merely to a proposed account of its origin or earliest antecedents. For example: "Our nation cherishes freedom today, since many of the founders of the republic were men who prized freedom more than life itself."

Genetic fallacies overlook the development or regression of ideas and movements. The assumption is made that the heart or essence of an idea, subject area, or movement is found in the state of affairs in which it arose and that no significant difference is to be found in the contemporary situation.

Thus, the essence of contemporary science would be accounted for on the basis of its origin in Greece, and the nature of art would be explained by reference to its origin in primitive societies.

Some cases of the genetic fallacy propose initial evaluations of the source of an idea and carry over this evaluation to any subsequent notion, process, or act attributed to such a source. "The movement to lower taxes and improve local government is a worthy endeavor, since it was begun by the 'Informed Citizens Grass Roots Committee for Fair Taxation'—a group of public-minded citizens."

False Cause. The fallacy of false cause oversimplifies the relevant antecedents of a given series of events. The actual occasion for the occurrence of an event is reduced to factors that are insufficient or irrelevant to account for it, and the context fails to present fully the relevant conditions that are sufficient and necessary for the event. Many instances of false cause either overemphasize the role of one particular factor or include too many general conditions. Examples of the fallacy of false cause would be "Smith drowned because he did not learn to swim when he was young" and "Rome fell because her leaders quarreled among themselves." (Causal fallacies are discussed in more detail in Section 18.5.)

False Analogy. An analogy finds similar characteristics in two or more objects and suggests that the objects share additional similarities that are not immediately obvious. Since such objects are alike in certain known respects, it is inferred that they must be similar in additional respects as well. A false analogy makes an unwarranted inference about the additional ways in which such objects are said to be similar. A property known to characterize one of the objects is unjustifiably attributed to the other. In a false analogy the error is made of overlooking possible significant differences between objects that share either apparent or relevant similarities.

Analogies have legitimate uses in both scientific and other creative work. They may be particularly useful for illustrative purposes and for suggesting clues in developing hypotheses. Proper precautions must be taken to prevent their abuse. (Analogies are discussed in greater detail in Section 16.5.)

The following argument illustrates the fallacy of false analogy:

> Minds, like rivers, can be broad.
> The broader the river, the shallower it is.
> Therefore, the broader the mind, the less depth it has.

Black-and-White Fallacies. Black-and-white fallacies are arguments based upon the application of only two extreme categories to a subject matter capable of having multiple evaluative categories. Such evaluations use extremes such as absolutely good or absolutely bad. Degrees of desirability or undesirability are ignored. For example: "All politicians are either highly efficient or completely inept."

Black-and-white fallacies overlook both gradations and additional alternatives between extreme positions. The universe of discourse is bifurcated into only two possible value considerations or states of affairs. But situations in the real world seldom are simple dichotomies. In an international crisis, for example, the alternatives usually are not limited to acts of war on the one hand and complete permissiveness on the other. Steps short of armed conflict or complete acquiescence are sought. Before accepting a statement proposing only "either this or that," one should seek additional relevant alternatives so that the statement becomes "either this or that or something else."

Accident.   The fallacy of accident and the fallacy of converse accident relate to inferences derived from general principles or from exceptions to such principles. The fallacy of accident applies a general principle to an exceptional case, as in the following examples: "All property in this city should be subject to the same tax rate. Therefore, this particular charity hospital which operates at a net loss should be taxed at the same rate as any other property held in the community." "A citizen should be allowed to express his own views freely. Therefore, he should be permitted to yell 'Fire!' in a theatre if he chooses to do so."

Instances in which the fallacy of accident occurs fail to take into account the restricted range of some generalizations. Generalizations that need qualification are interpreted as if they were unqualified. Absolute rules or principles are applied without critical examination and without regard to contexts: "If it is wrong to break into a cabin, then a cabin should not be entered to save a party from freezing even though they are caught in a blizzard." Such generalizations are applied to cases for which they are not intended or in a manner that is too inclusive.

Converse Accident.   The fallacy of converse accident takes an exceptional or "accidental" case and seeks to make a general rule out of the unusual state of affairs. Consider the following examples: "Since it is permissible for a student to delay handing in his assignment if he is called home on an emergency, it is permissible for a student to delay handing in an assignment whenever he chooses to do so." "Since the government is permitted to exercise the right of condemnation of property for public roads, it is also right for the government to condemn property for any reason believed desirable."

The fallacy of converse accident generalizes from an exceptional case to a proposed general principle. Special pleading, as we have seen, stacks the deck with a group or series of favorable cases—that is, the evidence is not so much exceptional as it is one-sided. Converse accident, on the other hand, takes an instance of what is more obviously unusual and formulates a general principle, which is then universalized and applied uniformly to a class of objects or actions that are not recognized as exceptional cases and to which another principle is more relevant. If deceit is permitted in protecting a small girl from being attacked by a mentally deranged man, it may then be proposed that deceit is always justifiable; this proposal overlooks the more general principle that deceit is morally unacceptable and that only highly unusual circumstances can support its justification. Exceptions in such cases remain exceptions and do not constitute a general principle for guiding behavior.

Hasty Generalization. The fallacy of hasty generalization reaches a generalized conclusion on the basis of too limited a range of examples. For example: "Smith, Jones, and Brown are members of labor unions and each of them is interested in gaining the maximum pay with the least amount of work. Therefore, all members of labor unions are interested only in gaining the highest wage with the least work." "I have talked with three professors who say they are so involved in completing research that they cannot give attention to individual students. Hence, all professors are so involved in research that they cannot give attention to individual students."

The person making a hasty generalization rushes to a conclusion without finding a sufficiently wide base to warrant it. He assumes that every case will be similar to the few that have come to his attention. Many instances of hasty generalization are superficial efforts to justify a preconceived notion or a prejudice. A person may want to believe that members of a particular social group are dishonest, that adherents to a particular religious community are dogmatic, or that persons who have gained wealth exploit the underprivileged. As a basis for justifying his point of view he produces a few cases and then generalizes, claiming that anyone falling in this general class shares the characteristics attributed to the few individuals he singles out.

Hasty generalization covers such a broad spectrum that many other informal fallacies are to some extent instances of it. Fallacies are properly classified under this heading if the thrust or emphasis of the argument is on cases that are too restricted in number or too limited in scope. The classification of some borderline cases remains a matter of judgment.

5.3 EXERCISES

Identify the fallacies in the following statements.
1. Right is right and wrong is wrong. Political compromise is not right. Therefore, it is wrong.
2. Since the government is permitted to exercise forms of censorship during times of war, it is permissible for the government to exercise censorship during any national emergency.
3. Since it is right for parents to guide the choices of their children, it is right for college teachers to guide the choices of their students.

4. Some depressions occur after a sharp drop in the stock market. Therefore, they occur because of a sharp drop in the stock market.

5. Science is sophisticated superstition, since one of the early precursors of science, the effort of man to control his environment, was based on magic.

6. Labor unions are undesirable, since some of their leaders have been convicted of income tax evasion, many of their supporters are known to be associated with criminal elements, and strikes are called to the great inconvenience of the public.

7. Since a mother survives on very little sleep to take care of a sick child, she can be expected to survive at any time on very little sleep.

8. On three occasions persons wearing bow ties have lied to me. Therefore, you can never trust a person wearing a bow tie.

9. Adults feel insecure because of childhood experiences.

10. Since human bodies become less active and then die, it is reasonable to expect political bodies to become less active and then die.

5.4 Fallacies of Misuse of Appeal to Emotions

The fallacy of misuse of appeal to emotion occurs if an argument appeals to emotion as a substitute for evidence, or to distract attention from poor evidence, or to make evidence appear more significant than it actually is.

We do not claim here that emotion is bad in itself. The expression of emotion is found in great works of literature and other forms of art. These works are appraised by criteria appropriate to the media. The use of emotion to motivate action not only is a normal occurrence but is regarded as praiseworthy under some circumstances—usually where the expression of emotion has a basis in the events, reflects honestly the feeling of the persons involved, and is appropriate in degree and manner.

The fallacy of the misuse of emotion occurs with cases of avoiding, replacing, or distorting the weight or significance of evidence as it relates to the conclusion of an argument. Feeling rather than evidence is offered to justify conclusions. The appeal to emotion may be effective in some forms of persuasive speech, but in the appraisal of argument it is no substitute for evidence. The story is told of an attorney whose trial notes were found by a janitor. At one point in the summary statement was the notation, "The case is weak here, tell a joke."

The Misuse of the Appeal to Laughter.   The misuse of the appeal to laughter consists in the use of humor as a substitute for relevant evidence, or as a basis for making evidence appear more significant than it is. An example of such an appeal in some contexts could be the following: "Anyone who accepts the conclusions of my opponent would also be forced to accept the view that the tail wags the dog."

Humor can be used effectively to secure acceptance of a conclusion in persuasive speech; it can be misused to introduce irrelevant considerations into a discussion. Humor can help relieve tensions at a critical point of a discussion and can help to focus attention on relevant issues, or it can divert attention from the central issues and can stifle serious thought and analysis.

The Appeal to Pity (Argumentum Ad Misericordiam). The appeal to pity, instead of presenting relevant evidence, attempts to elicit a feeling of sympathy to secure an emotional disposition to accept a conclusion. For example: "John deserves a 'C' in this class since his parents have sacrificed to send him to college and he will not graduate if he receives a lower grade." Appeal to pity can be more indirect; for example, a lawyer during his final argument may find occasion to relate to a jury an incident in which a car runs over a small boy's dog. A speaker seeking to secure acceptance of his views can digress to tell a story about his mother in emotional tones.

The fallacy of appeal to pity rests on the replacement of relevant evidence for a conclusion by a bid for the sympathy of an audience. Pity or sympathy is accepted as an appropriate emotional response under proper circumstances, and it can provide motivation for praiseworthy acts; nonetheless, the logician cannot accept it as a basis for inference.

The Appeal to Reverence. Respect for traditions and for the men and instrumentalities associated with them helps to maintain social stability and continuity. An appeal to reverence based upon such traditions, men, and instrumentalities can constitute a fallacy if it takes the place of relevant evidence supporting a conclusion. Consider the statement "We must beware of foreign entangling alliances since Washington, the founder of our nation, warned us against taking such a course of action." Past events suggesting a need for caution in foreign alliances can be indicated, but the evidence relevant to a decision must be related to a contemporary state of affairs and to current issues. The views of a historical figure who rendered significant service to his nation may not be applicable to problems of a later period.

Appeal to misplaced authority can be confused with the appeal to reverence. The latter appeal is more firmly imbedded in the traditions of a culture with strong emotional attachment to its heritage. Its emphasis is on the regard for the person as a major representative of a tradition held dear in a community of admirers.

The Bandwagon Fallacy. The bandwagon fallacy appeals to an interest in following the crowd and doing as they do rather than to adequate evidence justifying a conclusion. For example: "You ought to learn the bugaloo, as everyone bugaloos, and you will be left out if you don't." "You ought to buy a small European sports car as all members of the smart crowd now own one of these cars."

The bandwagon fallacy is a favorite ploy of advertisers and propagandists. The thrust of this appeal is to adopt the alleged preferences of the crowd. The suggestion is made that if everyone is doing a particular act, showing a particular preference, buying a given product, then this must be good. The "in group" or the "smart set" approves, and membership in such groups may follow from "doing as they do."

The Common-Folks Appeal.   The fallacy of the common-folks appeal attempts to secure acceptance of a conclusion by the speaker's identification with the everyday concerns and feelings of an audience rather than on the basis of adequate evidence. For example: "I'm sure you will recognize that I am more competent than my opponent. When I was in high school I had to get up at four-thirty every morning to deliver papers. In college I was barely able to make C's and had to do janitorial work in order to make ends meet to put myself through school. Therefore, I would make a better congressman."

An experienced public speaker interested in persuading an audience often seeks to identify himself with their concerns, interests, and way of life. The "common-folks" appeal becomes a fallacy when such techniques of identification are used as a substitute for relevant evidence in an argument.

Appeal to the Gallery (Argumentum Ad Populum).   An appeal to the gallery seeks acceptance of a point of view by an emotional reaffirmation of a speaker's support of values, traditions, interests, prejudices, or provincial concerns shared widely by members of an audience. In making this appeal the speaker frequently uses the terminology and clichés characteristic of the common discourse of the group. A speaker at a political rally might seek to secure acceptance of his program not by offering evidence in its support, but by appealing to the prejudices against "big business" or "vested interests" or "outside groups." The speaker at a businessmen's luncheon might elaborate upon his opposition to government control of business to secure support for his position on wildlife conservation. Likewise, a speaker to a labor group might begin by condemning the exploitation workers have undergone in order to win support for his views on agricultural legislation.

Appeal to the gallery is characterized frequently by a speaker's use of emotional anecdotes and glittering generalities. He presents himself as the champion of motherhood, liberty, justice, virtue, and religion. Such appeals constitute fallacies when they become substitutes for evidence needed for sound reasoning in attaining trustworthy conclusions.

5.5 EXERCISES

Identify the informal fallacies occurring in the following cases.

1. "You should join the switch to Taste Tells Cigarettes, since everybody is doing this and you are sure to be popular if you do."
2. Political speaker to a group of student demonstrators: "I have emphasized the need for respect for student rights. I believe students should have a voice on the Board of Regents of their colleges. I believe students should determine all the rules they are expected to observe in college and to be the jury and judge in cases

involving violations of these rules. I am confident that you will agree that I would make an effective representative in the state legislature."

3. "We must avoid entangling ourselves with foreign alliances. Our nation became great during the first one hundred years of its existence by avoiding such alliances."

4. "You must believe that I told the truth. Do not my tears indicate that I am not lying?"

5. "My client must be innocent. He worked hard to get through school. He has gone to church all his life. He has taken good care of his mother. He takes his son to the Little League ball games. He is an ordinary citizen and would do only those things that you, as self-respecting citizens, would do."

6. "You must agree that these students did not cheat on the exam. Think what effect their failure in the class would have on their subsequent careers."

7. In a famous debate on evolution one of the speakers asked the opposition a question of the following kind: "Would you please tell the audience whether you were descended from apes on your mother's side or your father's side of the family?"

8. "Protective tariffs are needed for the common good of the nation. Think what would happen to the economy of our region if tariffs were lowered and cheap foreign-labor goods were to compete with our products."

5.6 Fallacies of Involved or Complex Assumptions

Fallacies of involved assumptions presume a conclusion rather than prove a conclusion. A conclusion based on a complex assumption makes explicit the assumption contained in the proposed evidence. Instances of complex assumptions may occur without an argument. In such cases they are to be classified as abuse of the principles of inquiry rather than as informal fallacies.

Begging the Question (Petitio Principii). The fallacy of begging the question consists in stating an argument in which one of the statements offered as evidence assumes the conclusion and in claiming that such evidence justifies the conclusion. Consider the following example: "All the events in nature are determined, human events are part of the events in nature; therefore, human events are determined." The conclusion is assumed in the initial premise, which, in this context, would need to be established.

Begging the question assumes what needs to be proven and offers this assumption as evidence for a conclusion that only particularizes the assumption or that restates an equivalent form of the original assumption. To claim that a particular person is naive and offer as evidence that he is a liberal, with the assumption that to be liberal means to be naive, is to beg the question. If such evidence is to stand up, then it must be established that all liberals are naive. Begging the question can occur even though the technical form of the argument might not violate any formal rule of inference. What is being questioned in this case is not the validity of the form taken by the argument:

All liberals are naive.
Smith is a liberal.
Therefore, Smith is naive.

Rather, we question the justification of the provided evidence: "All liberals are naive." The assumption of this statement and its subsequent use to prove that Smith is naive "begs the question." To say, "All members of Bill's fraternity are foolish because they are stupid," is to beg the question by assuming their stupidity and then claiming they are foolish, which is a kind of restatement of the proposed evidence.

Arguing in a Circle.   The fallacy of arguing in a circle is a special case of the fallacy of begging the question; it is listed separately here for emphasis. Arguing in a circle makes explicit the assumption that is implicit in the more general fallacy of begging the question. A premise is used as evidence to establish a conclusion, and this conclusion is used as evidence to establish the original premise. This fallacy sometimes is called circular reasoning.

Consider the proposed argument: "Democracy is desirable because it promotes freedom of inquiry. But why is freedom of inquiry desirable? It is desirable because it promotes democracy." Arguing in a circle has the form: "*A* is true because *B* is true, and *B* is true because *A* is true." It also may be more complex: "*A* is true because *B* is true. *B* is true because *C* is true. And *C* is true because *A* is true."

Name-Tagging.   Name-tagging is the attaching of labels to persons or things. Such labels may suggest praiseworthy qualities ("good," "noble," "industrious," "fair-minded"), blameworthy qualities ("stupid," "irresponsible," "naive," "lazy"), or other qualities ("radical," "liberal," "conservative," "reactionary"). The fallacy of name-tagging occurs if it is assumed that such labels constitute evidence for conclusions about the objects to which the labels are applied. Consider the following examples: "Smith is a narrow-minded conservative because his opponent called him a 'narrow-minded conservative.'" "Jones is an irresponsible liberal because a newspaper columnist referred to him as 'an irresponsible liberal.'" "Black is a person with radical leanings as he was called a radical by the chairman of a legislative committee."

The fallacy of name-tagging occurs frequently in advertising. "This application is easy to use. Look at its label, 'Easy Applicator.'" "Our prices are the lowest in town since we have the name, 'The Cut Rate House.'"

Names, of course, cannot determine either what anything is or what value it has.

Poisoning the Wells.   The fallacy of "poisoning the wells" consists in discrediting the source of proposed evidence, so that the evidence is ruled out prior to any consideration of its merits. An example of this fallacy would be: "Anything that you say would be influenced by your interest in civil rights. You may make your statement, but we shall know beforehand that it will be distorted and unreliable." By "poisoning the wells" one establishes in advance that contrary evidence from an allegedly "contaminated" source will be given no weight in the argument. Some instances of "poisoning the wells" are better classified as improper ways of conducting an inquiry than as fallacies in argument.

Complex Question. A complex question, like a leading question (discussed below), is not strictly a fallacy of argument. Rather it represents a defective or improper manner of pursuing an investigation. A complex question makes an interrogation that assumes certain states of affairs; any answer involves the granting of the assumption. In answering the question "Have you stopped telling lies?" you would be accepting the assumption that you had been telling lies.

A complex question is loaded. Any answer involves accepting assumptions that prejudice the inquiry. If a defendant answered the question "Where did you put the knife after leaving the room?" he would be admitting both that he had such a knife and that he left the room.

Complex questions can be the source of fallacies in arguments if conclusions are inferred from them on the basis of inadequate evidence.

Leading Question. A leading question, which is an improper procedure in inquiry rather than essentially an error in argument, "plants" a proposed answer to a question by the manner in which the question is asked. The question "Did you turn out of your traffic lane only after you saw an accident was otherwise unavoidable?" suggests the desirability of answering, "Yes, I did." Consider another example: "You do believe that longer vacations are desirable, do you not?" Some questions can be loaded both by a prejudiced assumption and a suggested answer: "You planned to return the money you embezzled, did you not?" Leading questions, like complex questions and other forms of complex assumptions, are ruled out of order when used by an attorney in courts of law.

Contradictory Assumptions. The fallacy of contradictory assumptions is another incorrect procedure in inquiry. A traditional example is the question: "What would happen if an irresistible force met an immovable object?" The assumption of either an irresistible force or an immovable object excludes the possibility of the other. The mother who tells her son to go out and play football but not to get dirty is confusing him by the same fallacy: the playing of football precludes the possibility of keeping clean. Politicians promising to increase government services and to reduce taxes obviously cannot achieve both goals.

5.7 EXERCISES

Identify the assumptions or fallacies in the following examples.

1. "You must accept my belief in the freedom of speech, since freedom of speech is the cornerstone of liberal principles. But why should one accept liberal principles? One should accept liberal principles because this assures freedom of speech."

2. "Have you decided to begin to pay attention in class?"

3. "Only men of real taste smoke Smooth Cigarettes. How do you know this is the case? Because a man of real taste told me so. But how do you know he is a man of real taste? He is a man of real taste because he smokes Smooth Cigarettes."

4. "My socialist opponent refuses to state why he believes in Social Security legislation."

5. Any person who disagrees with me is a Give-Away International Do-Gooder. Representative Smith disagrees with me. You know what kind of person he must be."

6. "You did study your lesson, didn't you?"

7. "Since you are known to be an advocate of liberal views, your ideas on this issue will not be worthy of consideration in our arriving at a conclusion."

8. "We should increase our military preparedness, but we should decrease military expenditures."

Chapter 6
Informal Fallacies
(Continued)

6.1 Fallacies of Imprecision in the Use of Language

Informal fallacies due to imprecision in language occur if conclusions not justified by the evidence are based upon ambiguity or vagueness in a given word, phrase, or statement in an argument.

The Misuse of Vague Expressions. The informal fallacy of misuse of vague expressions occurs if a conclusion not justified by evidence is attributable to the misinterpretation of a vague expression. Consider the following example: "You claim that you believe in free enterprise, yet you accept socialistic practices of government like the War on Poverty and Medicare. The American way of life has never endorsed a policy of providing something for nothing." In this statement, expressions such as "the American way of life" and "free enterprise" conceivably have differing ranges of applicability. They could be interpreted to exclude a War on Poverty or a Medicare program on the basis that these had never been done in the past, or they could be interpreted to include these programs as a reasonable development of principles already accepted on the American scene. Most glittering generalities of this sort are so vague that differing interpretations of their meaning can lead to widely differing conclusions.

The Fallacy of Simple Ambiguity. The fallacy of simple ambiguity is the drawing of an improper conclusion from a statement having more than one possible meaning. However, in this case the ambiguity does not have as its source inadequacies of grammar or errors of punctuation. The fallacy of simple ambiguity is exemplified in the following statement: "We cannot

54

expect John to come since he said, 'Nothing will deter me from coming.' "

The fallacy of simple ambiguity results from an effort to establish a conclusion by interpreting a statement in a manner not justified by the context. If the context does not provide a basis for clarifying a statement and the probable intention of the author remains obscure, then an interpretation of the statement does not entail this fallacy, even though objections to the interpretation might be made by other parties. Usually the fallacy of simple ambiguity occurs only if interpretation is either deliberate or careless—and an act of judgment be required to determine whether it is.

The Fallacy of Equivocation.   In the fallacy of equivocation the meaning of a key expression changes or shifts its meaning in an argument. Consider the following argument: "Everything subject to law is subject to a lawgiver. The natural order is subject to a law. Therefore, the natural order is subject to a lawgiver." In this argument "law" is used in two different ways. In one case it refers to statutory or legislative law, and in the second case it refers to a statistical uniformity that provides a basis for prediction and control of events of the natural order.

In the foregoing example a formal fallacy also occurs in the equivocal use of the middle term "subject to law." It is a four-term fallacy to be discussed under the rules of the categorical syllogism.

Some words lend themselves readily to shifts in meaning in ordinary discourse. Expressions used in the same context in figurative and nonfigurative senses, or moral and nonmoral ones, are especially subject to this error.

The Fallacy of Amphiboly.   The fallacy of amphiboly occurs if a conclusion not justified by evidence is based upon ambiguity attributed to the syntax of a sentence. An example of this fallacy is the following: "No cat has nine tails. Any cat has one more tail than no cat. Therefore, any cat has ten tails." Such ambiguity is due to the grammatical structure of the sentence. The statement is interpreted in a manner not justified by the context or by the intention of the author.

The Fallacy of Ambiguity of Significance.   Ambiguity of significance occurs in the drawing of an improper conclusion by misinterpretation of the significance of a statement. Suppose a speaker makes the following claim: "A period of higher unemployment is developing, since there was a one percent increase in the rate of unemployment in January." The significance of an increased rate of unemployment in January can be determined only if it is compared with such rates during the same month in previous years. If a two percent decline in employment during January is customary, a decline of one percent represents a relative increase rather than a decline in employment. Evidence not only is insufficient to support the proposed inference, but additional information may justify an opposing conclusion.

The Fallacy of Accent. The fallacy of accent occurs when improper emphasis is placed upon a word, phrase, or a sentence and on this basis a conclusion is inferred. One may commit this fallacy by stressing a word or a phrase, by using italics, by underlining, by the inflection of the voice, or by taking a statement out of context ("excerpt lifting").

The fallacy of accent occurs in the following examples. A theme was returned to a student with the notation, "Some parts of this theme are good and other parts interesting. The interesting parts are inaccurate and the good parts were copied." The student wrote his parents, "The grader wrote that my theme was 'good' and 'interesting.'" A newspaper headline declares, "NATIONAL EMERGENCY ARISES." The accompanying story recounts an interview with a congressman who states, "If inflation is not held in check, a national emergency may arise." As another example, a person might claim that he need not respect the rights of the underprivileged living in the slums across town, since his religious principles only require him to love his neighbor as himself.

The Fallacy of Division. The fallacy of division and the fallacy of composition are concerned with the relation of parts and wholes or with the collective and distributive senses or meanings of terms. The collective meaning of a term refers to the total group characterized by the term. Examples are found in the extensions of such terms as "students," "professors," "logicians," "physicians," or "attorneys." The distributive meaning of a term refers to each individual denoted by the term, such as each student, each professor, or each attorney. The fallacy of division is an argument inferring that the property of an organized whole also characterizes the parts of the whole. It also occurs if a property characteristic of the collective meaning of a term is said to apply necessarily to the distributive meaning of a term. Consider the following examples: "Since this is one of the best logic classes I have ever had, each student in this class is one of the best students in logic that I have ever had." "Since surgeons have spent many years in perfecting appendectomies, Dr. James Doe, the new surgeon in our town, has spent many years in perfecting his technique in performing appendectomies." In the fallacy of division an argument erroneously assumes that any characteristic or quality applicable to a collectivity or organized whole is applicable to each member of the collectivity. Although Professor Smith may be a member of an outstanding department of physics he may not be an outstanding physicist.

The Fallacy of Composition. The fallacy of composition is an argument inferring that the qualities or characteristics of parts of a whole must also characterize the whole itself. It also occurs when the characteristics of the distributive meaning of a term are claimed to apply necessarily to the collective sense of the term. Consider these examples: "Since the members of this team are the best players of their respective positions in the conference, a team composed of these players would be the best team in the conference." "Since individual athletes grow too old to remain in competition, athletes as a group will grow too old to compete for new records."

Arguments in fallacies of composition proceed in an opposite manner from arguments involving fallacies of division. In a fallacy of composition an argument holds that if each member of a collectivity or an organized whole has a particular characteristic or quality, then the collectivity will have the same characteristics or properties. A group of musicians may be highly skilled individually as players of particular instruments. It does not follow that if they play together they will constitute a superior band or orchestra.

The fallacy of composition also is to be distinguished from the fallacy of hasty generalization. The latter is a generalization from too few instances —that is, the number of cases having the property in common is not sufficient to justify the conclusion that each member of the class has this property in common. Thus it would constitute a fallacy of hasty generalization to argue that since three parolees were involved in subsequent crimes, all parolees become involved in subsequent crimes. The fallacy of composition is not concerned with an argument whose fault is merely that of having too few instances to justify the conclusion; rather, it applies to arguments assuming that a collectivity or whole necessarily has the properties assigned to any of its parts.

Some instances of the fallacies of composition and division could be classified as fallacies of equivocation. This holds if there is a shift in the argument from the distributive sense of a term to its collective sense or vice versa. This is exemplified in the terms "surgeons" and "athletes" used above to illustrate the fallacies of division and composition. Consider also the following example: "Organized labor is opposed to racial discrimination; therefore, organized labor in each of its branches is opposed to racial discrimination." "Organized labor" is used in a collective sense in the premise and in a distributive sense in the conclusion. This is a fallacy of division, since the argument attributes a characteristic of the collective sense of the term "organized labor" to the distributive sense of the term. However, it is also a fallacy of equivocation, since a key expression in the argument is used with two different meanings. Such cases show how certain errors of reasoning may be instances of more than a single informal fallacy.

6.2 EXERCISES

Identify the informal fallacies found in the following statements.

1. Since the principles of liberal education have made our educational institutions so strong, we should not experiment with changing entrance requirements in colleges, as any change would be more likely to weaken than strengthen these principles.

2. Since professors become too old to be effective teachers, we can expect professors to become ineffective in teaching.

3. All rational beings are men. Women are not men. Therefore, women are not rational beings.

4. Since the players are all bushed, they will not feel like going to the dance tonight.

5. You are to obey all traffic regulations if a policeman is watching.

6. " 'The number of newspapers in the United States declined from 2202 in 1909–10 to 1760 in 1953–4. The number of cities with competing daily newspapers declined from 689 to only 87. The number of cities with non-competing dailies increased from 518 to 1301. Eighteen states are now without any locally competing daily newspapers.' "[1]

7. She ran to meet her mother, happy and excited.

8. Since John is on the right side, he must be conservative.

9. Since this rope is strong, each piece of twine in the rope is strong.

10. No man has two heads. Any man has one more head than no man. Therefore, any man has three heads.

11. Since each premise in this argument is relevant, we can expect the argument to be relevant.

12. Since there was a 4 percent drop in enrollment during the second semester, there must be a decline in enrollment in the college.

13. Since attorneys are professional persons concerned with the defense of human rights, Attorney Smith is a professional person concerned with the defense of human rights.

14. Professor Jones must be a good man since he is a good teacher.

15. The bankers say that money is tight, but all of mine gets away before I can save any of it.

6.3 Fallacies of Irrelevance

Fallacies of irrelevance violate the general principle that evidence presented in support of a conclusion should be related to the issue under discussion. The proposed evidence in such cases does not support a conclusion in the manner claimed by the proponent. Fallacies of irrelevance are not always obvious, and different appraisals, changing perspectives, or additional information may affect our judgments of relevance.

Irrelevances are distinguishable as internal and external. If the irrelevance is internal to the argument, the evidence misses the point in need of proof within the argument. If the irrelevance is external to the argument, the evidence fails to support the conclusion by ignoring the point at issue; that is, it is "beside the point at issue," and a conclusion other than the point at issue may be drawn. In specialized cases, discussed later in this section, the fallacy of *non sequitur* is concerned with internal irrelevance and the fallacy of *ignoratio elenchi* ("ignoring the point at issue") is concerned

---

[1] Quoted by Robert U. Brown in "Shop Talk at Thirty," *Editor & Publisher*, January 6, 1968, p. 52.

with external irrelevance. These names are usually reserved to fallacies whose contexts are developed at some length. No hard and fast line can be drawn in all cases with regard to the internal or external character of the irrelevance.

In a broad sense many of the informal fallacies discussed elsewhere also could be classified as fallacies of irrelevance. The fallacies discussed in this section have been traditionally classified as "fallacies of irrelevance," and they are distinguished in part by their degree of irrelevance.

Fallacies Misusing Appeals to Authoritative Sources.　The use of statements from authoritative sources as evidence to support a conclusion does not in itself constitute a fallacy of argument. The views and opinions of qualified authorities can have significance when evidence is weighed. Problems do emerge if the point at issue is in dispute among different competent authorities; in such cases we must appeal to original data. In basic research the appeal to an authority relative to a point at issue would not be accepted as adequate or satisfactory evidence.

Fallacies based upon misusing appeals to authoritative sources consist in supporting a conclusion by appeals to documents, generally held beliefs, or the opinions of well-known persons that are not particularly germane or qualified to deal with the point at issue. The statements of a physician about matters of health, of an attorney about law, of an economist about economics, of a biologist about biology, or of a theologian about theology may be relevant and appropriate in an argument concerned with an issue bearing on these areas. However, the statement of a physician about sports, of a lawyer about economics, of an economist about politics, or of a theologian about biology are fallacies of irrelevance (assuming such persons have achieved recognized professional competence only in one field). If such persons have achieved competence in the field to which reference is made, the appeal is to a sports authority who is also a physician or to an economist who is also a lawyer, or to a scientist who is also a theologian.

For purposes of analysis we can distinguish three major variations of the fallacies misusing appeals to authoritative sources. The first is the *appeal to misplaced authority,* in which the views of an authority in one field are adduced as evidence about a point at issue in another subject area, for which the alleged authority has no particular competence. Consider the argument, "We need to support the formation of a common market among the countries of Latin America because the great nuclear scientist, Juan Fulano, stated that this would help strengthen the economy of these countries."

A second kind of fallacy of the misuse of appeal to authorities is the *appeal to celebrity*. This consists in the proposed settlement of a point at issue in an argument by reference to a well-known or popular public figure, relying upon his fame or popularity rather than his competence in any particular subject matter. "Flying saucers carrying creatures from outer space have landed in this country because the great television newscaster, John Doe, reported on his show that this was undoubtedly a fact."

A third kind of misuse of appeal to authoritative sources is the *appeal to common consensus*. This appeal seeks to resolve a point at issue in an argument by introducing evidence based on an alleged general belief of mankind. Thus, it might be claimed "Man must be immortal because this belief has tended to be present in such widely differing societies in highly divergent circumstances over such a long span of history." A belief that is widespread may not be well supported by primary evidence. The point at issue is not whether a given view is commonly held but rather whether there is solid evidence to support such a belief.

The Appeal to Force (Argumentum Ad Baculum). The fallacy of appeal to force takes the form "If you do not accept this conclusion, then certain unfortunate circumstances will fall to your lot." For example: "You should accept the view that our protection society can strengthen the sales of your product. Otherwise you might find that your machinery has been damaged and that your labor troubles increase."

The *argumentum ad baculum,* or the appeal to a club, substitutes force or the threat of its use for rational evidence in the support of a conclusion. Although the appeal to force may be effective in achieving a limited goal, it abandons rational procedures in gaining an objective. In some instances this kind of appeal may be successfully opposed by rational argument. Persuasive speech and even counterforce have been used to oppose such tactics particularly if the issues are concerned with immediate practical objectives.

The Appeal to the Man (Argumentum Ad Hominem). The fallacy of the appeal to the man seeks to prove a conclusion false by attacking the character, reputation, associations, or social situations of the person proposing it. An *ad hominem* argument shifts the point at issue from evidence related to the conclusion of the argument to the person making the opposing argument. The effort is made to discredit an argument by discrediting its proponent.

Two forms of *ad hominem* arguments are traditionally distinguished: the abusive *ad hominem* and the circumstantial *ad hominem*. The *abusive ad hominem* seeks to discredit the person proposing an argument by an attack upon his character. Vilifying reference may be made to character defects, such as alleged tendencies to lie, to deceive, or to steal. Guilt by association may be suggested by proposed identification of the opposition with hoodlums, by reference to unpopular activities of his relatives or close acquaintances. Consider the following abusive *ad hominem* arguments: "My opponent's view that we should increase taxes is wrong, since he supported Senator Doe who was censured by his colleagues for improper accounting for funds raised at testimonial dinners." "The statement of this witness cannot be accepted as reliable, since he participated in a protest demonstration against the United States' foreign policy when he was a student in college." Abusive *ad hominem* appeals can attempt to direct social prejudice against the person making the statement. "The views of Mr. Smith relative to antipoverty measures cannot be sound, since he supports granting full voting opportunities to the minority groups in this section of the country." Rather than advancing evidence to support an issue, abusive *ad hominem* appeals attempt to undermine opposing views by discrediting the character of the person advancing them.

Circumstantial ad hominem arguments discredit the person advancing opposing arguments by claiming that his circumstances or groups with which he is identified warrant rejection of his views. Thus, it may be claimed that certain views are to be rejected because they merely reflect the opinion of the speaker's social or professional group. Consider the following argument: "The recommendations of Attorney Smith to file suit for damages in this case are unsound, since he is a lawyer and lawyers are expected to recommend that suits be filed when persons claim to have been injured by the action of another party." A special case of a circumstantial *ad hominem* argument is the *tu quoque* (you also) or appeal to similar circumstances. This seeks to discredit views of an opposing party by pointing to discrepancies between his circumstances and views he is advocating or between a previous and present position. Charges are made that the opposing party does the kind of thing he is claiming to be against or that he has held the same views that he is now rejecting. "You cannot believe what you say in favor of desegregated housing, since you live in a neighborhood where there is *de facto* segregated housing."

Some arguments that bring in evidence relevant to the character or circumstances of the person representing opposing views may not constitute a fallacy of irrelevance. If a person is shown to distort and misrepresent evidence in a habitual fashion, his testimony can be discredited. The appeal to similar circumstances can show bad faith or hypocrisy of a person advocating an opposing view. However, a given position must be justified by evidence rather than merely by discrediting an opponent. The critical factor in deciding the justifiability of arguments, including references to the character or circumstances of the person offering opposing views, is their relevance to the issue at hand. It is the unusual case if such attacks do not introduce considerations irrelevant to the point at issue in an argument.

The Appeal to Ignorance (Argumentum Ad Ignorantium).   The fallacy of the appeal to ignorance advances the position that if one conclusion in an argument cannot be established convincingly, then the opposing view can be accepted. "X is true because you are unable to establish convincingly that it is false." Consider the following examples: "Since you cannot disprove that there are flying saucers, you should accept as reliable the reports of those claiming to have seen such objects." "Since you cannot prove with absolute certainty that the amount of radioactive fallout from past explosions of nuclear test devices is significantly injurious to human life, it must therefore be the case that the radioactive fallout has not been injurious."

A difficulty with arguments using appeals to ignorance is that the same kind of argument can be used to establish opposing views. "Since you cannot prove reliable the reports of those who claim to have seen flying saucers, you should agree that there are no objects of this kind." Furthermore, circumstances in which a given conclusion cannot be established do not constitute evidence that the opposing view is worthy of acceptance, but only that a rationally convincing position has not been put forward.

Objections can be offered that legal procedures of assuming a defendant innocent until he is proven guilty are instances of appeal to ignorance. Legal guilt is to be proven in a judicial system. The prosecution has to present convincing evidence to support a verdict of guilty. Technically speaking, requirements for establishing such convincing evidence, beyond a reasonable doubt, mean that the legal status of the defendant remains what it has been prior to the accusation until legal proof demonstrates otherwise. Prior to such proof the defendant remains legally innocent. Both "guilt" and "innocence" in this case have technical meanings. They do not refer to the specific conduct of the defendant but rather to the verdict rendered, based upon the ability of the prosecution to establish a position beyond a reasonable doubt by using the rules of evidence accepted in a court of law. Unless such evidence is established, no change occurs in the legal status of the defendant.

The Fallacy of an Irrelevant Conclusion or of "Missing the Point" of the Evidence (Ignoratio Elenchi).   The fallacy of an irrelevant conclusion establishes the wrong conclusion—that is, a conclusion that is not the issue. The traditional name of this fallacy, *ignoratio elenchi,* means "ignoring the point at issue." This fallacy misses the point to be established. Consider the following example (which is oversimplified): "Collective bargaining ought to be abolished. Collective bargaining gives the labor unions strength. Collective bargaining makes possible corruption of government officials. Collective bargaining strengthens the power of the leaders of the unions." On the basis of such premises, a conclusion supporting the need for legislation abolishing collective bargaining can be proposed. Such a conclusion does not follow from these premises, however.

Consider another example: "Any high school graduate should be admitted to any university supported by taxes in his state, since he should be assured of all privileges of citizenship guaranteed to him by the Constitution, his family also pays taxes in that particular state, and he can get a better job if he is a graduate of a university." The evidence may justify a conclusion supporting the provision of additional colleges or vocational training for qualified graduates of high schools in institutions in their state, but it does not justify adequately the conclusion that any high school graduate regardless of high school grades and admissions tests should be admitted to a state-supported university.

An irrelevant conclusion is not germane to the issue at hand and stresses factors that may support a conclusion other than the one proposed. The fallacy of an irrelevant conclusion in a general sense can include various informal fallacies discussed elsewhere in this text. However, in practice the classification of a fallacy under this heading tends to be restricted to fallacies with a developed context. The most appropriate examples frequently occur in illustrations, digressions, and repetitions. The issues tend to become obscured by a constant flow of words and a sense of bewilderment created about the central topic. Irrelevant conclusions are a favorite device of persons resorting to persuasion if they are hard pressed to establish a particular conclusion or to offer an effective counterargument.

The Argumentative Leap (Non Sequitur).   The fallacy of an argumentative leap "jumps to a conclusion." No immediate basis for drawing the proposed conclusion is provided internally within the argument. For example: "The electoral college is subject to extreme criticism. Therefore, presidential candidates should be nominated by popular votes rather than by political conventions."

The argumentative leap may include evidence related in some general manner to the point being discussed, but the premises fail to provide either a logical basis or a relevant connection with the conclusion. The evidence is not sufficiently germane to establish the point at issue. Fallacies properly classified as argumentative leaps tend to occur primarily in contexts that are highly developed. Many other informal fallacies discussed elsewhere could be classified as *non sequitur* arguments. The appropriate classification of some fallacies—whether special pleading or *non sequitur,* for example—may be a matter of judgment based in part on interpretation of the context of the proposed argument.

The claim that an argument constitutes an informal fallacy needs to be examined carefully. Fallacies are mistakes in reasoning. In a strict sense a fallacy is concerned with an error in an inference rather than an error in the use of language. A statement may be loaded; there may be obvious equivocation; an improper question may be asked. Such errors in the use of language or in conducting inquiry are technical fallacies in argument only if they contribute to a further error in inference.

The determination of fallacious arguments often requires an analysis of the broader context in which the alleged fallacy occurs. The use of fallacies in some forms of persuasive speech may be effective because of their resemblance to acceptable forms of inference. If an opposing case has not been proven, it is proper to point this out as one means of establishing that a conclusion other than the opposing view can be accepted and be consistent with other reasonable positions.

Fallacies may be alleged to characterize an argument without adequate justification. The use of information relative to a disputant's circumstances can be relevant in limiting the weight of his argument without constituting a circumstantial *ad hominem* argument if it can be shown that persons in such circumstances are restricted to one point of view. Pointing to such factors does not establish that the opposing party has made an error in reasoning, but it emphasizes that whatever the evidence might be, only one conclusion would be acceptable to him. In the application of a general principle to specific cases, the case chosen may be extreme without constituting an exceptional case or a fallacy of accident. If the general principle is held that all adult citizens are permitted to vote in national elections, then it might be regarded as an extreme case to apply this principle to illiterate persons. But the fallacy of accident has not been committed merely because this is an extreme (rather than an exceptional) case.

Since some errors in reasoning can be instances of several different kinds of fallacies, the context needs to be examined for the main thrust of the proposed argument. Determination of the primary kind of error may be a matter of judgment. It is preferable in making such judgments to restrict fallacies of irrelevant conclusion and argumentative leap primarily to cases with a context that is developed, and to use names of other fallacies where these are applicable. In a general sense many abusive *ad hominem* arguments, appeals to ignorance, and various kinds of appeals to emotion are fallacies of irrelevant conclusions.

6.4 EXERCISES

Identify the informal fallacies in the following examples.
1. Increased federal spending is good for the economy, since you cannot prove it is bad.
2. Man must be free, since this has been a commonly accepted view for centuries.
3. You cannot accept his view that there is need to increase the size of the armed forces, since he is a military officer and military officers are expected to recommend an increase in military personnel.
4. We must reduce the size of the public debt, since George Stradivarius, the great orchestral conductor, pointed out this is essential.
5. If you do not agree that this business merger is a good deal, you may find yourself in a price war.
6. The increase in the cost of living is inevitable in an expanding economy. Therefore, it is a good thing for the economy.
7. We have not developed the kind of foreign policy that is respected either by

critics at home or by other governments. Therefore, we need a change of administration.

8. Since the great movie star, John Gable, said there was fiscal irresponsibility in government, we should accept this point of view.

9. The statement of the witness that the driver of the automobile ran the red light cannot be accepted, since he was convicted of perjury twenty years ago.

10. Students are anxious to get a good education. They also want qualified teachers and interesting classes. Therefore, students should be permitted to receive a college degree only by taking four years of undergraduate courses regardless of the selection of courses they might take.

11. You cannot be serious in stating that the military involvement in Southeast Asia should be supported, since you have not enlisted in the military forces in support of the military activities there.

12. Since you cannot prove intelligence tests are inaccurate, they must be accurate.

13. It is true that God is only a projection of a father-image into the universe, since Freud, the father of psychoanalysis, stated this was so.

14. Books are expensive and books are necessary for making good grades in college. Therefore, the government should provide texts for all college students.

Identify the fallacies or complex assumptions in the following statements.

15. The United States Chamber of Commerce is a wealthy organization; therefore, every member of the United States Chamber of Commerce is a wealthy person.

16. Any student has the right of a citizen. Students have an obligation to do the right thing. Citizens have a right to protest the actions of government. Therefore, students have an obligation to criticize the actions of government.

17. Any great musical composition is beautiful because if it isn't beautiful, then it is not a great musical composition.

18. The natives here must be barbarians, since John heard one of them say that as they were eating a friend the nephew of their chief came in.

19. Research has failed to prove that cigarette smoking is really harmful to health. Therefore, it is reasonable to conclude that cigarette smoking in moderation is not harmful.

20. Physician Smith must be a poor medical doctor. Did not the newspapers report his involvement in a nightclub brawl, and is he not divorced?

21. This ruling of the Supreme Court is unfair to reporters, since reporters keep the public informed and a well-informed public is necessary for justice.

22. Councilman Smith's plea that the city needs more industry cannot be accepted as worthy of serious consideration, since he is a member of the Chamber of Commerce and any member of the Chamber of Commerce is expected to make this kind of plea.

23. Since the officer said that no more leaves would be given, we can expect a leave next weekend, since we have been getting leaves on weekends in the past.

24. Have you not learned your lesson by this time?

25. A person is entitled to use what is his own property. This automobile is the property of John's uncle, who is drunk. Therefore, John's uncle is entitled to the use and possession of the automobile now.

26. How can you accept his recommendation that surgery be performed? After all, Dr. Blank is a surgeon and surgeons are expected to recommend operations.

27. Any measures that might lead to war should not be taken, since no mother wishes her son to be killed fighting in a foreign land.

28. A crumb is better than nothing. Nothing is better than strawberry shortcake. Therefore, a crumb is better than strawberry shortcake.

29. Since it cannot be proven that John copied his term theme from the work of a student in a previous class, we can be sure that John did not do this.

30. Morphine is habit-forming; therefore, physicians should not use this drug in easing pain.

31. Each member of the committee on civic improvement is a hard-working person; therefore, we can be assured that the committee on civic improvement is a hard-working committee.

32. You must accept mental telepathy as a fact, since no one has ever proven that there is nothing to it.

33. Your arguments against the draft cannot be accepted, since you are a pacifist and all pacifists are opposed to the draft.

34. Teacher to the student: "If you don't accept my reason for marking your answer wrong, I shall regrade your paper; but you can be sure that your score will not be as high as it is now."

35. Any extension of the coverage of Social Security is wrong. People should plan for the future, and if they fall on hard times it's their own fault.

36. If you don't support my candidacy for Congress, then I will see to it that no new reservoirs are built in your area.

37. "We should not have escalated the war in Vietnam." "But there were many reasons to justify this action." "But can you demonstrate absolutely that there were no other alternatives?" "But these appear to be the best alternatives we had at the time." "See, you cannot prove beyond any doubt that we should have escalated the war in Vietnam; therefore, this proves conclusively that we shouldn't have."

38. Glistening Glitter is the most revolutionary toothpaste on the market. Ima Starr stated on television that she had been trying this for six months and that no other toothpaste had ever cleaned her teeth so effectively.

39. Salesman to undecided customer: "Shall I charge this TV set to your account or do you wish to pay cash?"

40. You must agree that this weekly news magazine is the best in the country. Seven out of ten of the top executives in the country read it every week.

41. My client cannot be guilty of this crime. See how honest his eyes appear. Notice what a clean-cut, square-jawed countenance he has.

42. If you elect me to this office, I promise to be faithful to the principles on which George Washington founded this great Republic and to be faithful to the causes for which our sons fought so nobly in battle.

43. Did not Emerson say, "A foolish consistency is the hobgoblin of little minds, little statesmen, and little divines"? Therefore, you should not be concerned if all my statements are not consistent.

44. Every book in his library is a good book. Therefore, he has a good library.

45. This problem is wrong. It's wrong because there is a mistake in it. There is a mistake in it because it's incorrect and it's incorrect because it's wrong.

46. Child: "Since my mother said for me to be in bed when she gets home, it will be all right for me to get up after she comes home."

47. Cooperation made this nation great. Therefore, the merger of large corporations will make this nation even greater.

48. Since the candidate has not clearly indicated his opposition to the government's meddling in our local affairs by insisting upon equal economic opportunities for all local citizens, he obviously is strongly in favor of this.

49. When did you stop losing half of your weekly paycheck at the race track?

50. Democratic institutions are to be supported. Therefore, the Democratic party is to be supported.

51. Jones pitched an excellent game after he had an argument with his wife; therefore, he pitched the excellent game because he had the argument with his wife.

52. Since nothing is better than blue-chip stock and poor returns are better than nothing, poor returns are better than blue-chip stock.

53. This building is a splendid architectural masterpiece. It combines the best features of Early American, French Provincial, and Italian Renaissance architecture.

54. The men of the Executive Committee exercise superior judgment in their personal affairs. Therefore, we can be assured that the Executive Committee will exercise superior judgment in handling the affairs of the club.

55. Either it's all right or it's all wrong. You will admit that it is not all right, therefore, it must be all wrong.

56. Children alone are not permitted to see the movie. Therefore, they can go if accompanied by other children.

57. Some professors teach crime courses. Therefore, some persons learn how to become criminals in college.

58. You can't possibly accept his views that the employees need a raise. After all, he is the executive secretary of the labor union, and he is paid to make these kinds of statements.

59. Since many persons claim to have extrasensory perception, we must conclude that they have extrasensory perception, since no one has ever disproven that they do not have this ability.

60. "Son, why are your grades so low?" "Father, did you ever make a low grade in school?"

61. Mr. Smith's credit can't be any good because we have no record of his meeting monthly installment payments.

62. The company obviously is solvent. You haven't heard of any one filing bankruptcy charges against it, have you?

63. Candidate Blank would make an excellent legislator. When he was in college, he worked such long hours as a salesman that he was barely able to keep a passing average.

64. You should surely agree that my work deserves an "A" because if I do not make an "A" in this course I cannot graduate with honors.

65. If you convict this man of perjury, who will feed the mouths of his three hungry children and who will keep a roof over the heads of these bright children?

66. "I only go to good movies." "But how do you know that they are good?" "Well, I don't choose to go to them unless they are good."

67. When you know the applicant as well as I do, you will be convinced of his abilities as I am.

68. Since I shall demonstrate for you beyond any possibility of a doubt that my client is a strong upstanding red-blooded American, you must agree that he cannot have been involved in any way with the falsification of records.

69. Every peace-loving citizen will abhor the suffering found in war. Therefore, you will agree that our mothers' sons should not be sent to fight in conflicts on foreign soil.

70. You can be sure that I am behind you, yes, far behind.

71. Persons who subscribe to our stock-market analyses have an annual income far greater than the average citizen. Therefore, this higher income is due to their use of our market reports.

72. Since inflation hurts people on fixed incomes and decreases the purchasing power of the dollar, inflation is always bad for the economy.

73. You did throw the revolver in the river, did you not?

74. Youngster: "Mother, I do not believe in Santa Claus any more." Mother: "Well, I guess you will not get any presents for Christmas." Youngster: "I have changed my mind. I do believe in Santa Claus."

75. We should spend our vacation in the mountains because we need to have a rest and a visit to the mountains is restful.

76. The Republican party is for the working man, since labor groups helped to organize it.

77. Since rulers are like parents in that both desire the well-being of those responsible to them, rulers should require obedience to their wishes, since parents can require obedience from their children.

78. You must agree that our section of the country needs lower freight rates, since those who establish freight rates all live in comfortable houses in Washington.

79. We must operate on a balanced budget, because the Founding Fathers of our republic insisted that nations can be strong only as they stay clear of debt, and they insisted on great national sacrifices to pay off the original debt.

80. Our region is entitled to the use of all water in this river basin, because the development of both agriculture and industry in this area is dependent upon our having available every drop of this water for our own use.

81. Since the Democratic Party supports the war on poverty, we can expect Congressman Smith, who is a member of the Democratic Party, to support the war on poverty.

82. Exercise is excellent for health. Therefore, Charles Jones who has a serious heart ailment ought to take more exercise.

83. The strongest motive always determines a person's choice. But how do you know what the strongest motive is? You can determine the strongest motive by the choice that is made.

84. We should increase the quality of our public schools and make certain that only texts that meet the approval of the most conservative members of our community are adopted.

Part II
Deductive
Logic

Part II
Deductive
Logic

Chapter 7
The Categorical
Syllogism

7.1 Arguments

In Part I we discussed elementary factors in the analysis of language and of informal fallacies. The proper use of language and the avoidance of such fallacies are prerequisites to sound reasoning. However, reliable inference also requires that conclusions be supported by adequate evidence. Consider the following syllogism:

> All strikers are persons wanting higher wages.
> No truck drivers are strikers.
> Therefore, no truck drivers are persons wanting higher wages.

A glance at this conclusion and an analysis of the evidence given to justify it indicates that some error in reasoning is present. However, the source of the error is not so immediately obvious. The analysis of forms of valid reasoning provides a basis for identifying and determining the source of such errors. In the present example a term, "persons wanting higher wages," refers only to some such persons in the premises but it refers to all such persons in the conclusion. A formal fallacy—known as an illicit major term —has occurred.

The use of reliable forms for structuring arguments and the detection of improper procedures in other cases requires an ability to analyze the structure of arguments. Part II of this book presents material related to such an analysis. The study of deductive logic requires a development of technical material whose usefulness is not always immediately obvious, although it must be mastered for the proper analysis of valid as well as invalid arguments.

This chapter discusses the use of categorical propositions in Aristotelian logic. Later chapters present material related to other kinds of propositions that offer greater flexibility in making reliable inferences. This part of the book is not concerned with the procedures for determining the reliability of statements offered as evidence; these are considered in Part III. Part II analyzes the structure that relations between propositions must take in order to justify the drawing of a conclusion in a deductive argument.

Deductive logic analyzes and develops the principles and procedures of necessary inference. A *necessary inference* is a properly derived conclusion that must be true if its premises are true. *Premises* are statements offered as evidence to justify a conclusion.

> EVIDENCE:
> All physicians are college graduates.
> All surgeons are physicians.
> CONCLUSION:
> Therefore, all surgeons are college graduates.

In this example, the two propositions offered as evidence are premises. The premises together with the conclusion constitute the argument. *Argument* has a technical meaning in logic: it refers to a statement or set of statements that provide evidence to support a conclusion claimed to be derived from them or justified by them. The logical use of "argument" is to be distinguished from other uses of the word. For example, in logic an argument does not refer to a disagreement or a quarrel as such.

Arguments are appraised as valid or invalid. A *valid* argument has a logical structure or form such that in all cases in which its conclusion is false, one or more premises are false. The propositions stating the evidence formally justify the conclusion by virtue of the meaning and relation holding between such propositions. An *invalid* argument is one whose logical form permits a false conclusion with true premises. A *sound* argument is valid and its premises are true. An *unsound* argument has either an invalid form or at least one false premise. These distinctions will be clarified as different types of arguments are developed.

7.2 The Meaning of "Proposition"

The premises and the conclusion of an argument are sentences expressing propositions. A *proposition* is the meaning of a declarative sentence. A *sentence* is a combination of words formulated according to accepted linguistic uses and setting forth a complete expression.

As the meanings of declarative sentences, propositions can be classified as "mental" or "intellectual" objects and relate to such activities as knowing, doubting, believing, and denying belief. The following sentences express propositions: "All physicians are college graduates" and "No surgeons are unprepared." A proposition is true or false but not both true and false.

Statements refer to the assertions of declarative sentences. Different declarative sentences can assert the same proposition; consider the following examples: "All students are intelligent." "Todos los estudiantes son inteligentes." In different contexts the same sentence (or sentence token) can assert different propositions. Consider the meanings or propositions that are possible in different contexts for such sentences as "He caught a fly" and "He is a skilled operator."

7.3 The Principles of Thought and Propositions

Since propositions are true or false, three traditional principles with regard to their truth or falsity may be formulated. Since the time of Aristotle these principles have been called the *laws of thought*. Aristotle applied these laws not only to propositions but also to things; their application to things, however, has been rejected by many modern philosophers.

1. *The principle of identity.* The principle of identity holds that the truth value of a proposition remains constant. If proposition P is true, then proposition P is true.

2. *The principle of excluded middle.* The principle of excluded middle holds that the truth value of a proposition is limited to one of two values, truth or falsity. Either proposition P is false or proposition P is true.

3. *The principle of contradiction.* The principle of contradiction holds that the truth value of a proposition cannot be both true and false. It is impossible both for proposition P to be true and for proposition P to be false.

These principles of thought are fundamental in reasoning. They assure the constancy and definiteness of the truth value of a given proposition in a given context. Any effort to deny these principles presupposes the use of the principles in the attempt to deny them.

7.4 Categorical Propositions

The conventional meaning of *proposition* is the meaning of a declarative sentence. Traditional or Aristotelian logic is concerned with the *categorical proposition*. Examples of categorical propositions are the following: "All physicists are scientists." "No biologists are astrologers." "Some athletes are accounting majors." "Some citizens are not soldiers." In each of these propositions the subject term and the predicate term are connected by a copula, "is" or "are." Some of them also have the negatives, "no" or "not," used in conjunction with the "is" or "are."

In a categorical proposition the copula, unqualified by "not" or "no," means "is (are) included in the class of." The copula qualified by "no" or "not" means "is (are) not included in the class of" or "is (are) excluded from the class of." All categorical propositions are characterized by this notion of class inclusion or of class exclusion.

Categorical propositions have (1) a subject term, (2) a predicate term, (3) a sign denoting class inclusion or class exclusion, such as "are," "is," "are not," "is not," "no . . . is," "no . . . are," and (4) quantifiers, such as "all" or "some." The subject term of a categorical proposition refers to a class included in or excluded from the class indicated by the predicate term. In the sentence "All logicians are philosophers" the subject term is "logicians," the predicate term is "philosophers," the term of class inclusion is "is," and the quantifier is "all." In the sentence "No Greeks are barbarians" the term of class exclusion is "No . . . are," and the sign "no" functions also as a quantifier to determine the distribution of the subject term, "Greeks."

The *quality* of a categorical proposition is affirmative or negative. *Affirmative* categorical propositions characterize the relation of "included in the class of," and *negative* propositions characterize the relation of "is excluded from the class of." The following two propositions are affirmative in quality: "All statesmen are politicians" and "Some rodents are mice." The following propositions are negative in quality: "No gorillas are peace-loving" and "Some Vietnamese are not Buddhists." Thus, a categorical proposition is the meaning of a declarative sentence in which a part or all of the class of the subject term is related to the class of the predicate term by a form of the copula "to be" signifying either "is included in the class of" in affirmative cases or "is excluded from the class of" in negative cases.

The terms of propositions also vary in quality. The subject and predicate terms in the proposition "Some steel alloys are rustproof materials" are affirmative in character. In the proposition "No logicians are nonphilosophers" and in the proposition "Some nonstatesmen are demagogues" the terms "nonphilosophers" and "nonstatesmen" are negative in quality, but the quality of such terms does not determine the quality of the proposition as a whole.

The *quantity* of a categorical proposition is determined by the distribution of the subject term. A categorical proposition is *universal* in quantity if it includes all the members of the class of its subject term—that is, if it has a distributed subject term. "All logicians," "no logicians," "all demagogues," and "no demagogues" are distributed terms, and propositions introduced by such terms are universal. A categorical proposition whose subject term refers to less than all members of its class is *particular* in quantity. In the propositions "Some men are mortal" and "Some professors are logicians" the subject terms "Some men" and "some professors" are undistributed and introduce particular propositions.

A general universal categorical proposition has a distributed general and nonsingular term as its subject: "All college students are adults." "All students in this room are logic students." A singular universal categorical proposition has a subject consisting of a proper name or a term introduced by a personal pronoun, the definite article "the," or a demonstrative expression such as "this" and "those": "Smith is an attorney." "Mary is an English major." "The present president of Smithville College is a bachelor." "This student is alert." "Those test tubes are dirty."

By distinguishing their quality and their quantity, logicians divide categorical propositions into four different types: (1) universal in quantity, affirmative in quality; (2) universal in quantity, negative in quality; (3) particular in quantity, affirmative in quality; (4) particular in quantity, negative in quality. These categorical propositions are (1) universal-affirmative, (2) universal-negative, (3) particular-affirmative, and (4) particular-negative. The letters **A**, **E**, **I**, and **O** have been used traditionally to refer to the four different types of propositions.

An **A** proposition is universal and affirmative.
An **E** proposition is universal and negative.
An **I** proposition is particular and affirmative.
An **O** proposition is particular and negative.

These symbols traditionally were based upon the first vowels in the Latin word *"affirmo"* for the affirmative propositions and the comparable vowels in the Latin *"nego"* for the negative propositions.

Examples of **A** propositions are: "All actors are interpreters of life" and "All professors are liberals." Examples of **E** propositions are: "No actors are interpreters of life" and "No professors are liberals." Examples of **I** propositions are: "Some actors are interpreters of life" and "Some professors are liberals." Examples of **O** propositions are: "Some actors are not interpreters of life" and "Some professors are not liberals."

The subject term is distributed in the **A** and the **E** propositions; it is undistributed in the **I** and the **O** propositions. The predicate term is undistributed in affirmative categorical propositions and is distributed in negative categorical propositions. If the letter S stands for any subject term whatsoever of a categorical proposition, and the letter P stands for any predicate term of such a proposition, and d stands for a distributed term, and u stands for an undistributed term, the distribution of terms in the four types of categorical propositions is as follows:

A propositions	Sd	Pu
E propositions	Sd	Pd
I propositions	Su	Pu
O propositions	Su	Pd

The convention that the predicate term of an **A** proposition is undistributed is based on the principle of following the lesser meaning of a propositional form. Consider the statement: "All enlisted soldiers are military personnel." The term "military personnel" in this statement is undistributed. Less than all military personnel are included in the class of enlisted soldiers. In this case the predicate term of an affirmative proposition is clearly undistributed. In a few cases the predicate term of an **A** proposition could be distributed; for example, consider the propositions "All squares are plane figures with four right angles and four equal sides" and "Mr. Smith's favorite chair is the easy chair in his den." Such propositions would require special consideration. For purposes of this introductory treatment we shall follow the usual procedure of regarding the predicate term of an **A** proposition as undistributed.

Several traditional ways of symbolizing the structure of categorical propositions are shown in Table 7.1. In the third column, the sign "$<$"

Table 7.1   Symbolization of Categorical Propositions

Type of proposition	Traditional Aristotelian form	Form with quality and quantity designated	Boolean form
A	All S is P	$Sd < Pu$	$S\bar{P} = 0$
E	No S is P	$Sd \not< Pd$	$SP = 0$
I	Some S is P	$Su < Pu$	$SP \neq 0$
O	Some S is not P	$Su \not< Pd$	$S\bar{P} \neq 0$

means "included in the class of" and the sign "$\not<$" means "excluded from the class of." These two forms have certain advantages in focusing attention upon the distribution of terms, and we shall find them particularly helpful in dealing with material presented later in such operations as obversion, conversion, and contraposition, in putting categorical syllogisms into logical form, and in working with sorites. The last column assists in the construction of Venn diagrams as well as in analysis of the premises and conclusion of an argument. The bar over a letter negates the class designated by the letter; for example, $S\bar{P} = 0$ means that the class of S and not P is null. The sign "$=$" means "is," and "$\neq$" means "is not." "0" means "null" or "empty." A null class has no members. A class that is not null has at least one member.

7.5 EXERCISES

Analyze each of the following categorical propositions, naming the type of proposition, the traditional Aristotelian form, the form with quality and quantity designated, and the Boolean form. For example, the proposition, "Op art is a passing fad," is an A proposition, universal affirmative, "All S is P," Sd < Pu, $S\bar{P} = 0$.
1. All air pollution is a threat to the national health.

2. Some international peace-keeping proposals are not practical.

3. Some disarmament proposals are feasible alternatives.

4. No nuclear disarmament plan based on the concept of inviolable state sovereignty is a practical plan.

5. Some accommodations are political compromises.

6. Those chemists are professionally competent.

7. All nations are political entities.

8. Some supporters of the United Nations are persons who do not accept the view of the self-determination of peoples.

9. Some high school counselors are highly knowledgeable about college admission requirements.

10. No committees on accreditation are policy-making bodies.

11. Mr. Jones is not welcome.

7.6 Circles for Boolean Analysis of Propositions

We can show the class distinctions of categorical propositions by drawing two overlapping circles, labeling one circle S for the subject term and the other P for the predicate term. (These are circles for Boolean analysis.) See Fig. 7.1.

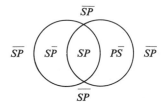

FIGURE 7.1

The part of the circles overlapping can be denoted as the class of SP. To the left of the class of SP is the class of $S\overline{P}$; to the right of the class of SP is the class of $P\overline{S}$. The part outside all of the circles is the class of $\overline{SP}$. A universal-affirmative proposition states that the part of the circle designated S and not P ($S\overline{P}$) is null: it has no members. A universal-negative proposition states that the part of the circle designated S that is common to P (SP) is null. A particular-affirmative proposition states that the part of the circle designated S that is common to P (SP) is not null: it has at least one member. A particular-negative proposition states that the part of the circle designated S and not P ($S\overline{P}$) is not null: it has at least one member. To signify that a class is known to be empty, we shall use a shaded area, and to indicate that a class has a member, we shall insert a letter "x" in that place. On the basis of this Boolean analysis, the different types of categorical propositions are exemplified in Figs. 7.2–7.5.

All S is P
$Sd < Pu$

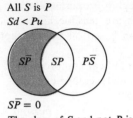

$S\overline{P} = 0$
The class of S and not P is null.

FIGURE 7.2.   Universal Affirmative

No S is P
$Sd \not< Pd$

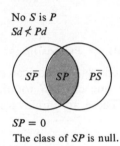

$SP = 0$
The class of SP is null.

FIGURE 7.3.   Universal Negative

Some S is P
$Su < Pu$

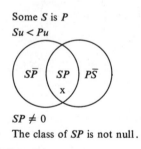

$SP \neq 0$
The class of SP is not null.

FIGURE 7.4.   Particular Affirmative

Some S is not P
$Su \not< Pd$

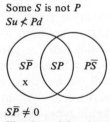

$S\overline{P} \neq 0$
The class of S and not P is not null.

FIGURE 7.5.   Particular Negative

Table 7.2 provides an analysis of the types of categorical propositions.

Table 7.2   Types of Categorical Propositions

A	Universal-affirmative	All S is P	$Sd < Pu$	$S\overline{P} = 0$	S		P
E	Universal-negative	No S is P	$Sd \not< Pd$	$SP = 0$	S		P
I	Particular-affirmative	Some S is P	$Su < Pu$	$SP \neq 0$	S		P
O	Particular-negative	Some S is not P	$Su \not< Pd$	$S\overline{P} \neq 0$	S		P

7.7 The Existentialist Assumption and Aristotelian Logic

Aristotelian or traditional logic apparently assumes two postulates regarding the existence of members of classes of the subject and predicate terms: (1) any class has members, (2) a complementary class of a subject or predicate term also has members. In Aristotelian logic, for example, the class of all mammals has some members and the class of all nonmammals also has some members. A *complementary class* in this sense refers to members of any class that are other than members of the specific class to which reference is made. The complementary class of professors is nonprofessors and the complementary class of students is nonstudents. These two existentialist assumptions have been questioned in modern logic.

The convention holds in modern logic that universal categorical propositions are hypothetical and class membership of the subject and predicate terms remains an open question. Thus, the statements "All graduates are qualified persons" and "All gremlins are strange creatures" are interpreted to mean "If any person is a graduate, then he is a qualified person" and "If any creature is a gremlin, then it is a strange creature." The existence of graduates, of qualified persons, of gremlins, or of strange creatures is left undetermined by the *form* of the original statement.

The convention also is followed in modern logic that the subject terms of a particular proposition and the predicate term of a particular affirmative proposition have class membership; that is, there is at least one member of the indicated class. Thus, the statements "Some dogs have fleas" and "Some persons who play Santa Claus are not elves" are interpreted in the following manner: "There are some creatures (at least one) that are dogs and these creatures have fleas (at least one)," and "Some persons who play Santa Claus (at least one) are not elves." The existence of creatures that are dogs, of creatures that are fleas, and of persons who play Santa Claus is specified by the *form* of the original statement. In this book we shall follow this convention regarding the existential import of class membership of universal or particular propositions, with the possible variation noted in Section 7.16.

A proposition interpreted as having a singular subject containing a proper name, a personal pronoun, a definite description used with the definite article "the" or with demonstrative expressions such as "this," "that," "these," and "those" is classified as a universal proposition. Hence, statements such as "John is a senior" and "The red shoes are objects in the closet" are universal propositions interpreted as meaning: "All persons identical with the individual John are seniors" and "All shoes identical with the red shoes to which reference is made are objects in the closet." The context in which singular-type propositions occur gives rise to special problems regarding existential import. This provides the basis for the possible variation noted in Section 7.16 regarding their use as minor premises in categorical syllogisms in Figure III.

7.8 EXERCISES

1. Draw the Boolean circles for the propositions listed in Section 7.5.
2. Give a complete analysis of the following propositions.
   (a) Mr. Smith is a man with strong beliefs.
   (b) Some research projects are interesting.
   (c) The molecular orbital theory is a description of paths taken by electrons.
   (d) Some students are not science majors.
   (e) No computers are animate objects.
   (f) Fermi is not an unknown physicist.
   (g) All diamonds are hard jewels.
   (h) Some students given a second chance are able to pass.

7.9 Premises and Terms of a Categorical Syllogism

A categorical syllogism has an argument using two categorical propositions as premises and a third such proposition as a conclusion. A categorical syllogism is valid if its structure always prevents the occurrence of a false conclusion with true premises; it is invalid if its structure permits the occurrence of true premises and a false conclusion. The rules of the categorical syllogism specify the conditions of its validity. To determine the formal structures of valid categorical syllogisms and to distinguish these from invalid forms requires a detailed analysis.

The key to the analysis of the categorical proposition is the conclusion. Consider the following categorical syllogism.

> All *physicians* are *college graduates*.
> All *surgeons* are *physicians*.
> Therefore, all *surgeons* are *college graduates*.

Each categorical syllogism has three terms, and each term occurs twice in the syllogism. These terms are the major term, the minor term, and the middle term.

The *major term* of a categorical syllogism is the predicate term of the conclusion. The *minor term* of a categorical syllogism is the subject term of the conclusion. The *middle term* is the term common to each of the premises; it does not appear in the conclusion. The *major premise* for the syllogism is the premise containing the major term. In the example above, the major premise is "All physicians are college graduates." The *minor premise* is the premise with the minor term. The minor premise above is "All surgeons are physicians." In ordinary usage, the premises and the conclusion may appear in any order. When they are analyzed logically, however, the major premise is placed first, the minor premise second, and the conclusion last.

Words such as "therefore," "hence," and "thus" introduce conclusions. Words such as "since," "as," "granted that," "given that," and "because" introduce premises. The premises count as evidence, and in a valid syllogism they logically justify the conclusion derived from them. If the conclusion is to be justified, the basic rules of the categorical syllogism must be met.

7.10 The Rules of the Categorical Syllogism

For a traditional categorical syllogism to be valid, it must conform to the following rules. (These rules are discussed in Section 8.4).

1. A valid categorical syllogism must have three and only three terms, each of which occurs twice with the same meaning in the syllogism.

2. A valid categorical syllogism must have the middle term distributed at least once.

3. A valid categorical syllogism must have every term that is distributed in the conclusion also distributed in the premises.

4. A valid categorical syllogism must have a negative conclusion if either premise is negative.

5. A valid categorical syllogism must have at least one affirmative premise.

6. A valid categorical syllogism cannot have a conclusion with existential import unless one of the premises has existential import.

7.11 EXERCISES

Identify the major term, the minor term, and the middle term in each of the following syllogisms. Determine the validity of the syllogisms.
1. All underdogs are persons having to fight harder. No popular heroes are underdogs. Therefore, no popular heroes are persons having to fight harder.
2. All land conservation is in the national interest. All planting of forests is land conservation. Therefore, all planting of forests is in the national interest.

3. Any industry in a rut is stunting its own growth. No electronic industry is in a rut. Hence, no electronic industry is stunting its own growth.

4. All quixotic programs are risks and many creative programs are quixotic. Therefore, many creative programs are risks.

5. All activities exciting the imagination of people are conducive to progress. All explorations of frontiers are activities exciting to the imagination of people. Hence, all explorations of frontiers are conducive to progress.

7.12 The Figures of Categorical Syllogisms

Categorical propositions in proper logical order have the major premise first, the minor premise second, and the conclusion last. The *figure* of a categorical syllogism is identified by the order of occurrence of the middle term in each of the premises. Consider the following possible arrangements of the middle term, where M refers to the middle term, P refers to the major term, and S refers to the minor term.

	I	II	III	IV
Major premise	M P	P M	M P	P M
Minor premise	S M	S M	M S	M S

There are four possible positions of the middle term. Each different manner of occurrence is a separate figure of the syllogism. In Figure I the middle term is the subject term in the major premise and the predicate term in the minor premise. In Figure II the middle term is the predicate term in both premises. In Figure III the middle term is the subject term in both premises. In Figure IV the middle term is the predicate term in the major premise and the subject term in the minor premise.

Figure I	Figure II	Figure III	Figure IV
M P	P M	M P	P M
S M	S M	M S	M S
S P	S P	S P	S P

The following examples are illustrative of these four figures:

FIGURE I:

       (M)
No scientists are superstitious persons.
              (M)
Some teachers are scientists.

Therefore, some teachers are not superstitious persons.

FIGURE II:

                             (M)
No superstitious persons are scientists.

(*M*)
Some teachers are scientists.

Therefore, some teachers are not superstitious persons.

FIGURE III:

(*M*)
No scientists are superstitious persons.
(*M*)
Some scientists are teachers.

Therefore, some teachers are not superstitious persons.

FIGURE IV:

(*M*)
No superstitious persons are scientists.
(*M*)
Some scientists are teachers.

Therefore, some teachers are not superstitious persons.

7.13 The Mood of a Categorical Syllogism

The *mood* of a categorical syllogism is determined by the types of **A**, **E**, **I**, or **O** propositions found in properly ordered premises and the conclusion. Consider the propositions in the following categorical syllogism in Figure II.

E No oligarchies are democratic.
A All liberal governments are democratic.
E Therefore, no liberal governments are oligarchies.

Here the major premise is an **E** proposition, the minor premise is an **A** proposition, and the conclusion is an **E** proposition. The figure and mood of this syllogism is written II-**EAE**.

In making a logical analysis of a categorical syllogism, we must state the syllogism's figure and mood. Although there are 256 ways in which propositions in categorical syllogisms can be arranged, less than 8 percent of these can occur in a valid categorical syllogism. For example, any syllogism with combinations of **E** and **O** propositions in the premises is invalid. Any syllogism with an **E** or an **O** proposition in the conclusion without an **E** or an **O** proposition in the premises is invalid. Any syllogism with an **E** or an **O** proposition in the premises and an **A** or an **I** proposition in the conclusion is invalid. Each of these cases violates rules of valid categorical syllogisms.

The figure and mood of a syllogism provide a basis for immediate recognition and analysis of the logical structure of its argument form (see Sections 8.2 and 8.4).

7.14 EXERCISES

Give a complete analysis of each of the following syllogisms and of each of its propositions. Identify the figure and mood, determine the validity of the syllogism, and specify any rule of the categorical syllogism that is violated.

1. All actions subject to law are subject to a lawgiver. All movements of planets are actions subject to law. Therefore, all movements of planets are subject to a lawgiver.

2. All atoms are in movement. Some atoms are not subject to experimental control. Therefore, some things subject to experimental control are in movement.

3. No theories are moral commands. All categorical imperatives are moral commands. Therefore, no categorical imperatives are theories.

4. Nothing infinite is an expanding sphere. The universe is an expanding sphere. Therefore, the universe is not infinite.

5. All control of behavior is control of volition. Some control of volition is a consequence of redirecting interests. Therefore, some consequence of redirecting interests is control of behavior.

6. Some theories of probability are rationalistic. All rationalistic theories are *a priori*. Therefore, some *a priori* theories are theories of probability.

7. All pre-med students are interested in biology. George is a pre-med student. Therefore, George is interested in biology.

8. All forms of social control are instances of social determination. The urban renewal program is a form of social control. Therefore, urban renewal is an instance of social determination.

9. No upright animals are quadrupeds. All dogs are quadrupeds. Therefore, no dogs are upright.

10. All cases of justice are matters for the courts. Some cases of justice are cases of alleviation of poverty. Therefore, some cases of alleviation of poverty are matters for the courts.

11. All elderly persons are trustworthy. Some trustworthy persons are talkative. Therefore, some talkative persons are elderly.

12. All parapsychologists are optimistic about ESP. No experimental psychologists are optimistic about ESP. Therefore, no experimental psychologists are parapsychologists.

13. All experiments are proposed solutions to an experimental question. No experiments are projects undertaken without tentative identification of relevant variables. Therefore, no projects undertaken without tentative identification of relevant variables are proposed solutions to an experimental question.

14. Some psychotherapists are not experimentalists. No experimentalist is an investigator indifferent to laboratory techniques. Therefore, some investigators indifferent to laboratory techniques are psychotherapists.

15. Some chess players are engineers. Mr. Smith is an engineer. Therefore, Mr. Smith is a chess player.

7.15 Suppressed Propositions in an Argument

An argument may have one or more propositions suppressed. The completion of the argument requires the making explicit of the suppressed proposition.

An *enthymeme,* meaning "in the mind," is an argument with a suppressed premise or conclusion. In a categorical syllogism, these suppressed propositions may occur in one of four instances.

1. The major premise may be suppressed.
2. The minor premise may be suppressed.
3. The conclusion may be suppressed.
4. The minor premise and the conclusion may be suppressed.

The major premise is suppressed in the following enthymeme: "You diversify your investments; therefore, you are a good investor." The missing major premise can be "All persons who diversify their investments are good investors."

The minor premise is missing in the following argument: "All persons who diversify their investments are good investors; therefore, you are a good investor."

The conclusion is missing in the following enthymeme: "All persons who diversify their investments are good investors and you diversify your investments."

If the minor premise and the conclusion are both missing in an enthymeme, we examine the context in which the major premise occurs. The suppressed minor premise and the conclusion are implicit in the context. After an investor who does not diversify his investments has suffered a severe reversal on the stock market, someone may remark, "All good investors diversify their investments." The minor premise and the conclusion implicit in this context would be, "Mr. X does not diversify his investments; therefore, Mr. X is not a good investor."

The suppressed proposition of an enthymeme can become a source of formal fallacies, particularly in cases of *ad populum* appeals. Consider the following example: "All enemies of the Constitution are persons who appeal to the Bill of Rights for protection. Therefore, members of X Society are enemies of the Constitution." The suppressed premise is "All members of X Society are persons who appeal to the Bill of Rights for their protection." As this enthymeme is stated, it has an undistributed middle term and is therefore invalid.

7.16 Singular Universal Propositions and Existential Import

The convention we have been following interprets universal propositions as hypothetical in form. An exception can be made with regard to a restricted number of cases in which the subject term of a proposition is an affirmative singular-type universal proposition and the syllogism in which this singular-type proposition occurs has identical subject terms in each premise (Figure III).

This alternative convention makes allowance for the apparent existential intent of many singular-type universal propositions. Consider such cases as "This chair is white," "Smith is an architect," "His family is anxious," and "The Viet Cong are a determined adversary." Such affirmative universal statements (comparable to particular categorical propositions) apparently refer to the classes of existent objects expressed by their subject and predicate terms.

The form of a singular universal statement is not sufficient to justify interpretation of existential import. Consider such statements as "The present king of France is an artist" and "This elf is mischievous." There does not seem to be any intention to attribute existence to the class of "this elf" and to "the present king of France." To use this convention permitting an exception to the hypothetical interpretation of universal propositions, we must exercise judgment, considering the context of the statement just as in the case of an enthymeme.

The use of this convention is subject to three restrictions:

1. The subject term of the minor affirmative premise uses a proper name, a personal pronoun, or a definite description used with the definite article "the" or with demonstrative expressions such as "this, "these," "that," and "those."

2. The subject term of both premises is the middle term of the syllogism; that is, the syllogism has the form of Figure III.

3. The context of the sentence provides a basis for justifying a judgment attributing class membership to the subject and predicate terms of the minor premise.

When these restrictions are met, this convention permits the use of Moods **AAI** and **EAO** in Figure III. In using the circles for Boolean analysis in such cases the minor premise is written and drawn first as an **A** premise and then as an **I** premise (see Section 8.1).

7.17 EXERCISES

Write the appropriate premises or conclusion and determine the validity of the following enthymemes.

1. All good lawyers read fine print in contracts. Therefore, John reads fine print in contracts.

2. Background: Mr. Brown makes a foolish assertion in a conference. Later one of the participants remarks to another: "Any person making such a statement is uninformed."

3. All civil wars promote future internal division. Therefore, this war will promote future internal division.

4. All romanticists are idealistic. The "New Left" is idealistic.

5. Many folk-oriented songs are popular. Therefore, this song will be popular.

6. Picasso's works have strong imagery. Therefore, Picasso's works are superior works of art.

7. All persons sleeping have minds that are active. Therefore, persons who have died have minds that are active.

8. Some dreams are events resulting in higher blood pressure. Therefore, Mr. Blank is dreaming.

9. No careful driver "tailgates" another car. Therefore, Mr. Jones is not a careful driver.

10. No man with a poor credit rating can secure personal loans readily. Therefore, Mr. Smith can secure personal loans readily.

Chapter 8
Venn Diagrams and
Categorical Syllogisms

8.1 The Use of Venn Diagrams

The validity of categorical syllogisms can be determined by the use of Venn diagrams. We construct such diagrams by drawing the circles representing the Boolean analysis of the propositions in the premises and imposing these circles on a common set of circles. If a categorical syllogism is valid, we can draw the conclusion by drawing the circles for the premises. If a categorical syllogism is invalid, such circles will not fully draw the conclusion.

Consider the following categorical syllogisms.

(1) All Greeks are wise.
   All Athenians are Greeks.
   Therefore, all Athenians are wise.

(2) All conservatives believe the world is round.
   All liberals believe the world is round.
   Therefore, all liberals are conservatives.

The first syllogism in Figure I, Mood **AAA,** has the Boolean analysis shown in Fig. 8.1. A common set of circles can be drawn as in Fig. 8.2. The major premise and the minor premise can be drawn on the common set of circles as in Fig. 8.3. The circles for the Boolean analysis of the conclusion are compared with the common set of circles for both premises (Fig. 8.4). The common circles drawn only for the premises also draw the conclusion. Thus, the syllogism is valid.

$M\overline{P} = 0$

Major premise

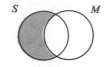

$S\overline{M} = 0$

Minor premise

$S\overline{P} = 0$

Conclusion

FIGURE 8.1

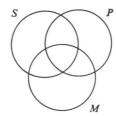

FIGURE 8.2

$M\overline{P} = 0$

Major premise

$S\overline{M} = 0$

Minor premise

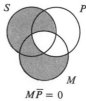

$M\overline{P} = 0$
$S\overline{M} = 0$

Both premises

FIGURE 8.3

$M\overline{P} = 0$
$S\overline{M} = 0$

Both premises

$S\overline{P} = 0$

Conclusion

FIGURE 8.4

$P\overline{M} = 0$
Major premise

$S\overline{M} = 0$
Minor premise

$S\overline{P} = 0$
Conclusion

FIGURE 8.5

$P\overline{M} = 0$
Major premise

$S\overline{M} = 0$
Minor premise

$P\overline{M} = 0$
$S\overline{M} = 0$
Both premises

FIGURE 8.6

$P\overline{M} = 0$
$S\overline{M} = 0$
Both premises

$S\overline{P} = 0$
Conclusion

FIGURE 8.7

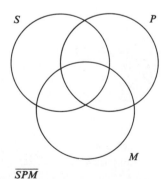

$\overline{SPM}$

FIGURE 8.8

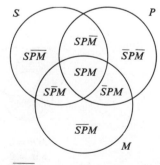

$\overline{SPM}$

The second syllogism in Figure II, Mood **AAA,** has the analysis shown in Fig. 8.5. The premises drawn on a common set of circles are shown in Fig. 8.6. The circles for both premises and the conclusion are compared in Fig. 8.7. We see that the drawing of the premises did not fully draw the conclusion. A part of the class of S and not P is not shown to be null by the drawing of the premises, but all of this class is shown to be null in the conclusion. Thus, this syllogism is invalid.

The different sections of the composite circles in the Venn diagrams can be analyzed into classes, as shown in Fig. 8.8. In this diagram a number of classes and subclasses can be distinguished:

SM refers to the class of SPM and the class of $S\overline{P}M$.
PM refers to the class of SPM and the class of $\overline{S}PM$.
SP refers to the class of SPM and the class of $SP\overline{M}$.
$S\overline{P}$ refers to the class of $S\overline{P}\overline{M}$ and the class of $S\overline{P}M$.
$S\overline{M}$ refers to the class of $S\overline{P}\overline{M}$ and the class of $SP\overline{M}$.
$P\overline{S}$ refers to the class of $\overline{S}PM$ and the class of $\overline{S}P\overline{M}$.
$P\overline{M}$ refers to the class of $SP\overline{M}$ and the class of $\overline{S}P\overline{M}$.
$M\overline{S}$ refers to the class of $\overline{S}PM$ and the class of $\overline{S}\overline{P}M$.
$M\overline{P}$ refers to the class of $S\overline{P}M$ and the class of $\overline{S}\overline{P}M$.

$\overline{S}\overline{P}\overline{M}$ refers to all classes other than class S or class P or class M or some combination of such classes.

These subclasses are useful in the analysis of Venn diagrams to determine the validity of syllogisms.

8.2 Propositions With Existential Import and Venn Diagrams

Propositions with existential import require that the universal propositions be drawn on the combined circles before the "x" is placed on a circle. Consider the following syllogism in Figure III, Mood **IAI:**

Some humanists are novelists.
All humanists are defenders of human rights.
Therefore, some defenders of human rights are novelists.

If the "x" denoting class membership were drawn on the combined circle first, it might fall in the section later indicated as null. Therefore, the universal premise needs to be shown first and the "x" placed in the part of the circle that is not shown to be null (Fig. 8.9).

A special problem arises if a line crosses a section where an "x" is to be placed after any universal premise has been drawn. Consider the analysis of the following syllogism in Figure I, Mood **AOO:**

All employees are eligible for social security benefits.
Some stockholders are not employees.

Therefore, some stockholders are not eligible for social security benefits.

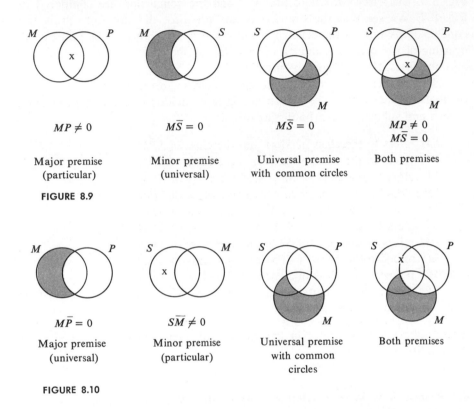

MP ≠ 0	M$\overline{S}$ = 0	M$\overline{S}$ = 0	MP ≠ 0 M$\overline{S}$ = 0
Major premise (particular)	Minor premise (universal)	Universal premise with common circles	Both premises

FIGURE 8.9

M$\overline{P}$ = 0	S$\overline{M}$ ≠ 0		
Major premise (universal)	Minor premise (particular)	Universal premise with common circles	Both premises

FIGURE 8.10

Look at Fig. 8.10. The minor premise requires that the "x" be placed in the class of S and not M. After the universal premise has been drawn, a line divides the class of S and not M. The class membership signified by the "x" might apply only to one class of the two classes, SPM and SPM, in the larger class of SM. Owing to this possibility, the "x" is placed on the line dividing the classes SPM and SPM. However, the conclusion (Fig. 8.11) requires that the "x" definitely appear in the class signified as SP and not merely on a line that would signify possible but not necessary membership in the class of SP. Since the "x" appears only on the line and not definitely in the class indicated by the conclusion, the syllogism is invalid.

Venn diagrams for syllogisms in Figure III with universal affirmative singular-type propositions as minor premises (Section 7.16) are constructed by drawing the major and minor premises as universal premises and drawing the minor premise a second time on the diagram as an **I** proposition. (The "x" is placed in the class of MS that is not indicated as null.)

After the technique of drawing the Venn diagram has been mastered,

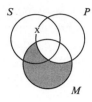

Both premises   Conclusion

FIGURE 8.11

it is necessary to draw only the one set of common circles in testing the validity of the syllogism.

8.3 EXERCISES

Draw the Venn diagrams for the following figures and moods. State the rule violated for any invalid case.
1. Figure I, **AEE, EAE, AII, AOI, OAO, EIO.**
2. Figure II, **OAO, EIO, AAA, AEE, AOO.**
3. Figure III, **AOO, IAI, OOO, EAE.**
4. Figure IV, **AAA, IAI, OAO, AEE.**

8.4 Discussion of the Rules of the Categorical Syllogism

The rules of the categorical syllogism were stated previously without discussion. An understanding of their justification develops as one uses them and applies the Venn diagrams. Let us now examine these rules in greater detail.

RULE ONE: *A valid categorical syllogism must have three and only three terms, each of which occurs twice with the same meaning in the syllogism.* The middle term provides a relationship between the major term and the minor term. If the middle term changes its meaning, there is no adequate basis for relating the major term to the minor term. Consider the following example:

> All jewels are precious stones.
> Jane is a jewel.
> Therefore, Jane is a precious stone.

This syllogism is invalid, since the middle term is used with two different meanings. When this fallacy occurs, it is known as the "fallacy of four terms." It is also possible to have a four-term fallacy if the major term or the minor term is used in this equivocal manner. A two-term fallacy can occur when the major term and the minor term or one of these terms and the middle term have the identical meaning. This fallacy does not occur as often as the four-term fallacy.

RULE TWO: *A valid categorical syllogism must have the middle term distributed at least once.* If the middle term is not distributed at least once, then the basis for relating the major term and the minor term is missing, since the middle term could refer to different parts or subclasses in each occurrence. Consider the following syllogism and the analysis of its Venn diagram:

> All capitalists are persons believing the world is round.
> All communists are persons believing the world is round.
> Therefore, all communists are capitalists.

In this syllogism the middle term, "persons believing the world is round," comprises many groups, many of which may have little in common except that they do believe the world is round. The class of "all capitalists" here could be entirely other than the class of "all communists." Since the middle term is undistributed, it provides no satisfactory basis for relating the minor term to the major term.

Consider the Venn diagram for Figure II, Mood **AAA** (Fig. 8.12). In

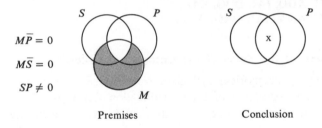

$M\overline{P} = 0$

$M\overline{S} = 0$

$SP \neq 0$

Premises Conclusion

FIGURE 8.12

this case the middle term is undistributed. If the conclusion, $S\overline{P} = 0$, were true, then all of the class section of $S\overline{P}$ would be shaded. However, there is a portion, $S\overline{P}M$, that is not shaded. This demonstrates that for any case of an undistributed middle term in this figure it is possible for the class of $S\overline{P}$ to have members (it is possible that the class of $S\overline{P}$ is not null). A comparable type of problem arises in any other figure in which the middle term is not distributed. The fallacy in this instance is called the "fallacy of the undistributed middle term."

RULE THREE: *A valid categorical syllogism must have every term that is distributed in the conclusion also distributed in the premises.* If a term is undistributed in the premise, it refers to less than all members of its class. However, if the same term is distributed in the conclusion, some of the members of the class referred to in the conclusion may vary significantly from other members in the class referred to by the undistributed term in the premise. This would permit an erroneous logical procedure of including more in the conclusion than was contained in the premises. Consider the following example:

> All conservatives are persons believing in human rights.
> No conservative is a liberal.
> Therefore, no liberal is a person believing in human rights.

In this syllogism, "persons believing in human rights" is distributed in the conclusion, but it is undistributed in the premises. The major premise states that among the persons who believe in human rights is to be included any conservative. This does not exclude other classes such as liberals from being persons believing in human rights, nor does the minor premise exclude liberals from believing in human rights. Therefore, the evidence presented in the premises does not justify the conclusion, "No liberal is a person believing in human rights."

Figure 8.13 shows this syllogism, Figure III, Mood **AEE,** in a Venn

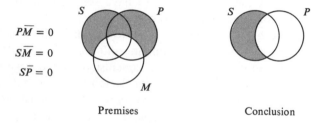

$$P\overline{M} = 0$$
$$S\overline{M} = 0$$
$$S\overline{P} = 0$$

Premises   Conclusion

FIGURE 8.13

diagram. The class of *SPM* is null, but some of the class of *SP,* namely *SPM̄,* is not known to be null. The conclusion states, however, that the class of *SP* is null. Thus, Figure III, Mood **AEE,** is invalid. A comparable problem occurs whenever a term undistributed in the premises is distributed in the conclusion. If the major term is undistributed in the premise, but distributed in the conclusion, this is the "fallacy of the illicit major." If the minor term is undistributed in the premise, but distributed in the conclusion, this is the "fallacy of the illicit minor."

RULE FOUR: *A valid categorical syllogism must have a negative conclusion if either premise is negative.* If this rule is violated, an affirmative conclusion is reached from a negative premise. An affirmative conclusion states a relation of class inclusion between the subject and predicate terms. However, if one of the premises is negative, there is no manner in which class inclusion can be inferred necessarily by the relations holding between two premises. Consider the following syllogism, which has a negative premise and an affirmative conclusion:

> No humanitarian is a person who ignores human suffering.

All physicians are humanitarians.
Therefore, all physicians are persons who ignore human suffering.

The error in this syllogism is readily discernible in a Venn diagram, in Figure I, Mood **EAA.** Look at Fig. 8.14. The class of $S\overline{P}M$ has not been marked

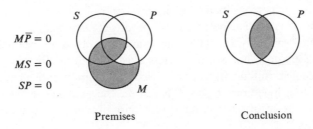

$$M\overline{P} = 0$$

$$MS = 0$$

$$SP = 0$$

Premises   Conclusion

FIGURE 8.14

out; it is possible for this class section to have some members. Not only is it not possible to conclude validly from these premises, "All physicians are persons who ignore human suffering," but we can infer the conclusion, "No physicians are persons who ignore human suffering." The violation of the fourth rule by the use of an affirmative conclusion with a negative premise is called the "fallacy of an affirmative conclusion with a negative premise."

RULE FIVE: *A valid categorical syllogism must have at least one affirmative premise.* The exclusion of part or all of the major and minor terms from the middle term does not make possible any inference about the relation of the major and minor terms to each other. These terms could be wholly or partially included in or excluded from each other, if their only stated relation to the middle term is complete or incomplete exclusion. In such cases we may reach conclusions that are obviously absurd. Consider the invalid syllogism:

No stones are sentient creatures.
No men are stones.
Therefore, no men are sentient creatures.

In this syllogism in Figure I, Mood **EEE,** the class of $SP\overline{M}$ is not marked out in the Venn diagram (Fig. 8.15), and it is possible for it to have members. A valid conclusion would require all the class of *SP,* including $SP\overline{M}$, to be null. The violation of the fifth rule by the use of two negative premises is called the "fallacy of two negative premises."

RULE SIX: *A valid categorical syllogism cannot have a conclusion with existential import unless a premise has existential import.* This rule is a convention based upon the development of modern logic; traditional Aristotelian logic did not adhere to it. The convention was established to prevent the introduction of class membership in the terms found in the conclusion

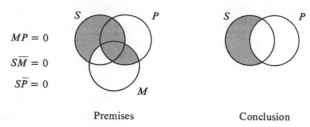

$MP = 0$

$S\overline{M} = 0$

$S\overline{P} = 0$

Premises   Conclusion

FIGURE 8.15

without the introduction of class membership in the terms found in the premises. The particular proposition asserts the existence of classes, but this can be a part of a conclusion only if the existence of such classes has been introduced in the premises. This rule excludes conclusions with existential import if the premises are only general universal propositions. (Many of the more intricate problems dealing with existential import can be dealt with adequately only in a refined system of notation of modern logic.) As an example of the kind of problem that can emerge if this rule is violated, consider the following syllogism in Figure III, Mood **AAI:**

All professors with complete mastery of their subject matter and pedagogical techniques are perfect professors.

All professors with complete mastery of their subject matter and pedagogical techniques are highly popular with their students.

Therefore, some professors who are highly popular with their students are perfect professors.

Each of the above premises is conditioned by the notion: "if there are any professors with complete mastery of their subject matter and pedagogical techniques." No membership is required in the classes of "perfect professors" and "professors who are highly popular with their students." Neither premise specifically holds that as a matter of fact there exist professors of this kind. The conclusion in the form of a particular proposition definitely states that there are (exist) some professors who are both highly popular with their students and who are perfect. In this case, an existential assumption is made in the conclusion and is not warranted by the premises.

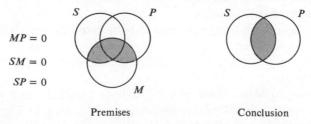

$MP = 0$

$SM = 0$

$SP = 0$

Premises   Conclusion

FIGURE 8.16

Consider the Venn diagrams for this syllogism in Figure III, Mood **AAI** (Fig. 8.16). For the conclusion to be valid, there needs to be an "x" in some part of the class of *SP* to indicate that this class is not null. The violation of this rule is the "fallacy of an illicit existential assumption."

8.5 Some Corollaries of the Rules for the Categorical Syllogism

In addition to the rules previously given, a number of corollaries hold with regard to categorical propositions and with regard to different figures in categorical propositions. These corollaries can be derived from the rules of the categorical syllogism by proofs. If there is doubt as to the manner of establishing a proof for one of these corollaries, it can be helpful to violate the principles in each of the four figures and to note what happens in each case. On the basis of these observations, the construction of a proof can be begun.

Consider the following case:

The first corollary mentioned later is, "No categorical syllogism is valid if the major premise is particular and the minor premise is negative." This corollary means that the following moods are invalid in any figure:

IEA	**OEA**	**IOA**	**OOA**
IEE	**OEE**	**IOE**	**OOE**
IEI	**OEI**	**IOI**	**OOI**
IEO	**OEO**	**IOO**	**OOO**

In the column with premises having the forms **IE,** an affirmative conclusion occurs with a negative premise in the moods **IEA** and **IEI.** The fallacy of an illicit major term occurs with the moods **IEE** and **IEO.** These identical fallacies are repeated in the third column. The moods **IOA** and **IOI** have an affirmative conclusion with a negative premise, and the moods **IOE** and **IOO** have illicit major terms. All the moods in the second column and in the fourth column commit the fallacy of two negative premises. In every possible instance a categorical syllogism with a particular major premise and a negative minor premise violates a rule of the categorical syllogism.

Among the corollaries that follow from the rules of the categorical syllogism are the following (we could give more):

1. No categorical syllogism is valid if the major premise is particular and the minor premise is negative.
2. No categorical syllogism is valid if both premises are affirmative and the conclusion is negative.
3. No categorical syllogism is valid if a conclusion is universal and a premise is particular.
4. No categorical syllogism is valid if both premises are particular.
5. A universal affirmative conclusion is possible only in Figure I.
6. The conclusions of all categorical syllogisms in Figure II are negative.

7. The conclusions of all categorical propositions in Figure III are particular.

8. The major premise in Figure IV is always universal if the conclusion is negative.

8.6 EXERCISES

1. Prove each of the corollaries mentioned for the categorical syllogism. Also prove the statement: "Only one mood is valid in all four figures of the categorical syllogism."

2. Give a complete analysis of the following syllogisms. Include figure, mood, validity, Venn diagrams, and proper logical order. If the syllogism is invalid, state the rule violated.

(a)   Some militarists are not inured to war. No pacifists are inured to war. Therefore, some pacifists are not militarists.

(b)   All fixed costs are expenses that rise in inflation. No gambling losses are fixed costs. Therefore, no gambling losses are expenses that rise in inflation.

(c)   James is a mathematician. James is a reporter. Therefore, some mathematicians are reporters.

(d)   Pilots are short. Mr. Brown is a pilot. Therefore, Mr. Brown is short.

(e)   All conditioned reflexes are learned. No conditioned reflex is innate. Therefore, nothing innate is learned.

(f)   All hawkish policies are dangerous. "Dovey policies" are not hawkish. Therefore, "dovey policies" are not dangerous.

(g)   Pythagoras believes numbers are the key to the universe. Pythagoras is a wise man. Therefore, some wise men believe numbers are the key to the universe.

(h)   Some policemen are persons riding a motorscooter. Mr. Smith is a policeman. Therefore, Mr. Smith is a person riding a motorscooter.

(i)   All persons who study insects scientifically are biologists. All entomologists are persons who study insects scientifically. Therefore, all entomologists are biologists.

(j)   All electrons are in motion. All electrons are parts of the atom. Therefore, some parts of the atom are in motion.

(k)   All air carriers are companies maintaining expensive ground schools. All major air companies are air carriers. Therefore, all major air companies maintain expensive ground schools.

(l)   No flight engineer is poorly paid. No pilots are flight engineers. Therefore, no pilots are poorly paid.

(m)   Rudolph is a reindeer of Santa Claus. Rudolph is a reindeer with a red nose. Therefore, some reindeer with a red nose are reindeer of Santa Claus.

Chapter 9
Reduction of
Categorical Syllogisms
to Proper Form

9.1 Categorical Syllogisms in Irregular Form

Categorical syllogisms may occur in ordinary discourse in irregular form. The analysis of such syllogisms for validity requires their reduction to standard form. Consider the following syllogism:

> Only syllogisms having three terms are valid categorical syllogisms.
> This syllogism is not an invalid categorical syllogism.
> Therefore, this syllogism has three terms.

In its present form this syllogism is improperly stated if it is appraised by the relevant rules of the categorical syllogism. The first premise reverses the order of the subject and predicate terms by the use of "only" at the beginning of the premise. The second premise introduces a negative term, "invalid," of a term appearing in the first premise. The conclusion uses the verb form of "has" rather than the verb form of the copula, "to be." The conclusion also is affirmative and the second premise is negative.

By restating the first premise and the conclusion in the form of proper categorical propositions and by writing an equivalent form for the proposition stating the second premise, we can reduce this syllogism to a valid form.

> All valid categorical syllogisms are syllogisms having three terms.
> This syllogism is a valid categorical syllogism.
> Therefore, this syllogism is a syllogism having three terms.

This chapter discusses the manner in which such restatements of propositions can be made in logically equivalent forms for analysis by the rules of the categorical syllogism.

9.2 The Meaning of Equivalent Categorical Propositions

Propositions are equivalent if they have identical truth values. They have identical truth values if in all instances in which one is true the other is true and if in all instances in which one is false the other is false. Consider the following example.

> Some uses of make-up are factors in increasing productivity of women factory workers.
> Some factors in increasing productivity of women factory workers are uses of make-up.

These propositions have the same truth value. Since they are logical equivalents, one can replace the other in any context without altering the logical meaning of the contexts.

The equivalents for some propositions are derived by operations requiring the interchange of the subject and predicate terms or the negation of both the proposition and the predicate term. For example, these propositions are equivalents:

> All powder-puff working girls are female employees showing less fatigue.
> All female employees not showing less fatigue are non-powder-puff working girls.

Other propositions that are not in standard categorical form have logical equivalent propositions in standard form. Consider the following example of equivalent propositions:

> None but the prepared are nations that survive.
> All nations that survive are nations that are prepared.

The extended analysis of the syllogism requires development of techniques for using such equivalent forms. First we shall consider propositions requiring obversion, conversion, and contraposition, then those requiring restatement of propositions in ordinary language into standard categorical form.

9.3 Obversion

Obversion is a logical operation of double negation. Given the proposition, "All commercial banks are lending institutions," its obverse is "No commercial banks are non-lending institutions." The quality of the proposition as a whole is changed and the quality of the predicate term is changed; that is, the proposition as a whole is negated, and the predicate term is negated.

The quality and distribution of the subject term remain unchanged. Since the distribution of the predicate term is determined by the quality of the proposition as a whole and this quality is changed in obversion, the distribution of the predicate term always changes in obversion.

These considerations can be noted in the following examples of obversion. If the original proposition is "No artist is a color-blind person," the obverse is "All artists are non-color-blind persons." The obverse of "Some Byzantine churches are buildings constructed on top of mountains" is "Some Byzantine churches are not buildings that are not constructed on top of mountains." The obverse of "Some peasants are not workers who plow with a donkey team" is "Some peasants are workers who do not plow with a donkey team."

Thus the formal structure of the obverse of the **A** proposition "All S is P" is "No S is non-P," or $Sd < Pu$ and $Sd \nless -Pd$. The use of the minus sign negates the term that it precedes; it designates the complementary term of the original term. The obverse of the **E** proposition "No S is P" is "All S is non-P"—that is, $Sd \nless Pd$ and $Sd < -Pu$.

The obverse of the **I** proposition "Some S is P" is "Some S is not non-P," or $Su < Pu$ and $Su \nless -Pd$. The obverse of the **O** proposition "Some S is not P" is "Some S is non-P," or $Su \nless Pd$ and $Su < -Pu$.

The negation of the predicate term may be accomplished in a variety of ways besides by the use of "non-" in front of it. One must be careful to make certain that the predicate term is fully negated rather than only partly negated and that the complementary class is designated. The obverse of "John is a person without malice" may be written: "John is not a person with malice. " However, the expression "John is a rational being" would have as its obverse: "John is not a non-rational being." If the obverse were proposed as "John is not an irrational being," this formulation might leave some kind of middle ground between an "irrational being" and a "rational being," particularly since "non-rational" has connotations other than merely "irrational."

Ordinary language sometimes compromises in the negation of a term by not adhering strictly to the notion of a complementary class. Consider the obverse of the following statement: "All accountants are professionally trained persons." The complementary class of the predicate term is "non-professionally trained persons"—that is, "anything that is not a professionally trained person." In a rigorous sense the complementary class is more inclusive than "persons without professional training" or "persons who are not professionally trained."

If the obverse of the above statement is given as, "No accountants are persons without professional training," a compromise of the complete negation of the predicate term has been made for the sake of a linguistic form more in accordance with ordinary usage. The alternative would be a strict adherence to the more cumbersome form of stating a complementary class:

"No accountants are things that are not professionally trained persons." Although compromise of this sort is permitted in the exercises and examples given in this section, it is desirable to recognize the need for a more rigorous procedure in dealing with more advanced problems in logic.

9.4 Conversion

A second logical operation on categorical propositions is *conversion*. This consists of an interchange of the subject term and the predicate term of the proposition, but under two restrictions: (1) the quality of the proposition remains the same, and (2) there can be no increase in the distribution of any term. In modern logic a universal affirmative proposition cannot be converted to a particular one. An **A** proposition has only a partial conversion that is not valid by itself in modern logic. The partial conversion of the statement "All demogogues are persons who prey upon the emotions of people" is "Some persons who prey upon the emotions of people are demogogues." To propose "All persons who prey upon the emotions of people are demogogues" as the converse of the original statement would violate the rule prohibiting the increase in the distribution of a term in conversion.

The converse of the **E** proposition "No Oxford don is an illiterate person" is "No illiterate person is an Oxford don." The **E** proposition converts without difficulty. The converse of the **I** proposition "Some persuasive speakers are persons who achieve identification with their audience" is "Some persons who achieve identification with their audiences are persuasive speakers." The **I** proposition converts with no problems. Consider the **O** proposition "Some teachers are not stimulating lecturers." To propose as the converse "Some stimulating lecturers are not teachers" is to increase the distribution of the original subject term when it becomes the predicate term of the proposed converse; this violates a rule of conversion. An **O** proposition does not have a valid converse form.

The converse of the **E** proposition "No S is P" is "No P is S," or $Sd \not< Pd$ and $Pd \not< Sd$. The converse of the **I** proposition "Some S is P" is "Some P is S," or $Su < Pu$ and $Pu < Su$. The partial converse of the **A** proposition "All S is P" is "Some P is S," or $Sd < Pu$ and $Pu < Su$. This form is not valid in modern logic. The **O** proposition "Some S is not P" has no valid converse.

9.5 Contraposition

Contraposition is a logical operation of interchange and negation of terms. The original proposition is obverted, the obverse is converted, and then this proposition is obverted. This last form is the contraposition. For example, take the following propositions through these operations:

1. *Original proposition*: All labor leaders are collective bargainists.
2. *Obverse*: No labor leader is a non-collective bargainist.
3. *Converse of step 2*: No non-collective bargainist is a labor leader.
4. *Obverse of step 3 and contraposition of step 1*: All non-collective bargainists are non-labor leaders.

The **A** proposition and the **O** proposition have full contrapositives. The contrapositive of the **A** proposition "All *S* is *P*" *is* "All non-*P* is non-*S*," or $Sd < Pu$ and $-Pd < -Su$. The contrapositive of the **O** proposition "Some *S* is not *P*" is "Some non-*P* is not non-*S*," or $Su \not< Pd$ and $-Pu \not< -Sd$.

The **E** proposition has only a partial contrapositive—to an **O** proposition—and is not valid in modern logic. The partial contrapositive of an **E** proposition comes about in the following way. "No *S* is *P*" becomes obverted to "All *S* is non-*P*." The converse of "All *S* is non-*P*" is only partial: "Some non-*P* is *S*." The obverse of "Some non-*P* is *S*" is "Some non-*P* is not non-*S*." This is the partial contrapositive.

The **I** proposition has no contrapositive for the following reason. The obverse of "Some *S* is *P*" is "Some *S* is not non-*P*." But "Some *S* is not non-*P*" has no converse. It is an **O** proposition.

9.6 Tables For Obversion, Conversion, and Contraposition

Tables 9.1, 9.2, and 9.3 show the obversion, conversion, and contraposition, respectively, of the different types of categorical propositions.

Table 9.1   Table for Obversion

A	$Sd < Pu$		All men are rational.
	$Sd \not< -Pd$	Obverse	No men are nonrational.
E	$Sd \not< Pd$		No men are rational.
	$Sd < -Pu$	Observe	All men are nonrational.
I	$Su < Pu$		Some men are rational.
	$Su \not< -Pd$	Obverse	Some men are not nonrational.
O	$Su \not< Pd$		Some men are not rational.
	$Su < -Pu$	Obverse	Some men are nonrational.

Table 9.2   Table for Conversion

A	$Sd < Pu$		All men are mortals.
	$*Pu < Su$	Partial converse	*Some mortals are men.
E	$Sd \not< Pd$		No men are mortals.
	$Pd \not< Sd$	Converse	No mortals are men.
I	$Su < Pu$		Some men are mortals.
	$Pu < Su$	Converse	Some mortals are men.
O	$Su \not< Pd$		(There is no converse for an
	(None)		**O** proposition.)

* Not valid in modern logic.

Table 9.3 Table for Contraposition

A	$Sd < Pu$		All students are intelligent.
	$-Pd < -Su$	Contrapositive	All non-intelligent persons are nonstudents.
E	$Sd \not< Pd$		No students are intelligent.
	$*-Pu \not< -Sd$	Partial contrapositive	*Some non-intelligent persons are not nonstudents.
I	$Su < Pu$ (None)		(There is no contrapositive for an **I** proposition.)
O	$Su \not< Pd$		Some students are not intelligent.
	$-Pu \not< -Sd$	Contrapositive	Some non-intelligent persons are not nonstudents.

* Not valid in modern logic.

9.7 EXERCISES

1. Write the obverse of the following propositions.
   (a) The platoon system is popular.
   (b) No relief pitcher is a regular starter.
   (c) Some catchers are slow.
   (d) Some coaches are not lenient.
2. Write (where possible) the converse of the following propositions.
   (a) All programs are things to be evaluated.
   (b) No waves are particles.
   (c) Some interference patterns are irregular.
   (d) Some photographic plates are not rough.
3. Write (where possible) the contraposition of the following propositions.
   (a) Some recessive characteristics are transmitted to the young.
   (b) All viruses are nucleoprotein.
   (c) No gene is capable of multiplying outside a cell.
   (d) Some plants are not mutations.

9.8 Reduction of Categorical Syllogisms to Three Terms

In logical analysis of a categorical syllogism the propositions are to be placed in standard form and arranged in proper order. If a syllogism can be shown to be valid by obversion, conversion, contraposition, or some combination of these operations, then an analysis of the syllogism should include the form of the proposition in which the syllogism can be valid. Once a syllogism has been reduced to three and only three terms without any violation of the rule with regard to negative premises, it can be evaluated for its validity. If, in this case, the syllogism is invalid, there are no operations of obversion, conversion, and contraposition that can make it valid. If, however, there are more than three terms and they can be reduced to three terms by operations involving obversion, conversion, contraposition, or some combination of these operations, or if there is some violation of the rule about negative premises, every effort needs to be made to remove the conditions that interfere with our stating the syllogism in a valid form.

In the analysis of the categorical syllogism in an irregular form, the following steps should be taken:

1. The conclusion should be identified. (Words such as "so," "hence," "thus," and "therefore" frequently introduce conclusions.)

2. The major term and the minor term should be identified. (The major term is the predicate term of the conclusion. The minor term is the subject term of the conclusion.) In ordinary circumstances, no operation, such as conversion or contraposition, involving the interchange of the subject term and the predicate term of the conclusion is to be performed. The reasons for this recommendation are essentially practical in character. To convert or to contrapose the conclusion would result in loss of uniformity in the analysis of the syllogism and affect more radically other considerations such as its figure and its mood. (If corresponding changes are made in the premises, a valid syllogism remains valid if the conclusion is expressed by an equivalent proposition by obversion, conversion, or contraposition.) It will facilitate the analysis of the syllogism if the minor term is marked with S and the major term is marked with P. In this analysis of the syllogism, the S term means "minor term" and the P means "major term."

3. The major premise, the minor premise, and the middle term should be identified. (The major premise is the premise with the major term. The minor premise is the premise with the minor term.) The letter P (or $-P$) can be placed over the major term and the letter S (or $-S$) over the minor term. (The minus sign indicates the negation of a term. Thus, "$-P$" means "non-P.") The term appearing in both of the premises but not in the conclusion is marked with the letter M (or $-M$). This is the middle term. If either the major term or the minor term is the complementary class of the respective major term or minor term in the conclusion, then it will be designated by a $-S$ or a $-P$. Likewise, if one of the middle terms is a complementary class of the other middle term, one of the middle terms should be marked as an M and the second as a $-M$.

4. The premises and the conclusion of the categorical syllogism need to be placed in logical order—the major premise first, the minor premise second, and the conclusion last.

5. The syllogism should be reduced to three terms, and any violation of the rule with regard to negative premises should be eliminated. If there is any doubt as to the point at which to begin the analysis of the syllogism in order to state it in logical order, then an effort may be made to have the syllogism conform to Figure I. Figure I is the strongest of all four figures and the only one in which an affirmative universal proposition is possible in the conclusion. In the original analysis of propositions the S term referred to any subject term whatsoever. The meaning of the letters S and P changes in the analysis of the categorical syllogism. The S term now refers to the

minor term and the P now refers to the major term. The M refers to the middle term of the syllogism. The use of the forms "$<$" and "$\not<$" together with the d and the u to indicate distribution of terms is particularly helpful in identifying affirmative and negative premises, in identifying the distribution of terms in the proposition, in reducing to three terms any complementary terms, and in performing operations of obversion, conversion, and contraposition.

6. A complete analysis of the syllogism states the proper order of the premises, its figure and mood, its forms and Venn diagram, and its validity. If any of the rules of the categorical syllogism is violated, the rule also should be stated.

The foregoing steps are illustrated in the analysis of the following syllogism: "Since all college students are high school graduates, all philosophy majors are high school graduates because no philosophy majors are noncollege students."

1. Identify the conclusion: "All philosophy majors are high school graduates." Although the conclusion in the syllogism above is not introduced by words such as "thus," "hence," or "therefore," the other propositions are introduced by "since" and "because," which introduce premises.

2. Identify the major terms and minor terms. The subject term of the conclusion is the minor term, which is "philosophy majors." The predicate term in the conclusion introduces the major term, which is "high school graduates." An S is placed over the minor term and a P is placed over the major term.

$$\overset{S}{\text{"All philosophy majors}} \text{ are high} \overset{P}{\text{school}} \text{ graduates."}$$

3. Identify the major premise, minor premise, and middle term. The major premise is the premise with the major term, "high school graduates." The major premise is "All college students are high school graduates." The minor premise is the premise with the minor term, "philosophy majors." The minor premise is "No philosophy majors are non-college students." The middle term is "college students."

4. The premises are stated in logical order:

$$\overset{M}{\text{All college students}} \text{ are high} \overset{P}{\text{school graduates.}} \quad \text{(Major)}$$

$$\overset{S}{\text{No philosophy majors}} \text{ are non-} \overset{-M}{\text{college students.}} \quad \text{(Minor)}$$

$$\overset{S}{\text{All philosophy majors}} \text{ are high} \overset{P}{\text{school students.}} \quad \text{(Conclusion)}$$

5. Reduce to three terms and eliminate violations of rule with regard to negative premises. Restate in proper form:

Original form	Final form
$Md < Pu$	$Md < Pu$
$Sd \not< -Md$	$Sd < Mu$ (Obverse of $Sd \not< -Md$
$Sd < Pu$	$Sd < Pu$

All college students are high school graduates.

All philosophy majors are college students.
Therefore, all philosophy majors are high school graduates.
6. Analyze the structure of the syllogism (Fig. 9.1).

Figure I, $Md < Pu$
                     $Sd < Mu$
Mood **AAA** $Sd < Pu$
Venn diagram: $M\overline{P} = 0$
                     $S\overline{M} = 0$
                     $S\overline{P} = 0$
VALID. No rules violated.

FIGURE 9.1

9.9 EXERCISES

Give a complete analysis of each of the following syllogisms. If the syllogism can be made valid by obversion, conversion, contraposition, or some combination of these operations, make it valid. Arrange the premises so that the major premise is first, the minor premise second, and the conclusion last. In the analysis, give the figure, the mood, the forms showing class inclusion and distribution of terms, the Boolean forms, and the Venn diagrams. Identify valid and invalid syllogisms. If the syllogism is invalid, state the rule violated. It is helpful to use the symbols, such as Sd < Pu, in placing the propositions in proper forms.

1. Since all political experiments are things involving risks, all democratic movements in Southeast Asia are things involving risks, because no democratic movements in Southeast Asia are non-political experiments.
2. Since all non-profitable sources of revenue are non-sales taxes and all sales taxes are taxes hitting the hardest the persons less able to pay, therefore, all taxes hitting the hardest the persons less able to pay are profitable sources of revenue.
3. No person who is easy to trap is a person leading a risky life, because all double agents are difficult to trap and no double agent is a person not leading a risky life.
4. Since no reduction of supply of needed goods is a non-inflationary practice, a reduction in supply of needed goods is harmful to persons with fixed incomes, because all inflationary practices are harmful to persons with fixed incomes.
5. All persons of ability are competent, hence no incompetent person is a cabinet member, since all cabinet members are persons of ability.
6. The Northeast is an area not having a heat wave, since the Northeast is not in a high-pressure area and all areas having heat waves are high-pressure areas.
7. Some justifiable acts of government are actions accompanied by protest, since some increases in taxes are not unjustifiable acts of government and no increases in taxes are actions of government not accompanied by protest.
8. The forecasting of weather is an activity that cannot predict with accuracy, hence the forecasting of weather is an inexact science, as no activity that cannot predict with accuracy is an exact science.
9. All illegal practices are things that can cause trouble and some acts of opening fire hydrants for fun are not legal practices, therefore some acts of opening fire hydrants for fun are things that can cause trouble.

10. All cases of inequity are protestable, since all cases of unequal tax rates are cases of inequity and no cases of unequal tax rates are nonprotestable.

11. Mr. Able is a controversial architect, as he is not an uncreative architect and all noncontroversial architects are noncreative.

12. Since some acts of nonviolent resistance are successful and this demonstration against housing discrimination is not an act of violent resistance, this demonstration against housing discrimination is successful.

13. No opponents of radar to detect traffic violations are safety officers, hence all safety officers are persons who are opposed by speeders, since all persons who are not opposed by speeders are opponents of radar to detect traffic violations.

14. All persons who are not good proofreaders are non-editors. Therefore, all good proofreaders are informed, since no uninformed person is an editor.

9.10 Categorical Propositions and Ordinary Language

Many propositions expressed in ordinary language need to be restated if they are to function as categorical propositions. In stating the proposition in standard categorical form, we must make the subject and the predicate terms explicit, make their distribution precise, and make definite the relation of class inclusion or class exclusion by the copula. Some of the procedures to be followed are included in the following eleven recommendations:

1. The distribution of the subject term is to be made explicit. Consider the statement, "Men are mortals." We need to make explicit the distribution of the subject term by placing "All" or "Some" in front of "men." Such a decision must be made in light of the context. If there is serious doubt about which of the two meanings is intended, the usual procedure is to use the more restricted quantifier ("some") rather than the universal quantifier ("all") for the statement. However, if "some" is used with the subject term in modern logic, the proposition is particular and the existence of class membership of the subject and predicate term is implied; one must consider this implication in deciding how to quantify the subject term. In the case of the statement, "Men are mortal," there is little room for serious doubt about the meaning of the sentence: "all men" customarily would be meant. The proposition would be restated, "All men are mortal."

Consider the expressions, "Many scholars are professors," "Most teachers are college graduates," "A few seniors are candidates for high honors," "Several students are absent." The expressions "many," "most," "a few," and "several" are translated for the categorical proposition by the word "some," whose minimal meaning is "at least one." Although the substitution of "some" in these statements diminishes their original force, this form indicates that the subject term is undistributed and that the proposition is particular. The original statement is written in categorical form: "Some scholars are professors," "Some teachers are college graduates," "Some seniors are candidates for high honors," and "Some students are absent."

2. The notion of class inclusion or class exclusion needs to be made explicit by the verb form of the copula. The proposition needs to be stated in the present tense of the verb "to be." The class inclusion or class exclusion of the subject term in the predicate term needs to be made definite. Take the statement, "Old generals fade away." This needs to be restated as, "All old generals are persons who fade away." Consider the expression, "Librarians read widely." A proper categorical form for this statement is, "All librarians are persons reading widely."

3. The subject term and the predicate term have to be made explicit. Consider the statement, "On the table are many dishes." This statement needs to be stated, "Some dishes are objects on the table." Consider the statement, "From many sources comes evidence of the invasion of Britain by William the Conqueror." The subject and predicate terms here need to be made definite. This statement may be rendered in categorical form as follows: "The invasion of Britain by William the Conqueror is an event attested by evidence from many sources." Consider the statement, "Fools rush in where angels fear to tread." In this case, several decisions have to be made. Will the proposition be universal or particular? What will constitute the proper subject term and what the proper predicate term? One might propose either of the two following statements before making a decision: "All occasions in which angels fear to tread are occasions in which fools rush in." "Some circumstances in which angels fear to tread are occasions in which fools rush in." According to the rules of modern logic, the latter statement also holds "there are some circumstances in which angels fear to tread."

4. The predicate term needs to be made explicit, and the class of objects to which it refers needs to be specified clearly. Consider the following statements: "Students are curious," "Birds fly," "John's car hit a deer." If these are to be made into categorical propositions, a definite predicate term is needed. The class of things to which adjectives in the predicate term pertain needs to be made specific. The contexts of the statements above suggest the following ways of stating them in the proper form: "All students are curious persons," "All birds are creatures that fly," "John's car is a vehicle that hit a deer."

5. The meaning of singular propositions has to be made explicit. Consider the propositions "Socrates is mortal" and "Charles DeGaulle was a leader of the French Resistance Movement." These are singular propositions in which the subject term refers to all the members of its class, but in which there is only one member. Technically speaking, the meaning here would be "The class of men of whom Socrates is the only member is mortal" and "The class of men of whom Charles DeGaulle is the only member is included in the class of persons who were leaders in the French Resistance Movement." However, in ordinary language, this way of constructing a proposition would become rather cumbersome, so the propositions remain "Socrates is mortal" and "Charles DeGaulle is a person who was a leader of the French Resistance Movement."

6. Universal negative propositions need to be distinguished from particular negative propositions in some cases. Consider the statement "All engineers are not scientists." The expression "All . . . are not . . ." is not clear. Is the proposition universal or particular? Judgment must be based upon the context. Again, if there is serious doubt remaining, the more limited meaning of the expression should be used. The statement above may be rendered properly "Some engineers are not scientists." On the other hand, the context of the statement "All freshmen are not permitted to participate in varsity sports" might indicate the appropriateness of an **E** proposition in many intercollegiate athletic conferences: "No freshmen are permitted to participate in varsity sports in the X conference."

7. The meaning of expressions such as "only" and "none but" has to be clarified. Consider the expression "Only good mathematicians are good theoretical physicists." The proper form for this statement is "All good theoretical physicists are good mathematicians." The form "Only *A*'s are *B*'s" or "None but *A*'s are *B*'s" is rendered in the categorical proposition "All *B*'s are *A*'s." Thus, the statement "None but the courageous are victorious" is given in categorical form as "All victorious persons are courageous ones."

Expressions using the form "the only" require further consideration. "The only clothes I have are out of date." In this case "the only" introduces the subject term of the categorical proposition, whose restated form is "All my clothes are materials out of date." Likewise the statement "Fingerprints are the only clue to the robbery" is restated "All clues to the robbery are fingerprints." An expression using the form "only some" may require both an **I** and an **O** proposition for the rendering of its complete meaning. The statement "Only some hard-nosed guys win" becomes "Some hard-nosed guys win" and "Some hard-nosed guys do not win." Both forms of these statements need to be tested in determining the validity of a syllogism.

8. Exceptive statements need to be clarified. These statements occur with the use of expressions such as "except," "but," and "all . . . except some."

Consider the following statements for analysis:

All freshmen except (but) honor students may leave.

No students but (except) seniors are excused.

The first statement clearly includes the meaning "All freshmen who are not honor students are persons who can leave." It apparently also means but does not state explicitly, "No freshmen who are honor students may leave." If such an expression occurs in a syllogism, the testing of the first meaning is required. If this form does not provide a valid syllogism, the second form can be tested as a premise for an enthymeme with the notation that this premise is suppressed.

The second statement clearly includes the meaning "No non-senior students are excused." It does not state explicitly that "All senior students are excused." We can use this last form by acknowledging that a suppressed premise is being used in the context.

Consider the statement "No students but some seniors are excused." Two statements are clearly intended and are to be tested as premises: "No non-senior students are excused" and "Some senior students are excused." The original sentence also suggests the statement "Some senior students are not excused." However, we can use this form only by regarding it as a suppressed premise in an enthymeme, and in some contexts this may not be justified.

The clarification of exceptive statements may be summarized as follows:

(1) All *A*'s except *B*'s are *C*'s. *Restated as:*
    (a) All *A*'s that are non-*B*'s are *C*'s. (In all cases)
    (b) No *B*'s that are *A*'s are *C*'s. (Suppressed proposition in some cases)

(2) No *A*'s except *B*'s are *C*'s. *Restated as:*
    (a) No *A*'s that are non-*B*'s are *C*'s. (In all cases)
    (b) All *A*'s that are *B*'s are *C*'s. (Suppressed proposition in some cases)

(3) All *A*'s except some *B*'s are *C*'s. *Restated as:*
    (a) All *A*'s that are non-*B*'s are *C*'s. (In all cases)
    (b) Some *A*'s that are *B*'s are not *C*'s. (In all cases)
    (c) Some *A*'s that are *B*'s are *C*'s. (Suppressed proposition in some cases)

(4) No *A*'s except some *B*'s are *C*'s. *Restated as:*
    (a) No *A*'s that are non-*B*'s are *C*'s. (In all cases)
    (b) Some *A*'s that are *B*'s are *C*'s. (In all cases)
    (c) Some *A*'s that are *B*'s are not *C*'s. (Suppressed proposition in some cases)

9. Some statements using conjunctive expressions can be rendered in the form of a categorical statement. Statements with clauses introduced by expressions like "when" and "if" can be placed in the form of a categorical proposition, in which expressions following "when" and "if" introduce the subject term. However, "only when" and "only if" introduced the predicate term. "When he comes I shall be ready" can be rendered "All occasions of his coming are occasions when I shall be ready." "Only if you put forth an extra effort can you win the game" can be rendered "All occasions of your winning the game are circumstances in which you put forth an extra effort."

Statements using "unless" to introduce a clause are troublesome. Consider the statement: "John goes home on weekends unless a fraternity dance is held." This expression clearly states, "If a fraternity dance is not held, then John goes home on weekends." It also appears to mean but does not explicitly state, "If a fraternity dance is held, then John does not go home on weekends." With this interpretation the original statement can be rendered "All occasions on which a fraternity dance is not held are occasions on which John goes home on weekends." The second form can be tested as a suppressed premise for an enthymeme. This form is "All occasions on which a fraternity dance is held are occasions on which John does not go home on weekends." The following forms may assist in clarifying this use of "unless" in an expression such as "*A* unless *B*":

(a) All non-*B*'s are *A*'s. (In all cases)
(b) All *B*'s are non-*A*'s. (As a suppressed proposition in some cases)

10. Statements involving notions of time, place, and circumstances need to be clarified. Consider the statements "There are boys playing in the streets" and "There are several visitors arriving." In such expressions, references to time, place, occasion, or circumstances have to be added to make the meaning of the sentence explicit and to arrange it in the form of a categorical proposition. These statements may be clarified follows: "This time is included in the class of occasions in which boys are playing in the street" and "This occasion is included in the class of circumstances in which several visitors are arriving."

11. Statements involving other forms of ambiguity need to be clarified. Consider the statement "Nothing is too good for you." This statement is ambiguous and its meaning has to be clarified. It could mean either that "You are included in the class of persons deserving the very best" or "You are included in the class of persons deserving the worst." If the context itself is indeterminate, then both meanings of the premise need to be tested and each meaning applied to a syllogism and tested for validity.

Language indeed is much more varied than the logical forms into which it is structured for appraisal in the form of categorical propositions. Yet, such rephrasing or restating is essential if the logical notions that language conveys are to be checked by rigorous analysis.

9.11 EXERCISES

1. Write the following propositions in proper categorical form.
   (a) Crows are black.
   (b) Youth dares where old men fear to plunge.
   (c) Only the prepared survive.
   (d) Old dogs do not learn new tricks.
   (e) There is never a dull moment in Professor Smith's class.
   (f) Times change.
   (g) Many a former student wished he had studied more and played less.
   (h) There are several books on the shelf.
   (i) Puzzles intrigue Henry.
   (j) The only survivors are small children.
   (k) Mr. Bird hunts quail in the fall of the year.
   (l) None but seniors are invited.
   (m) First come, first served.
   (n) Birds of a feather flock together.

(o)   All seniors except those not graduating attended the banquet.

(p)   Fish have fins.

(q)   Goblins are invisible.

(r)   I shall lose no time in returning this manuscript.

(s)   No members except the executive committee left the room.

(t)   Skeletons need not be brought out of the closet.

(u)   Only some questions are difficult.

(v)   If Tom sinks his putt, he wins the match.

(w)   This experiment works unless contamination is present.

(x)   No one would take that risk unless he is a fool.

(y)   Cars washed any day except Sunday.

(z)   The students are not working all day.

(a′)   All college students are not pressed financially.

(b′)   All exercises except some requiring advanced math are easy.

(c′)   There are two visitors at the door.

(d′)   Gone are the days of yore.

(e′)   Charles missed the bus.

2. Write the following syllogisms in proper propositional form and in logical order. Make a complete analysis of each syllogism and determine its validity. State any rule that is violated in the invalid syllogisms.

(a) Jungle societies do not cultivate the arts, therefore societies concerned with only their own economic interests do not cultivate the arts, since such societies are jungle societies.

(b) Only in cases where "the bayonet strikes the bone" are you to fail to advance. "The bayonet strikes the bone" in cases of strong military support from the outside. Therefore, when there is strong military support from the outside you can fail to advance.

(c) There is concern by the courts about stop-and-frisk laws, but stop-and-frisk laws are supported by police officers as a prevention against crime. Thus, some laws that are sought by police officers as a prevention against crime are of concern to the courts.

(d) Some particles repay the energy balance in nature; therefore, some things that repay the energy balance in nature are extremely short-lived, since many particles have very short lives.

(e) Since a wrong unprotested festers, radar traps will not fester, since they are protested.

(f) All civilians except those active in the war effort were evacuated, thus no civilians active in the war effort were permitted to leave the country, because only evacuated persons were permitted to leave the country.

(g) As common-sense notions of time and space are uncritical and they do not fit into quantum-theory experiments, some notions that do not fit into quantum-theory experiments are uncritical.

(h) All downtown businesses except those with off-street parking facilities will find it difficult to survive. Therefore, downtown businesses in Boomtown will not find it difficult to survive, since they have off-street parking.

(i) These are difficult times, since the only easy times were before the development of nuclear explosives and those days have gone forever.

(j) Racial troubles are not good for business, and community Smithville has conditions bad for business; therefore, community Smithville has racial troubles.

(k) All uncommitted nations form a neutral block in the United Nations, since none but the unaligned countries form a neutral block in the United Nations and the uncommitted nations alone do not align themselves with the East or West.

(l) Many physicists are well trained and no physicist is untrained. Therefore, many well-trained persons are untrained.

3. Give a complete analysis of the following syllogisms. Write them in logical form. Identify validity. If the syllogism is invalid, state the rule violated.

(a) Mr. Derby is a voter, since he is a citizen and only citizens are voters.

(b) No loans not approved by the credit department are granted; therefore, some loans approved by the credit department are not paid back, since some loans that are granted are defaulted.

(c) Since many strikes are difficult to resolve, many situations that are difficult to resolve work hardships on families of workers, since all strikes are hard on families of workers.

(d) Any pain is to be avoided if possible and Johnny is a pain. Therefore, Johnny is to be avoided if possible.

(e) New issues grow out of changing conditions. Therefore, there should be new issues, since there are changing conditions.

(f) Anyone who does not have time on his side is other than the struggling masses, and the struggling masses cannot afford to ignore the need to improve slums. Therefore, the groups who have time on their side cannot afford to ignore the need to work to improve the slums.

(g) All except wise men make hasty decisions, therefore all statesmen are wise, since no statesmen make hasty decisions.

(h) Since some persons who study the stock market make errors, bankers make errors, since they study the stock market.

(i) Mastery of the principles of reasoning requires work, since many good things require work and mastery of the principles of reasoning is a good thing.

(j) Men who seek money also seek power; therefore, men who seek money cannot ignore politics, since no one who seeks power can ignore politics.

(k) The discovery of penicillin was a scientific accident, but scientific accidents are made possible only where minds are trained. Therefore, the discovery of penicillin was made possible by minds that were trained.

(l) Since activity that contributed to the defeat of the U-boats in World War II made possible the successful invasion of Europe, Operations Research made possible the successful invasion of Europe inasmuch as it contributed to the defeat of the U-boats in World War II.

(m) Nothing that is without nutritional value helps to develop strong bones. Therefore, vitamins help to develop strong bones, since anything that does not have nutritional value is certainly something other than a vitamin.

(n) Muckrakers need to know when to stop raking the muck, Therefore, Mr. Charles needs to know when to stop raking the muck, since he is a muckraker.

(o) Only where there is order is political freedom able to flourish, but political freedom is not able to flourish in a totalitarian state. Therefore, there is no order in a totalitarian state.

(p) Anyone except players, coaches, and officials is permitted to wager on games. Therefore, players, coaches, and officials are not gamblers, since gamblers are permitted to wager on games.

(q) No program approving of exposed lots for wrecked cars is worthy of support, since any program unworthy of support is other than a program of national beautification and a program of national beautification disapproves of exposed lots for wrecked cars.

(r) Some anemic persons are unhealthy. Therefore, some persons who do not take exercise are anemic, since none but persons who take exercise are healthy.

(s) Since Professor Donothing is a fossil and all fossils are remains of past life, Professor Donothing is a remains of past life.

(t) Advocates of unrest and discontent are following self-defeating programs, since no one who is not following a self-defeating program sows the seeds of his own undoing and only those who are not sowing the seeds of their own undoing are persons who are not advocates of unrest and discontent.

(u) All reactions against excesses tend to become excesses themselves, since reactions against excesses evoke excesses and things that evoke excesses tend to become excesses.

(v) Since sound judgment is a source of wealth and some wealth is a source of leisure, sound judgment is a source of leisure.

(w) Unless there is compromise there is no growth in cooperation, and only where there is growth in cooperation is there strength in interdependence. Therefore, there is strength in interdependence only where there are compromises.

(x) DMSO is a drug whose use is not authorized except under carefully controlled and limited conditions, since DMSO has extensive and unknown side effects and no drug having extensive and unknown side effects is one whose use is authorized except under carefully controlled and limited conditions.

Chapter 10
Sorites

10.1 The Reducing of Sorites to Categorical Syllogisms

Categorical propositions sometimes are used in *sorites*—chain arguments in which several categorical syllogisms are telescoped into one. Consider the following sorites:

> Some registered materials are subject to inspection.
> All materials subject to inspection are supported by documentation.
> All materials supported by documentation are analyzable.
> No material that is analyzable is meaningless.
> Therefore, some registered materials are not meaningless.

In ordinary discourse these premises might occur in any order. One way of analyzing the argument consists in breaking down the propositions of the sorites into syllogisms. The subject term of the conclusion becomes the minor term of each successive syllogism. The middle term of the first syllogism is the second term appearing in the proposition in the sorites with the subject term (minor term) of the conclusion. The major term of the first syllogism is the term appearing in the proposition with the other occurrence of the indicated middle term. In the sorites above the minor term of each syllogism is "some registered materials." This minor term occurs in the premise "Some registered materials are subject to inspection." The middle term of the first syllogism is "(materials) subject to inspection." Thus, the original syllogism of this sorites is:

> All materials subject to inspection are supported by documentation.
> Some registered materials are subject to inspection.

Therefore, some registered materials are supported by documentation.

The next syllogism will have as its minor premise the conclusion of the immediately preceding syllogism. The new middle term is the second term in the conclusion of the preceding syllogism, and the major term is the additional term occurring in the premise with the new middle term. This analysis is followed with the remaining premises, and we obtain the remaining syllogisms as follows:

All materials supported by documentation are analyzable.
Some registered materials are supported by documentation.
Therefore, some registered materials are analyzable.

No material that is analyzable is meaningless.
Some registered materials are analyzable.
Therefore, some registered materials are not meaningless.

If any one of the syllogisms into which the sorites is broken down is invalid, the sorites is invalid.

A second way of reducing the sorites to syllogisms consists in using the predicate term of the conclusion as the major term in each categorical syllogism constructed. In some cases the propositions have to be reduced to proper form. If a sorites is incomplete in that no conclusion is stated, the two terms appearing only once in the premises are the subject and predicate terms of the conclusion.

10.2 Aristotelian and Goclenian Forms of Sorites

Sorites also are analyzed by their forms. One valid form is the Aristotelian sorites; another is the Goclenian. These are illustrated in the following examples.

Aristotelian sorites:
(a) All students are restless.
(b) All restless persons are excitable.
(c) All excitable persons are activists.
(d) All activists are demonstrators.
(e) Therefore, all students are demonstrators.

Goclenian sorites:
(d) All activists are demonstrators.
(c) All excitable persons are activists.
(b) All restless persons are excitable.
(a) All students are restless.
(e) Therefore, all students are demonstrators.

A valid sorites has one more term than there are premises. (In the previous sorites there were four premises and five terms.) The key to the analysis of the sorites is the conclusion. A simple way of determining the structure of a sorites is to use capital letters in sequence (beginning with A) for the various terms. In the Aristotelian sorites the letter A can stand for the subject term of the conclusion. The predicate term of the conclusion has the letter corresponding to the last alphabetical term used in the sorites. For example, if three premises are used in the sorites, the last term is the fourth term; the fourth letter in the alphabet is D. If there are four premises in the sorites, there are five terms marked in; the last term would be E. Beginning with the term listed as A in the conclusion, which is the subject term of the conclusion in an Aristotelian sorites, the same term is listed as A in the premises. The other term of the same proposition in the premise is marked as B. The B term is marked again in its second appearance and the term in the same proposition with it is listed as C. This process is continued for the remaining premises in the sorites.

Consider the Aristotelian form of the sorites given previously.

$$\overset{A}{} \qquad \overset{E}{}$$
Conclusion: All students are demonstrators.

$$\overset{A}{} \qquad \overset{B}{}$$
All students are restless.

$$\overset{B}{} \qquad \overset{C}{}$$
All restless persons are excitable.

$$\overset{C}{} \qquad \overset{D}{}$$
All excitable persons are activists.

$$\overset{D}{} \qquad \overset{E}{}$$
All activists are demonstrators.

$$\overset{A}{} \qquad \overset{E}{}$$
Therefore, all students are demonstrators.

The form of this sorites may be given as follows:

All A is B	$Ad < Bu$
All B is C	$Bd < Cu$
All C is D	$Cd < Du$
All D is E	$Dd < Eu$
Therefore, all A is E	$Ad < Eu$

In the Aristotelian sorites the subject term of the conclusion is also the subject term of the first premise. New terms are always introduced in the predicate term.

In the Goclenian sorites let the letter A stand for the predicate term of the conclusion. Let the letter of the alphabet corresponding to the last term used in the sorites stand for the subject term of the conclusion. If there were four premises, there would be five terms, and the subject term of the conclusion would be designated by the letter E. Proceed by finding the A term (the term with the predicate term of the conclusion) in the premises, and label the other term appearing in the same proposition the *B* term. Follow same procedure for the remaining propositions, using the letters *C, D,* and *E* (or as many as necessary).

The key to the analysis of the Goclenian sorites, obviously, is the subject and predicate terms of the conclusion, which should be identified first. Consider the following example:

$$\overset{E}{}\qquad\overset{A}{}$$
Conclusion: Therefore, all students are demonstrators.

$$\overset{B}{}\qquad\overset{A}{}$$
All activists are demonstrators.

$$\overset{C}{}\qquad\overset{B}{}$$
All excitable persons are activists.

$$\overset{D}{}\qquad\overset{C}{}$$
All restless persons are excitable.

$$\overset{E}{}\qquad\overset{D}{}$$
All students are restless.

$$\overset{E}{}\qquad\overset{A}{}$$
Therefore, all students are demonstrators.

This Goclenian sorites has the following form:

All *B* is *A*	$Bd < Au$
All *C* is *B*	$Cd < Bu$
All *D* is *C*	$Dd < Cu$
All *E* is *D*	$Ed < Du$
Therefore, all *E* is *A*	$Ed < Au$

In the Goclenian sorites the predicate term of the conclusion is the predicate term of the first premise. The subject term of the conclusion is the subject term of the last premise. The new term is introduced in the subject term of each succeeding premise.

In reducing a sorites to its component syllogisms, we first arrange it in proper order. The subject term of the conclusion becomes the minor term in each successive syllogism in the Aristotelian sorites. The predicate term of the conclusion becomes the major term in each successive syllogism for the Goclenian sorites. The following syllogisms are telescoped in the previous Goclenian sorites.

$$\overset{B}{}\qquad\overset{A}{}$$
All activists are demonstrators.

$$\overset{C}{}\qquad\overset{B}{}$$
All excitable persons are activists.

$$\overset{C}{}\qquad\overset{A}{}$$
Therefore, all excitable persons are demonstrators.

$$\overset{C}{}\qquad\overset{A}{}$$
All excitable persons are demonstrators.

$$\overset{D}{}\qquad\overset{C}{}$$
All restless persons are excitable.

$$\overset{D}{\text{Therefore, all restless}}\ \text{persons are}\ \overset{A}{\text{demonstrators.}}$$

$$\overset{D}{\text{All restless}}\ \text{persons are}\ \overset{A}{\text{demonstrators.}}$$

$$\overset{E}{\text{All students are}}\ \overset{D}{\text{restless.}}$$

$$\overset{E}{\text{Therefore, all students are}}\ \overset{A}{\text{demonstrators.}}$$

The following form of an Aristotelian sorites

$$Ad\ <\ Bu$$
$$Bd\ <\ Cu$$
$$Cd\ <\ Du$$
$$Dd\ <\ Eu$$
$$\overline{\therefore\ Ad\ <\ Eu}$$

is reduced to separate syllogisms in the following steps:

(1) $Bd\ <\ Cu$
$Ad\ <\ Bu$
$\overline{\therefore\ Ad\ <\ Cu}$

(2) $Cd\ <\ Du$
$Ad\ <\ Cu$
$\overline{\therefore\ Ad\ <\ Du}$

(3) $Dd\ <\ Eu$
$Ad\ <\ Du$
$\overline{\therefore\ Ad\ <\ Eu}$

A sorites is valid if it can be reduced to a proper Aristotelian or Goclenian form. If it cannot be reduced to these forms, we must break it down into its component syllogisms to determine the reason for its invalidity.

10.3 Sorites with Particular or Negative Premises

In valid sorites only one premise can be particular and only one premise can be negative. If a premise is particular, it occurs first in an Aristotelian sorites and last in a Goclenian sorites. If a premise is negative, it occurs last in an Aristotelian sorites and first in a Goclenian sorites.

	Particular premise	Negative premise
Aristotelian sorites	First	Last
Goclenian sorites	Last	First

Consider the direction of argument of the different sorites shown by the modified Euler circles in Figs. 10.1 and 10.2. The Aristotelian argument progresses from the center of the circle outwards, and the Goclenian from the outside circle to the center. A negative premise always will be related

$Ad < Bu$

$Bd < Cu$

$Cd < Du$

$Dd < Eu$

$\therefore Ad < Eu$

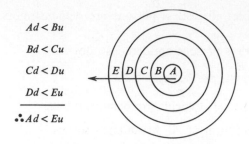

Direction of argument

FIGURE 10.1

$Bd < Au$

$Cd < Bu$

$Dd < Cu$

$Ed < Du$

$\therefore Ed < Au$

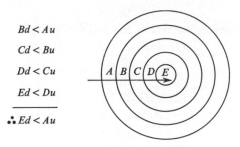

Direction of argument

FIGURE 10.2

to the outside circle. A particular premise always will be related to the inner-most circle. Consider the sets of circles shown in Figs. 10.3, 10.4, and 10.5.

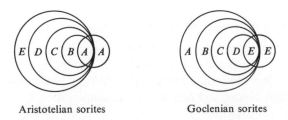

Aristotelian sorites   Goclenian sorites

FIGURE 10.3

In writing sorites in proper categorical form we may need to convert, obvert, or contrapose some of the propositions. If the sorites can be made valid by such operations, then a logical analysis of its structure includes the performing of such operations.

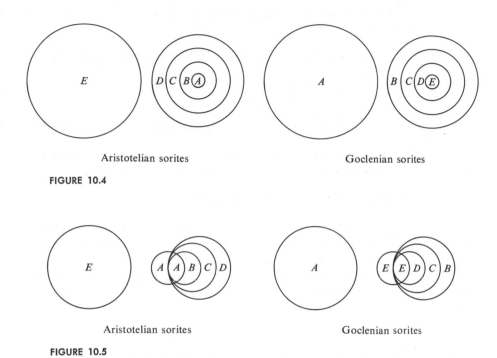

Aristotelian sorites   Goclenian sorites

FIGURE 10.4

Aristotelian sorites   Goclenian sorites

FIGURE 10.5

10.4 Sorites with Suppressed Conclusions

A sorites may occur with the conclusion suppressed. In this case we must find a conclusion as a basis for determining the structure of the sorites and its validity. To find the conclusion, we first identify the terms appearing twice in the premises. These terms, including the possibility of a complementary or negated term, can be underlined or circled. The two terms remaining constitute the subject and predicate term of the conclusion.

We may need to decide which term is the proper subject of the conclusion and which the predicate. If a term appears in the subject of the premise, it may be tried for the subject of the conclusion. If both terms appear as the subject terms of their propositions, then the term that is the subject of a negative proposition or that apparently is a complementary term can be tested as the predicate term of the conclusion. If both terms appear in the predicate, then the term appearing as the predicate term of a negative proposition or as a negated term might be tried as the subject term of the conclusion. Consider the following sorites, which is not in logical order:

> All persons concerned for fair play are sensitive.
> All students are demonstrators.
> All sensitive persons are imaginative.

All demonstrators are concerned for fair play.
Therefore, ?

The terms appearing twice are italicized. The sorites appears as follows:

All persons *concerned for fair play* are *sensitive*.
All students are *demonstrators*.
All *sensitive* persons are imaginative.
All *demonstrators* are *concerned for fair play*.

Two terms not italicized above are "students" and "imaginative." Thus, the following conclusion could be formulated and tested for its validity.

All students are imaginative (persons).

If the third premise had read, "No non-imaginative persons are sensitive," then each of the terms found in the conclusion is in the subject term of the premises. However, "non-imaginative" is both the negation of a term and a subject term of a negative proposition. Either of these suggests the possibility that this term might become the predicate term of the conclusion (by conversion and then by obversion).

10.5 EXERCISES

1. Analyze the following sorites. Write each in a proper Aristotelian or Goclenian form. If a sorites is invalid, reduce it to separate syllogisms and state the rule that is violated.

(a) Television programs provide escape. All things that have unexpected side effects can be factors in producing social changes. All things providing escape play down human misery. All things that play down human misery have unexpected side effects. Therefore, some television programs can be factors in producing social changes.

(b) No person who does not express stimulating ideas is an interesting conversationalist. All literary critics are well informed on contemporary novels. Anyone well grounded in the contemporary theater expresses stimulating ideas. Anyone who is not an interesting conversationalist is a person who is not well informed on contemporary novels. Therefore, all literary critics are persons well grounded in the contemporary theater.

(c) No satisfied person is a disillusioned idealist. Any dissatisfied person is frustrated. No cynics are persons who are not disillusioned idealists. Anyone who is enthusiastic about the future is a person not frustrated. Therefore, no cynics are enthusiastic about the future.

(d) Without inquiry facts are not secured. Intelligence requires insight. Good judgment requires facts. There is no insight without good judgment. Therefore, intelligence requires inquiry.

(e) Any programs that are not intellectually boring are programs not designed for mass audiences. Nothing that increases the appreciation for the arts is unworthy of support. No program that is intellectually boring increases appreciation for the arts. All TV serials are designed for mass audiences. Therefore no TV serials are worth supporting.

(f) All multibillion-dollar enterprises are industries that are the wave of the future. No industry that is the wave of the future is a source of poor investment in stocks. The data-processing industries are a multibillion-dollar enterprise. Some stocks that are subject to wide fluctuation in their value over a limited period of time are sources of poor investments in stock. Therefore, some data-processing industries are not subject to wide fluctuations in the value of stocks over a limited period of time.

2. Find the conclusion of the following sorites and determine the validity of the argument. To find the conclusion determine the two terms that occur only once in the premises; these terms will be the subject term and the predicate term of the conclusion. Give a complete analysis of the sorites. State it in proper Aristotelian or Goclenian form. If a sorites is invalid, break it down into syllogisms and state the rule of the syllogism that has been violated.

(a) All situations requiring the asking of proper questions require persons skillful in formulating questions. All situations requiring persons with background knowledge also require persons who understand current problems in the area. Superior use of computers involves situations requiring the asking of proper questions. All situations requiring persons skillful in formulating questions also require persons with background knowledge. Therefore, . . .

(b) Any problem that cannot be worked immediately is complex. Any problem that is easy to solve is simple. Sorites are chain arguments. Chain arguments are easy to solve. Therefore, . . .

(c) Talent banks can ignore individual differences in computer selection. Any selection process that obscures superior leadership abilities cannot ignore individual differences in computer selection. Any computer is a talent bank. No selection process that obscures superior leadership abilities is without need to be supplemented by other tested means of evaluating competence. Therefore, . . .

(d) Elections not requiring information and judgment do not focus on issues. The need for an informed public with ability to analyze issues requires accurate reporting on newspapers and television. Elections requiring both information and judgment are situations needing an informed public with an ability to analyze issues. Elections that do not focus on candidates focus on issues. Therefore, . . .

(e) Instruments requiring the application of know-how and skill in devising proper learning situations also may be used in creating games that are exciting. Computers are instruments that can assist the student to learn by discovery. An instrument that is useless under proper programming conditions cannot assist the student to learn by discovery. No useful instrument under proper programming conditions fails to require the application of know-how and skills in devising a proper learning situation. Therefore, . . .

(f) No opinion poll is a survey that is not designed to test public reaction to current questions. The use of any sample is reliable only if it is a random sample that has been properly collected and analyzed. Some surveys designed to test public reactions to current questions use samples that are reliable. No sample can be a reliable guide of current public opinion if it is not a random sample properly collected and analyzed. Therefore, . . .

(g) Computers developed to transmit the data by the use of satellites can make health and financial data available at the push of a button anywhere in the country. Things that can be useful in the treatment of diseases and in economic development can help to improve health and provide time for the enjoyment of leisure. Things that can help to improve health and provide time for the enjoyment of leisure cannot assure the growth of the mind's creativity or the enjoyment of its fruits. Computers developed to transmit data by the use of satellites can be useful in the treatment of diseases and in promoting economic development. Therefore, . . .

Chapter 11
Mediate and
Immediate
Inference

11.1 The Meaning of Mediate and Immediate Inference

A *mediate* inference requires the use as evidence of two or more premises or conjunctive statements for the justification of a conclusion. Categorical syllogisms are a form of mediate inference.

An *immediate* inference is made by the use of only one premise or statement as evidence. Obversion, conversion, and contraposition are forms of immediate inference. If the truth or falsity of one proposition is known in immediate inference, the truth or falsity of a second statement or proposition may be inferred directly, that is, without the use of other premises. Given that the statement "All men are mortal" is true, then it can be inferred immediately that the obverse of this proposition, "No men are non-mortal," also is true.

11.2 Relations Between Propositions Based on Their Truth Values

There are seven possible relations of truth values between propositions. Six of these involve some form of immediate inference with regard to the truth or falsity of a second proposition if the truth value of one proposition is known. These seven relations are the following:

1. *Independence.* The truth or falsity of one proposition does not permit an inference about the truth or falsity of a second proposition. Consider the truth-value relation between these two statements: "Washington was the first President of the United States." "President Lincoln was assassinated." Even

though the truth or falsity of one of these propositions is known, no inference from this can be made about the truth or falsity of the second proposition.

2. *Equivalence.* Two propositions are equivalent if their truth values are identical. If one of these propositions is known to be true, the truth of the second can be inferred directly. If one of these propositions is known to be false, the falsity of the second can be inferred immediately. Consider the propositions "All democracies are forms of government that permit dissent" and "All governments that do not permit dissent are nondemocratic." These propositions are equivalent and they also are contrapositives. An obverted proposition is equivalent to its original proposition. The **E** form or the **I** form of conversion yields an equivalent proposition.

3. *Contradiction.* One proposition is the contradiction of another if the truth of either proposition requires the falsity of the second and the falsity of either proposition requires the truth of the second. Both propositions cannot be true, and both propositions cannot be false. One proposition must be true, the other false. The propositions in each of the following sets are contradictory: "All physicians are surgeons" and "Some physicians are not surgeons." "No engineers are scientists" and "Some engineers are scientists." "All philosophy students are logic students" and "Some philosophy students are not logic students."

4. *Contrariety.* The relation of contrariety between two propositions holds if both propositions cannot be true, but both may be false. If one proposition is true, one can immediately infer the falsity of the other. If one proposition is known to be false, no inference can be made about the truth or falsity of the second. Each of the following sets of propositions is an example of contrariety: "All library books are in open stacks" and "No library books are in open stacks." "All pre-med students are majors in chemistry" and "No pre-med students are majors in chemistry." "All lawyers are students of the Constitution" and "No lawyers are students of the Constitution."

In the foregoing examples of contrariety as well as in subsequent examples through the discussion of superimplication, the problem of class membership of terms or of existential import is not taken into account.

5. *Subcontrariety.* Two propositions are subcontraries if at least one proposition is true and both propositions cannot be false. If one subcontrary is false, the other subcontrary must be true. If one subcontrary is true, the truth or falsity of the other is undetermined. Each of the following is a set of subcontrary propositions: "Some animals are mammals" and "Some animals are not mammals." "Some TV programs are educational" and "Some TV programs are not educational." "Some logic assignments are easy" and "Some logic assignments are not easy."

6. *Subimplication.* Two propositions are subimplicants if the falsity of the first requires also the falsity of the second. However, if the first propo-

sition is true, nothing can be inferred about the truth or falsity of the second. In this relationship, the order of the propositions cannot be reversed. Consider the examples: "Some milk cows are Longhorns" and "All milk cows are Longhorns." "Some presidents are statesmen" and "All presidents are statesmen." If the first proposition is false, then the second proposition also must be false. If the first proposition is true, nothing can be inferred about the truth of the second. We cannot change the order of the propositions above and still maintain these truth relations.

7. *Superimplication.* Two propositions are in a relation of superimplication if the truth of the first requires the truth of the second and if the falsity of the first does not warrant an inference about the truth or the falsity of the second. The order of the propositions is not reversible. The first proposition in each of the following sets is a superimplicant of the second proposition: "All athletes are strong persons" and "Some athletes are strong persons." "All deep-sea diving is dangerous" and "Some deep-sea diving is dangerous." Superimplication is particularly vulnerable to the question of existential import in relations between categorical propositions.

11.3 The Traditional Square of Opposition

The relation of contradiction, contrariety, subcontrariety, subimplication, and superimplication can be shown on the traditional square of opposition to which the principle of existential import is not applied (Fig. 11.1).

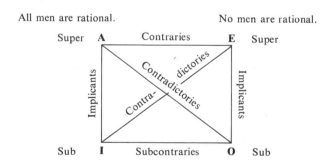

FIGURE 11.1

Contradictories: A and O; E and I. If the **A** form, "All men are rational," is true, then the **O** form is false.

    If the **A** form is false, then the **O** form is true.
    If the **O** form is true, the **A** form is false.
    If the **O** form is false, then the **A** form is true.

The **E** form of the proposition, "No men are rational," and the **I** form, "Some men are rational," also have opposite truth values in every case.

If the principle of existential import is applied to the relations on the square of opposition, the relation of contradiction is the only one of the five relations that continues to hold.

Contraries.   If the **A** form, "All men are rational," is true, the **E** form, "No men are rational," is false.

If the **A** form is false, the **E** form is undetermined.

If the **E** form is true, the **A** form is false.

If the **E** form is false, the **A** form is undetermined.

Subcontraries.   If the **I** form, "Some men are rational," is true, the **O** form is undetermined.

If the **I** form is false, the **O** form is true.

If the **O** form is true, the **I** form is undetermined.

If the **O** form is false, the **I** form is true.

Subimplicants (or subalternates).   If the **I** form, "Some men are mortal," is true, the **A** form, "All men are mortal," is undetermined.

If the **I** form is false, the **A** form is false.

If the **O** form is true, the **E** form is undetermined.

If the **O** form is false, the **E** form is false.

Superimplicants (or superalternates).   If the **A** form, "All men are rational," is true, the **I** form is true.

If the **A** form is false, the **I** form is undetermined.

If the **E** form is true, the **O** form is true.

If the **E** form is false, the **O** form is undetermined.

11.4 The Principle of Existential Import and the Square of Opposition

If the principle of existential import is used, the **A** and the **E** forms on the square of opposition can be true and the relation of contrariety does not hold between them. For example, if there does not exist any form of life on the planet Mercury, then both the following statements could be true: "All forms of life on the planet Mercury are primitive" and "No form of life on the planet Mercury is primitive." This is more obvious if the propositions are rendered in equivalent hypothetical forms: "If there is any life on the planet Mercury, it is primitive" and "If there is any life on Mercury, it is not primitive."

Likewise, if the principle of existential import is used, the **I** and the **O** can both be false. Consider the examples "Some forms of life on the planet

Mercury are primitive" and "Some forms of life on the planet Mercury are not primitive." Again, we may make this more obvious by writing these propositions in equivalent conjunctive statements: "There is a form of life on the planet Mercury and it is primitive." "There is a form of life on the planet Mercury and it is not primitive." Each of these statements is false if the first conjunct, "There is a form of life on the planet Mercury," is false.

The relations of subimplication and superimplication do not hold on the square of opposition when the principle of existential import is applied. An **I** proposition may be false and the **A** true, and the **O** may be false and the **E** true. If, for example, the **I** proposition, "Some goblins are grotesque," is false, the **A** proposition, "All goblins are grotesque," can be true. Likewise, the **O** form, "Some goblins are not grotesque," can be false, and the **E** form, "No goblins are grotesque," can be true. The possible truth values of the propositions are more obvious if they are rendered in equivalent propositions. If the statement "There are goblins and they are grotesque" is false, the statement "If there are any goblins, they are grotesque" can be true.

The categorical proposition's lack of flexibility and the problems posed by the existential import emphasize the need for developing argument forms that can consider a wider range of applicability and flexibility than the categorical syllogisms.

11.5 EXERCISES

If the original proposition is true, state the truth values of the succeeding propositions, using the traditional square of opposition, but disregarding the principle of existential import.

1. Original proposition: All plays are entertaining.
   (a) Some plays are entertaining.
   (b) Some plays are not entertaining.
   (c) No plays are entertaining.
2. Original proposition: Some logic problems are not difficult.
   (a) All logic problems are difficult.
   (b) No logic problems are difficult.
   (c) Some logic problems are difficult.
3. Original proposition: All bankers are capitalists.
   (a) Some bankers are not noncapitalists.
   (b) No bankers are capitalists.
   (c) All capitalists are nonbankers.
   (d) Some noncapitalists are not nonbankers.
   (e) All noncapitalists are nonbankers.
   (f) Some capitalists are bankers.
   (g) Some bankers are not capitalists.
   (h) All capitalists are bankers.
   (i) No noncapitalists are bankers.
4. Original proposition: No crows are white.
   (a) Some white things are crows.

    (b) All crows are nonwhite.
    (c) Some white things are not crows.
    (d) No white things are crows.
    (e) All crows are black.
    (f) All white things are noncrows.
    (g) All noncrows are white things.
    (h) Some nonwhite things are crows.
    (i) Some noncrows are white.

5. Original proposition: No carriages are blue.
    (a) Some carriages are blue.
    (b) No noncarriage is nonblue.
    (c) Some noncarriages are not nonblue.
    (d) No blue objects are carriages.
    (e) Some blue objects are not carriages.
    (f) All blue objects are carriages.
    (g) Some carriages are black.
    (h) All carriages are nonblue.
    (i) Some blue objects are not noncarriages.
    (j) All blue objects are noncarriages.

If the original proposition is true, determine the truth values of the succeeding propositions in the following statements, applying the principle of existential import.

6. Original proposition: All perfect students are well rounded.
    (a) Some perfect students are not well rounded.
    (b) No perfect students are well rounded.
    (c) Some perfect students are well rounded.

7. Original proposition: All poltergeists are noisy.
    (a) No poltergeists are noisy.
    (b) Some poltergeists are not noisy.
    (c) Some poltergeists are noisy.
    (d) Some nonnoisy things are not nonpoltergeists.
    (e) All poltergeists are nonnoisy.
    (f) All nonnoisy things are nonpoltergeists.
    (g) Some nonnoisy things are poltergeists.
    (h) No nonnoisy things are poltergeists.
    (i) Some poltergeists are nonnoisy.
    (j) All nonpoltergeists are nonnoisy.

8. Original proposition: Some babies are hungry.
    (a) All hungry creatures are nonbabies.
    (b) Some babies are not nonhungry.
    (c) No babies are hungry.
    (d) No nonhungry creatures are babies.
    (e) Some babies are not hungry.
    (f) Some hungry creatures are babies.
    (g) Some nonhungry creatures are not nonbabies.
    (h) All nonhungry creatures are nonbabies.
    (i) Some hungry creatures are nonbabies.
    (j) All babies are hungry.

11.6 Relational Terms

Relational terms occurring in propositions make possible further inferences in which the relational terms are used. Let R mean any relational term and the letters a, b, c refer to the terms related. The symbols aRb signify that a has relation R to b. If a refers to Smith, b to Jones, and R is the relational term "is older than," the meaning of the symbols aRb would be "Smith is older than Jones."

If a refers to "the weight of the gallon of water in the green bottle," and b refers to "the weight of the gallon of water in the black bottle," and R means "is equal to," then the symbols aRb mean "the weight of the water in the green bottle is equal to the weight of the water in the black bottle." Other relational terms include such expressions as "is greater than," "is a cousin of," "is a friend of," "is on the left of," "is included in the class of," and "is a member of the class of." Some forms of immediate inference and of mediate inference are made logically possible by these relational terms.

For example, "greater than" is a relational term. If it is given as true that A is greater than B, then it will be false that B is greater than A. If it is true that Susan is a cousin of Betty, it must be true that Betty is a cousin of Susan. A relational term can relate a second term either to itself or to additional terms. The same relational term may be used to relate a third term to additional terms. Three types of relational situations often encountered are reflexivity, symmetry, and transitivity.

Reflexivity concerns the applicability of a related term in a relation involving itself. If "equals" is the relational term, then "A equals A" is a relationship involving reflexivity. Relations of reflexivity are reflexive, irreflexive, and nonreflexive. In a *reflexive* relation the relational term is always applicable to the related term, which appears on both sides of the relational term. In a reflexive relation, aRa always holds. For example, in the statement "A is equal to A" the relational term "is equal to" is reflexive. Other examples of reflexive relations are "B is not greater than B" and "John is not taller than himself."

A relational term is *irreflexive* if the application of the relational term to the related term in the form aRa cannot hold. Some examples of irreflexive relational terms are "is unequal to," "is taller than," and "is the father of." Since, in an irreflexive relation, aRa cannot hold, statements such as the following are necessarily false: "X is unequal to X." "John is taller than himself." "Smith is the father of himself."

A relational term is *nonreflexive* if it may or may not hold in cases of relating a related term to itself. In each case the meaning of the relational term alone cannot determine whether the relation holds or does not hold. Some statements exemplifying the use of nonreflexive terms are "Smith is a despiser of himself," "Mrs. Jones is an admirer of herself," and "Mr. Able is not critical of himself."

Symmetery is concerned with the use of a relational expression to relate two other terms, such as "*A* loves *B*." A term is *symmetrical* if the relation between the two related terms is interchangeable. A symmetrical relation is expressed in the statements "If *A* is equal to *B*, then *B* is equal to *A*" and "If John is a cousin of Mary, then Mary is a cousin of John." If *aRb* holds, then *bRa* holds in a symmetrical relation. A term is *asymmetrical* if the relationship between the related terms cannot be interchanged: "If *A* is greater than *B*, then *B* cannot be greater than *A*." "If Jane is older than Sybil, then Sybil cannot be older than Jane." In each case of an asymmetrical relation, if *aRb* holds, then *bRa* cannot hold. A *nonsymmetrical* relation does not provide a basis for a judgment about a statement in which the related terms are reversed. If a term is nonsymmetrical and *aRb* is true, *bRa* may or may not hold. In this case the truth of *bRa* would be undetermined on the basis of the meaning of the relational term alone: "If Mr. Jones loves Miss Smith, then Miss Smith may or may not love Mr. Jones." "If *A* is the brother of *B*, then *B* may or may not be the brother of *A*." "If the Smiths are the nearest neighbors of the Joneses, then the Joneses may or may not be the nearest neighbors of the Smiths."

Immediate inference is possible in relations denoting reflexivity and symmetry. Mediate inference is possible in the next relational term discussed, since we determine the truth value of the conclusion by considering the truth or falsity of more than one atomic statement used as a premise.

Transitivity involves the relation between three related terms. If a relation holds between the first related term and a second related term, and between the second related term and a third related term, the relation of transitivity concerns the relation of the first related term to the third. A term is *transitive* if the relationship signified by the relational term holds between a first term and a second and between a second term and a third and then between the first related term and the third. In each transitive relation if *aRb* holds and *bRc* holds, then *aRc* holds. "If *A* equals *B* and *B* equals *C*, then *A* equals *C*." "Greater than" is a transitive term: "If *A* is greater than *B* and if *B* is greater than *C*, then *A* is greater than *C*." Other transitive relational terms are "is older than," "is a descendent of," "is more experienced in politics than," "has fewer errors than," and "has better judgment than."

In an *intransitive* relation the following conditions hold. If a particular relation holds between the first related term and the second, and the same relation holds between the second related term and the third, then the first related term cannot hold this relation to the third related term. In an intransitive relation, if *aRb* and *bRc* hold, then it is not possible for the relation *aRc* to hold: "If Susan is the closest friend of Mary, and Mary is the closest friend of Kate, then Susan cannot be the closest friend of

Kate." "If John is the father of Bill, and Bill is the father of George, then John cannot be the father of George."

A term is *nontransitive* if the first term has a specified relation to a second and the second term has the same relation to a third and if it cannot be determined by the meaning of the relational term alone whether this relation holds between the first related term and the third. Some non-transitive relational terms are "is unequal to," "is fond of," "is a cousin of," and "is a member of the class of." Thus: "If George is a friend of Jim and Jim is a friend of Henry, then George may or may not be a friend of Henry." "If *A* is a member of the class *B,* and if *B* is a member of the class *C,* then *A* may or may not be a member of the class *C.*" In any nontransitive relation if *aRb* and *bRc* hold, then *aRc* may or may not hold.

Although it frequently is claimed that "included in the class of" is a transitive relation, this is not the case in a rigorous sense. With a distributed subject term or with **A** categorical proposition, "is included in the class of" expresses a transitive relation. However, with an undistributed subject term or with an **I** categorical proposition, "are included in the class of" is a non-transitive relation. "Some *A*'s are included in the class of *B* and some *B*'s are included in the class of *C*" does not provide logical grounds for justifying the conclusion, "some *A*'s are included in the class of *C*."

It is important to note that with a distributed subject term the relational term "is included in the class of" is transitive and the relational term "is a member of the class of" is nontransitive. The rules of the categorical syllogism are justifiable on the basis of the different relations expressed by class inclusion and class exclusion.

Any given relational term can be classified on the basis of its reflexivity, symmetry, and transitivity. Thus, the relational term "is unequal to" is irreflexive, symmetrical, and nontransitive. The relational term "is a sister of" is irreflexive, nonsymmetrical, and transitive. Many different relational terms are employed in modern logic to make it more flexible and more useful than traditional Aristotelian logic in dealing with many problems of inference. (See Section 16.5.)

11.7 EXERCISES

Identify the type of relational terms exemplified in each of the following. Include reflexivity, symmetry, and transitivity.

1. Greater than.
2. Brother of.
3. A cousin of.
4. Not less than.
5. An enemy of.
6. East of.
7. A secret admirer of.
8. A sibling of.
9. A predecessor of.
10. The same as.
11. The disappointed lover of.
12. On the left of.
13. A better student in logic than.
14. The nearest neighbor of.
15. Is excluded from the class of.

Chapter 12
Arguments Using
Compound Propositions[1]

12.1 Types of Compound Propositions

Categorical syllogisms are restricted to the relations expressed by the meaning of "included in the class of" or "excluded from the class of." The analysis of reflexivity, symmetry, and transitivity shows that inferences are much broader in scope than those expressed only by the use of class inclusion or class exclusion.

Modern logic develops the use of symbols in a more complex and varied manner than traditional Aristotelian logic, and it employs more involved argument forms dependent upon the use of statements and their properties, relations, and functions rather than only class terms restricted to class inclusion or class exclusion. The use of symbols of formal logic makes possible precise definition of logical relations and avoids the ambiguities of ordinary discourse. These symbols facilitate the analysis of highly complex arguments in a clear and precise manner. The forms of symbolic logic can be fed into computers, which can be programmed to determine the validity of arguments.

Modern logic uses both simple and compound statements. Compound statements are composed of simple statements joined together with connectives such as "if . . . then," "or," "either . . . or . . . ," "and," "not both . . . and . . . ," "if and only if . . . then . . . ." Statements using such connec-

---

[1] A more rigorous approach to the material presented in Chapters 12 and 13 is given in Chapter 14. Chapter 14 can be studied concurrently with Chapters 12 and 13 or with only occasional reference to them.

tives have a minimal logical meaning. When these statements are used in combination with other statements, many valid inferences are possible.

Illustrations of propositions using these connectives may be helpful.

Hypothetical propositions. Hypothetical propositions use the connective "If . . . then . . . ." The symbol for this connective is the horseshoe, "⊃." An example of a hypothetical proposition is: "If the injury is serious, then John will go to the hospital."

A hypothetical proposition can be divided into two parts, the antecedent and the consequent. The *antecedent* is introduced by the connective "if" and the *consequent* by the connective "then." The antecedent in the statement above is "the injury is serious"; the consequent is "John will go to the hospital." Designating the antecedent as p and the consequent as q, we can express the hypothetical proposition symbolically as $p ⊃ q$—that is, if p then q. However, the expression "only if" introduces the consequent, and "then" following "only if" introduces the antecedent. Consider the meaning of the proposition "Only seniors are graduating," or "All graduating students are seniors." Thus, the expression "Only if a student is a senior does he graduate" becomes "If a student graduates, then he is a senior."

Disjunctive propositions. Disjunctive propositions use the connectives "or" or "either . . . . or . . . ." The symbol for this connective is the wedge, " ." An example of a disjunctive proposition is: "Either he had an accident or he is not coming."

The atomic parts of a disjunctive proposition are called *disjuncts*. In the proposition above, "either" introduces the first disjunct, "he had an accident"; "or" introduces the second disjunct, "he is not coming." In some propositions "either" is understood but not expressed: "He had an accident or he is not coming." Designating the first disjunct as p and the second disjunct as q, we can express the disjunctive proposition symbolically as $p \quad q$—that is, either p or q.

Conjunctive propositions. Conjunctive propositions use the connective " . . . and . . . ." to join two propositions. The symbol for this connective is the dot, " · ". An example of a conjunctive proposition is: "He is a logic student and he is intelligent."

The atomic parts of a conjunctive proposition are *conjuncts*. The first conjunct in the statement above is "He is a logic student," and the second conjunct is "he is intelligent." Designating the first conjunct by p and the second conjunct by q we can express the conjunctive proposition symbolically as $p · q$— that is, p and q.

Denial-of-conjunction propositions. Propositions denying the conjunction of two propositions use connectives such as "It is not the case both that

. . . and that . . . ." Another expression stating the same logical meaning is, "Not both . . . and . . . ." An illustration of a proposition denying conjunction is: "It is not the case both that it is raining and that the field is dry."

The atomic parts of such expressions are conjuncts of propositions denying the conjunction of two propositions. Enclosing the conjuncts in parentheses and placing the tilde symbol, "∼," in front of the first parenthesis to signify "not," we can express a proposition denying the conjunction of two propositions symbolically as ∼(p · q)—that is, it is not the case both that p and that q, or not both p and q.

Materially equivalent propositions. Materially equivalent propositions use the connectives ". . . is (materially) equivalent to . . ." or "if and only if . . . ." An example of a materially equivalent proposition is: "If and only if we are without a misadventure, do we arrive on time."

The atomic parts of such expressions are material equivalents. Letting the letter p symbolize the first materially equivalent proposition and the letter q symbolize the second materially equivalent proposition, and using the symbol "≡" to signify "is (materially) equivalent to," we can represent the materially equivalent proposition symbolically as $p \equiv q$—that is, p is materially equivalent to q. It also can be expressed as $(p \supset q) \cdot (q \supset p)$— that is, if p then q and if q then p, or if and only if p then q. Materially equivalent propositions are sometimes referred to as biconditional propositions.

12.2 The Logical Meaning of Symbols Used in Compound Propositions

The hypothetical proposition. The symbol "⊃," used to express a hypothetical proposition, signifies material implication. In a hypothetical proposition, the antecedent materially implies the consequent. In all cases in which a hypothetical proposition is true, the truth of the antecedent requires the truth of the consequent. Likewise, the falsity of the consequent requires the falsity of the antecedent.

Consider the hypothetical proposition: "If wages rise, then prices increase." If this proposition is true, then the truth of the atomic statement "wages rise" requires the truth of the atomic statement "prices increase." Likewise, the falsity of the statement "prices increase" requires the falsity of the statement "wages rise." The connective "if . . . then . . ." or the symbol "⊃" means that a true proposition using these forms will never have an antecedent that is true and a consequent that is false. However, the falsity of the antecedent does not require the falsity of the consequent and the truth of the consequent does not require the truth of the antecedent.

The disjunctive proposition. The disjunctive proposition, symbolized by "∨" is true if at least one disjunct is true. If one of the disjuncts is false, and the disjunctive proposition is true, then the other disjunct must be true.

Consider the disjunctive proposition: "Either he is brave or he is unaware of the risks." If the proposition is true, and the statement "He is brave" is false, then the statement "He is unaware of the risks" is necessarily true. Likewise, if "He is unaware of the risks" is false, then "He is brave" is necessarily true. The connectives "either . . . or . . ." or the symbol "$\vee$" means that a true proposition using these forms always will have at least one true disjunct. However, the truth of one disjunct does not require the falsity of the other disjunct. The meaning given above for the wedge, "$\vee$," does not exhaust all meanings of statements using the expression "either . . . or . . . ." This meaning, strictly speaking, is for inclusive disjunction. If the disjunction is exclusive, with one and only one disjunct that is true and with the other disjunct false, another symbolization with a different interpretation of meaning is possible. [Such symbolization can be $(p \vee q) \cdot (\sim p \vee \sim q)$ or $p \equiv \sim q$.]

The conjunctive proposition. The conjunctive proposition, using the connective " $\cdot$ ", is true only in those cases in which each conjunct is true.

Consider the conjunctive proposition: "Smith is a scholar and Smith is married." If the proposition is true, then the statement "Smith is a scholar" is true. Likewise, the statement "Smith is married" is true. The conjoined statements are true separately. Separate true statements also can be conjoined into a true statement.

The proposition denying the conjunction of two propositions. Propositions denying the conjunction of two propositions, having the logical form $\sim (p \cdot q)$, are true only in those cases in which one of the conjuncts symbolized within the parentheses is false. Propositions denying conjunctions are true even though both the indicated conjuncts are false.

Consider as true the proposition: "Not both can you have your cake and eat your cake." If the statement "You can have your cake" is true, then the statement "You can eat your cake" is false. If the statement "You can eat your cake" is true, then the statement "You can have your cake" is false. If one of the conjuncts of a true proposition denying the conjunction of two propositions is known to be false, nothing can be inferred about the truth or falsity of the second conjunct.

The materially equivalent proposition. A materially equivalent proposition, expressed by the form $p \equiv q$ or $(p \supset q) \cdot (q \supset p)$, means that if the indicated proposition is true, the propositions identified as materially equivalent have identical truth values. In a true materially equivalent proposition the truth of one of the equivalent propositions requires the truth of the other and the falsity of one requires the falsity of another.

Consider the following proposition: "If and only if we increase our effort can we win." If this is a true proposition, then the truth of the state-ment "We increase our effort" requires the truth of the statement "We can win." The truth of the statement "We can win" requires the truth of the statement "We increase our effort." The falsity of the statement "We increase our effort" requires the falsity of the statement "We can win." The falsity of the latter statement requires the falsity of the former.

12.3 EXERCISES

Identify the types of compound propositions in the following examples. Assign the value of "true" to the compound propositions. If the first atomic proposition is true, determine the truth value of the second. If the first atomic proposition is false, determine the truth value of the second. Assign similar values to the second atomic proposition, and in each case determine the truth value of the first proposition.

1. If and only if the research is completed can the thesis be written.
2. Either he is distracted or he does not care.
3. The fleet was attacked and many ships were sunk.
4. Not both can we be careless and we not suffer losses.
5. Only if great expenditure of funds is made can cities be rebuilt.
6. Sporotrichosis is a disease and it is caused by a fungus.
7. If and only if the probe is successful can we land on the moon.
8. Not both can satisfactory progress be made and social experimentation be retarded.
9. If the turmoil increases in the Middle East, then each side will become more aggressive.
10. He has an Oedipus complex and he is unwilling to fight.
11. Only if we find and anticipate all major questions that come up can we be prepared.
12. If the variables are controlled properly, then the experiment is successful.

12.4 The Denial of the Truth of a Proposition

We deny a proposition by affirming its contradiction. The contradiction of a proposition is false in all cases in which the original proposition is true, and in all cases in which the original proposition is false the contradiction is true. Likewise, if the contradiction is true, the original statement is false, and if the contradiction is false, the original statement is true. Thus, a propo-sition and its contradiction have opposite truth values.

If the original proposition has added to it an expression such as "It is not the case that" or if the symbols for the statement are enclosed in paren-theses and preceded by a tilde, the resulting proposition is the contradiction of the original. The contradiction of "$p \supset q$" is "$\sim(p \supset q)$." The con-tradiction of $p \lor q$ is "$\sim(p \lor q)$." The contradiction of "$\sim(p \cdot q)$" is "$\sim\sim(p \cdot q)$" or simply "$p \cdot q$."

There is a simpler manner of writing the contradiction for the hypothetical and disjunctive proposition. The form "$p \cdot \sim q$" asserts the same thing as "$\sim(p \supset q)$." The original form "$p \supset q$" holds that in all cases in which p is true q also is true. The form "$p \cdot \sim q$" simply denies this. The form "$\sim p \cdot \sim q$" asserts the same thing as "$\sim(p \vee q)$." The original form "$p \vee q$" asserts that at least one of the disjuncts, p or q, is true. The denial of this is the assertion "$\sim p$ and $\sim q$." Thus, "$\sim p \cdot \sim q$" is the denial of "$p \vee q$."

Table 12.1 shows the simplest way of writing the contradictory form

Table 12.1 Contradictory Forms of Propositions

Type of proposition	Original form	Contradictory form
Hypothetical	$p \supset q$	$p \cdot \sim q$
Disjunctive	$p \vee q$	$\sim p \cdot \sim q$
Conjunctive	$p \cdot q$	$\sim(p \cdot q)$
Denial of conjunction	$\sim(p \cdot q)$	$p \cdot q$
Equivalent materially	$p \equiv q$	$(p \cdot \sim q) \vee (q \cdot \sim p)$

of each of the propositions discussed. Consider the following examples:

Original: If you work hard, then you succeed.
Contradiction: You work hard and you do not succeed.

Original: Either he made a mistake or he forgot.
Contradiction: He did not make a mistake and he did not forget.

Original: He is honest and he is sincere.
Contradiction: It is not the case both that he is honest and that he is sincere.

Original: If and only if these forms are understood can they be used properly.
Contradiction: These forms are understood and they are not used properly or these forms are used properly and they are not understood.

12.5 The Equivalent Forms of Hypothetical, Disjunctive, and Denial-of-Conjunction Propositions

Hypothetical, disjunctive, and denial-of-conjunction propositions can be expressed in forms that are logically equivalent. The following forms have identical truth values and are logically equivalent:

$$p \supset q \qquad \sim p \vee q \qquad \sim(p \cdot \sim q)$$

Consider the following equivalent statements expressed in the forms indicated above.

If the metal is aluminum, it is a good conductor of heat.
Either the metal is not aluminum or it is a good conductor of heat.
Not both is the metal aluminum and not a good conductor of heat.

Each of these propositions holds:

In all cases of metal's being aluminum it is a good conductor of heat.
In all cases of a metal's not being a good conductor of heat it is not aluminum.

In every case in which one of these propositions is true, the other is true.
Consider the contradictory form of the propositions above:

Original form	Contradictory form	Contradictory form (simplified)
$p \supset q$	$p \cdot \sim q$	$p \cdot \sim q$
$\sim p \lor q$	$\sim\sim p \cdot \sim q$	$p \cdot \sim q$
$\sim(p \cdot \sim q)$	$p \cdot \sim q$	$p \cdot \sim q$

Original: If the metal is aluminum, it is a good conductor of heat.

Contradiction: The metal is aluminum and it is not a good conductor of heat.

Original: Either the metal is not aluminum or it is a good conductor of heat.

Contradiction: The metal is aluminum and it is not a good conductor of heat.

Original: Not both is the metal aluminum and not a good conductor of heat.

Contradiction: The metal is aluminum and is not a good conductor of heat.

The contradictions of the original propositions are identical. Since each of the original propositions has the same proposition for its contradiction, in any case in which one of the original propositions is false, the other forms also will be false.

The original propositions are equivalent to each other, since in each case in which one is true the others are true and in each case in which one is false the others are false. Propositions that are logically equivalent can be substituted for each other wherever they occur in an argument without affecting the logical meaning of the argument.

It also can be shown that $p \supset q$ is logically equivalent to $\sim q \supset \sim p$. Since $p \supset q$ means that for the proposition p to be true q also is true, then in any case where q is false p also must be false. Thus, if $p \supset q$ is true, then $\sim q \supset \sim p$ also must be true. The contradiction of $\sim q \supset \sim p$ is

$\sim q \cdot p$. The contradiction of $p \supset q$ is $p \cdot \sim q$. In all cases in which $p \cdot \sim q$ is false $\sim q \cdot p$ also will be false. Thus if $p \supset q$ is false, $\sim q \cdot p$ also will be false. Since $p \supset q$ and $\sim q \supset \sim p$ have identical truth values, they are equivalent propositions. The following two propositions exemplify these two equivalences:

> If the metal is aluminum, it is a good conductor of heat.
> If the metal is not a good conductor of heat, it is not aluminum.

The following propositions have now been shown to be equivalent:

$$\left. \begin{array}{l} p \supset q \\ \sim p \vee q \\ \sim (p \cdot q) \\ \sim q \supset \sim p \end{array} \right\} \text{Elementary propositional equivalents (EPE)}$$

Other forms that are equivalent to each other are the following:

$(p \cdot q) \equiv (q \cdot p)$	(Commutation) (Comm.)
$(p \vee q) \equiv (q \vee p)$	(Commutation) (Comm.)
$(p \equiv q) \equiv [(p \supset q) \cdot (q \supset p)]$	(Material equivalence) (ME)
$(p \vee p) \equiv p$	(Repetition) (Rep.)
$(p \cdot p) \equiv p$	(Repetition) (Rep.)

12.6 The Use of the Hypothetical Proposition in Argument Forms *modus ponens* and *modus tollens*

The logical structure of compound propositions allows us to use them in different kinds of argument forms and more flexibly than we can categorical propositions and the categorical syllogism. Using the minimal meaning of the different compound propositions, we can reach valid conclusions by the proper application of the following argument forms.

The minimal meaning of the hypothetical proposition is that in all cases in which the antecedent is true the consequent is true.

Modus ponens.   The argument form for *modus ponens* is

$$\begin{array}{l} p \supset q \\ \underline{p} \\ \therefore q \end{array}$$

In this argument form the hypothetical proposition is affirmed. Then its antecedent is affirmed. This permits the affirmation of the consequent. Consider the following example of the argument form *modus ponens*.

> If the metal is lead, it is a poor conductor.
> The metal is lead.
> Therefore, it is a poor conductor.

Modus tollens.   The argument form for *modus tollens* is

$$p \supset q$$
$$\sim q$$
$$\therefore \sim p$$

In this argument form the hypothetical proposition is affirmed and then the consequent is denied. This permits the denial of the antecedent. Consider the following example:

> If this gas is helium, it has an atomic weight of four.
> This gas does not have an atomic weight of four.
> Therefore, it is not helium.

If a hypothetical proposition is affirmed, and then the antecedent is denied, no conclusion can be validly inferred. To do so is to commit the formal "fallacy of denying the antecedent." If a hypothetical proposition is affirmed and then the consequent is affirmed, no conclusion can be validly inferred. To do so is to commit the formal "fallacy of affirming the consequent." These two fallacies are exemplified in the following invalid argument forms:

$$p \supset q$$
$$\sim p \quad \text{(INVALID)}$$
$$\therefore \sim q$$

$$p \supset q$$
$$q \quad \text{(INVALID)}$$
$$\therefore p$$

12.7 The Use of Disjunctive Propositions in Arguments

The minimal meaning of the disjunctive proposition is that at least one of the disjuncts is true. In a rigorous sense this minimal meaning is for an inclusive disjunction whose logical form is expressed by the use of the wedge, "v." The argument forms for a disjunctive argument are the following:

$$p \lor q$$
$$\sim p$$
$$\therefore q$$

$$p \lor q$$
$$\sim q$$
$$\therefore p$$

The disjunctive proposition is affirmed to be true and one of the disjuncts is denied. This permits the affirmation of the other disjunct. Consider the following examples:

> Either we explore the sea, or we fail to exploit its resources.
> We do not explore the sea.
> Therefore, we fail to exploit its resources.

> Either we take the bus or we take an airplane.
> We do not take an airplane.
> Therefore, we take the bus.

The formal "fallacy of affirming a disjunct" occurs if an original disjunctive proposition is affirmed and then one of the disjuncts is affirmed and the other disjunct is denied in the conclusion. This fallacy is illustrated in the following invalid forms:

$$\frac{\begin{array}{l} p \vee q \\ p \end{array}}{\therefore \sim q} \quad \text{(INVALID)} \qquad \frac{\begin{array}{l} p \vee q \\ q \end{array}}{\therefore \sim p} \quad \text{(INVALID)}$$

12.8 The Use of Propositions Denying Conjunctions in Arguments

The minimal meaning of a proposition denying the conjunction of two propositions is that at least one of the conjuncts in the denied proposition is false. The forms for a valid argument using a proposition denying the conjunction of two propositions are the following:

$$\frac{\begin{array}{l} \sim(p \cdot q) \\ p \end{array}}{\therefore \sim q} \qquad\qquad \frac{\begin{array}{l} \sim(p \cdot q) \\ q \end{array}}{\therefore \sim p}$$

The proposition denying the conjunction of two propositions is affirmed to be true and one of the conjuncts within the proposition is affirmed. This permits the denial of the remaining conjunct within the original proposition. Consider the following example:

It is not the case both that we are careless and that we succeed.
We are careless.
Therefore, we do not succeed.

The "fallacy of denying a conjunct in a proposition denying the conjunction of two propositions" occurs in the following invalid argument forms:

$$\frac{\begin{array}{l} \sim(p \cdot q) \\ \sim p \end{array}}{\therefore q} \quad \text{(INVALID)} \qquad \frac{\begin{array}{l} \sim(p \cdot q) \\ \sim q \end{array}}{\therefore p} \quad \text{(INVALID)}$$

12.9 EXERCISES

Analyze the following arguments. Identify arguments whose form is valid. Identify any fallacies in the arguments using invalid forms.

1. If the gas is nitrogen, it is colorless and tasteless. The gas is colorless and tasteless. Therefore, it is nitrogen.

2. Not both can this be a crawfish and not be a crustacean. This is not a crustacean. Therefore, it is not a crawfish.

3. Either we develop faster supersonic jets or we lose out in competition. We lose out in competition. Therefore, we do not develop faster supersonic jets.

4. It is not true both that the conference is successful and that the war continues. The war continues. Therefore, the conference is not successful.

5. Either conflict is inevitable or peaceful solutions can be found. Conflict is not inevitable. Therefore, peaceful solutions can be found.

6. If rapid changes occur, social stability is threatened. Social stability is threatened. Therefore, rapid changes occur.

7. Not both can the government increase taxes and the cost of living be reduced. The cost of living is not reduced. Therefore, the government increases taxes.

8. Either the Incas had no written language, or they left records of a written language. They left no records of a written language. Therefore, they had no written language.

9. If the corruption is not corrected, the government will fall. The government will not fall. Therefore, the corruption is corrected.

10. If the market drops, Smith will borrow more money. Smith does not borrow more money. Therefore, the market does not drop.

12.10 Reductions of Argument Form to *modus ponens*

We can reduce the argument forms designated as disjunctive, a denial of conjunction, and *modus tollens* to the form of *modus ponens* by replacing the original proposition with an equivalent one.

Original proposition	*Equivalent disjunctive form*	*Equivalent form denial of conjunction*
$p \supset q$	$\sim p \lor q$	$\sim(p \cdot \sim q)$
p	p	p
$\therefore q$	$\therefore q$	$\therefore q$

Consider the following valid arguments:

(1) If the bough breaks, the cradle will fall.
The bough breaks.
Therefore, the cradle will fall.

(2) Either the bough does not break or the cradle will fall.
The bough breaks.
Therefore, the cradle will fall.

(3) Not both does the bough break and the cradle not fall.
The bough breaks.
Therefore, the cradle will fall.

The disjunctive proposition in the second example and the proposition denying conjunction in the third example are equivalents of the hypothetical proposition in the first example. When the first premise in the second and third examples replaces the hypothetical proposition, the *modus ponens* argument form results.

It has been shown that the argument form $p \supset q$ is equivalent to $\sim q \supset \sim p$. Consider the following argument forms:

$$(1) \quad p \supset q$$
$$\frac{\sim q}{\therefore \sim p}$$

$$(2) \quad \sim q \supset \sim p$$
$$\frac{\sim q}{\therefore \sim p}$$

The second example has the logical form of a *modus ponens* argument, since the antecedent is affirmed in the second statement and the consequent is affirmed in the conclusion. When $\sim q \supset \sim p$ replaces $p \supset q$ for the premise of the hypothetical proposition, a *modus ponens* form can be used in the place of a *modus tollens* form. Consider the following arguments:

(1) If the bough breaks, the cradle will fall.
   The cradle will not fall.
   Therefore, the bough does not break.

(2) If the cradle will not fall, the bough will not break.
   The cradle will not fall.
   Therefore, the bough will not break.

The other possible arguments in the disjunctive and denial-of-conjunction forms have comparable results. Consider the following argument forms:

$$(1) \quad p \supset q \qquad (2) \quad \sim q \supset \sim p \qquad (3) \quad \sim p \vee q \qquad (4) \quad \sim(p \cdot \sim q)$$
$$\frac{\sim q}{\therefore \sim p} \qquad\qquad \frac{\sim q}{\therefore \sim p} \qquad\qquad \frac{\sim q}{\therefore \sim p} \qquad\qquad \frac{\sim q}{\therefore \sim p}$$

The propositions $p \supset q$, $\sim q \supset \sim p$, $\sim p \vee q$, and $\sim(p \cdot \sim q)$ are equivalent forms. The form of the second argument is the *modus ponens* form of the argument *modus tollens* shown in the first example. The disjunctive propositional form in the third example and the denial-of-conjunction form in the fourth example are logical equivalents of the hypothetical propositional form in the second example. The remaining parts of the arguments in the third and fourth example are the same as in the second example. Thus, when the form $\sim q \supset \sim p$ replaces $\sim p \vee q$ or $\sim(p \cdot \sim q)$, it is possible to have a *modus ponens* argument form. Consider the following examples:

(1) If the support is not strong, we do not win the election.
   The support is not strong.
   Therefore, we do not win the election.

(2) Either we do not win the election or the support is strong.
   The support is not strong.
   Therefore, we do not win the election.

(3) Not both do we win the election and the support not be strong.
   The support is not strong.
   Therefore, we do not win the election.

By substituting a logically equivalent hypothetical form for a disjunctive premise using a disjunctive or denial-of-conjunction proposition, we can develop the same argument in the form of *modus ponens*. Therefore, the other argument forms can be reduced to the form of a *modus ponens* argument.

It also would be possible to reduce such argument forms to one basic type with either the disjunctive or the denial-of-conjunction proposition as a major premise. This has particular significance in the programming of computers to solve problems in logic. By the use of disjunctive and conjunctive forms of atomic forms with values for negation, computers can be programmed to solve complex problems in logic.

12.11 EXERCISES

Analyze the following arguments. Identify the invalid arguments and state the reason for invalidity. Identify the valid arguments and restate these valid arguments in the form of modus ponens.

1. Either there is educational innovation or there is educational stagnation. There is not educational stagnation. Therefore, there is educational innovation.
2. Not both can the weather prediction be reliable and a storm develop. A storm develops. Therefore, the weather prediction is not reliable.
3. If conservation is not practiced, the fields will turn into deserts. The fields will not turn into deserts. Therefore, conservation will be practiced.
4. Not both can the blooms develop and the plants not be sprayed against red spider mites. The blooms do not develop. Therefore, they are not sprayed against red spider mites.
5. Either the destruction of their native habitat by drainage and development will cease or alligators will not survive. Alligators will survive. Therefore, the destruction of their native habitat will cease.
6. If the exploiters do not refrain from cutting the trees to make syrup from the sap, the forest will be destroyed. The exploiters do refrain from cutting the trees to make syrup from the sap. Therefore, the forest will not be destroyed.
7. Only if the actress is cast properly will she be a success. She is not cast properly. Therefore, she is not a success.
8. Either the student is a poor reader or he is distracted easily. The student is a poor reader. Therefore, he is not distracted easily.
9. Not both can the board be abolished and the complaints be considered fairly. The complaints are considered fairly. Therefore, the board is not abolished.
10. Only if the fares are reduced will the market develop. The fares are not reduced. Therefore, the market does not develop.

12.12 The Use of Conjunctive Propositions in Arguments

The logical meaning of a conjunctive proposition is that each (major) conjunct must be true for the proposition to be true. A conjunctive proposition is false if any (major) conjunct is false. Thus, the propositional form $p \cdot q$ is true only if p has the value of true and q has the value of true.

Simplification (or separation). Any major conjunct of a true conjunctive proposition may be separated from the conjunctive proposition and remain true. If the propositional form $p \cdot q$ is true, then p is true. Likewise q is true.

Consider the following proposition to be true: "Lincoln was elected president and Lincoln was married." Each proposition is true by separation (simplification): "Lincoln was elected president." "Lincoln was married."

Conjunction.   The principle of conjunction states that any true proposition can be combined with any other true proposition in a conjunctive proposition and the resulting proposition will be true. If the propositional form p is given as true and the propositional form q is given as true, then the conjunctive propositional form $p \cdot q$ is true.

Consider the following propositions to be true: "Eisenhower was a general." "Eisenhower was president." The following conjunctive proposition also is true: "Eisenhower was a general and Eisenhower was president."

Another valid argument form using a conjunctive expression is *absorption*. This can be derived readily from other valid argument forms and the use of equivalent forms. Absorption has the argument form: $p \supset q$, therefore, $p \supset (p \cdot q)$. Thus, granted the truth of the statement "If the thesis is completed, John will graduate in June," it is also true that "If the thesis is completed, then the thesis is completed and John will graduate in June." Although this argument form appears obvious, it has definite value in the use of extended proofs.

12.13 Addition

Since a disjunctive proposition has the minimal meaning that at least one disjunct must be true, any proposition can be added by forming a disjunction with a true proposition and the resulting disjunctive proposition will be true. If the propositional form p is true, then the propositional form $p \lor q$ is true. Consider the following example:

> Calcium is a light yellow metal.
> Therefore, either calcium is a light yellow metal or this piece of metal is not calcium.

The principle of addition makes possible the formulation of disjunctive propositions that may appear to be unusual. Thus, if the proposition "Silver is one of the oldest known metals" is true, the proposition "Either silver is one of the oldest known metals or a space ship from Mars landed at Kennedy International Airport" is also true.

12.14 Hypothetical Syllogisms

The hypothetical syllogism has two premises and a conclusion in the form of hypothetical propositions. An original hypothetical proposition is affirmed. A second hypothetical proposition whose antecedent is the same as the consequent of the first proposition is also affirmed. This permits a conclusion in the form of a hypothetical proposition. The antecedent of the conclusion has the antecedent of the first proposition and the consequent of the second proposition. The hypothetical proposition has the following argument form:

$$p \supset q$$
$$q \supset r$$
$$\therefore p \supset r$$

Consider this example:

If exhaust fumes are not controlled, the air is contaminated.
If the air is contaminated, respiratory diseases increase.
Therefore, if exhaust fumes are not controlled, then respiratory diseases increase.

By replacing one logically equivalent proposition with another one, we can reduce argument forms such as the following to a valid form for hypothetical syllogisms.

(1) $p \supset q$
$q \supset r$
$\therefore \sim r \supset \sim p$

(2) $\sim p \vee q$
$\sim q \vee r$
$\therefore \sim p \vee r$

(3) $p \supset q$
$r \vee \sim q$
$\therefore \sim (\sim r \cdot p)$

(4) $\sim (p \cdot \sim q)$
$\sim (q \cdot \sim r)$
$\therefore \sim (p \cdot \sim r)$

(5) $\sim (p \cdot \sim q)$
$\sim q \vee r$
$\therefore p \supset r$

(6) $\sim (p \cdot \sim q)$
$\sim r \supset \sim q$
$\therefore \sim (p \cdot \sim r)$

The following forms are invalid and their use constitutes a formal fallacy.

$p \supset q$
$p \supset r$ (INVALID)
$\therefore q \supset r$

$p \supset q$
$q \supset r$ (INVALID)
$\therefore \sim p \supset \sim r$

$p \supset q$
$q \supset r$ (INVALID)
$\therefore r \supset q$

12.15 The Dilemma

The dilemma makes use of hypothetical, disjunctive, conjunctive, and (in some cases) simple propositions. The major premise sets forth two hypothetical propositions joined in the form of a conjunctive proposition. The minor premise is a disjunctive proposition selecting alternatives set forth in the major premise. The conclusion sets forth the logical alternatives remaining after the choice of the minor premise. In practical use the conclusion of a dilemma frequently sets forth a situation constituting a predicament or an unfavorable set of alternatives. For example:

If we give help to our allies, our own economic stability is threatened, and if we fail to help our allies, our political security is threatened.

Either we give help to our allies or we fail to help our allies.

Therefore, either our own economic stability is threatened or our political security is threatened.

Traditionally, four major variants of the dilemma are distinguished. These are expressed in the following forms:

1. The simple constructive dilemma:

$$(p \supset q) \cdot (r \supset q)$$
$$p \vee r$$
$$\overline{\therefore q}$$

2. The simple destructive dilemma:

$$(p \supset q) \cdot (p \supset r)$$
$$\sim q \vee \sim r$$
$$\overline{\therefore \sim p}$$

3. The complex constructive dilemma:

$$(p \supset q) \cdot (r \supset s)$$
$$p \vee r$$
$$\overline{\therefore q \vee s}$$

4. The complex destructive dilemma:

$$(p \supset q) \cdot (r \supset s)$$
$$\sim q \vee \sim s$$
$$\overline{\therefore \sim p \vee \sim r}$$

By replacing the original propositions with equivalent propositions in the major premise, we can reduce the number of forms for the dilemma to the structure of the simple and the complex constructive dilemma. The major premise of the original simple destructive dilemma would become $(\sim q \supset \sim p) \cdot (\sim r \supset \sim p)$. The major premise of the original complex destructive dilemma would become $(\sim q \supset \sim p) \cdot (\sim s \supset \sim r)$. The minor premise in each case remains the same as in the original dilemma—that is, $\sim q \vee \sim r$ for the simple dilemma and $\sim q \vee \sim s$ for the compound dilemma.

Rebuttals of a dilemma take three forms: (1) attacking it by going through the horns, (2) attacking it by taking it by the horns, (3) attacking it by proposing a counterdilemma.

Attack by going through the horns.   The attack on the dilemma by going through the horns consists in adding another disjunct to the minor premise. In such a case the argument is no longer valid. However, in practical use another disjunct may be added to the conclusion to show that another alternative is possible as a consequence of the proposition added in the minor premise. Consider the following examples:

Original constructive dilemma:

$$(p \supset q) \cdot (r \supset s)$$
$$\underline{p \vee r}$$
$$\therefore q \vee s$$

Attack by going through the horns:

$$(p \supset q) \cdot (r \supset s)$$
$$\underline{p \vee r \vee t}$$
$$\therefore q \vee s \quad \text{or} \quad q \vee s \vee u$$

Original constructive dilemma:

If we are aggressive, we are accused of hostile acts and if we are passive, we are threatened by disaster.

Either we are aggressive or we are passive.

Therefore, either we are accused of hostile acts or we are threatened by disaster.

Attack by going through the horns:

If we are aggressive, we are accused of hostile acts and if we are passive, we are threatened by disaster.

Either we are aggressive or we are passive or we are patiently firm.

Therefore, either we are accused of hostile acts or we are threatened with disaster or we remain strong without being accused of hostile acts and being threatened by disaster.

If the disjuncts in the minor premise are contradictory propositions or express exclusive alternatives in which only one can be chosen, it is difficult to provide a satisfactory argument going through the horns. However, in some cases a division can be made in one of the disjuncts to form a third alternative. Consider the following disjunctive proposition as a minor premise of a dilemma. "Either we aid our allies or we do not." The first disjunct could be divided and the attacking premise expressed as follows: "Either we aid our allies to the point of threatening our economic stability, or we aid our allies only to a point that does not threaten our economic stability, or we do not aid our allies." (In some cases also one of the horns of the major premise may be divided.)

Attack by taking the dilemma by the horns. In attacking a dilemma by the horns, we call into question the truth of the major premise. At least one of the hypothetical propositions in the major premise is denied. This can be done in one of three ways:

(a) Denial of the first hypothetical proposition:

$$(p \cdot \sim q) \cdot (r \supset s)$$

(b) Denial of the second hypothetical proposition:

$$(p \supset q) \cdot (r \cdot \sim s)$$

(c) Denial of both first and second hypothetical propositions:
$$(p \cdot \sim q) \cdot (r \cdot \sim s)$$
Consider the application of these procedures in attacking the major premise of a traditional statement of a proposed dilemma:

> If the book teaches what is written in the Koran, it is not needed; and if it teaches what is contrary to the Koran, it is harmful.

(a) Denial of the first hypothetical proposition:

> The book teaches what is written in the Koran and it is needed, and if it teaches what is contrary to it, it is harmful.

(b) Denial of the second hypothetical proposition:

> If the book teaches what is written in the Koran, it is not needed; and it teaches what is contrary to the Koran and it is not harmful.

(c) Denial of both the first and the second hypothetical propositions:

> The book teaches what is written in the Koran and is needed, and it teaches what is contrary to the Koran and is not harmful.

The denial of one of the hypothetical propositions makes a major conjunct in the original premise false, and the resulting argument based upon it becomes invalid. In most cases only one of the horns of the dilemma is attacked. In a few cases in practical situations the attacking of both horns adds an emphasis to the rebuttal.

Attack by proposing a counterdilemma. In the proposal of a counterdilemma, the major premise is altered. The consequents of the hypothetical propositions are interchanged and negated. The minor premise remains the same. The disjuncts in the conclusion are interchanged and negated.

Original form:	*Counterdilemma:*
$(p \supset q) \cdot (r \supset s)$	$(p \supset \sim s) \cdot (r \supset \sim q)$
$p \vee r$	$p \vee r$
$\therefore q \vee s$	$\therefore \sim s \vee \sim q$

The classical illustration of the counterdilemma concerns a teacher who desired that the court order his former student to pay him for logic lessons. The student originally had agreed to pay the teacher for the lessons after winning his first case in court. The teacher proposed the following argument:

> If the court decides in favor of the teacher, the student must pay for the lessons because of the decision of the court, and if the court decides in favor of the student, the student must pay for the lessons because of his original agreement.
>
> Either the court decides in favor of the teacher or it decides in favor of the student.

Therefore, either the student must pay for the lessons because of the decision of the court, or he must pay because of his original agreement.

The student proposed as a rebuttal a counterdilemma:

If the court decides in favor of the teacher, the student does not have to pay for his lessons because of his original agreement, and

If the court decides in favor of the student, the student does not have to pay because of the decision of the court.

Either the court decides in favor of the teacher or it decides in favor of the student.

Therefore, either the student does not have to pay for his lessons because of his original agreement or he does not have to pay because of the decision of the court.

A counterdilemma has definite limitations as a sound procedure in rebutting an original dilemma. It is a rebuttal in a strict sense only if the conclusion of the counterdilemma denies the conclusion of the original dilemma. However, such a denial rarely occurs. When it does happen there is reason to question the consistency of the original premises stated in hypothetical form. The conclusion of the counterdilemma in such cases helps to focus on this original inconsistency.

A counterdilemma does present another side to the proposed predicament. In this situation it is not technically a rebuttal but it emphasizes the other (usually more favorable) viewpoint. Consider the following pessimistic conclusion:

If we permit freedom of ideas, we are threatened with an attack on our security; and if we restrain the free expression of ideas, we are confronted with an attack upon our basic rights.

Either we permit freedom of ideas or we restrain their free expression.

Therefore, either we are threatened with an attack on our security or we are confronted with an attack on our basic rights.

The use of the form of the counterdilemma makes possible a more optimistic conclusion:

If we permit freedom of ideas, we are not confronted with an attack on our basic rights; and if we restrain the free expression of ideas, we are not threatened with an attack on our security.

Either we permit freedom of ideas or we restrain their free expression.

Therefore, either we are not confronted with an attack upon our basic rights or we are not threatened with an attack on our security.

The more optimistic conclusion of the counterdilemma does not rebut in a theoretical sense the conclusion of the original dilemma. Both conclusions could hold without any inconsistency. However, in popular speech the counterdilemma might subjectively persuade the listener toward putting aside the original dilemma.

Some dilemmas do not have an effective rebuttal. This is most likely to occur in the following situation: (1) the alternatives presented in the premise with the disjunctive form of "either . . . or" are exhaustive, (2) the premises expressed in hypothetical form represent genuine entailments so that the consequents are the case given the truth of the antecedent, and (3) no counterdilemma is proper.

12.16 EXERCISES

Analyze the following dilemmas for validity. Use symbols to show the different types of possible rebuttals and state in words the key premise in a rebuttal that might be used in each of the valid dilemmas.
1. If sufficient time is given to preparation of the defense, then preparation of the offense is neglected, and if adequate preparation for the offense is made, the defense is neglected. Either sufficient time is given to the preparation of the defense, or adequate preparation for the offense is made. Therefore, either the preparation for the offense is neglected or preparation for the defense is neglected.
2. If taxes rise, then the cost of living rises, and if inflation continues, the cost of living rises. Either taxes rise or inflation continues. Therefore, the cost of living rises.
3. If the bonds are approved, the needed civic improvements can be made, and if the bond issue does not carry, then conditions essential for growth will not be attained. Either the bonds are approved or the bond issue does not carry. Therefore, either the needed civic improvements can be made or conditions essential for growth will not be attained.
4. If you compete and win, you have the satisfaction of victory, and if you compete and lose, you have gained valuable experience. Either you compete and win or you compete and lose. Therefore, you have the satisfaction of victory or you have gained valuable experience.
5. If the problem is solved, its answer is accepted, and if its statement is not correct, a new statement has to be formulated. Either the problem is solved or a new statement has to be formulated. Therefore, either its answer is accepted or its statement is not correct.
6. If the crime is admitted, then a prison sentence will be given, and if the case is tried, the defendant will be found guilty. Either the prison sentence will not be given or the defendant will not be found guilty. Therefore, either the crime is not admitted or the case is not tried.
7. If you know the material, you need not read outside material to make a good grade, and if you do not understand the material, outside reading is useless. Either you know the material or you do not understand it. Therefore, either you need not read outside material to make good grades or outside reading is useless.
8. If freedom of speech is permitted, then extremist groups can advocate undemocratic practices, and if freedom of speech is curtailed, then democratic institu-

tions are threatened. Either freedom of speech is permitted or it is curtailed. Therefore, either extremist groups can advocate undemocratic practices or democratic institutions are threatened.

9. If wages are permitted to rise, inflation will result in increased costs of goods, and if wages are frozen, popular unrest will result in a change in the elected representatives to Congress. Either wages are permitted to rise or wages are frozen. Therefore, either inflation will result in increased costs of goods or popular unrest will result in a change in the elected representatives to Congress.

10. If I lead the six of hearts and the bidder plays his ace of hearts, he makes his bid; and if I lead my low trump and the bidder plays his high trump, he makes his bid. Either I lead the six of hearts and the bidder plays his ace of hearts or I lead my low trump and the bidder plays his high trump. Therefore, he makes his bid. (Can this dilemma be rebutted?)

Chapter 13
Proofs of
Extended Arguments

13.1 Valid Propositional Argument Forms and Equivalences

The propositional argument forms discussed in Chapter 12 can be used to justify the validity of an argument consisting of a series of propositions. Consider the following argument:

(1) If we have an opportunity to expand, then we must act.
(2) If we must act, then we must take risks.
(3) We have an opportunity to expand.
    Therefore, we must take risks.

By combining statements (1) and (3) with the use of the argument form *modus ponens* we can draw the conclusion: (4) "We must act." By use of statements (2) and (4) and *modus ponens* we can draw the conclusion: "We must take risks." The use of such form in extended arguments can be examined for validity by showing that the conclusion follows necessarily from the premises and from the application of relevant and valid argument forms. This chapter discusses the elementary use of propositional argument forms in the analysis and proofs in extended arguments.

The following argument forms, given here together with their names and abbreviations, have been shown to be valid:

1. *Modus ponens* (MP):

$$p \supset q$$
$$\underline{p}$$
$$\therefore q$$

2. *Modus tollens* (MT):

$$p \supset q$$
$$\sim q$$
$$\overline{\therefore \sim p}$$

3. Disjunctive argument (DA):

$$p \vee q \qquad p \vee q$$
$$\sim p \qquad \sim q$$
$$\overline{\therefore q} \qquad \overline{\therefore p}$$

4. Denial-of-conjunction argument (DCA):

$$\sim (p \cdot q) \qquad \sim (p \cdot q)$$
$$p \qquad\qquad q$$
$$\overline{\therefore \sim q} \qquad \overline{\therefore \sim p}$$

5. Hypothetical syllogism (HS):

$$p \supset q$$
$$q \supset r$$
$$\overline{\therefore p \supset r}$$

6. Complex (constructive) dilemma (CCD):

$$(p \supset q) \cdot (r \supset s)$$
$$p \vee r$$
$$\overline{\therefore q \vee s}$$

7. Addition (Add.):

$$p$$
$$\overline{\therefore p \vee q}$$

8. Conjunction (Conj.):

$$p$$
$$q$$
$$\overline{\therefore p \cdot q}$$

9. Simplification (Simp.):

$$p \cdot q \qquad p \cdot q$$
$$\overline{\therefore p} \qquad \overline{\therefore q}$$

The following forms are logically equivalent.

1. Elementary propositional equivalents (EPE):

$$(p \supset q) \equiv (\sim p \vee q)$$
$$\equiv \sim (p \cdot \sim q)$$
$$\equiv (\sim q \supset \sim p)$$

2. Commutation equivalents (Comm.):

$$(p \vee q) \equiv (q \vee p)$$
$$(p \cdot q) \equiv (q \cdot p)$$

3. Material equivalents (ME):
$$(p \equiv q) \equiv [(p \supset q) \cdot (q \supset p)]$$
$$(p \equiv q) \equiv [p \cdot q) \vee (\sim p \cdot \sim q)] \qquad \text{(alternative form)}$$

4. Repetition (Rep.):
$$(p \vee p) \equiv p$$
$$(p \cdot p) \equiv p$$

5. Distribution (Dist.):
$$[p \vee (q \cdot r)] \equiv [(p \vee q) \cdot (p \vee r)]$$
$$[p \cdot (q \vee r)] \equiv [(p \cdot q) \vee (p \cdot r)]$$

6. Association (Assoc.):
$$[p \vee (q \vee r)] \equiv [(p \vee q) \vee r]$$
$$[p \cdot (q \cdot r)] \equiv [(p \cdot q) \cdot r]$$

Propositional argument forms that are equivalent may replace each other wherever they occur. Thus, if $p \equiv q$ and $q \vee r$ are given, p can replace q with the resultant form $p \vee r$. Likewise, if it is given that $(p \cdot q) \equiv r$, and $s \supset (p \cdot q)$, then r can replace $p \cdot q$ with the resultant form $s \supset r$.

Elementary propositional equivalents can be broken down further. The use of the specific names of these forms is preferable after the technique of writing proofs is developed.

7. Material implication (MI):
$$(p \supset q) \equiv (\sim p \vee q)$$

8. De Morgan's law (DeM):
$$(p \vee q) \equiv \sim (\sim p \cdot \sim q)$$
$$(p \cdot q) \equiv \sim (\sim p \vee \sim q)$$

9. De Morgan's law and material implication (DeM & MI):
$$(p \supset q) \equiv \sim (p \cdot \sim q)$$

10. Contraposition (Contrap.):
$$(p \supset q) \equiv (\sim q \supset \sim p)$$

The commutation equivalents are particularly useful in reducing arguments using forms of disjunction, denial of conjunction, or *modus tollens* to the form of *modus ponens*. Since the method of proof introduced in this section is not as rigorous as it becomes in more advanced logic, the use of commutation equivalents will not be applied as often as it would be in stricter procedures.

Parentheses are used to identify the more elementary parts within a statement in order to keep the logical relations clear. Brackets and braces also can be used. The statement "If either p or q, then r" is written

$(p \lor q) \supset r$. The statement "If either p and q, or r, then s" is written $[(p \cdot q) \lor r] \supset s$.

An argument is valid if it has a valid argument form. By convention, capital letters are used to designate propositions in arguments and small letters beginning with p are used to designate propositional variables in argument forms. Consider the argument:

> If the cat's away, the mice will play.
> The cat's away.
> Therefore, the mice will play.

Letting the letter C symbolize "the cat's away" and the letter M symbolize "the mice will play," we can express the argument and the argument form as follows:

Argument	Argument form
$C \supset M$	$p \supset q$
C	p
$\therefore M$	$\therefore q$

This argument has the argument form of *modus ponens*. Since its argument form is valid, the argument is valid.

A proof for an argument consists in showing that it has a valid argument form or that it can be derived from a series of argument forms that are valid. Consider the following argument:

> If John is a graduate, he is eligible for the job. (G, E)
> John is a graduate.
> If John is eligible for the job, he will apply for it. (A)
> Therefore, he will apply for the job.

Column I	Column II	Column III
(1) $G \supset E$		
(2) G		
(3) $E \supset A$		
$\therefore A$		
(4) E	(1), (2) $p \supset q$, p, / $\therefore q$	(1), (2) MP
(5) A	(3), (4) $p \supset q$, p, / $\therefore q$	(3), (4) MP

Column I states the argument and steps used in the proof of the conclusion. Column II refers to the argument forms or the equivalences used in lines (4) and (5). Column III refers to the name of the argument. The numbers in columns II and III refer to the line numbers in column I to show which propositions were used for the argument forms or equivalences in column II and column III.

Consider the following argument:

If Mary goes to town, then she will cut class. (G, C)
Not both can she cut class and see her boy friend. (S)
Mary sees her boy friend.
Therefore, she does not go to town.

Column I	Column II	Column III
(1) $G \supset C$		
(2) $\sim(C \cdot S)$		
(3) S		
$\therefore \ \sim G$		
(4) $\sim C$	(2), (3) $\sim(p \cdot q)$, q, / $\therefore \sim p$	(2), (3) DCA
(5) $\sim G$	(1), (4) $p \supset q$, $\sim q$, / $\therefore \sim p$	(1), (4) MT

Not both can it be plutonium and not be a transuranium element. (P, T)

Either it is not a transuranium element or it has atomic number 94. (N)

Therefore, if it is plutonium, it has atomic number 94.

Column I	Column II	Column III
(1) $\sim(P \cdot \sim T)$		
(2) $\sim T \lor N$		
$\therefore P \supset N$		
(3) $P \supset T$	(1) $p \supset q \equiv (p \cdot \sim q)$	(1) EPE
(4) $T \supset N$	(2) $p \supset q \equiv \sim p \lor q$	(2) EPE
(5) $P \supset N$	(3), (4) $p \supset q$, $q \supset r$, / $\therefore p \supset r$	(3), (4) HS

Line (3), column II, shows that $P \supset T$ replaces $\sim(P \cdot \sim T)$ as an equivalent. Column II can be eliminated or combined with column III after the technique has been learned. In line (4), $T \supset N$ replaces $\sim T \lor N$ in line (2) as its equivalent. Line (5) shows that the conclusion is derived from lines (3) and (4) by the use of a hypothetical syllogism.

Here is another example:

Column I	Column II	Column III
(1) $B \supset C$		
(2) $(\sim C \lor D) \cdot \sim D$		
(3) $\sim(\sim B \cdot E)$		
$\therefore \ \sim E$		
(4) $\sim C \lor D$	(2) $p \cdot q$, / $\therefore p$	(2) Simp.
(5) $\sim D$	(2) $p \cdot q$, / $\therefore q$	(2) Simp.
(6) $\sim C$	(4), (5) $p \lor q$, $\sim q$, / $\therefore p$	(4), (5) DA
(7) $\sim B$	(1), (6) $p \supset q$, $\sim q$, / $\therefore \sim p$	(1), (6) MT
(8) $\sim E$	(3), (7) $\sim(p \cdot q)$, p, / $\therefore \sim q$	(3), (7) DCA

13.2 EXERCISES

1. Complete columns II and III in the following arguments:

(a)

	Column I	Column II	Column III
(1)	$A \supset B$		
(2)	$\sim B \vee C$		
(3)	A		
	$\therefore C$		
(4)	B		
(5)	C		

(b)

	Column I	Column II	Column III
(1)	$B \vee C$		
(2)	$C \supset (D \vee E)$		
(3)	$\sim B$		
(4)	$\sim E$		
	$\therefore D$		
(5)	C		
(6)	$D \vee E$		
(7)	D		

(c)

	Column I	Column II	Column III
(1)	$(A \cdot B) \supset C$		
(2)	$\sim C \vee D$		
(3)	$\sim D$		
	$\therefore \sim A \vee \sim B$		
(4)	$C \supset D$		
(5)	$(A \cdot B) \supset D$		
(6)	$\sim (A \cdot B)$		
(7)	$\sim A \vee \sim B$		

(d)

	Column I	Column II	Column III
(1)	$(E \supset F) \cdot (G \supset H)$		
(2)	$\sim (\sim E \cdot \sim G)$		
(3)	$(F \vee H) \supset K$		
	$\therefore K$		
(4)	$E \vee G$		
(5)	$F \vee H$		
(6)	K		

(e)

	Column I	Column II	Column III
(1)	$(H \vee K) \supset L$		
(2)	$\sim (L \cdot \sim M)$		
(3)	$\sim M$		

(4) $\sim H \supset N$

      $\therefore N$

(5) $L \supset M$

(6) $(H \lor K) \supset M$

(7) $\sim(H \lor K)$

(8) $\sim H \cdot \sim K$

(9) $\sim H$

(10) N

2. Construct proofs for the following arguments:

(a) Either we do not attack or our position is in jeopardy. (A, J) If our position is in jeopardy, then we need to be alert. (N) Therefore, if we attack, then we need to be alert.

(b) It is impossible both that Smith be elected and that he not campaign vigorously. (E, C) If he campaigns vigorously, then he must spend considerable money on TV announcements. (S) He will not spend considerable money on TV announcements. Therefore, Smith will not be elected.

(c) James is in class and either he is wearing a coat or he is wearing a sweater. (C, W, S) If he is in class, then he forgot his glasses. (F) It is not possible both that he forgot his glasses and that he is wearing a sweater. Therefore, he is wearing a coat.

(d) If Susan is either ill or sleepy, then she is in her room. (I, S, R) Not both can she be in her room and be in the drug store. (D) She is in the drug store. Therefore, she is not ill.

(e) If I study all night, I shall not be alert, and if I am not prepared, I shall fail the test. (S, A, P, F). Either I study all night or I am not prepared. Not both can I either not be alert or fail the test and make a good grade in the course. (G) Therefore, I shall not make a good grade in the course.

(f) Either the team does not win the game or they will win the title. (W, T) Not both can they win the title and not play in a bowl game. (P) If either they get the breaks or play in a bowl game, then they will have a high ranking. (B, R) They will not have a high ranking. Therefore, they do not win the title and they do not win the game.

(g) If the students are indifferent, then they do not indicate strong interest. (I, S) Not both can they not indicate strong interest and not be concerned (C). The students are not concerned. If they are not indifferent, they will not miss classes. (M) Therefore, they will not miss classes.

(h) If it is not possible both that Charles attend the movie and prepare his assignment, then he will visit friends. (A, P, V) If he visits friends, he will be detained. (D) Either he is not detained, or he will watch a late TV show. (W) He will not watch a late TV show. Therefore, he does prepare his assignment.

(i) If this arugment is valid, then addition will be helpful. (V, A) Either this argument is valid or it is difficult. (D) It is not difficult. Therefore, either addition will be helpful or it will be useless. (U)

(j) If and only if the hypothetical form of equivalence is used with this problem can this problem be solved. (H, S) The hypothetical form of equivalence is used with this problem. Either this problem is not solved or it is valid. (V) Therefore it is valid.

13.3 Inconsistency

Although the proper use of argument forms assures the validity of an argument, it cannot assure a sound argument. If some of the premises used in a valid argument are false, the argument is not sound. This situation becomes particularly obvious if an internal inconsistency or contradiction occurs in the argument itself.

Consider the following argument:

> Either John returns on time or he has an accident. (R, A)
> Either John does not return on time or he stops to play. (P)
> John does not have an accident.
> John does not stop to play.
> Therefore, John bought a new car. (B)

(1) $R \lor A$
(2) $\sim R \lor P$
(3) $\sim A$
(4) $\underline{\sim P}$
$\therefore B$

(5) R	(1), (3) $p \lor q, \sim q, / \therefore p$	(1), (3) DA
(6) $\sim R$	(2), (4) $p \lor q, \sim q, / \therefore p$	(2), (4) DA
(7) $R \lor B$	(5) $p, / \therefore p \lor q$	(5) Add.
(8) B	(7), (6) $p \lor q, \sim p, / \therefore q$	(7), (6) Add.

The argument above is valid but it cannot be sound. In step (5) R is proven and in step (6) $\sim R$ is proven. Both R and $\sim R$ cannot be true, since they are contradictory. With the introduction of such an inconsistency and the use of addition, as shown above, any proposition can be established as the conclusion. Since a sound argument not only is valid but has true premises, the argument above cannot be sound, as all of its premises cannot be true.

13.4 Invalidity

Although extended proofs of the type we have studied thus far can prove validity, this procedure does not permit an adequate procedure for determining invalidity in all the cases. The argument is valid if it can be proven that the conclusion can be derived properly from the premises given. It is possible that the argument is valid even though on any particular occasion the procedure for proving its validity is not found. Likewise, in some cases, an instance of an *apparently* invalid procedure might be detected and yet the argument would be valid.

Consider the following example:

> If silicon with its many compounds makes up approximately 25 percent of the earth's crust, then it is one of the elements in greatest abundance. (M, A)

If silicon has atomic number 14, then silicon with its many compounds makes up approximately 25 percent of the earth's crust. (*N*)

Silicon is one of the elements of greatest abundance.

Silicon has atomic number 14.

Therefore, silicon with its many compounds makes up approximately 25 percent of the earth's crust.

(1)	$M \supset A$		
(2)	$N \supset M$		
(3)	A		
(4)	N		
	$\therefore M$		
(5)	M	(2), (4) $p \supset q, p, / \therefore q$	(2), (4) MP

This argument is valid. Only two of the forms were used to prove the conclusion. However, in the premises that were given it might be noticed that $M \supset A$ and A were affirmed. On this basis it might appear that the fallacy of affirming the consequent had occurred. However, the conclusion, M, was derived validly from other forms: $N \supset M, N$, therefore M.

If all alternative procedures for drawing possible inferences from the argument have been exhausted, and the conclusion has not been established but an apparently fallacious procedure in the premises has been found, this would provide a basis for a claim of invalidity. The substitution of hypothetical propositions for other kinds of propositions would facilitate the exhaustion of possible inferences in the argument. Many fallacious arguments can be shown to be instances of the fallacy of affirming the consequent. However, this procedure can become cumbersome. A more rigorous way of proving invalidity is discussed in Sections 14.5 and 14.9.

13.5 EXERCISES

Determine the validity of the following arguments. Write proofs for valid arguments. If an argument appears to be invalid, indicate the apparent reason for invalidity after reducing all following forms of disjunctive, denial-of-conjunction, and modus tollens *arguments to the fallacy of affirming the consequent.*

1. (1) $\sim A \lor B$
   (2) $\underline{\sim B \lor C}$
   $\therefore \sim C \supset \sim A$

2. (1) $\sim (B \cdot C)$
   (2) $D \supset C$
   (3) $\underline{(D \lor E) \cdot \sim E}$
   $\therefore \sim B$

3. (1) $C \supset (D \cdot E)$
   (2) $F \supset \sim (D \cdot E)$
   (3) $\underline{\sim (G \cdot \sim F) \cdot G}$
   $\therefore \sim C$

4. (1) $D \supset E$
   (2) $D \supset F$
   (3) $E \supset \sim F$
   (4) $\underline{D}$
   $\therefore G$

5. (1) $A \supset B$
   (2) $\sim(B \cdot \sim C) \cdot \sim C$
   ∴ $\sim A \lor D$

6. (1) $\sim(E \cdot \sim F)$
   (2) $\sim F \lor G$
   (3) $\sim G$
   ∴ $\sim E$

7. (1) $(A \supset B) \cdot (A \supset C)$
   (2) $\sim(B \cdot C)$
   (3) $D \lor A$
   ∴ D

8. (1) $G \cdot (K \lor L)$
   (2) $\sim H \supset \sim I$
   (3) $\sim H$
   (4) $\sim(K \cdot G)$
   ∴ $L \cdot \sim I$

9. (1) $(H \supset I) \cdot (J \supset K)$
   (2) $L \supset (\sim I \lor \sim K)$
   (3) L
   ∴ $H \supset \sim J$

10. (1) $I \supset (J \supset K)$
    (2) $L \supset (J \cdot \sim K)$
    (3) $I \cdot L$
    ∴ M

11. (1) $J \equiv K$
    (2) $\sim K \lor L$
    (3) $(L \supset M) \cdot \sim M$
    ∴ $\sim J$

12. (1) $(P \supset Q) \cdot (R \supset Q)$
    (2) $P \lor R$
    ∴ Q

13. Either there is not free interchange of information or the advancement of science is helped. (I, A) Not both can the advancement of science be helped and censorship of scientific publications be practiced. (C) There is free interchange of information. Therefore, the censorship of scientific publications is not practiced.

14. If the scientist is honest, then he will make true statements and will indicate evidence that is difficult to account for by his views. (H, T, I) If he makes true statements and he indicates evidence that is difficult to account for by his views, then he supports thoroughness of inquiry. (S) The scientist is honest. Therefore, he supports thoroughness of inquiry.

15. Not both can research methods be sound and not provide some basis for verification. (S, V) If research methods are sound, then appeals to guesses will not be made. (G) Appeals to guesses are not made. Therefore, research methods provide some basis for verification.

16. If the experiment is carried out properly, then the results are confirmable. (E, R) Either the results of the experiment are not confirmable or appropriate techniques have been used. (T) The experiment is carried out properly and appropriate techniques have not been used. Therefore, the experiment is a landmark in scientific investigation. (L)

17. If and only if an acceptable theory is supported by evidence can it be verified. (E, V) If there are sound reasons to hold to an acceptable theory, then it is supported by evidence. (R) It is not the case both that there are not sound reasons to hold an acceptable theory and that unfavorable evidence is not ignored in scientific investigation. (I) Unfavorable evidence is not ignored in scientific investigation. Therefore, an acceptable theory can be verified.

18. If an overdose of irradiated ergosterol has been given these adult rats, then either widespread metastatic calcification occurs in their cardiovascular system or it occurs in other organs of their bodies. (E, C, O) If no symptoms of calcification occur, then widespread metastatic calcification has not occurred in their

cardiovascular system and it has not occurred in other organs of their bodies. (S) No symptoms of calcification occur. Either an overdose of irradiated ergosterol has been given these adult rats or a vitamin C preparation was given them. (V) Therefore, a vitamin C preparation was given to them.

19. Not both can a person be an activist and not be a demonstrator. (A, D) Either one is not an excitable person or he is an activist. (E) If a person is restless, then he is excitable. (R) Either a person is restless or he is not a student. (S) Therefore, if anyone is not a demonstrator, then he is not a student.

20. Either we go to the coast for our vacation or we shall invite friends to join us, and either we go to the mountains or we shall rest quietly in the cabin for two weeks. (C, F, M, R) If we go to the coast for our vacation, we shall not go to the mountains. Therefore, if we do not invite friends to join us, we shall rest quietly in the cabin for two weeks.

21. Either proper techniques are not followed or the experiment is sound. (F, S) If the experiment does not provide a basis for testing hypotheses, it is not sound. (T) The experiment provides a basis for testing hypotheses. Therefore, proper techniques are followed.

22. Either Smith wins the award or, if Jones' work was recognized as superior and his discovery was regarded as highly significant, then Jones wins the award. (S, W, D, J) Smith does not win the award and Jones' work was recognized as superior. If Jones' discovery was not regarded as highly significant, then his work was not recognized as superior. If Jones' work was regarded as superior he will be given additional research grants. (R) Therefore, Jones wins the award and Jones will be given additional research grants.

23. If both the forms are understood and the problem is not solved, then the statements are not clear. (F, P, S) The forms are understood and the work is complete. (C) If the work is complete, then the answers are not correct. (A) Either the problem is not solved or the answers are correct. Therefore, the statements are not clear.

24. If there are no focal points of urban dissatisfaction, there is no fear of large-scale riots. (D, R) Either there is no need to take extra precautions in assuring order in impoverished urban areas or it is not the case both that there are no focal points of urban dissatisfaction and that there is no fear of large-scale riots. (P) There is need to take extra precautions in assuring order in impoverished urban areas. Therefore, there is fear of large-scale riots.

25. It is the case that either the decision was made in ignorance or the decision was made on poor judgment and that the decision was costly. (I, P, C) The decision was not made in ignorance and if the decision was made on poor judgment, a more experienced administrator is needed. (E) Therefore, it is not the case either that the decision was not made on poor judgment or that a more experienced administrator is not needed.

26. It is not the case both that there are price increases and that there are not any inflationary tendencies. (P, T) If there are any inflationary tendencies, then the real income of pensioners declines. (R) Either the real income of pensioners does not decline or additional sources of revenue are provided to increase the income of pensioners. (A) If it is the case that if there are price increases, additional sources of revenue are provided to increase the income of pensioners, then either there will be a marked increase in taxes or there will be a decrease in government

spending on national defense. (*M, D*) There will not be a decrease in government spending on national defense. Therefore, there will be a marked increase in taxes.

13.6 Conditional Proofs and *Reductio ad Absurdum* Proofs

Another way to establish the validity of an argument is by the use of conditional proofs. Such proofs are relevant to cases in which the conclusion has the form of a hypothetical statement or can be replaced by a hypothetical statement.

Consider the following argument:

Not both can some sedimentary rocks be weakly magnetized and this factor be irrelevant to the original formation of these rocks. (*W, F*)

If this factor is not irrelevant to the original formation of these rocks, then the magnetism in sedimentary rocks provides evidence for determining the direction of the earth's magnetic field at the time of the formation of these rocks. (*D*)

Either the magnetism in sedimentary rocks does not provide evidence for determining the direction of the earth's magnetic field at the time of the formation of these rocks, or there is strong evidence to support the hypothesis of a continental drift. (*H*)

Therefore, if some sedimentary rocks are weakly magnetized, then there is strong evidence to support the hypothesis of a continental drift.

A validation of this argument using the form of a conditional proof is as follows:

$$(1) \quad \sim(W \cdot F)$$
$$(2) \quad \sim F \supset D$$
$$(3) \quad \sim D \lor H$$
$$\overline{\therefore \ W \supset H}$$

⌈(4)	W	Add. cond. prem.
(5)	$\sim F$	(1), (4) DCA
(6)	D	(2), (5) MP
⌊(7)	H	(3), (6) DA
(8)	$\overline{W \supset H}$	(4)–(7) Cond. proof

The conclusion, "$W \supset H$," is in the form of a hypothetical statement. The first step in the proof states the antecedent of this proposition as an added premise, the conditional nature of this premise and the steps dependent upon its addition being indicated by indentation and two right-angle markings. The added (and conditional) premise is labeled with the abbreviation "Add. cond. prem.," indicating an added conditional premise. The citations of forms of proof within this indented section refer to forms that logically follow from the added or assumed premise taken together with the original premises. Thus, in the case above, if W as the added premise is true, then $\sim F$ is also true, as in D and H. The final step in the conclusion shows that, by the use of this conditional proof, it must be the case that if the premises are true, then $W \supset H$ also is true. This is established by the proof that $W \supset H$ is a necessary conclusion if W is assumed to be true. This type of validation is optional and is useful in simplifying some forms of proof.

Another form of proof is the *reductio ad absurdum*. This kind of argument establishes that the negation of the conclusion requires the negation of a premise, thus causing a contradiction to occur in the argument. Therefore, in order to avoid this absurdity (of establishing by denial of the conclusion that a premise that is given as true is also false), this argument shows that the conclusion must be true.

The proof begins by showing that the consequence of accepting the conclusion is false. Consider the following argument:

> If the intelligence information is correct, then racial tension is building up in this metropolitan area. (I, T)
>
> If racial tension is building up in this metropolitan area, then greater effort to achieve conditions lessening tensions is to be made. (A)
>
> Either greater effort to achieve conditions lessening tensions is not to be made or peaceful settlement of issues is attained. (P)
>
> The intelligence information is correct.
>
> Therefore, peaceful settlement of issues is attained.

$$(1)\ I \supset T$$
$$(2)\ T \supset A$$
$$(3)\ {\sim}A \lor P$$
$$(4)\ I$$

$$\therefore P$$

(5)	${\sim}P$	Add. *reductio* prem.
(6)	${\sim}A$	(3), (5) DA
(7)	${\sim}T$	(2), (6) MT
(8)	${\sim}I$	(1), (7) MT
(9)	$I \cdot {\sim}I$	(4), (8) Conj.
(10)	P	(5)–(9) *Reductio* prem. absurd

The proof above shows that if the conclusion P is assumed to be false $({\sim}P)$, then I must be false $({\sim}I)$. However, the premises require I to be true. Therefore, the added *reductio* premise, ${\sim}P$, must be false, since the assumption of its truth introduces a contradiction in the premises.

The *reductio ad absurdum* form of proof adds the denial of the conclusion as a *reductio* premise and marks this premise and any other statement derived by its use by two right angle markings and indentation in the proof. The *reductio* proof is acceptable only if it shows that a conclusion derived by the *reductio* premise introduces a contradiction in the argument.

The example above shows that if the *reductio* premise were accepted, the following contradictions would develop in the argument:

(5) Peaceful settlement of issues is not attained.

(6) Greater effort to achieve conditions lessening tension is not to be made.
(7) Greater racial tension is not being built up in large cities.
(8) The intelligence information is not correct.
(9) The intelligence information is correct and the intelligence information is not correct.

The adoption of the *reductio* premise in the fifth statement leads to the contradiction in the ninth statement. Hence the *reductio* premise must be false.

Conditional and *reductio ad absurdum* forms of proof are also useful in justifying a step needed within a proof. In such cases the proof can begin prior to the introduction of these procedures and extend beyond them.

13.7 EXERCISES

Construct conditional or reductio ad absurdum *proofs for the following arguments.*

1. (1) $D \supset E$
   (2) $E \supset F$
   (3) $F \supset G$
   $\therefore D \supset G$

2. (1) $\sim A \lor B$
   (2) $\sim (B \cdot \sim C)$
   (3) $\sim C$
   $\therefore \sim A$

3. (1) $\sim A \lor B$
   (2) $\sim (B \cdot \sim C)$
   (3) $\sim D \supset \sim C$
   $\therefore A \supset D$

4. (1) $D \supset C$
   (2) $\sim E \supset \sim C$
   (3) $\sim E$
   (4) $\sim D \supset (F \supset G)$
   $\therefore \sim (F \cdot \sim G)$

5. (1) $(A \cdot \sim B) \supset C$
   (2) $C \supset D$
   (3) $E \lor \sim D$
   (4) $\sim E \cdot A$
   $\therefore B$

6. (1) $A \cdot (B \supset C)$
   (2) $C \supset D$
   (3) $\sim (A \cdot \sim B)$
   (4) $\sim D \lor (\sim E \lor F)$
   $\therefore E \supset F$

7. Either more taxes are not asked or there will be controversy. (T, C) Not both can there be controversy and not be congressional hearings. (H) If there are congressional hearings, then there will be greater voter discontent. (D) Therefore, if there is not greater voter discontent, then more taxes will not be asked.

8. Not both will there be strong opposition to the legislation and there not be a fight on the floor. (O, F) If there is a floor fight, then there will be executive pressure and party division will occur. (P, D) Party division will not occur. Either there will be strong opposition to the legislation or stronger Social Security benefits will be made available. (S) Therefore, stronger Social Security benefits will be made available.

9. Either the strike is not successful or wages will rise. (S, R) If wages do rise, then there will be an increase in the cost of producing automobiles. (C) Not both can there be an increase in the cost of producing automobiles and the price of automobiles not increase. (P) If the price of automobiles increases, then

the cost-of-living index will rise. (*I*) Therefore, if the strike is successful, the cost-of-living index will rise.

10. If either a public announcement is made about opening bids or kickbacks are not made, then the prices paid for goods and services are noted in public documents. (*A, K, D*) The prices paid for goods and services are not noted in public documents. If kickbacks are made and a public announcement is not made about opening bids, then a public investigation is held. (*I*) Therefore, a public investigation is held.

Chapter 14
Definitions and
Proofs Using
Truth Tables

14.1 Truth Tables and Truth Values

The defining of propositions and the determining of valid argument forms discussed in Chapters 12 and 13 are based upon the minimal meaning of hypothetical, disjunctive, conjunctive, denial-of-conjunction, and equivalent propositions. A more rigorous manner of defining these propositions, of determining valid argument forms, and of identifying cases of invalidity is through the use of truth tables.

A truth table exhausts the possible relations of the values of true or false in a proposition or in a series of propositions. In its extended use it provides a basis for determining the validity of arguments. It is based on the postulate of a two-valued logic in which the truth value of any proposition is limited to true or false. Such a postulate is in keeping with the "laws of thought": the principle of identity, the principle of excluded middle, and the principle of contradiction. The *principle of identity* asserts that the truth value of a given proposition (in a given context) remains constant; that is, the truth values do not shift from being true to being false. The *principle of excluded middle* asserts that the truth value of a given proposition is limited to one of two values, true or false, and that any given proposition has only one of these values in a given context. The *principle of contradiction* asserts that the truth value of any one of these propositions is limited to one of these values in a given context; it is not possible both that a given proposition is true and that it is false.

The truth value of only one proposition is limited to the possibilities expressed in the following table, in which "T" refers to the value of true and "F" to the value of false.

$$\frac{p}{\begin{array}{c} T \\ F \end{array}}$$

If the truth values of both p and not p are considered, the following table results:

p	not p
T	F
F	T

Compare the possibilities of tossing heads on a coin. On any possible toss of the coin the following possibilities occur if *"H"* refers to heads, "not *H*" to not heads, "T" to the occurrence of heads and "F" to the occurrence of not heads (or tails).

H	not H
T	F
F	T

In each of these cases the logical possibilities of specific values, p or not p, H or not H, are exhausted. The table is used to specify all possible occurrences of the values of p and of H.

14.2 Truth Tables and Elementary Definitions

The symbols used in logic are definable in terms of the truth tables. Consider the following definition of the dot ($\cdot$) used for conjunction:

p	q	$p \cdot q$
T	T	T
T	F	F
F	T	F
F	F	F

The vertical columns under the letters p and q exhaust the possible values of true and false as these relate to any two propositions designated by the propositional forms p and q. The column under the conjunctive proposition $p \cdot q$ is formed by reference to the values found in the columns under p and q. This table defines the logical symbol for "and" by showing that a proposition joined by the connective ($\cdot$) is true only in the case in which each proposition is true; in all other cases the proposition is false.

A *row* on the truth table is formed by the entries along any given horizontal line. The truth table above has four rows with the values TTT, TFF, FTF, and FFF. The value assigned to any compound proposition containing as elements the propositions listed in the part of the table exhausting the possible truth relations between the propositions (in the present example the columns under p and q) is determined by the truth value of the different elementary propositions (designated above by p and q) found on the same row with the truth value assigned to the compound proposition. Thus, if the value of p is T and of q is T on any row in the table above, the value of $p \cdot q$ is T. If the value of p is F or the value of q is F, the value of $p \cdot q$ is F on that particular row.

The meaning of the tilde ($\sim$), the sign of negation, is defined as follows:

p	$\sim p$
T	F
F	T

The use of the tilde before any proposition negates that proposition; the opposite truth value is assigned to the proposition. Thus, if $p \cdot q$ is T, then its negation, $\sim(p \cdot q)$, is F.

The meaning of the wedge ($\vee$) is defined by the truth table as follows:

p	q	$p \vee q$
T	T	T
T	F	T
F	T	T
F	F	F

The proposition $p \vee q$ is true in all cases where p is true or q is true (including cases where both are true).

The meaning of the horseshoe ($\supset$) is defined by the truth table as follows:

p	q	$p \supset q$
T	T	T
T	F	F
F	T	T
F	F	T

The definition above also can be called the definition of the truth function of "$\supset$" or the definition of material implication. *Material implication* asserts that any proposition having the form $p \supset q$ is true in every instance except where p has the value of T and q has the value of F. The meaning of the symbol "$\supset$" is difficult to grasp intuitively, but additional practice will make its usefulness apparent.

Material equivalence ($\equiv$) is defined as follows:

p	q	$p \equiv q$
T	T	T
T	F	F
F	T	F
F	F	T

An alternate manner of defining material equivalence, which gives the same results, is $(p \supset q) \cdot (q \supset p)$.

p	q	$p \supset q$	$q \supset p$	$(p \supset q) \cdot (q \supset p)$
T	T	T	T	T
T	F	F	T	F
F	T	T	F	F
F	F	T	T	T

The propositional form $(p \supset q) \cdot (q \supset p)$ is a conjunctive proposition and is true only if both conjuncts, $(p \supset q)$ and $(q \supset p)$, are true.

14.3 A Tautologous Statement, a Contradictory Statement, and a Contingent Statement

A statement whose logical form yields only instances of true statements is a *tautologous* statement.[1] Consider the forms $p \vee \sim p$ and $\sim(p \cdot \sim p)$.

p	$\sim p$	$p \cdot \sim p$	$p \vee \sim p$	$\sim(p \cdot \sim p)$
T	F	F	T	T
F	T	F	T	T

The columns under the forms $p \vee \sim p$ and $\sim(p \cdot \sim p)$ yield only true values. Thus, any statement having this form is false on logical grounds alone.

A statement whose logical form yields only instances of a false statement is *contradictory*. Consider the possible truth values for the form $p \cdot \sim p$ in the truth table above. The truth value for each possible occurrence is false. Thus, any statement having this form is false on logical grounds alone.

A statement whose logical form yields instances that may be either true or false is *contingent*. Examine the forms p, q, $p \vee q$, $p \cdot q$, $p \supset q$ given in previous uses of the truth table. The truth or falsity of instances of these forms cannot be determined by logical considerations alone; rather it is contingent upon the material content of statements using these forms.

14.4 The Determination of Contradictory or Equivalent Relations Between Two or More Propositions

Two propositions are *contradictory* if they have opposite truth values in each case of their occurrence. Consider the relation of $p \cdot q$ and $\sim(p \cdot q)$ or of $p \vee q$ and $\sim p \cdot \sim q$.

p	q	$\sim p$	$\sim q$	$p \cdot q$	$\sim(p \cdot q)$	$p \vee q$	$\sim p \cdot \sim q$
T	T	F	F	T	F	T	F
T	F	F	T	F	T	T	F
F	T	T	F	F	T	T	F
F	F	T	T	F	T	F	T

---

[1] Although each of the equivalent forms "$(p \cdot p) / \therefore p$" and "$(p \vee p) / \therefore p$" is sometimes called a "tautology" (Taut.), they are not tautologies as we define the term here; rather, they are tautologous in the sense of "repetition" or "redundancy." The following sentence has a tautologous expression in the latter sense: "The essential essentials are prepared."

In each case where $p \cdot q$ is true, $\sim(p \cdot q)$ is false, and where one is false, the other is true. In each case where $p \vee q$ is true, $\sim p \cdot \sim q$ is false. Since the designated forms have opposite truth values in every case, they are contradictory propositional forms. The denial of a proposition consists in the affirmation of its contradiction.

Two propositions are *equivalent* if they have identical truth values in all cases. Consider the forms $p \supset q$, $\sim p \vee q$, $\sim(p \cdot \sim q)$ in the following table:

p	q	$\sim p$	$\sim q$	$p \cdot \sim q$	$p \supset q$	$\sim p \vee q$	$\sim(p \cdot \sim q)$
T	T	F	F	F	T	T	T
T	F	F	T	T	F	F	F
F	T	T	F	F	T	T	T
F	F	T	T	F	T	T	T

In each case the indicated forms have identical truth values; in the rows in which one is true, the others are true, and in the row in which one is false, the others are false. Thus, these propositional forms are equivalent. Equivalent forms may replace each other wherever they occur, either as propositions or as elements in propositions.

14.5 Argument Forms and the Truth Table

An argument form is valid if there cannot be an instance in which the conclusion is false and the premises are true. An argument form is invalid if there is at least one instance in which the premises can be true and the conclusion is false. Consider the argument form of *modus ponens*, $p \supset q$, p, $/ \therefore q$.

p	q	$p \supset q$	p	$/ \therefore q$
T	T	T	T	T
T	F	F	T	F
F	T	T	F	T
F	F	T	F	F

In the analysis of this argument form on the truth table the conclusion, q, is false in the second row and one premise, $p \supset q$, is false. The conclusion also is false in the fourth row. Again one of the premises, p, is false. There is no case (that is, no row) in which the conclusion is false and the premises are true. This demonstrates that the argument form is valid, since in no case is it possible both for the conclusion to be false and the premises to be true.

Consider the invalid argument form $p \vee q$, p, $/ \therefore \sim q$.

p	q	$\sim q$	$p \vee q$	p	$/ \therefore \sim q$
T	T	F	T	T	F
T	F	T	T	T	T
F	T	F	T	F	F
F	F	T	F	F	T

In the first row the conclusion, ~q, is false, and the premises, p ∨ q and p, are true. Since this argument form has at least one instance in which the conclusion can be false and the premises true, it is invalid.

In constructing a table for proofs, we write the values T or F under the indicated form by reference to the values originally assigned to the variables (in the cases above, p and q) in the initial columns of the truth table. It is helpful to separate the original analysis of possible truth relations between the atomic parts of the proposition (p and q above) and the remaining portion of the truth table. Likewise, it is helpful to separate the conclusion from other portions of the truth table. The premises can be identified more readily if they are adjacent. If additional forms are needed to assist in the determination of the truth values of the premises, it is well to separate these from the premises by drawing a vertical line. Thus, for the sake of convenience vertical lines can be drawn in the truth table (1) after the listing of the truth values of the original atomic propositions used in the argument, (2) after the forms helpful in the analysis of the truth values of the premises, and (3) after the premises. It also is helpful to draw horizontal lines under the original propositions that are analyzed, and under every second or fourth row in the proof (to facilitate reading the rows).

The number of rows in a truth table is determined by the number of elementary or atomic propositions occurring in the argument. If two elementary propositions are used, the number of rows is 2 × 2 or 4. If three elementary propositions are used, the number of rows needed is 2 × 2 × 2 or 8. If four elementary propositions are used, the number of rows needed is 2 × 2 × 2 × 2 or 16, and so on. If sixteen rows are needed, the first eight rows under the first elementary proposition can be assigned the value of T, and the value of F can be assigned to the last eight rows. Under the second elementary proposition, the first set of four rows and the third set of four rows can be assigned the value of T, and the second and fourth sets of rows can be assigned the value of F. In each succeeding case the number of consecutive rows with the value of T is one-half the number in the sequence of the preceeding elementary proposition. The column under the last elementary proposition will alternate T and F on each successive row.

Consider the argument form for the constructive complex dilemma, (p ⊃ q) · (r ⊃ s), p ∨ r, therefore q ∨ s. This argument form has four elementary propositions, and its truth table will have sixteen rows. The number of consecutive T's under the first elementary proposition, p, will be eight, under the second elementary proposition, q, will be four, under the third elementary proposition, r, will be two, and under the last elementary proposition, s, will be one. The conclusion has the value of F in the sixth, eighth, fourteenth, and sixteenth rows. In each of these cases at least one premise is false. Since there is no instance in which it is possible for the conclusion to have a value of F and each premise in the same row to have a value of T, the argument form is valid.

Table 14.1 Truth Table for a Constructive Complex Dilemma

p	q	r	s	$p \supset q$	$r \supset s$	$(p \supset q) \cdot (r \supset s)$	$p \vee r$	$/ \therefore q \vee s$
T	T	T	T	T	T	T	T	T
T	T	T	F	T	F	F	T	T
T	T	F	T	T	T	T	T	T
T	T	F	F	T	T	T	T	T
T	F	T	T	F	T	F	T	T
T	F	T	F	F	F	F	T	F
T	F	F	T	F	T	F	T	T
T	F	F	F	F	T	F	T	F
F	T	T	T	T	T	T	T	T
F	T	T	F	T	F	F	T	T
F	T	F	T	T	T	T	F	T
F	T	F	F	T	T	T	F	T
F	F	T	T	T	T	T	T	T
F	F	T	F	T	F	F	T	F
F	F	F	T	T	T	T	F	T
F	F	F	F	T	T	T	F	F

14.6 EXERCISES

Determine the validity of the following argument forms by the use of the truth table.

1. $p \supset q$
   $p \supset r$
   $\therefore q \supset r$

2. $(p \supset q) \cdot (p \supset r)$
   $\sim p \vee \sim r$
   $\therefore \sim q$

3. $p \supset (q \cdot r)$
   $\sim q \vee \sim r$
   $\therefore \sim p$

4. $(p \vee q) \supset (r \vee s)$
   $\sim q \cdot \sim s$
   $\therefore p \supset r$

5. $\sim(p \cdot \sim q)$
   $q \vee \sim r$
   $\sim r$
   $\therefore p$

6. $(p \supset q) \cdot (r_0 \supset s)$
   $\sim s \vee \sim q$
   p
   $\therefore \sim r$

14.7 Extended Arguments

An argument can be shown to be valid by proofs other than the immediate use of the truth table. Such proofs are particularly helpful where there are a large number of variables to consider. For such extended arguments, the premises and each step in the proof are numbered consecutively. To the right of each step in the proof is listed the type of argument form or equivalence form used in the proof. These are used together with the numbers assigned to premises or to previous steps in the proof to show how any given step in the proof is established. The last step in the proof should establish the conclusion.

Consider the following argument:

> If the heart pump works, the patient recovers. (W, R)
> The heart pump works.
> If the patient recovers, he returns to his job. (J)
> Therefore, the patient returns to his job.

(1) $W \supset R$
(2) W
(3) $R \supset J$
        $\overline{\quad\quad}$
        $\therefore J$

(4) R (1), (2) $p \supset q,\ p,\ /\ \therefore\ q$ (1), (2) MP
(5) J (3), (4) $p \supset q,\ p,\ /\ \therefore\ q$ (3), (4) MP

The capital letters W, R, and J are used to refer to the propositions in the argument. The argument has a valid argument form as demonstrated in steps (4) and (5) of the proof. Therefore, the argument is valid.

The type of proof presented here is not as rigorous as those traditionally employed in symbolic logic. In a rigorous system of proofs the minimum number of argument forms are employed along with the minimum number of equivalent forms. Since *modus tollens,* disjunctive arguments, and denial-of-conjunction arguments can occur with some frequency in ordinary discourse, these forms are included in the following list of elementary valid argument forms demonstrated by the truth table.

Basic argument forms:

1. *Modus ponens* (MP):

$$p \supset q$$
$$\underline{p\qquad}$$
$$\therefore q$$

2. Hypothetical syllogism (HS):

$$p \supset q$$
$$\underline{q \supset r}$$
$$\therefore p \supset r$$

3. Addition (Add.):

$$\underline{p\qquad}$$
$$\therefore p \vee q$$

4. Simplification (Simp.):

$$\underline{p \cdot q}$$
$$\therefore p$$

5. Conjunction (Conj.):

$$p$$
$$\underline{q\qquad}$$
$$\therefore p \cdot q$$

Derivable elementary argument forms:

6. *Modus tollens* (MT):

$$p \supset q$$
$$\underline{\sim q}$$
$$\therefore \sim p$$

7. Disjunctive argument (DA):

$$p \vee q$$
$$\underline{\sim p}$$
$$\therefore q$$

8. Denial-of-conjunction argument (DCA):

$$\sim (p \cdot q)$$
$$\underline{p}$$
$$\therefore \sim q$$

9. Constructive complex dilemma (CCD):

$$(p \supset q) \cdot (r \supset s)$$
$$\underline{p \vee r}$$
$$\therefore q \vee s$$

10. Constructive simple dilemma (CSD):

$$(p \supset q) \cdot (r \supset q)$$
$$\underline{p \vee r}$$
$$\therefore q$$

11. Absorption (Abs.):

$$\underline{p \supset q}$$
$$\therefore p \supset (p \cdot q)$$

The following lists of equivalences, also demonstrable by the use of the truth table, are useful in developing proofs.

1. Elementary propositional equivalents (EPE):

$$(p \supset q) \equiv (\sim p \vee q)$$
$$\equiv \sim (p \cdot \sim q)$$
$$\equiv (\sim q \supset \sim p)$$

2. Commutation equivalents (Comm.):

$$(p \vee q) \equiv (q \vee p)$$
$$(p \cdot q) \equiv (q \cdot p)$$

3. Material equivalence (ME):

$$(p \equiv q) \equiv [(p \supset q) \cdot (q \supset p)]$$
$$(p \equiv q) \equiv [(p \cdot q) \vee (\sim p \cdot \sim q)]$$

4. Double negation equivalents (DN):

$$p \equiv \sim \sim p$$

5. Repetition (Rep.):
$$(p \lor q) \equiv p$$
$$(p \cdot p) \equiv p$$

6. Distribution (Dist.):
$$[p \lor (q \cdot r)] \equiv [(p \lor q) \cdot (p \lor r)]$$
$$[p \cdot (q \lor r)] \equiv [(p \cdot q) \lor (p \cdot r)]$$

7. Association (Assoc.):
$$[p \lor (q \lor r)] \equiv [(p \lor q) \lor r]$$
$$[p \cdot (q \cdot r)] \equiv [(p \cdot q) \cdot r]$$

8. Exportation (Exp.):
$$[p \supset (q \supset r)] \equiv [(p \cdot q) \supset r]$$

The elementary propositional equivalents can be broken down into equivalent propositions with more specific names:

9. Material implication (MI):
$$(p \supset q) \equiv (\sim p \lor q)$$

10. De Morgan's law (DeM):
$$(p \lor q) \equiv \sim(\sim p \cdot \sim q)$$

11. De Morgan's law and material implication (DeM & MI):
$$(p \supset q) \equiv \sim(p \cdot \sim q)$$

12. Contraposition (Contrap.):
$$(p \supset q) \equiv (\sim q \supset \sim p)$$

In the construction of proofs based upon these valid argument forms and equivalences, only one form of the disjunctive argument and one form of the denial-of-conjunction argument are permitted. Commutation is needed to prove the validity of a disjunctive argument in which the second disjunct is denied in a premise. Commutation also is needed to establish the validity of a denial-of-conjunction argument if the second conjunct of the denied conjunct is affirmed. Likewise, the principle of double negation must be used rather than merely assumed. Consider the following examples:

(1) $A \lor B$
(2) $\sim B$
(3) $C \supset \sim A$
$\overline{\qquad\qquad\qquad}$
$\therefore \sim C$

(4)	$B \lor A$	(1) $(p \lor q) \equiv (q \lor p)$	Comm.
(5)	A	(4), (2) $p \lor q, \sim p, / \therefore q$	DA
(6)	$\sim\sim A$	(5) $\sim\sim p \equiv p$	DN
(7)	$\sim C$	(3), (6) $p \supset q, \sim q, / \therefore \sim p$	MT

(1)	$(F \cdot G) \supset H$		
(2)	$H \supset (I \lor J)$		
(3)	$\sim J$		
(4)	$I \supset K$		
(5)	$\sim K$		
	$\therefore \sim G \lor \sim F$		
(6)	$(F \cdot G) \supset (I \lor J)$	(1), (2) $p \supset q, q \supset r, / \therefore p \supset r$	HS
(7)	$\sim I$	(4), (5) $p \supset q, \sim q, / \therefore \sim p$	MT
(8)	$\sim I \cdot \sim J$	(7), (3) $p, q, / \therefore p \cdot q$	Conj.
(9)	$\sim (I \lor J)$	(8) $p \lor q \equiv \sim(\sim p \cdot \sim q)$	EPE (or DeM)
(10)	$\sim (F \cdot G)$	(6), (9) $p \supset q, \sim q, / \therefore \sim p$	MT
(11)	$\sim F \lor \sim G$	(10) $(p \lor q) \equiv \sim(\sim p \cdot \sim q)$	EPE (or DeM)
(12)	$\sim G \lor \sim F$	(11) $(p \lor q) \equiv (q \lor p)$	Comm.

In a more rigorous proof it can be specified that the derived elementary argument forms not be used. It can be specified further that the names of the particular types of elementary proposition equivalents be given and that the argument forms after the names of the argument forms of propositional equivalents be eliminated. Consider the following example:

(1)	$D \supset (E \lor F)$		
(2)	$\sim (G \lor \sim H) \lor I$		
(3)	$\sim I \cdot \sim E$		
(4)	$\sim G \supset D$		
	$\therefore F$		
(5)	$I \lor \sim (G \lor \sim H)$	(2)	Comm.
(6)	$\sim I$	(3)	Simp.
(7)	$\sim I \supset \sim (G \lor \sim H)$	(5)	MI
(8)	$\sim (G \lor \sim H)$	(7), (6)	MP
(9)	$\sim G \cdot H$	(8)	DeM
(10)	$\sim G$	(9)	Simp.
(11)	D	(4), (10)	MP
(12)	$E \lor F$	(1), (11)	MP
(13)	$\sim E \cdot \sim I$	(3)	Comm.
(14)	$\sim E$	(13)	Simp.
(15)	$\sim E \supset F$	(12)	MI
(16)	F	(15), (14)	MP

The argument forms listed as derivable elementary argument forms can be proven by use of the basic argument forms and equivalent forms. Consider the form of the complex constructive dilemma:

(1)	$(p \supset q) \cdot (r \supset s)$		
(2)	$p \lor r$		
	$\therefore q \lor s$		
(3)	$p \supset q$	(1)	Simp.
(4)	$(r \supset s) \cdot (p \supset q)$	(1)	Comm.
(5)	$r \supset s$	(4)	Simp.

(6)	$\sim q \supset \sim p$	(3)		Contrap.
(7)	$\sim p \supset r$	(2)		MI
(8)	$\sim q \supset r$	(6), (7)		HS
(9)	$\sim q \supset s$	(8), (5)		HS
(10)	$q \lor s$	(9)		MI

The derived argument forms can be used for convenience in the working of problems in this text, unless the context specifies otherwise.

If an argument has an inconsistency within its premises, we can prove any conclusion by using addition. Although the argument is valid, it cannot be sound, since all of its premises cannot be true. Consider the following argument:

If the movie has a haunting melodic theme, it will be popular. (H, P)

The movie has a haunting melodic theme and it is not popular. Therefore, the movie will be a great success. (S)

(1)	$H \supset P$		
(2)	$H \cdot \sim P$		
	$\therefore S$		
(3)	H	(2) $p \cdot q / \therefore p$	Simp.
(4)	P	(1), (3) $p \supset q, p / \therefore q$	MP
(5)	$\sim P \cdot H$	(2) $(p \cdot q) \equiv (q \cdot p)$	Comm.
(6)	$\sim P$	(5) $p \cdot q / \therefore p$	Simp.
(7)	$P \ \ S$	(4) $p / \therefore p \lor q$	Add.
(8)	S	(7), (6) $p \lor q, \sim p / \therefore q$	DA

14.8 EXERCISES

Write proofs for the following arguments. For problems 16 to 20 do not use the argument forms for modus tollens, *disjunctive argument, or denial-of-conjunction arguments, and use the names for material implication and De Morgan's law rather than merely elementary propositional equivalents.*

1. (1) $A \supset B$
   (2) $\sim B \lor C$
   (3) $\sim C$
   $\therefore \sim A$

2. (1) $\sim (D \cdot \sim E)$
   (2) $\sim E$
   (3) $D \lor F$
   $\therefore F$

3. (1) $G \supset (H \lor I)$
   (2) $(H \lor I) \supset J$
   (3) $\sim J$
   $\therefore \sim G$

4. (1) $\sim [(A \cdot B) \supset C] \supset D$
   (2) $D \supset (E \lor F)$
   (3) $\sim E \cdot \sim F$
   (4) $C \supset E$
   $\therefore \sim A \lor \sim B$

5. (1) $A \equiv B$
   (2) $B \supset (C \cdot D)$
   (3) A
   $\therefore D$

6. (1) $E \supset [F \lor (G \cdot H)]$
   (2) $I \supset (E \lor \sim G)$
   (3) $I \cdot \sim (\sim G \lor F)$
   $\therefore H$

7. (1) $A \supset (B \cdot C)$
   (2) $A \cdot D$
   (3) $D \supset \sim C$
   $\overline{}$
   $\therefore E$

8. Either a job is not interesting or it is challenging. (I, C) Not both is a job challenging and it fails to provide an opportunity for developing abilities. (O) Therefore, if a job fails to provide an opportunity for developing abilities, it is not interesting.

9. If greater benefits are made possible, then both payments are higher and the sense of security is stronger. (B, P, S) Greater benefits are made possible. Either the sense of security is not stronger or less fear of catastrophic illness occurs. (F) Therefore, less fear of catastrophic illness occurs.

10. If an actor does not have an agent, then he has to negotiate contracts for himself. (A, N) It is not possible both that an actor has to negotiate contracts for himself and that he not need to secure satisfactory provisions in the contract. (P) If an actor needs to secure satisfactory provisions in the contract, then he needs to be satisfied with his working arrangements. (W) Therefore, if he does not have an agent, he needs to be satisfied with his working arrangements.

11. If the domestic difficulties continue, then either troublesome issues do not come to the surface or the account of their intensity is unreliable. (D, T, A) Either the account of their intensity is reliable, or the troubles of the President are exaggerated. (E) The domestic difficulties continue and troublesome issues do come to the surface. Therefore, the troubles of the President are exaggerated.

12. If inflation is curtailed, then income taxes are increased and interest rates are reduced. (C, T, R) If widespread unemployment threatens, then interest rates are not reduced. (U) If income taxes are increased, then increased dissatisfaction among voters will spread and widespread unemployment threatens. (D) Income taxes are increased. Therefore, inflation is not curtailed.

13. If the Republicans are successful in the election, then they will strengthen their position in the House. (E, P) Either the Republicans do not strengthen their position in the House, or they have gained the support of the younger generation. (G) The Republicans are successful in the election and they have not gained the support of the younger generation. Therefore, both the Democratic and Republican parties are confronted with strong internal dissention. (D)

14. Either the demands of the demonstrators are met or the police are called and the demonstrators are removed by the police. (D, C, R) If the demonstrators threaten violence, then their demands are not met. (T) It is not possible both that the demonstrators are removed by police and the board meeting not occur. (M) The demonstrators threaten violence. Therefore, the board meeting will occur.

15. If the demands of the demonstrators are met, then the police are not called; and either the demonstrators do not threaten violence or they are removed by the police. (D, C, T, R) Either the demands of the demonstrators are met, or the demonstrators threaten violence. If either the police are not called or the demonstrators are removed by the police, then the board meeting will not be held. (M) Therefore, the board meeting will not be held.

16. If the issues are compromised, then either the strike is called off or the in-

come of the strikers is raised. (*C, S, I*) Either the strike is not called off or the issues of satisfactory working conditions are settled. (*W*) If the income of the strikers is raised, then the strike is called off. The issues of satisfactory working conditions are not settled. Therefore, the issue is not compromised.

17. If the support of the Prime Minister does not fade away, then either he has the strong support of labor or he has the strong support of industry. (*F, L, I*) If either the Prime Minister supports policies essential for strengthening economic conditions or he supports conditions essential for strengthening foreign policy, then his support does not fade away. (*E, C*) He supports policies essential for strengthening economic conditions. Therefore, it is not the case both that he does not have the strong support of labor and that he does not have the strong support of industry.

18. If either Russia's split with Communist China continues or Communist China continues her policy of seeking to expand her sphere of influence, then Russia's security will be threatened. (*S, E, T*) If Russia's security is threatened, then if Communist China continues her policy of seeking to expand her sphere of influence, China will not refrain from further nuclear experiments. (*N*) Russia's split with Communist China continues and Communist China continues her policy of seeking to expand her sphere of influence. Therefore, China will not refrain from further nuclear experiments.

19. If it is the case that if this book either is full of obscure references or deals with trivialities, it is tedious to read, then this book is not provocative. (*R, D, T, P*) Not both can this book not be provocative and be relevant to contemporary issues. (*C*) This book is relevant to contemporary issues and it is not tedious to read. Therefore, this book is not full of obscure references and it does not deal in trivialities.

20. If and only if higher education becomes less concerned with research will it provide the optimum learning situations in freshman and sophomore courses. (*R, L*) If higher education provides the optimum learning situations in freshman and sophomore courses, then innovations in the curriculum will be accelerated. (*I*) It is not true both that there is no major breakthrough in the relation of faculties to students and that innovations in the curriculum will be accelerated. (*B*) There is no major breakthrough in the relation of faculties to students. Therefore, higher education does not become less concerned with research.

Write proofs for the following argument forms without using any derived elementary argument forms.

21. $p \supset q$
$\dfrac{\sim q}{\therefore \sim p}$

22. $\sim(p \cdot q)$
$\dfrac{p}{\therefore \sim q}$

23. $p \lor q$
$\dfrac{\sim p}{\therefore q}$

24. $(p \supset q) \cdot (r \supset q)$
   $p \vee r$
   ──────
   $\therefore q$ (simple constructive dilemma)

25. $(p \supset q) \cdot (r \supset s)$
   $\sim q \vee \sim s$
   ──────
   $\therefore \sim p \vee \sim r$ (complex destructive dilemma)

26. $p \supset q$
   ──────
   $\therefore p \supset (p \cdot q)$ (absorption)

14.9 Proving Invalidity by a Cross Section of the Truth Table

We can establish invalidity by showing an instance of a false conclusion with true premises on a row or cross section of the truth table. Consider the following argument:

$$A \supset B$$
$$B \vee C$$
$$\sim(C \cdot \sim D)$$
$$D$$
$$\overline{\therefore A}$$

The elementary propositions, the forms helpful in determining the truth values of the premises, the premises, and the conclusion are written on a line as in the first step in constructing a truth table. The conclusion is assigned the value of F and the premises are assigned the value of T.

A	B	C	D	$\sim D$	$(C \cdot \sim D)$	$A \supset B$	$B \vee C$	$\sim(C \cdot \sim D)$	D	$/ \therefore A$
						T	T	T	T	F

A proof of invalidity consists in finding truth values for A, B, C, and D that will make possible the truth values assigned above to the premises and the conclusion. If the conclusion is false, then A is false, and this is noted in the column under the first A. Since D is given as a premise and must be true if the argument is invalid, the value of T is also placed under the original D column. The cross section now appears as follows:

A	B	C	D	$\sim D$	$(C \cdot \sim D)$	$A \supset B$	$B \vee C$	$\sim(C \cdot \sim D)$	D	$/ \therefore A$
F			T	F		T	T	T	T	F

The remaining problem is to find values for B and C. If the premise $A \supset B$ is true and A is false, B can be true or false. For the premise B C to be true one of the disjuncts B or C must be true. Since $\sim D$ is false, the conjunctive $(C \cdot \sim D)$ is false, regardless of the value assigned to C, and the premise $\sim(C \cdot \sim D)$ is true. There is need to assign the value of T to B or C.

By assigning the value of T to B, we can assign T or F to C. Another alternative would be to assign the value of T to C and either T or F to B. Thus, any one of the following rows could be drawn as a cross section of the truth table to demonstrate invalidity of the argument.

A	B	C	D	$\sim D$	$(C \cdot \sim D)$	$A \supset B$	$B \vee C$	$\sim(C \cdot \sim D)$	D	$/ \therefore A$
F	T	T	T	F	F	T	T	T	T	F
F	T	F	T	F	F	T	T	T	T	F
F	F	T	T	F	F	T	T	T	T	F

14.10 EXERCISES

Prove the invalidity of the following arguments by the use of a cross section of the truth table.

1. $(A \vee B) \vee C$
   $\underline{\sim C}$
   $\therefore B$

2. $A \vee (B \cdot C)$
   $(B \supset C) \supset (D \vee E)$
   $\underline{\sim A}$
   $\therefore D$

3. $(A \supset B) \cdot (C \supset D)$
   $A \vee D$
   $(B \vee C) \supset E$
   $\underline{E}$
   $\therefore \sim B \vee \sim D$

4. If we work in the slums, then we are involved as activists. (S, I) If we are involved as activists, we are concerned about the future. (F) Therefore, if we are concerned about the future, we work in the slums.

5. Either we shall strengthen our space program or we shall strengthen our anti-poverty program. (S, A) If we are concerned for our long-range defense, we shall strengthen our space program. (D) We are concerned for our long-range defense. Therefore, we shall not strengthen our antipoverty program.

6. If the price of the automobile is within 25 percent of your annual income, then the purchase can be budgeted properly. (A, B) If its purchase is properly budgeted, then the payments will come from savings or the payments will come from salary income. (S, I) If the payments come from salary income, then a limit on monthly payments will have to be fixed at a reasonable sum. (R) The price of the automobile is not within 25 percent of your annual income. Therefore, a limit on monthly payments will have to be fixed at a reasonable sum.

14.11 An Indirect Method of Proof

Arguments can be proved by an indirect procedure comparable to the method of proving invalidity by a cross section of the truth table. The indirect procedure establishes that no combination of truth values assigned to the elementary propositions in the argument can provide a false conclusion with true premises.

Consider, for example, the following argument: $A \supset B$, $\sim B \lor C$, A, $/ \therefore C$. The elementary propositions, the forms helpful in determining the truth of the premises, the premises, and the conclusion are written in the same form used in the procedure to establish invalidity by a cross section of the truth table.

A	B	C	$\sim B$	$A \supset B$	$\sim B \lor C$	A	$/ \therefore C$
				T	T	T	F

To prove validity by this method, we shall have to establish that no truth values can be assigned to the elementary propositions (A, B, and C in our example) such that the truth values of T for each premise and F for the conclusion hold. For the argument above to be invalid, we must assign the following truth values:

1. C is false, since it is a conclusion.
2. A is true, since it is a premise.
3. B is true, since $A \supset B$ is true as a premise, and A is true (step 2).
4. $\sim B$ is false, since B is true (step 3).
5. $\sim B$ would be false and C would be false (steps 1 and 4).
6. However, step 5 is not possible, since it would make the premise $\sim B \lor C$ false, and the premises must be true.

Therefore, it is not possible to assign truth values to the elementary propositions and have a false conclusion with true premises.

Consider the following argument: $A \supset B$, $\sim B \lor C$, $\sim (C \cdot \sim D)$, $\sim D \lor (E \cdot F)$, $\sim E$, $/ \therefore \sim A$.

$A\,B\,C\,D\,E\,F$	$\sim B$	$\sim D$	$\sim E$	$A \supset B$	$\sim B \lor C$	$\sim(C \cdot \sim D)$	$\sim D \lor (E \cdot F)$	$\sim E$	$\therefore / \sim A$
				T	T	T	T	T	F

If this argument is to be invalid, the following truth values must be assigned:

1. $\sim A$ is false, since it is the conclusion, and A is true.
2. $\sim E$ is true, since it is a premise, and E is false.
3. B is true, since $A \supset B$ is true as a premise and A is true in step 1.
4. $\sim B$ is false, since B is true (step 3).
5. C is true, since $\sim B \lor C$ is true as a premise, and $\sim B$ is false (step 4).
6. $\sim D$ is false, since $C \cdot \sim D$ is false for the premise $\sim (C \cdot \sim D)$ to be true, and C is true (step 5).
7. E and F are true, since the premise $\sim D \lor (E \cdot F)$ is true and $\sim D$ is false (step 6).
8. E would be true (step 7).
9. However, step 8 is not possible, since E must be false (step 2).

Therefore, it is not possible to assign truth values to the elementary propositions and have a false conclusion with true premises in this argument.

This indirect method of establishing validity is an adaptation of the *reductio ad absurdum* type of proof; it is of some use in dealing with highly complex arguments that are difficult to prove by other means. Usually, however, unless it is specified otherwise, it is preferable to follow one of the other methods that include the *reductio ad absurdum* type of proof.

Conditional proofs and *reductio ad absurdum* proofs are discussed in Section 13.6.

14.12 EXERCISES

Use the indirect method of proof to prove the validity of the following arguments.

1. $A \lor B$
   $\sim B \lor C$
   $\sim A$
   $\overline{\quad\quad}$
   $\therefore C$

2. $(A \cdot B) \supset C$
   $C \supset D$
   $\sim D$
   $\overline{\quad\quad\quad}$
   $\therefore \sim A \lor \sim B$

3. $A \lor (B \cdot C)$
   $(B \cdot C) \supset \sim D$
   $D \lor E$
   $\sim A$
   $\overline{\quad\quad}$
   $\therefore E$

4. If dividends increase, stock prices are higher. (D, S) If the market does not slump, stock prices are higher. (M) Either dividends increase or the market does not slump. Therefore, stock prices are higher.

5. Either the Peace Corps is successful or it is poorly administered, and either the Peace Corps is successful or it has a poor selective process. (S, A, P) Either the Peace Corps is not poorly administered, or it does not have a poor selective process. Therefore, the Peace Corps is successful.

6. Either it is the case that if wholesale prices drop, then food shortages do not continue, or boycotts by housewives continue. (D, F, B) It is not possible both that boycotts by housewives continue and that the level of wholesale prices is attributable to inflation. (I) The level of wholesale prices is attributable to inflation and food shortages do continue. Therefore, wholesale prices do not drop.

Determine which of the following arguments are valid. Use the form of extended proof, where possible, to prove validity. Prove invalidity by a cross section of the truth table. In writing proofs, do not use the EPE as a designation for equivalences.

7. If it is the case that if resolutions are reasonable, resolutions are made habitual, then New Year's resolutions are kept. (R, H, K) New Year's resolutions are not kept. Either resolutions are reasonable or old habits return. (O) Therefore, old habits return.

8. If the care of the soul is the most significant task for man, then Plato was correct. (T, C) If Plato was correct, then the proper care of the soul becomes a highly significant question. (Q) If the proper care of the soul becomes a highly significant question, then the care of the soul is the most significant task for man.

Therefore, if and only if the care of the soul is the most significant task for man does the proper care of the soul become a highly significant question.

9. Not both can Epictetus go back to the traditions of Zeno and not be concerned about apathy on occasions of tension. (*Z, A*) If Epictetus is concerned about apathy on occasions of tension, then he taught that man should be the master and not the victim of circumstances. (*M*) Either Epictetus was a Stoic philosopher, or he did not teach that man should be the master and not the victim of circumstances. (*S*) Not both was he a Stoic philosopher and not a Roman slave. (*R*) He goes back to the tradition of Zeno. Therefore, he was a Roman slave.

10. If Aristotle formulated the rules of the categorical syllogism, then the categorical syllogism is a very old form of argument. (*A, O*) Not both should not other arguments supplement the categorical syllogism and the categorical syllogism be a very old form of argument. (*S*) If other arguments should supplement the categorical syllogism, then modern logic should be studied. (*M*) Therefore, if Aristotle formulated the rules of the categorical syllogism, then modern logic should be studied.

11. If there is a healthy interaction between the arts and the sciences, then both fields are enriched. (*H, E*) If there is no opportunity for a healthy interaction between the arts and the sciences, then both fields are impoverishd. (*O, I*) Either there is a healthy interaction between the arts and the sciences or there is no opportunity for healthy interaction between them. If either both fields are enriched or both fields are impoverished, then there is need for efforts of mutual appreciation of the accomplishments of the other. (*A*) Therefore, there is need for efforts of mutual appreciation of the accomplishments of the other.

12. Not both can an action be rational and not anticipate a desired result. (*A, D*) Not both can a desired result be anticipated and not satisfy some interest or not meet some need. (*I, N*) If a result meets some need and satisfies some interest, then adequate motivation is needed for encouraging the action. (*M*) Therefore, if adequate motivation is not needed for encouraging the action, the action is not rational.

13. If Judge Smith's decision is arbitrary or if it is uninformed, then the decision can be appealed successfully. (*A, U, S*) If the decision can be appealed successfully, then if a competent attorney appeals the case and he exercises good judgment, the decision will be reversed. (*C, E, R*) The decision will not be reversed. A competent attorney appeals the case and he exercises good judgment. Therefore, Judge Smith's decision is not arbitrary and it is not uninformed.

14. If air pollution continues in large cities, then this is a political issue and corrections will be made. (*P, I, M*) If no control is exercised over automobile and industrial wastes, then air pollution continues in large cities. (*E*) No control is exercised over automobile and industrial wastes and corrections are not made. Therefore, there will be mass movement away from the major cities. (*A*)

15. Not both can a movement be extremist and not be schismatic. (*E, S*) Either a movement is schismatic or it has a general sense of unity. (*U*) If a movement has a general sense of unity, it can achieve significant results. (*R*) Therefore, if a movement is extremist, it can achieve significant results.

16. If either op art becomes dehumanized or becomes trivial, then either op art becomes meaningless or becomes irrelevant. (*D, T, M, I*) Op art does become

trivial and it does not become meaningless. Not both can op art become irrelevant and gain the support of the majority of the art critics. (S) Therefore, op art does not gain the support of the majority of art critics.

17. If Smith is guilty of the crime, then he was aware of the floor plan of the house and he was not out of town on the night of the crime. (G, F, T) If he had visited in the house, he was aware of the floor plan, and if he was in a local bar an hour after the crime, he was not out of town on the night of the crime. (V, B) He had visited in the house and he was in a local bar an hour after the crime. Therefore, Smith is guilty of the crime.

18. If the argument is correct, then no error of inference has been made. (A, I) Not both can no error of inference have been made and the procedure in making proofs be faulty. (P) If the procedure in making proofs is not faulty, then either a careless mistake was made or a deliberate mistake was made. (C, D) If John understands logic, then a careless mistake was not made and a deliberate mistake was not made. (J) John understands logic. Therefore, the argument is not correct.

19. Either the governor is not aware of the primary interests of the voters or, if he is interested in winning the election, then he needs to pay more attention to the polls. (A, W, P) If either the governor is not interested in winning the election or he needs to pay more attention to the polls, then he needs to be more critical of his advisors. (C) Either he does not need to be more critical of his advisors or he needs to bring in men with newer ideas. (N) The governor is aware of the primary interests of voters. Therefore, he needs to bring in men with newer ideas.

20. Either the injections were harmless or their side effects were not obvious immediately. (H, O) If their side effects were not obvious immediately, then either counteracting agents were present or the dose was small. (C, S) If either counteracting agents were present or the dose was small, then there are no visible symptoms of disturbance. (D) There are no visible symptoms of disturbance. Therefore, the injections were harmless.

21. If Watts can be ignored as an issue and attention can be focused on other problems, then greater popular support can be secured. (W, A, S) If the issue of desegregated housing is not significant and the rate of contributions increases, then the interest in the election will become stronger. (D, C, I) It is not the case that either attention cannot be focused on other problems or the rate of contributions does not increase. It is not the case that either greater popular support can be secured or interest in the election becomes stronger. Therefore, Watts cannot be ignored and the issue of desegregated housing is significant.

22. It is the case either that, if the report is not accurate, we are not lagging behind in the military capacity to destroy an aggressor or that we cannot penetrate enemy defenses. (A, W, D) The report is not accurate and we can penetrate enemy defenses. If we are not lagging behind in the military capacity to destroy an aggressor, then we can hope to survive an enemy attack. (H) Therefore, we can hope to survive an enemy attack.

23. If we do not develop an antiballistic-missile system, we are threatened with a delivery gap, and if we do not develop nuclear-powered space vehicles, we lose out in the control of space for national defense. (S, G, V, D) Either we are not threatened with a delivery gap or we do not lose out in the control of space for national defense. If we develop an antiballistic-missile system, there will be 30

billion dollars appropriated for this purpose. (A) There will not be a 30-billion-dollar appropriation for this purpose. Therefore, we develop nuclear-powered space vehicles.

24. Either it is true that either we have followed the proper procedure for peace or peace is not assured by making agreements, or else peace does not require greater economic productivity in less-developed nations. (F, A, E) If the threats of war continue, it is the case both that we have not followed the proper procedures for peace and that peace requires more economic productivity in less-developed nations. (T) It is the case both that either peace is not assured by making agreements or peace does not require more economic productivity in less-developed nations and that threats of war continue. Therefore, peace is not assured by making agreements.

Symbols other than those used in this text sometimes are used in writing arguments and argument forms in symbolic logic. Some alternate symbols used with greatest frequency, particularly in works in mathematics, are the following: → *for* ⊃, ↔ *for* ≡, *and* & *for* ·.

25. Symbolize and write proofs for problems 1, 3, and 5 in Exercise 14.8 using these alternate symbols.

Open and closed circuits are used in computers to solve problems in symbolic logic. A minus sign (−) indicates an open circuit and a plus sign (+) indicates a closed circuit. An argument form is valid only if there is no open circuit for a conclusion when all premises are connected with a closed circuit. In using this form with truth tables an F has the value of a minus sign (−), and a T has the value of a plus sign (+).

26. Write truth tables in Exercise 14.8 for problems 2, 6, 8, 9, 10, and 11 using the minus sign for F and the plus sign for T.

Chapter 15
Elementary
Quantificational
Logic

15.1 Existential Quantifiers and Universal Quantifiers

Earlier chapters have discussed arguments using compound and categorical propositions and have analyzed propositions as entire expressions. This chapter examines procedures for breaking down propositions into more elementary units and for developing a unitary approach or system to analyze statements and arguments. Such procedures, developed by *quantificational logic,* are discussed here in an elementary way as they apply to the analysis of statements and the use of such analyses in validating arguments. This material requires further refinement for more complex problems in the subject area. A detailed treatment of quantificational logic falls beyond the scope of this presentation.

Quantificational logic makes explicit the meaning of expressions involving quantifying words such as "all" and "some." It utilizes in proofs the truth-functional connectives such as "and," "if . . . then . . . ," and "either . . . or." It also develops additional rules and equivalent forms for use in proofs.

A basic consideration in quantificational logic is the development of a technique for precise analyses of statements. Consider the sentence:

> Some ores are iron (ores).

This statement can be expressed in the form:

> There is at least one thing such that this thing is ore and this thing is iron (ore).

The statement also can be expressed in the form:

There is at least one thing x such that x is ore and x is iron (ore).

A variable x has been introduced into the sentence and in this context refers to the "at least one thing" referred to by the expression "there is."[1] This use of x shows that reference is being made to the same thing throughout the sentence wherever x occurs. Words such as "this x" or "it" also express the meaning of (the variable) x:

There is at least one thing x such that this x (it) is ore and this x (it) is iron (ore).

The notion of "there is at least one thing x" or "there exists at least one thing x" is expressed by the symbol "$(\exists x)$," which is called the *existential quantifier*. Using this symbol, we can write the expression above as follows:

$$(\exists x)\ (x \text{ is ore} \cdot x \text{ is iron})$$

The symbol $(\exists x)$ provides existential quantification for the sentence. The *scope* of an existential quantifier is the part of an expression it covers or governs. The scope is indicated either by a single unified expression [such as "Fx" in the form "$(\exists x)Fx$"] after the quantifier or by the set of parentheses (or brackets) beginning immediately after the quantifier (or quantifiers). In the example above, the scope of the existential quantifier includes the remainder of the expression beginning with the parenthesis following the quantifier $(\exists x)$.

Universal quantification is symbolized by the form (x).

All miners are exploiters.

This statement can be rendered in the forms:

Everything is such that if it is a miner, then it is an exploiter.
Everything x is such that if x is a miner, then x is an exploiter.

$$(x)\ (x \text{ is a miner} \supset x \text{ is an exploiter})$$

The universal quantifier (x) can be expressed in various ways, such as "for anything x," "for any x," and "for each thing x." The scope of the universal quantifier also includes that part of a unified expression immediately following it or included in the parentheses or brackets immediately following the quantifier (or series of quantifiers). Its scope is determined by the range of symbols to which it is applicable. Parentheses are used to make explicit the range of applicability of the quantifier. If the two previous examples are combined and y is accepted as a proper replacement for x in one of the cases, the resultant expression can be developed in the following manner.

---

[1] Variables for individuals are expressed by lower-case letters beginning near the end of the alphabet; thus, x, y, z, w are variables for individuals. In a specific context lower-case letters beginning with a, b, c are individual constants and can represent substitution cases for individual variables such as x.

$(x)(x$ is a miner $\supset x$ is an exploiter) $\cdot$ $(\exists y)(y$ is ore $\cdot$ y is iron)

The scope of the universal quantifier (x) is $(x$ is a miner $\supset x$ is an exploiter), and the scope of the existential quantifier $(\exists y)$ is $(y$ is an ore $\cdot$ y is iron).

Since the position of the quantifier determines its range in a given expression, care must be exercised to write the meaning of a sentence correctly. Consider the following examples:

$(x)(x$ is smooth $\lor x$ is rough)
$(x)(x$ is smooth$) \lor (x)(x$ is rough$)$

The first expression states that "For everything x, this x is smooth or this x is rough" or "Everything is either smooth or rough." The second statement reads "Either for everything x, x is smooth or for everything x, x is rough" or "Either everything is smooth or everything is rough."

Consider the statements:

(1) Something is organic and is inorganic.
(2) Something is organic and something is inorganic.

The first statement is expressed:

(3) $(\exists x)(x$ is organic $\cdot$ x is inorganic)

The second statement can be expressed:

(4) $(\exists x)(x$ is organic$) \cdot (\exists y)(y$ is inorganic)

In the latter case y is another variable used like x; it is introduced in this context to help clarify the expression to show that different individuals are intended by $(\exists x)$ and $(\exists y)$.

A variable that falls within the scope of its quantifier is called a *bound* variable. A variable that is not covered or bound by its quantifier is called a *free* variable. Consider the following case:

$(x)(x$ is a vertebrate $\supset x$ is an animal)

Each x occurring within the parentheses is a bound variable.

$(\exists x)(x$ is a vertebrate $\cdot$ y is an animal)

In this example the x within the parentheses after $(\exists x)$ is bound by the existential quantifier $(\exists x)$. The y is a free variable since it is not bound by the quantifier (y).

$(\exists x)[x$ is a teacher $\cdot$ $(\exists y)(y$ is a student $\cdot$ x is older than $y)]$

In the example above the x occurring anywhere within the brackets and the y occurring within the parentheses after $(\exists y)$ are bound variables.

Now consider another case:

x is a friend $\lor x$ is a stranger

Here no variable is bound, and each occurrence of x is free.[2] This sentence can be restated, "It is a friend or it is a stranger." No reference for "it" is provided. In such a context the meaning of the statement is indeterminate.

An expression can be regarded as true or as false only if it does not contain a free variable. If an expression contains a free variable, its meaning cannot be definite, since a free variable has no referent in the context. An expression with a free variable cannot be assigned a specific truth value. (The rules formulated for quantificational logic later in this chapter place restrictions on the use of free variables.)

For an expression to have universal quantification the scope of the universal quantifier must include the complete expression. Likewise, for an expression to have existential quantification the scope of the existential quantifier must cover all the expression. Consider these statements:

> (1) $(x)(x$ is a peace officer$) \supset$ someone enforces the law
> (2) $(x)(x$ is a peace officer $\supset x$ enforces the law$)$

The first expression as a whole does not have universal quantification, since the quantifier applies only to part and *not* to the complete statement. The universal quantifier covers the entire scope of the second expression, which therefore is universally quantified. Rules for instantiation and generalization (*UI, EI, UG,* and *EG*) developed in Section 15.4 are applicable to quantified expressions—that is, to expressions that are completely governed by a quantifier.

We can further symbolize propositions by using a capital letter to signify properties or relations found in the statement. Consider the analysis of the following statements.

1. All executives are decision-makers.
    $(x)(x$ is an executive $\supset x$ is a decision-maker$)$
    $(x)(Ex \supset Dx)$

---

[2] The form of any sentence such as "x is a friend" can be symbolized Fx. In this case F represents a property ["(is a) friend"]. In some cases F represents a relation (for example, "is equal to."). The letter x designates a variable for the name of a thing. For example, if the expression above is changed to "John is a friend," this proposition can be expressed as Fj. In writing the forms that any similar proposition might take, we can use the expression Fx (or Fy, or Gx or Gy). In such cases capital letters beginning with F designate (variables for) properties or relations and lower-case letters $x, y, z, w, \ldots$ designate (variables for) things. The property designated by F is a function of the thing, and the thing (individual) designated by x is the argument of the function. In the preceding case F refers to the function of a thing and x to the argument of the function. Fx (or Fy, or Gx or Gy) is a *propositional function*. A propositional function consists of the letters used in accordance with specified rules to refer to a function of a thing (the property designated by F) and its arguments (the thing or individual designated by x). Propositional functions refer to language use, and in this sense they are linguistic functions and not functions of objects. A function such as Fxy is a two-place function. $Fxyz$ is a three-place function. Propositional functions sometimes are called *sentencial* functions.

2. Some decisions are sound.
$$(\exists x)(x \text{ is a decision} \cdot x \text{ is sound})$$
$$(\exists x)(Dx \cdot Sx)$$
3. Some persons like all dogs.
$$(\exists x)(x \text{ is a person} \cdot x \text{ likes all dogs})$$
$$(\exists x)[(x \text{ is a person} \cdot (y)(y \text{ is a dog} \supset x \text{ likes } y)]$$
$$(\exists x)[Px \cdot (y)(Dy \supset Lxy)]$$
4. Everything is round.
$$(x)x \text{ is round}$$
$$(x)Rx$$
5. If any students cheat, then they fail.
$$(x)[(x \text{ is a student} \cdot x \text{ cheats}) \supset (x \text{ fails})]$$
$$(x)[(Sx \cdot x \text{ cheats}) \supset (x \text{ fails})]$$
$$(x)[(Sx \cdot Cx) \supset (x \text{ fails})]$$
$$(x)[(Sx \cdot Cx) \supset Fx]$$

6. If some books are expensive, then if they are purchased then they are read.

$$(\exists x)[(x \text{ is a book} \cdot x \text{ is expensive}) \supset (x \text{ is purchased} \supset x \text{ is read})]$$
$$(\exists x)[(Bx \cdot x \text{ is expensive}) \supset (x \text{ is purchased} \supset x \text{ is read})]$$
$$(\exists x)[(Bx \cdot Ex) \supset (x \text{ is purchased} \supset x \text{ is read})]$$
$$(\exists x)[(Bx \cdot Ex) \supset (Px \supset x \text{ is read})]$$
$$(\exists x)[(Bx \cdot Ex) \supset (Px \supset Rx)]$$

7. If any initiatives are successful then some preparation is desirable.
$$(x)(x \text{ is initiative} \supset x \text{ is successful}) \supset \text{some preparation is desirable}$$
$$(x)(Ix \supset x \text{ is successful}) \supset \text{some preparation is desirable}$$
$$(x)(Ix \supset Sx) \supset \text{some preparation is desirable}$$
$$(x)(Ix \supset Sx) \supset (\exists y)(Py \cdot y \text{ is desirable})$$
$$(x)(Ix \supset Sx) \supset (\exists y)(Py \cdot Dy)$$

Capital letters in the instances above refer to specific properties (such as D for "decision-makers") or they refer to relations (such as L for "likes"). Careful study of such examples is essential for sound analysis of the meaning of statements. Ability to use the more complex arguments in quantificational logic requires ability to symbolize the original sentence in proper form. The following examples are shortened. (Try first to symbolize each statement into a satisfactory form before reading the proposed symbolism.[3])

1. All men are rational. [M (man), R (rational)]
$$(x)(x \text{ is a man}) \supset (x \text{ is rational})$$
$$(x)(Mx \supset Rx)$$

---

[3] "Each one," "everyone," and "anyone" traditionally are interpreted as requiring universal quantifiers in an affirmative context. "Not each one," "not everyone," and "not all" are interpreted as requiring existential quantifiers. "Not any," like "none," requires a universal quantifier. "Someone" may mean "anyone" in some sentences or "at least one" in other sentences. If it refers to "anyone," a universal quantifier is used. If it means "at least one," an existential quantifier is used. Examples in this book are limited to the meaning of "at least one."

2. Some men are apprehensive. [M (man), A (apprehensive)]
$$(\exists x)(x \text{ is a man} \cdot x \text{ is apprehensive})$$
$$(\exists x)(Mx \cdot Ax)$$

3. Some oranges are not ripe.
$$(\exists x)(Ox \cdot {\sim}Rx)$$

4. No documents are public.
$$(x)(Dx \supset {\sim}Px)$$

5. Some athletes are strong or fast.
$$(\exists x)[Ax \cdot (Sx \vee Fx)]$$

6. Everyone wants something.
$$(x)(\exists y)Wxy$$

7. Someone wants something.
$$(\exists x)(\exists y)Wxy$$

8. Someone wants everything.
$$(\exists x)(y)Wxy$$

9. Some teachers run faster than any students.
$$(\exists x)[Tx \cdot (y)(Sy \supset Rxy)]$$

10. Every graduate is either intelligent or persistent.
$$(x)[Gx \supset (Ix \vee Px)]$$

11. Some students are older than their teachers.
$$(\exists x)[Sx \cdot (\exists y)(Tyx \cdot Oxy)]$$

12. Some persons admire themselves.
$$(\exists x)Axx$$

13. It is false that all men are dishonest.
$${\sim}(x)(Mx \supset Dx)$$

14. It is false that some books are metal.
$${\sim}(\exists x)(Bx \cdot Mx)$$

15. If some person is excited, then some demonstrator has talked with him.
$(\exists x)[(x \text{ is a person} \cdot x \text{ is excited})$
$\qquad\qquad\qquad \supset (\exists y)(y \text{ is a demonstrator and } y \text{ has talked with } x)]$
$(\exists x)[(Px \cdot Ex) \supset (\exists y)(Dy \cdot Tyx)]$

16. If some person is angry, then something (some situation) is disturbing him. (If someone is angry, then something is disturbing him.)
$(\exists x)[(x \text{ is a person} \cdot x \text{ is angry}) \supset (\exists y)(y \text{ is a situation and } y \text{ disturbs } x)]$
$(\exists x)[(Px \cdot Ax) \supset (\exists y)(Sy \cdot Dyx)]$

17. If anyone is ill, then something is wrong with him.
$$(x)[Ix \supset (\exists y) \, Wyx]$$

Expressions containing the name of an individual use lower-case letters such as $a, b, c, \ldots, t$ to refer to the specific name of an individual and continue to use capital letters to refer to the indicated property or relation. Since a letter such as a designates a specific individual in this context, it is not a variable but a constant. Consider the symbolism for the following cases.

1. John is a teacher.

$$Tj$$

2. Adrian admires Blake.

$$Aab$$

3. Carl is older than Dan.

$$Ocd$$

4. No person visited the Smiths.

$$(x)(Px \supset \sim Vxs)$$

5. John is taller than any of his brothers.

$$(x)(Bxj \supset Tjx)$$

6. If George notifies Frank, then Frank notifies Larry.

$$Ngf \supset Nfl$$

15.2 EXERCISES

Write the proper symbolism in quantificational logic for each of the following statements. Use the longer form of symbolization for each expression and restate the final symbolization in the short form. If the form is complex, use several steps in breaking it down.

1. (*Example*) Some students learn slower than any teacher.
   $(\exists x)(x$ is a student $\cdot$ x learns slower than any teacher)
   $(\exists x)[x$ is a student. $\cdot$ $(y)(y$ is a teacher $\supset$ x learns slower than $y)]$
   $(\exists x)[Sx \cdot (y)(Ty \supset Lxy)]$
2. Some problems are easy. (*P, E*)
3. There are students who are either freshmen or sophomores. (*S, F, P*)
4. Anyone who reads the novel likes it. (*R, N, L*)
5. Something is despised by everyone. (*D*)
6. Some professionals are more skilled than any amateur. (*P, S, A*)
7. Smith is a golfer.
8. Everyone admires something.
9. No person assisted the Blacks.
10. It is false that some antiques are not expensive.
11. It is false that nobody works.
12. James is a better student than any of his classmates.
13. Good fishermen always catch fish.
14. It is false that nobody wants anything.
15. All answers are either correct or difficult.
16. If anyone is interested, then someone telephones him.
17. If John is interested, then he telephones Smith.
18. If the grain is ripe, then machines harvest it.

15.3 Quantifier Exchange, Negation, and Equivalent Expressions

In using quantifiers we need a procedure for replacing a universal quantifier with an existential quantifier or for replacing an existential quantifier with a universal quantifier. The justification of such a quantifier exchange is called the *principle of quantificational equivalences.* Briefly stated, this principle holds that we can replace a universal quantifier with an existential quantifier by placing the sign of negation before and after the existential quantifier (and vice versa). Thus, (x) can be replaced by $\sim(\exists x)\sim$, or $(\exists x)$ can be replaced by $\sim(x)\sim$, or $\sim(x)$ by $(\exists x)\sim$, or $\sim(\exists x)$ by $(x)\sim$.

We can see the justification for this principle by examining an original proposition, the contradiction of this proposition, and an alternative form of writing the denial of this contradiction. Consider the proposition

(1) All lawyers are politicians.
$$(x)(Lx \supset Px)$$

The contradiction of this proposition is

(2) Some lawyers are not politicians.
$$(\exists x)(Lx \cdot \sim Px)$$

The contradiction of (2) also can be written

(3) It is not the case that some lawyers are not politicians.
$$\sim(\exists x)(Lx \cdot \sim Px)$$

Statements (1) and (3) have the same truth value, since each is the contradiction of (2). Thus, statements (1) and (3) also are equivalent—that is,

$$(x)(Lx \supset Px) \equiv \sim(\exists x)(Lx \cdot \sim Px)$$

This equivalence leads to the following result:

(4) $(x)(Lx \supset Px)$ Given (1)
(5) $\sim(\exists x)(Lx \cdot \sim Px)$ Given (3)
(6) $\sim(\exists x)\sim(Lx \supset Px)$ (5) DeM & MI

Since the form in line (4) has been shown above to be equivalent to the form in line (5) and the form in line (5) is shown to be equivalent to the form in line (6), then the forms in lines (4) and (6) are equivalent. Thus,

$$(x)(Lx \supset Px) \equiv \sim(\exists x)\sim(Lx \supset Px)$$

The difference in the case above is that the one equivalent form has the quantifier (x) and the second equivalent form has the sign of negation on each side of, or flanking, the quantifier: $\sim(\exists x)\sim$. A comparable justification for quantifier exchange can be illustrated by the use of other propositions.

Traditional categorical propositions can be rendered in two forms with the use of the principle of quantification equivalences (QE). The equivalences for **A, E, I,** and **O** propositions in two different forms are shown below, where Lx means "x is a lawyer" and Px means "x is a politician."

A $(x)(Lx \supset Px)$ $\equiv \sim(\exists x)(Lx \cdot \sim Px)$
E $(x)(Lx \supset \sim Px)$ $\equiv \sim(\exists x)(Lx \cdot Px)$
I $(\exists x)(Lx \cdot Px)$ $\equiv \sim(x)(Lx \supset \sim Px)$
O $(\exists x)(Lx \cdot \sim Px)$ $\equiv \sim(x)(Lx \supset Px)$

The sign of negation on one flank of a quantifier can be rendered "it is not the case that." If the sign of negation occurs on each side of a quantifier, its second occurrence can be rendered "it is false that." $\sim(x)\sim(Lx \cdot Px)$

can be rendered "It is not the case that for any x it is false both that Lx and that Px."

The use of the sign of negation, "$\sim$," on a flank of a quantifier requires particular attention when we interpret the meaning of the expression form. Consider the following cases:

For any x if x is a lawyer, then x is a politician.

    1. $(x)(Lx \supset Px)$
    2. (1) $(x)\sim(Lx \supset Px)$ Given
         (2) $(x)(Lx \cdot \sim Px)$ (1) DeM & MI

For any x, x is a lawyer and x is not a politician.

    3. (1) $\sim(x)(Lx \supset Px)$ Given
         (2) $(\exists x)\sim(Lx \supset Px)$ (1) QE
         (3) $(\exists x)(Lx \cdot \sim Px)$ (2) DeM & MI

There is an x such that x is a lawyer and x is not a politician.

    4. (1) $\sim(x)\sim(Lx \supset Px)$ Given
         (2) $(\exists x)(Lx \supset Px)$ (1) QE

There is an x such that if x is a lawyer, then x is a politician.

The use of statements with existential and universal quantifiers extends the use of the arguments and proofs discussed in previous chapters. Premises and conclusions are written with quantifiers and follow the manner of development presented in the chapters dealing with truth-functional propositions (Chapters 12, 13, 14). Consider the following cases.

    1. (1) All men are rational.
        (2) All sailors are men.
            Therefore, all sailors are rational.

            (1) $(x)(Mx \supset Rx)$
            (2) $(x)(Sx \supset Mx)$
                    $\therefore (x)(Sx \supset Rx)$

    2. (1) No captives are happy.
        (2) All prisoners are captives.
        (3) Some prisoners are lonesome.
            Therefore, some lonesome persons are not happy.

            (1) $(x)(Cx \supset \sim Hx)$
                 $(x)(Px \supset Cx)$
                 $(\exists x)(Px \cdot Lx)$
                 $\therefore (\exists x)(Lx \cdot \sim Hx)$

In order to prove validity of arguments like those above, additional principles are needed. Some of these principles are discussed in the next section.

15.4 Principles Applied in Proofs Using Quantified Statements

We have referred to the writing of proofs for arguments using as premises quantified expressions such as "$(x)(Mx \supset Rx)$" and "$(x)(Sx \supset Mx)$." If some manner of removing the quantifier is found and appropriate individuals (substitution instances) are designated as having the indicated properties, an argument form such as the following can be stated.

$$Ma \supset Ra$$
$$\underline{Sa \supset Ma}$$
$$\therefore Sa \supset Ra$$

A hypothetical syllogism justifies the conclusion "$Sa \supset Ra$." Even if this form of conclusion is validly inferred, then we need some procedure to derive the quantified expression of the original conclusion "$(x)(Sx \supset Rx)$."

The procedure of specifying cases (instances) to which a quantified expression can refer is called *instantiation*. The procedure of inferring a quantified expression from specified cases (instances) is called *generalization*. This section discusses the proper use of these procedures together with other principles essential for proving quantified statements.

Proofs of arguments using quantified statements use argument forms and equivalences developed for propositional (or truth-functional) logic. These proofs also have to be supplemented by additional rules and restrictions, including the following:

1. A proof involving quantified statements as developed in this work must not contain free variables. (This rule is more restrictive than necessary, but its use precludes our having to make additional qualifications in discussing the principles of quantificational logic.) This rule is particularly relevant to the application of the principles of instantiation and generalization developed later in this section.

2. In any application of the principles of instantiation or of generalization (that is, of UI, EI, EG, and UG—discussed later) the entire expression must be included in (or governed by) the scope of the instantiated or generalized quantifier that is used. This restriction excludes these principles from being applied to an expression as long as it remains in the following form:

$$(x)(Hx \supset Ix) \supset (y)(Iy \supset Zy)$$

The entire expression is *not* governed by a single quantifier.

3. Any application of principles of instantiation or of generalization requires that the quantifier not be covered by any sign of negation. Instantiation (UI or EI) cannot be applied as long as an expression has forms such as "$\sim(\exists x)(Fx \cdot Gx)$" or "$\sim(x)(Fx \supset Gx)$."

The additional principles for proofs of arguments in quantificational logic are concerned with replacement, quantificational equivalences, instantiation, generalization, and quantifier manipulation.

The principle of replacement.   In propositional (truth-functional) logic any two propositions that are logically equivalent may replace each other whereever they occur in an argument. This principle is extended in quantificational logic to include quantified expressions. It is customary to apply this rule by noting the form of equivalence used. The use of the principle of replacement also includes use of any additional equivalences developed in this chapter.

The principle of quantificational equivalence (QE).   A universally quantified expression is equivalent to an existentially quantified expression if they are the same in all respects except in the quality (expressed by a negative sign or its absence) both before and after the quantifier (see Section 15.3). If the form Fx refers to any expression functioning as a proposition, then the application of this principle can be illustrated as follows:

$$(1) \quad \sim(x)Fx \quad \equiv (\exists x)\sim Fx$$
$$(2) \quad (x)\sim Fx \quad \equiv \sim(\exists x)Fx$$
$$(3) \quad \sim(\exists x)Fx \quad \equiv (x)\sim Fx$$
$$(4) \quad \sim(x)\sim Fx \equiv (\exists x)Fx$$

We can use the principle of quantificational equivalences in handling troublesome problems of negation in the construction of proofs and in finding some means of proceeding from a universally quantified statement to an existentially quantified statement or vice versa. Consider the following examples:

1. All problems are interesting things.
   It is not the case that all problems are difficult things.
   Therefore, some interesting things are not difficult.

(1)	$(x)(Px \supset Ix)$	
(2)	$\sim(x)(Px \supset Dx)$	
	$\therefore (\exists x)(Ix \cdot \sim Dx)$	
(3)	$(\exists x)\sim(Px \supset Dx)$	(2) QE
(4)	$(\exists x)(Px \cdot \sim Dx)$	(3) DeM & MI
(5)	$\ldots$	

2. It is not the case that some stocks are not risks.
   It is not the case that some risks are not exciting.
   Therefore, all stocks are exciting.

(1)	$\sim(\exists x)(Sx \cdot \sim Rx)$
(2)	$\sim(\exists x)(Rx \cdot \sim Ex)$
	$\therefore (x)(Sx \supset Ex)$

(3)	$(x) \sim (Sx \cdot \sim Rx)$	(1) QE
(4)	$(x)(Sx \supset Rx)$	(3) DeM & MI
(5)	$(x) \sim (Rx \cdot \sim Ex)$	(2) QE
(6)	$(x)(Rx \supset Ex)$	(5) DeM & MI
(7)	$\ldots$	

In the examples above we eliminated a negative sign before the quantifier by using the principle of quantificational equivalence (QE). A negative sign immediately after the quantifier can be eliminated by the use of an equivalent form of De Morgan's law.

The principles of instantiation and of generalization. The illustrative problems just given indicate a need for principles that make possible the continuation of the proof of an argument in quantificational logic. Some procedure to break down quantified expressions is required. We can accomplish this breaking down of the quantified expressions by providing instances to which the quantified expressions are applicable.

Consider the statement "All copies are paperbacks" with the quantified form "$(x)(Cx \supset Px)$." Any randomly designated instances or individual copies of editions can be designated as "copy a" or "copy b" or "copy c." In such a case "copy a" can serve as a name to refer to an instance of the designated edition. Similarly, lower-case letters (usually beginning with a) can be used as substitution instances for a variable, such as x, bound by a quantifier. Lower-case letters such as a used in such a context *serve as* individual constants. The designated lower-case letter such as a replaces each instance of the bound variable such as x for which it is a substitution instance, and the quantifier "(x)" in the expression is eliminated. In the example above the original symbols "$(x)(Cx \supset Px)$" can be instantiated by the form "$Ca \supset Pa$." In a similar manner the statement "Some copies are paperbacks," symbolized by the form "$(\exists x)(Cx \cdot Px)$," can be instantiated by the form "$Ca \cdot Pa$." The rules for using such procedures of instantiation are expressed by the principle of universal instantiation and the principle of existential instantiation.

Principle of universal instantiation (UI). The *principle of universal instantiation (UI)* holds that names of arbitrarily designated instances (individuals) of a universally quantified expression can be used in a substitution case for the original expression.[4] This can be symbolized by the following form, with

---

[4] These arbitrarily selected individuals, designated by lower-case letters such as a, serve as constants in the application of the principle of universal instantiation. However, in a strict sense they are not constants. In a rigorous sense a constant refers to a specific individual thing or name, such as "Charles." In the use of universal instantiation a lower-case letter such as a signifies any arbitrarily designated individual such as Charles. Additional refinement of this procedure is required in more technical discussion of instantiation.

Fx referring again (as in subsequent examples) to any expression that functions as a proposition:

$$\frac{(x)Fx}{\therefore Fa}$$

If an expression such as "Any student is ambitious" occurs as a premise, this can be expressed by the quantified expression

$$(x)(Sx \supset Ax)$$

The principle of universal instantiation can be applied to this quantified expression in the following manner:

$$Sa \supset Aa \qquad UI$$

The principle of universal instantiation makes possible the continuation of proofs like the one began in a previous example.

(1)	$\sim(\exists x)(Sx \cdot \sim Rx)$	
(2)	$\sim(\exists x)(Rx \cdot \sim Ex)$	
	$\therefore (x)(Sx \supset Ex)$	
(3)	$(x)\sim(Sx \cdot \sim Rx)$	(1) QE
(4)	$(x)(Sx \supset Rx)$	(3) DeM & MI
(5)	$(x)\sim(Rx \cdot \sim Ex)$	(2) QE
(6)	$(x)(Rx \supset Ex)$	(5) DeM & MI
(7)	$Sa \supset Ra$	(4) UI
(8)	$Ra \supset Ea$	(6) UI
(9)	$Sa \supset Ea$	(7), (8) HS
(10)	$\ldots$	

In the case above the proof is incomplete. A substitution instance of the conclusion is shown to hold, but the original conclusion has not yet been shown to hold.

In some arguments an individual name such as "Jones" occurs in a premise and this name is symbolized as a constant for a property or a relation occurring elsewhere in the argument. Consider the statement "Jones is president." This can be symbolized in a proof either as *Pj* or as *Pa*. If *Pa* is used, the *a* refers to a specific substitution instance of *P,* namely to Jones. This can be illustrated in the following case.

All presidents are citizens.
Jones is president.
Therefore, Jones is a citizen.

(1)	$(x)(Px \supset Cx)$	
(2)	Pa	
	$\therefore Ca$	

$$(3) \quad Pa \supset Ca \qquad\qquad (1) \ \text{UI}$$
$$(4) \quad Ca \qquad\qquad\qquad (3), (2) \ \text{MP}$$

In this case the proof is complete, since the conclusion is established. The argument also can be written as follows:

$$(1) \quad (x)(Px \supset Cx)$$
$$(2) \quad Pj$$
$$\qquad\qquad \overline{\qquad\qquad}$$
$$\qquad \therefore Cj$$
$$(3) \quad Pj \supset Cj \qquad\qquad (1) \ \text{UI}$$
$$(4) \quad Cj \qquad\qquad\qquad (3), (2) \ \text{MP}$$

In this case the j introduced in step (3) of the proof is interpreted as a substitution instance of the original quantified expression, $(x)(Px \supset Cx)$. The writing of the argument in the following form would not lead to fruitful results:

$$(1) \quad (x)(Px \supset Cx)$$
$$(2) \quad Pj$$
$$\qquad\qquad \overline{\qquad\qquad}$$
$$\qquad \therefore Ca$$
$$(3) \quad Pa \supset Ca \qquad\qquad (1) \quad \text{UI Not desirable}$$
$$(4) \quad \dots$$

In this case the use of two different individual constants in Jj and Ca does not provide an adequate basis for additional steps needed in the proof.

Principle of existential instantiation (EI).   In the foregoing discussion we have established a procedure for noting substitution instances for universally quantified expressions. A comparable procedure is needed for existentially quantified expressions. This latter procedure is called the *principle of existential instantiation (EI)*. It holds that names for relevant instances (individuals) of an existentially quantified expression can be substituted for the original expression provided that no previous use of the chosen individual constant or name (such as a) occurs in the context. That is, any lower-case letter (such as a) selected as the constant or name for the variable (such as x) in the quantified expression cannot have a prior occurrence either in the premises or in the steps in a proof. If an (individual) constant or name (such as a) occurs in the context, then we must use another lower-case letter (such as b) as the substitution instance in applying this principle. The principle of existential instantiation can be symbolized by the expression

$$\frac{(\exists x)Fx}{\therefore Fa}$$

However, the a must represent some relevant substitution instance in the context and cannot have a prior occurrence in it. This rule requires that the principle of existential instantiation be used in a proof prior to the principle of universal instantiation in all cases where the same (individual) constant, such as *a,* is used for both instantiations. Likewise, if the principle of existential instantiation occurs more than once in a proof, a different (individual) constant, such as *b* or *c* must be used for each additional use of the principle.

Consider the following examples.

1. All stereotypes are misleading.
   Some programs are stereotypes.
   Therefore, some programs are misleading.

(1)	$(x)(Sx \supset Mx)$	
(2)	$(\exists x)(Px \cdot Sx)$	
	$\therefore (\exists x)(Px \cdot Mx)$	
(3)	$Pa \cdot Sa$	(2) EI
(4)	$Sa \supset Ma$	(1) UI
(5)	$Sa \cdot Pa$	(3) Comm.
(6)	Sa	(5) Simp.
(7)	Ma	(4), (6) MP
(8)	Pa	(3) Simp.
(9)	$Pa \cdot Ma$	(8), (7) Conj.
(10)	. . .	

2. Some advisors are informed.
   Some wise persons are informed.
   Therefore, some wise persons are advisors.

(1)	$(\exists x)(Ax \cdot Ix)$	
(2)	$(\exists x)(Wx \cdot Ix)$	
	$\therefore (\exists x)(Wx \cdot Ax)$ (Invalid)	
(3)	$Aa \cdot Ia$	(1) EI
(4)	$Wa \cdot Ia$	(2) EI (Incorrect)

In the second example, step (3) provides a substitution instance for *x* with the individual name *a,* but *a* cannot be repeated in step (4) of the proof in another instance of existential instantiation since *a* is used in step (3). Step (4) requires a form such as "*Wb · Ab.*" The individual name *a* in this context has been assigned to an advisor who is also wise, and it is not to be repeated in another case of existential instantiation in the proof.

3. Some blacksmiths are strong.
   Alex is a blacksmith.
   Therefore, Alex is strong.

(1)	$(\exists x)(Bx \cdot Sx)$	
(2)	Ba	
	$\therefore Sa$ (Invalid)	
(3)	$Ba \cdot Sa$ (Incorrect)	(1) EI

In this example the letter *a* occurs as a name in the premise. In such instances the lower-case letter (such as *a* in this case) cannot be repeated as an instance of existential instantiation in the proof.

Principle of existential generalization (EG).   In examples given thus far for the instantiation of quantified expressions, a complete proof of the validity of an argument was given in only one case involving an individual name ("Jones") in the premise and the repetition of this name in the conclusion ("Jones is a citizen"). Principles are needed so that we can establish a conclusion in other cases.

Consider the proof we began in discussing the principle of existential instantiation.

$$(1)\quad (x)(Sx \supset Mx)$$
$$(2)\quad (\exists x)(Px \cdot Sx)$$
$$\therefore (\exists x)(Px \cdot Mx)$$

(3)	$Pa \cdot Sa$	(2) EI
(4)	$Sa \supset Ma$	(1) UI
(5)	$Sa \cdot Pa$	(3) Comm.
(6)	Sa	(5) Simp.
(7)	Ma	(4), (6) MP
(8)	Pa	(3) Simp.
(9)	$Pa \cdot Ma$	(8), (7) Conj.
(10)	...	

A procedure is yet to be established for proving the conclusion "$(\exists x)$ $(Px \cdot Mx)$." The principle of existential generalization makes available such a procedure.

The *principle of existential generalization* holds that an existentially quantified statement can be inferred from any of its relevant substitution instances. In such cases the relevant substitution instance needs to be a form either introduced in the proof by existential instantiation (EI) or derived properly from instances using EI in the proof.[5] This restriction is essential to prevent existential instantiation from being applied to an expression that has been used in the proof exclusively from forms introduced by universal instantiation (UI) or from forms derived only from other instances of universal instantiation. (This restriction is the basis for the rule of the categorical syllogism holding that conclusions with existential import are to be derived only if one premise has existential import.)

Subject to such restrictions the principle of existential generalization holds that if the form Fx refers to any completely quantified expression, the following inference holds:

$$Fa$$
$$\therefore (\exists x)Fx$$

---

[5] Existential generalization also can be applied to names introduced in the proof, provided such names are not fictitious. If this convention is added, we can use a notation for a fictitious name such as Fr (where r represents a fictitious name to which EI is not applicable). The adoption of this convention makes possible the proof of some categorical syllogisms in Figure III, Mood **AAI**. (Smith is a congressman. Smith is a lawyer. Therefore, some lawyers are congressmen.)

If this procedure is applied to an incomplete proof mentioned earlier, the final steps completing the proof are written as follows:

(9)	$Pa \cdot Ma$	(8), (7)	Conj.
(10)	$(\exists x)(Px \cdot Mx)$	(9)	EG

Additional examples of the use of this principle are given below.

1. All researchers are dedicated.
   Some insurance persons are researchers.
   Therefore, some insurance persons are dedicated persons.

(1)	$(x)(Rx \supset Dx)$		
(2)	$(\exists x)(Ix \cdot Rx)$		
	$\therefore (\exists x)(Ix \cdot Dx)$		
(3)	$Ia \cdot Ra$	(2)	EI
(4)	$Ra \supset Da$	(1)	UI
(5)	$Ra \cdot Ia$	(3)	Comm.
(6)	Ra	(5)	Simp.
(7)	Da	(4), (6)	MP
(8)	Ia	(3)	Simp.
(9)	$Ia \cdot Da$	(8), (7)	Conj.
(10)	$(\exists x)(Ix \cdot Dx)$	(9)	EG

2.

(1)	$(x)[(Fx \supset Gx) \cdot (Hx \supset Ix)]$		
(2)	$(x)(Fx \lor Hx)$		
	$\therefore (\exists x)(Gx \lor Ix)$ (Invalid)		
(3)	$(Fa \supset Ga) \cdot (Ha \supset Ia)$	(1)	UI
(4)	$Fa \lor Ha$	(2)	UI
(5)	$Ga \lor Ia$	(3), (4)	CCD
(6)	$(\exists x)(Gx \lor Ix)$	(5)	EG (Incorrect)

In the latter example the use of EG in step (6) is incorrect, since the name or (individual) constant, a, of step (5) has not been introduced into the argument by the use of existential instantiation (EI) and it has not been derived from a form introduced by existential instantiation.

The principle of universal generalization (UG). A principle is needed so that we can derive a universally quantified statement in a conclusion from a properly derived substitution instance of such a statement in a proof. In a previous example illustrating the principle of universal instantiation the last step derived in the proof from previous steps introduced by universal instantiation is

(9)	$Sa \supset Ea$	(7), (8)	HS

A procedure to complete the proof in this case needs to justify the derivation of "$(x)(Sx \supset Ex)$" from "$Sa \supset Ea$."

To make such a derivation properly we require several safeguards. An (individual) constant such as a (to which UG is applied) cannot be derived from forms introduced in the proof by existential instantiation (EI) or by a name introduced in the premises, such as Pj for a statement such as "Jones is president." An (individual) constant (such as a) in the proof needs to refer to any arbitrarily or randomly designated individual having the property or relation indicated in the form. In the case of the form

$$Sa \supset Ea$$

the S refers to "stocks" and the E refers to "exciting" in the original example. The constant, a, having been introduced in the proof by universal instantiation (UI), refers to any given individual instance of stocks that is named. Throughout the proof this meaning has remained unchanged. The principle of universal generalization makes possible the changing of this (individual) constant a to a variable such as x and for the universal quantification of the expression. The indicated proof can have the following satisfactory termination:

(9)	$Sa \supset Ea$	(7), (8)	HS
(10)	$(x)(Sx \supset Ex)$	(9)	UG

The principle of universal generalization holds that a universally quantified expression can be derived validly from a step in the proof only if (1) the step is derived from a form using UI and (2) the step is not derived from a form derived from the use of EI or an individual name in the proof. At this point a review and extension of the restrictions placed on the use of EG and UG may provide a useful reference.

1. EG and UG can be used on forms introduced in the proof only if the quantifier applied in UG or EG governs the complete expression on that line of the proof.

2. EG can be applied only on forms introduced in the proof by EI or derived from forms introduced by EI.

3. UG cannot be applied to forms derived either by the use of EI or by names of individuals.

4. UG cannot be applied to constants, such as a, that are introduced as part of a conditional or *reductio* premise within the sequence of a proof dependent exclusively on this assumed premise.

5. The use of EG or UG requires that if any constant expressed by the same letter, such as a, is being bound by a quantifier, such as (x), then all occurrences of a in the complete expression must be changed to the letter, such as x, of the binding quantifier.

6. If a given letter, such as x, is used with a quantifier, such as (x) or $(\exists x)$, to bind an expression, then this letter cannot be used again as a quantifier in a second application of EG or UG to that expression. If a constant, such as a, is already within the scope of a quantifier, such as (x) or $(\exists x)$, then another letter (variable), such as y, must be used in any applica-

tion of EG or UG to that expression. This restriction prohibits the following kinds of generalization:

1.   . . .
    (6) $(x)(Fx \supset Ga)$
    (7) $(\exists x)(x)(Fx \supset Gx)$ (6) EG (Incorrect)

2.   . . .
    (7) $(x)(Fx \supset Ga)$
    (8) $(x)(x)(Fx \supset Gx)$ (7) UG (Incorrect)

The following kinds of generalization are permitted if other rules are not violated:

1.   . . .
    (6) $(y)(Fy \supset Ga)$
    (7) $(\exists x)(y)(Fy \supset Gx)$ (6) EG

2.   . . .
    (7) $(y)(Fy \supset Ga)$
    (8) $(x)(y)(Fy \supset Gx)$ (7) UG

Subject to the restrictions above, the principle of universal generalization (UG) can be symbolized as follows:

$$\frac{Fa}{\therefore\ (x)Fx}$$

Consider the following examples relevant to the use of this principle.

1. All adventurers are brave.
   All mercenaries are adventurers.
   Therefore, all mercenaries are brave.

    (1) $(x)(Ax \supset Bx)$
    (2) $(x)(Mx \supset Ax)$
    $\overline{\therefore\ (x)(Mx \supset Bx)}$
    (3) $Aa \supset Ba$ (1) UI
    (4) $Ma \supset Aa$ (2) UI
    (5) $Ma \supset Ba$ (4), (3) HS
    (6) $(x)(Mx \supset Bx)$ (5) UG

2. All wise men are informed.
   Some rich men are not informed.
   Therefore, no rich men are wise.

    (1) $(x)(Wx \supset Ix)$
    (2) $(\exists x)(Rx \cdot \sim Ix)$
    $\overline{\therefore\ (x)(Rx \supset \sim Wx)}$ (Invalid)
    (3) $Ra \cdot \sim Ia$ (2) EI
    (4) $Wa \supset Ia$ (1) UI
    (5) $\sim Ia \cdot Ra$ (3) Comm.
    (6) $\sim Ia$ (5) Simp.

(7)	$\sim Wa$	(4), (6) MT
(8)	$\sim Wa \lor \sim Ra$	(7) Add.
(9)	$\sim Ra \lor \sim Wa$	(8) Comm.
(10)	$Ra \supset \sim Wa$	(9) MI
(11)	$(x)(Rx \supset \sim Wa)$	(10) UG (Incorrect)[6]

The last step in the proof above is incorrect, since it is an improper application of the principle of UG. The occurrence of a in the form $\sim Ra$ in step (8) is used with a form introduced in the proof by EI. UG cannot be applied subsequently to this form. The occurrence of Ra in step (11) is derived from the occurrence in step (3) of EI. There is no basis for justifying the application of Ra to any rich individual designated arbitrarily [in the use of UG in step (11)].

Consider another example with the use of a conditional proof.

3. All humans are mortal.
   All Greeks are human.
   All Athenians are Greeks.
   Therefore, all Athenians are mortal.

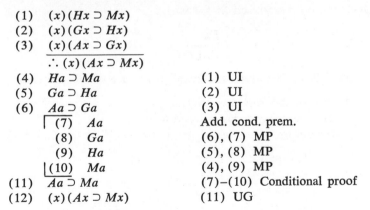

(1)	$(x)(Hx \supset Mx)$	
(2)	$(x)(Gx \supset Hx)$	
(3)	$(x)(Ax \supset Gx)$	
	$\therefore (x)(Ax \supset Mx)$	
(4)	$Ha \supset Ma$	(1) UI
(5)	$Ga \supset Ha$	(2) UI
(6)	$Aa \supset Ga$	(3) UI
(7)	Aa	Add. cond. prem.
(8)	Ga	(6), (7) MP
(9)	Ha	(5), (8) MP
(10)	Ma	(4), (9) MP
(11)	$Aa \supset Ma$	(7)–(10) Conditional proof
(12)	$(x)(Ax \supset Mx)$	(11) UG

A conditional proof is incorrect if UG is applied to a line exclusively dependent upon an assumed premise that has a constant (such as a) included as a part of the assumption. Consider, for example:

(4)	$Ha \supset Ma$	(1) UI
(5)	$Ga \supset Ha$	(2) UI
(6)	$Aa \supset Ga$	(3) UI
(7)	Ha	Add. cond. prem.
(8)	$Ha \supset Ga$	(4), (7) MP
(9)	$(x)(Hx \supset Gx)$	(8) UG (Incorrect)

---

[6] This erroneous application of UG is more obvious if the constants introduced by EI or by a name begin with a lower-case letter, such as m. Subsequent uses of UI can then use m or n rather than a or b if the latter refers to the same set of individuals. For example, step (3) would be "$Rm \cdot \sim Im$" and step (4) would be "$Wm \supset Im$."

(10) $Ha \supset (x)(Hx \supset Gx)$ (4)–(9) Cond. proof (Incorrect continuation)

(11) $(y)[Hy \supset (x)(Hx \supset Gx)]$ (10) UG (Incorrect continuation)

In this case a conditional proof is begun in line (7) and UG is incorrectly applied in line (9); lines (10) and (11) continue the error begun in line (9). However, if line (7) begins with the added conditional premise $(x)(Hx)$, lines (7) through (9) can be derived properly and UG can be used subsequently under the new assumption of step (7), if it is needed.

Principles applied in proofs using quantified statements can be summarized as follows:

1. The argument forms developed in propositional logic also are applicable in quantificational logic.

2. The principle of replacement holds that any two equivalent propositions may replace each other or any two equivalent quantified expressions may replace each other wherever they occur.

3. The principle of quantificational equivalence (QE) can be expressed by the following forms:

(a) $\sim(x)Fx \equiv (\exists x)\sim Fx.$

(b) $\sim(\exists x)Fx \equiv (x)\sim Fx.$

(c) $[(x)Fx \cdot (x)Gx] \equiv (x)(Fx \cdot Gx)$ [Section 15.10].

(d) $[(\exists x)Fx \lor (\exists x)Gx] \equiv (\exists x)(Fx \lor Gx)$ [Section 15.10].

4. The principles of instantiation and of generalization can be expressed by the following forms:

(a) Universal instantiation (UI):

$$(x)Fx$$
$$\overline{\therefore Fa}$$

(b) Existential instantiation (EI):

$$(\exists x)Fx$$
$$\overline{\therefore Fa}$$

The a cannot occur previously in the proof.

(c) Existential generalization (EG):

$$Fa$$
$$\overline{\therefore (\exists x)Fx}$$

The a must be introduced previously in the proof by EI or by a form derived by the use of EI (or by a nonfictitious name).

(d) Universal generalization (UG):

$$Fa$$
$$\overline{\therefore (x)Fx}$$

The a must not be introduced or derived previously in the proof by the use of EI and it must not be within the conditional part of a conditional (or *reductio*) proof having *a* as part of the added conditional premise.

The general restrictions placed on instantiation and generalization may be summarized as follows [see 4 above]:

1. The quantifier must govern the complete scope of the statement.
2. Steps taken in writing proofs cannot contain free variables (in this book).
3. Quantifiers covered by a sign of negation cannot be used in instantiation or generalization.
4. Substitutions in instantiations or generalizations in any given expression must include every occurrence of the relevant constant (such as *a*) and the relevant variable (such as *x*).
5. The values assigned in any complete expression to constants (such as *a* and *b*) and to variables (such as *x* and *y*) must remain uniform in successive applications of UI and EI or of EG and UG to that expression. [Within any complete expression a different constant is required for every different variable (such as *a* for *x* and *b* for *y*) in successive applications of EI or UI or of EG or UG. If a constant such as *a* is already within the scope of a quantifier, such as (x) or $(\exists x)$, then a second variable, such as *y*, must be used in any subsequent application of EG or UG to that constant.]

Two additional principles discussed in Section 15.10 are included here for convenient reference.

5. Principles of quantifier manipulation (QM):
   (a) $[(x)Fx \cdot P] \equiv (x)(Fx \cdot P)$.
   (b) $[(\exists x)Fx \cdot P] \equiv (\exists x)(Fx \cdot P)$.
   (c) $[(x)Fx \lor P] \equiv (x)(Fx \lor P)$.
   (d) $[(\exists x)Fx \lor P] \equiv (\exists x)(Fx \lor P)$.
   (e) $[P \supset (x)Fx] \equiv (x)(P \supset Fx)$.
   (f) $[P \supset (\exists v)Fx] \equiv (\exists x)(P \supset Fx)$.

P represents any expression that does not have *x* as a free variable or that does not have (x) or $(\exists x)$ as a quantifier. [It may have (y) or $(\exists y)$ as a quantifier with the above symbolization.]

6. Quantifier manipulation and principles of inference in special cases of disjunction, conjunction, and implication (QMI):

   (a) $\dfrac{(x)Fx \lor (x)Gx}{\therefore (x)(Fx \lor Gx)}$.

   (b) $\dfrac{(\exists x)(Fx \cdot Gx)}{\therefore (\exists x)Fx \cdot (\exists x)Gx}$.

   (c) $\dfrac{(x)(Fx \supset Gx)}{\therefore (x)Fx \supset (x)Gx}$.

(d) $\dfrac{(\exists x)Fx \supset (\exists x)Gx}{\therefore (\exists x)(Fx \supset Gx)}$.

(e) $\dfrac{(\exists x)Fx \supset P}{\therefore (x)(Fx \supset P)}$.

(f) $\dfrac{(\exists x)(Fx \supset P)}{\therefore (x)Fx \supset P}$.

15.5 EXERCISES

1. Complete the following proofs by making the proper notation for the justification of each step.

(a)
(1) $(x)(Fx \supset Gx)$
(2) $(x)(Gx \supset Hx)$
(3) $(x)(Hx \supset Ix)$
   $\therefore (x)(Fx \supset Ix)$
(4) $Fa \supset Ga$
(5) $Ga \supset Ha$
(6) $Ha \supset Ia$
(7) $Fa \supset Ha$
(8) $Fa \supset Ia$
(9) $(x)(Fx \supset Ix)$

(b)
(1) $\sim(x)\sim(Mx \cdot Nx)$
(2) $(x)(Mx \supset Px)$
(3) $(x)(Px \supset Rx)$
   $\therefore (\exists x)(Px \cdot Rx)$
(4) $\sim\sim(\exists x)\sim\sim(Mx \cdot Nx)$
(5) $(\exists x)\sim\sim(Mx \cdot Nx)$
(6) $(\exists x)(Mx \cdot Nx)$
(7) $Ma \cdot Na$
(8) $Ma \supset Pa$
(9) $Pa \supset Ra$
(10) Ma
(11) Pa
(12) Ra
(13) $Pa \cdot Ra$
(14) $(\exists x)(Px \cdot Rx)$

(c)
(1) $(\exists x)(Kx \cdot Mx)$
(2) $\sim(\exists x)(Kx \cdot \sim Lx)$
(3) $(x)[Lx \supset (Nx \supset Ox)]$
   $\therefore (\exists x)(Nx \cdot Ox)$
(4) $\sim\sim(x)\sim(Kx \cdot \sim Lx)$
(5) $(x)\sim(Kx \cdot \sim Lx)$[7]
(6) $(x)(Kx \supset Lx)$
(7) $Ka \cdot Ma$
(8) $Ka \supset La$
(9) $La \supset (Na \cdot Oa)$
(10) $Ka \supset (Na \cdot Oa)$
(11) Ka
(12) $Na \cdot Oa$
(13) $(\exists x)(Nx \cdot Ox)$

(d)
(1) $(x)[Rx \supset (Tx \vee Sx]$
(2) $(x)[Sx \supset (Ux \supset Wx)]$
(3) $(\exists x)(Rx \cdot \sim Tx)$
   $\therefore (\exists x)(Ux \supset Wx)$
(4) $Ra \cdot \sim Ta$
(5) $Ra \supset (Ta \vee Sa)$
(6) $Sa \supset (Ua \supset Wa)$
(7) Ra
(8) $Ta \vee Sa$
(9) $\sim Ta \cdot Ra$
(10) $\sim Ta$
(11) Sa
(12) $Ua \supset Wa$
(13) $(\exists x)(Ux \supset Wx)$

---

[7] After this technique of double negation has been mastered, steps like (4) can be eliminated and QE can be applied in the form of step (5). Thus step (4) above can be "$(x)\sim(Kx \cdot \sim Lx)$."

2. Write proofs for the following arguments. [Use a simplified form for symbolizing the subject term and predicate terms in problems (e) and (f). [For example,
write "$(x)(Tx \supset Lx)$" for the quantified form of the first premise in (f).]

(a) (1) $(\exists x)(Dx \cdot Cx)$
     (2) $(x)(Cx \supset Kx)$
          ∴ $(\exists x)(Kx \cdot Dx)$

(b) (1) $(x)(Lx \cdot Mx)$
     (2) $(x)(Nx \supset \sim Mx)$
     (3) $(x)[Nx \vee (Px \supset Qx)]$
          ∴ $(x)(Px \supset Qx)$

(c) (1) $(x)[Bx \supset (Cx \vee Dx)]$
     (2) $(\exists x)(\sim Cx \cdot \sim Dx)$
     (3) $(x)[Bx \vee (Jx \cdot Kx)]$
          ∴ $(\exists x)(Jx \cdot Kx)$

(d) (1) $\sim(x)\sim(Lx \cdot Mx)$
     (2) $(x)[Mx \supset (Nx \vee Px)]$
     (3) $(x)[\sim(\sim Nx \cdot \sim Px) \supset (Qx \cdot Rx)]$
          ∴ $(\exists x)(Qx \cdot Rx)$

(e) (1) All models are attractive. (M, A)
     (2) Some models are active in civil rights movements. (C)
     (3) All attractive persons are envied persons. (E)
          Therefore, some persons active in civil rights movements are envied
          persons.

(f) (1) Any actions increasing taxes are actions lowering purchasing
          power. (T, L)
     (2) Any actions lowering purchasing power are unpopular with voters.
          (U)
     (3) All actions unpopular with voters are actions threatening political
          careers. (P)
     (4) Some actions increasing taxes are a result of new demands for
          federal spending. (S)
          Therefore, some actions threatening political careers are a result
          of new demands for federal spending.

3. Write proofs for the valid categorical syllogisms in the exercises in Section 7.14.
Assume the simplicity of the subject term and of the predicate term of each
categorical proposition. [For example, $(x)(Mx \supset Px)$, $(\exists x)(Sx \cdot Mx)$ / ∴ $(\exists x)$
$(Sx \cdot Px)$.]

4. Write proofs for valid odd-lettered categorical syllogisms (a, c, e, . . .) in
Exercise 2, Section 8.6, and follow the instructions given in the immediately preceding case.

15.6 Proof of Invalidity

Invalidity is established in quantificational logic by the use of cross sections
of the truth tables. In proving an argument invalid in quantificational logic,

our aim is to establish truth values for the premises and the conclusion such that the premises can be true and the conclusion false. Use of the truth tables is more complex in quantificational logic than in propositional logic. Consider the following case, which is invalid according to the rules of the categorical syllogism (since the minor term is undistributed in the minor premise and is distributed in the conclusion):

> All problems are interesting.
> Some problems are easy.
> Therefore, all easy things are interesting.

$$(x)(Px \supset Ix)$$
$$(\exists x)(Px \cdot Ex)$$
$$\overline{\therefore (x)(Ex \supset Ix)}$$

The quantified expressions have to be replaced by (individual) constants, such as *a,* for checking on the truth table. If only one such constant is used, the results are as follows.

Values assigned if conclusion is false			$(x)(Px \supset Ix)$	$(\exists x)(Px \cdot Ex)$	/ $\therefore (x)(Ex \supset Ix)$
Pa	*Ia*	*Ea*	$Pa \supset Ia$	$Pa \cdot Ea$	$Ea \supset Ia$
F	F	T	F F	F T	T F
			T	F	F
T	F	T	T F	T T	T F
			F	T	F

For the argument to be invalid an instance must be established so that the conclusion, *Ea* $\supset$ *Ia,* is false and the premises are true. The conclusion is false only if *Ea* is true and *Ia* is false. However, if *Ia* is false in the conclusion, it also is false in the premise *Pa* $\supset$ *Ia.* If *Ia* is false, *Pa* must be false for the premise *Pa* $\supset$ *Ia* to be true. If *Pa* is false, the premise *Pa* $\cdot$ *Ea* must be false. Thus, no set of truth values can be assigned here where the premises are true and the conclusion is false.

Is the argument valid? It would be valid for a universe of only one member, but the original argument was not restricted to one member.

A universe of more than one member also must be tested. Since a universally quantified expression obviously includes all cases to which it is applicable, the expression $(x)(Px \supset Ix)$ in the premise includes not only the instance of *Pa* $\supset$ *Ia* but the conjunction of all other cases to which it is applicable. Thus, it includes *Pa* $\supset$ *In and Pb* $\supset$ *Ib and Pc* $\supset$ *Ic and . . . and Pn* $\supset$ *In.* It is also possible for the original universally quantified expression, $(x)(Px \supset Ix)$, to be empty. In such case it would have no substitution instances, so that $(x)(Px \supset Ix)$ can be true, and *Pa* $\supset$ *Ia* would be misleading.

Since an existentially quantified expression holds that there is at least one instance to which it is applicable, it includes the disjunction of its substitution instances. In the case of the premise $(\exists x)(Px \cdot Ex)$ its substitution instances include $Pa \cdot Ea$ or $Pb \cdot Eb$, or . . . or $Pn \cdot En$.

In a universe of at least two members a cross section of the truth table provides the following analysis for the previous argument.

Values assigned if conclusion is false Pa Pb Ia Ib Ea Eb	$(x)(Px \supset Ix)$ $(Pa \supset Ia) \cdot (Pb \supset Ib)$	$(\exists x)(Px \cdot Ex)$ $(Pa \cdot Ea) \vee (Pb \cdot Eb)$	$/\therefore (x)(Ex \supset Ix)$ $(Ea \supset Ia) \cdot (Eb \supset Ib)$
(1) T F T T	T F	T T	T T T F
(2) T F	T F	T F	
(3) T F T F T T	T T F F	T T F T	
(4)	T T	T F	T F
(5)	T	T	F

Line (1) shows truth values that hold if the premises are true and the conclusion is false. Line (2) shows values that can be assigned to other instances appearing in the premises so that each premise is true. Line (3) combines the truth values assigned in lines (1) and (2). Line (4) determines the truth values to be assigned to the conjuncts or disjuncts used for substitution cases of the original quantified expressions in the premises and the conclusion. Line (5) assigns the truth values of substitution instances of the premises and the conclusion. Line (5) also shows that given the original truth values noted in line (3), the premises in this case in a universe of two members can be true and the conclusion can be false. This demonstration establishes the invalidity of this argument for a universe of at least two members. After one has gained some experience, the procedure can be shortened to lines (3), (4), and (5).

In proving the invalidity of an argument in quantificational logic it is essential to test for a universe of at least two members if the test in a universe of only one member does not prove fruitful.

Testing for invalidity of premises that do not have substitution instances (that is, for null premises) requires a test for a universe without members. If a universe has no members, then the value of true can be assigned on a cross section of the truth table to the universally quantified expression and the value of false to an existentially quantified expression.

Consider the following argument:

All mischievous things are noisy (things).
All poltergeists are mischievous (things).
Therefore, if something is a poltergeist, then it is noisy.

$$(x)(Mx \supset Nx)$$
$$(x)(Px \supset Mx)$$
$$\therefore (\exists x)(Px \supset Nx)$$

This argument would be valid in a universe of one or more members. The following test shows that for a universe of no members the argument is invalid.

$$(x)(Mx \supset Nx) \qquad (x)(Px \supset Mx) \qquad (\exists x)(Px \supset Nx)$$
$$\text{T} \qquad\qquad\qquad \text{T} \qquad\qquad\qquad \text{F}$$

Since there are no proper substitution cases in a universe of no members, we can assign the quantified expressions truth values without using substitution instances such as $Ma \supset Na$, $Pa \supset Ma$, and $Pa \supset Na$.

In testing for null classes as well as in writing proofs, one should remove by proper procedures any negative signs flanking the quantifier. (We can remove the negative sign before the quantifier by finding the quantification equivalence.) For example,

$$\sim(x)(Lx \supset Mx) \equiv (\exists x)\sim(Lx \supset Mx)$$

The negative sign after the quantifier can be removed by the use of De Morgan's law. For example,

$$(\exists x)\sim(Lx \supset Mx) \equiv (\exists x)(Lx \cdot \sim Mx) \qquad \text{(DeM \& MI)}$$

15.7 EXERCISES

1. Determine the validity or invalidity of the following arguments. Write proofs in each case.

(a) $(x)(Mx \supset Nx)$
$(x)(Nx \supset Px)$
$\therefore (x)(Px \supset Mx)$

(b) $(x)(Px \supset Qx)$
$(\exists x)(Px \cdot Rx)$
$\therefore (\exists x)(Rx \cdot Qx)$

(c) $(x)(Px \supset Qx)$
$(x)(Rx \supset Qx)$
$\therefore (x)(Px \supset Rx)$

(d) $(\exists x)(Kx \cdot Lx)$
$(x)(Lx \supset Mx)$
$(x)(Kx \supset Nx)$
$\therefore (\exists x)(Mx \cdot Nx)$

(e) $\sim(x)(Kx \supset Lx)$
$(x)(Lx \supset Mx)$
$\therefore (x)(Kx \supset \sim Mx)$

(f) $(x)(Gx \supset Hx)$
$(\exists x)(Gx \cdot Ix)$
$(x)[(Ix \cdot Hx) \supset (Kx \cdot Lx)]$
$\therefore (\exists x)(Kx \cdot Lx)$

(g) $(x)(Mx \supset Nx)$
$(x)(Nx \supset Ox)$
$(x)(Px \supset Ox)$
$(\exists x)(Mx \cdot Rx)$
$\therefore (\exists x)(Px \cdot Rx)$

(h) All players are strong (P, S) All players are athletes. (A) Therefore, all athletes are strong.

(i) All reviews are brief. (R, B) All brief things are readable. (E) Some readable things are boresome. (O) Therefore, some reviews are boresome.

(j) All Egyptians are Arabs. (*E*, *A*) Some Moslems are Egyptians. (*M*) Therefore, all Moslems are Arabs.

(k) All sailors are travelers. (*S, T*) All travelers are knowledgeable. (*K*) All knowledgeable persons are broadminded. (*B*) Therefore, all sailors are broadminded.

2. In the following cases assume the simplicity of the subject term and of the predicate term in each proposition.

(a) Write proofs showing validity or invalidity of the even-lettered syllogisms, [(b), (d), (f), and so on] in Exercises 2 of Sections 8.6 and 9.11.

(b) Write proofs of validity or invalidity for sorites (a), (c), and (e) in Exercise 1 of Section 10.5.

15.8 Complex and Relational Arguments

Many of the examples we have given of the validation of arguments by quantificational logic make use of categorical propositions. Quantificational logic also makes possible the validation of more complex arguments. The rules given in this chapter for the use of quantificational logic can be applied reliably to many complex arguments, although some will require more precisely formulated rules than those given here. In every case the proper rendering of the original premises in accurate symbolic form is essential to a satisfactory validation of the argument. The following illustrations, involving more complex forms and validation procedures, should suggest the flexibility of quantificational logic in dealing with different kinds of statements.

The first example contains a premise that begins like a categorical proposition but has a conjunction uniting two terms in the predicate. It also has three premises and in this regard resembles a sorites.

1. All vacations are diversions and relaxing.
   All relaxing things are beneficial.
   Some vacations are expensive.
   Therefore, some diversions are beneficial.

(1)	$(x)[Vx \supset (Dx \cdot Rx)]$		
(2)	$(x)(Rx \supset Bx)$		
(3)	$(\exists x)(Vx \cdot Ex)$		
	$\therefore (\exists x)(Dx \cdot Bx)$		
(4)	$Va \cdot Ea$	(3)	EI
(5)	$Va \supset (Da \cdot Ra)$	(1)	UI
(6)	$Ra \supset Ba$	(2)	UI
(7)	Va	(4)	Simp.
(8)	$Da \cdot Ra$	(5), (7)	MP
(9)	Da	(8)	Simp.
(10)	$Ra \cdot Da$	(8)	Comm.
(11)	Ra	(10)	Simp.
(12)	Ba	(6), (11)	MP
(13)	$Da \cdot Ba$	(9), (12)	Conj.
(14)	$(\exists x)(Dx \cdot Bx)$	(13)	EG

2. Either John wins or Larry wins.
   Everyone who wins is lucky.
   Therefore, either John is lucky or Larry is lucky.

   (1) $Wj \lor Wl$
   (2) $(x)(Wx \supset Lx)$
   _____
   $\therefore Lj \lor Ll$

   (3) $Wj \supset Lj$ (2) UI
   (4) $Wl \supset Ll$ (2) UI
   (5) $(Wj \supset Lj) \cdot (Wl \supset Ll)$ (3), (4) Conj.
   (6) $Lj \lor Ll$ (5), (1) CCD

3. Anyone who used the lost credit card will be discovered by
   some officer.
   There is someone who used the lost credit card and who is
   culpable.
   Therefore, there is someone who is culpable and who will be
   discovered by some officer.

   (1) $(x)[Ux \supset (\exists y)(Oy \cdot Dxy)]$
   (2) $(\exists x)(Ux \cdot Cx)$
   _____
   $\therefore (\exists x)[Cx \cdot (\exists y)(Oy \cdot Dxy)]$

   (3) $Ua \cdot Ca$ (2) EI
   (4) $Ua \supset (\exists y)(Oy \cdot Day)$ (1) UI
   (5) Ua (3) Simp.
   (6) $(\exists y)(Oy \cdot Day)$ (4), (5) MP
   (7) $Ca \cdot Ua$ (3) Comm.
   (8) Ca (7) Simp.
   (9) $Ca \cdot (\exists y)(Oy \cdot Day)$ (8), (6) Conj.
   (10) $(\exists x)[(Cx) \cdot (\exists y)(Oy \cdot Dxy)]$ (9) EG

In the next example a suppressed premise must be added.

4. John is stronger than Eddie.
   Eddie is stronger than Bill.
   Therefore, John is stronger than Bill.

If only the stated premises and the conclusion are given, then formal
proof of the argument is not possible. The relation "is stronger than" is a
transitive relation and the assumed premise indicating this relation needs to
be stated.

   If John is stronger than Eddie, and Eddie is stronger than Bill,
   then John is stronger than Bill.

   (1) Sje
   (2) Seb
   (3) $(Sje \cdot Seb) \supset Sjb$
   _____
   $\therefore Sjb$

   (4) $Sje \cdot Seb$ (1), (2) Conj.
   (5) Sjb (3), (4) MP

The next example also contains a suppressed premise.

5. All Europeans are more talkative than Scotchmen.
   Therefore, all Frenchmen are more talkative than Scotchmen.
   (Suppressed premise—All Frenchmen are Europeans.)

(1)	$(x)[Ex \supset (y)(Sy \supset Txy)]$	
(2)	$(x)(Fx \supset Ex)$	
	$\therefore (x)[Fx \supset (y)(Sy \supset Txy)]$	
(4)	$Fa \supset Ea$	(2) UI
(5)	$Ea \supset (y)(Sy \supset Tay)$	(1) UI
(6)	$Fa \supset (y)(Sy \supset Tay)$	(4), (5) HS
(7)	$(x)[(Fx \supset (y)(Sy \supset Txy)]$	(6) UG

15.9 EXERCISES

1. Prove the validity or invalidity of the following arguments.

   (a) (1) $(x)[Ax \supset (Bx \cdot Cx)]$
       (2) $(x)[(Bx \cdot Cx) \supset Dx]$
       $\therefore (x)(\sim Ax \supset \sim Dx)$

   (b) (1) $(\exists x)(Dx \cdot \sim Ex)$
       (2) $(x)(Fx \supset Ex)$
       $\therefore (\exists x)(Dx \cdot \sim Fx)$

   (c) (1) $(x)(Hx \supset Ix)$
       (2) $(x)(Ix \supset Jx)$
       (3) $(x)(Jx \supset Kx)$
       $\therefore (\exists x)(\sim Kx \supset \sim Hx)$

   (d) (1) $(x)[Ax \supset (Bx \vee Cx)]$
       (2) $(x)[\sim (Bx \vee Cx) \vee (y)Dyx]$
       $\therefore (x)[Ax \supset (y)Dyx]$

   (e) (1) $(x)[Ox \supset (y)(Fxy \supset Sxy)]$
       (2) $(x)[Ox \cdot (y)Fxy]$
       (3) $(x)(y)[Sxy \supset (\exists z)Rxyz]$
       $\therefore (x)(y)(\exists z)Rxyz$

   (f) (1) $(x)[Ax \cdot Bx) \supset (Cx \cdot Dx)]$
       (2) $(\exists x)[(\sim Dx \vee Ex) \cdot \sim Ex]$
       $\therefore (\exists x)(\sim Ax \vee \sim Bx)$

   (g) (1) $(x)[Ax \supset (\exists y)Txy]$
       (2) $(x)(Bx \supset Ax)$
       (3) $(x)Bx$
       $\therefore (x)(\exists y)Txy$

2. Determine the validity of the following arguments by proofs and supply suppressed premises where necessary.

(a) Any primary sources are better than any secondary sources. (P, B, S) All eyewitnesses are primary sources. (E) Therefore, all eyewitnesses are better than secondary sources.

(b) Anyone buying the stock is either uninformed or incautious. (B, U, I) There is someone who is buying the stock and who is unable to suffer losses. (S) Therefore, there is someone who is unable to suffer losses and who is uninformed.

(c) Some problems are easy. Some problems are not interesting. Therefore, some easy things are not interesting. (P, E, I)

(d) Any Cadillac is faster than a Volkswagen. (C, V) Any Volkswagen is faster than a carriage. (F, R) Therefore any Cadillac is faster than a carriage.

(e) Any furniture in this room is clean. (F, C) Therefore, any chairs or tables in this room are clean. (H, T)

(f) Any violence is either dangerous or foolhardy. (V, D, F) Anything that is either dangerous or foolhardy is risky. (R) Anything that is risky is not safe. (S) Anything that is not safe is not advisable. (A) Therefore, no violence is advisable.

(g) Meaninglessness is boredom. (M, B) Boredom is frustration. (F) Frustration is despair. (D) Despair is anxiety. (A) Therefore, meaninglessness is anxiety.

(h) John is a physicist. (P) Some physicists are mathematicians. (M) All physicists are scientists. (S) Therefore John is a scientist and John is a mathematician.

(i) Either George drives or James drives. (D) Anyone who drives is licensed. (L) Anyone who is licensed is not inexperienced. (I) If James is not inexperienced, then George does not drive. James drives. Therefore, George does not drive.

3. In the following cases assume the simplicity of the subject terms and of the predicate term in each of the categorical propositions.

(a) Write proofs of validity or of invalidity for the odd-lettered syllogisms [(a), (c), (e), and so on] in Exercise 2 of Section 9.11.

(b) Write proofs of validity or of invalidity for sorites (b), (d), and (f) in Exercise 1 of Section 10.5.

(c) Determine the conclusion and write proofs of the validity or invalidity of the sorites in Exercise 2 of Section 10.5.

15.10 Additional Equivalences and Argument Forms

A restriction placed upon the use of the principles of instantiation (UI and EI) requires that a quantifier, such as (x) or $(\exists x)$, govern the complete expression. If expressions such as $(\exists x)Fx \lor (\exists x)Gx$ or $(x)Fx \cdot (x)Gx$ occur as premises or as steps in a proof, instantiation can be applied only if some means is found to extend the quantifier to govern the complete expression. In the case of the two expressions above additional quantificational equivalences (QE) can be provided as follows:

$$(1)\ [(x)Fx \cdot (x)Gx] \equiv (x)(Fx \cdot Gx)$$
$$(2)\ [(\exists x)Fx \lor (\exists x)Gx] \equiv (\exists x)(Fx \lor Gx)$$

These equivalences can be illustrated by reference to cross sections of the truth table.

	I		II			
(1)	$(x)Fx \cdot (x)Gx$		$(x)(Fx \cdot Gx)$			
(2)	$(Fa \cdot Fb \cdot \ldots \cdot Fn) \cdot (Ga \cdot Gb \cdot \ldots \cdot Gn)$		$(Fa \cdot Ga) \cdot (Fb \cdot Gb) \cdot (Fc \cdot Gc) \cdot \ldots \cdot (Fn \cdot Gn)$			
(3)			T	T	T	T
(4)	T	T				
(5)		T			T	

Column I represents the breaking down of truth values of substitution instances of $(x)Fx \cdot (x)Gx$, and column II represents a breaking down of truth values of substitution instances of $(x)(Fx \cdot Gx)$. In line (2), column I lists possible substitution instances of $(x)Fx \cdot (x)Gx$. In line (2), column II lists possible substitution instances of $(x)(Fx \cdot Gx)$. Line (3) shows that each substitution instance of $(x)(Fx \cdot Gx)$ must be assigned the value of T if $(x)(Fx \cdot Gx)$ is true as indicated in line (5). Likewise, line (4) shows the truth values that must hold for line (2) if the value of all substitution instances for $(x)Fx \cdot (x)Gx$ is true. All cases in which the series of substitution instances in line (2) yield a value of T for $(x)Fx \cdot (x)Gx$ also hold for $(x)(Fx \cdot Gx)$ and vice versa. If any substitution instance of $(x)Fx \cdot (x)Gx$ is false, then one of the conjuncts will be false in column I, and the use of this substitution instance in column II would be false. By similar analysis it can be seen that if an instance of false occurs in column II, then the same line in column I is false.

	I		II	
(1)	$(x)Fx \cdot (x)Gx$		$(x)(Fx \cdot Gx)$	
(2)	$(Fa \cdot Fb \cdot \ldots \cdot Fn) \cdot (Ga \cdot Gb \cdot \ldots \cdot Gn)$		$(Fa \cdot Ga) \cdot (Fb \cdot Gb) \cdot (Fc \cdot Gc) \cdot \ldots \cdot (Fn \cdot Gn)$	
(6)	F		F	
(7)		F		F

This illustrates the equivalence of $(x)Fx \cdot (x)Gx$ and $(x)(Fx \cdot Gx)$, since in every case in which one form is true the other is true and in every case in which one is false the other is false.

In subsequent examples we shall appeal to this type of illustrative use of cross sections of the truth table.

Consider the equivalent forms $(\exists x)Fx \vee (\exists x)Gx$ and $(\exists x)(Fx \vee Gx)$.

	I		II	
(1)	$(\exists x)Fx \vee (\exists x)Gx$		$(\exists x)(Fx \vee Gx)$	
(2)	$(Fa \vee Fb \vee \ldots \vee Fn) \vee (Ga \vee Gb \vee \ldots \vee Gn)$		$(Fa \vee Ga) \vee (Fb \vee Gb) \vee \ldots \vee (Fn \vee Gn)$	
(3)		T		T
(4)	T		T	

If any substitution instance in column I is true, then $(\exists x)Fx \vee (\exists x)Gx$ is true. The same substitution instance would be true in column II, and $(\exists x)(Fx \vee Gx)$ would be true. The same values hold if the analysis begins with column II. In all instances in which one of the forms is true the other is true.

If all disjuncts in the substitution instances of $(\exists x)Fx \lor (\exists x)Gx$ are false, then all substitution instances in $(\exists x)(Fx \lor Gx)$ also are false. In every case if either expression has the value of false, the other also has the value of false. Since the truth values of the expressions are the same, the following equivalence holds:

$$[(\exists x)Fx \lor (\exists x)Gx] \equiv (\exists x)(Fx \lor Gx)$$

In some cases there is need to manipulate a quantifier that covers only a part of an expression so that the quantifier covers the whole expression. For example, to apply UI in the case of $(x)Fx \cdot P$ we must find some means of manipulating the quantifier (x) to govern the range of the complete expression.

In our example, P refers to any expression that either does not contain a repetition of the original quantifier such as (x) or does not contain x as a free variable. The notation Fx in the form $(x)Fx \cdot P$ continues to refer to an expression governed by a quantifier. Consider the statement, "Either some scout is mistaken or some opponents are alert." This may be symbolized

$$(\exists x)(Sx \cdot Mx) \lor (\exists y)(Oy \cdot Ay)$$

In reference to the present discussion it is symbolized by the form

$$(\exists x)Fx \lor P$$

$(\exists x)Fx$ would refer to an expression such as $(\exists x)(Sx \cdot Mx)$, and P would refer to an expression such as $(\exists y)(Oy \cdot Ay)$.

The following equivalences hold in quantifier manipulation (QM).

	I		II
(1)	$[(x)Fx \cdot P] \equiv (x)(Fx \cdot P)$		$[P \cdot (x)Fx] \equiv (x)(P \cdot Fx)$
(2)	$[(\exists x)Fx \cdot P] \equiv \exists x(Fx \cdot P)$		$[P \cdot (\exists x)Fx] \equiv (\exists x)(P \cdot Fx)$
(3)	$[(x)Fx \lor P] \equiv (x)(Fx \lor P)$		$[P \lor (x)Fx] \equiv (x)(P \lor Fx)$
(4)	$[(\exists x)Fx \lor P] \equiv (\exists x)(Fx \lor P)$		$[P \lor (\exists x)Fx] \equiv (\exists x)(P \lor Fx)$
(5)	$[P \supset (x)Fx] \equiv (x)(P \supset Fx)$		
(6)	$[P \supset (\exists x)Fx] \equiv (\exists x)(P \supset Fx)$		

In the cases above any equivalent form may replace another in a proof with the designation of the step as QM. Column II can be derived from column I by commutation and is listed only for convenience.

A cross section of a truth table can help to illustrate why the equivalent forms above hold. Consider the following cases.

	I			II		
(1)	$(\exists x)Fx \cdot P$			$(\exists x)(Fx \cdot P)$		
(2)	$(Fa \lor Fb \lor \ldots \lor Fn) \cdot P$			$(Fa \cdot P) \lor (Fb \cdot P) \lor \ldots \lor (Fn \cdot P)$		
(3)			T	T	T	T
(4)	T				T	
(5)		T				T

Line (3) shows that P must be true as a condition for any complete series of forms in line (1) to be true. If any substitution instance of Fx (such as Fb)

holds in column I it also must hold in column II, and if such a substitution instance holds in column II it also must hold in column I. In any case in which a substitution instance of Fx in column I is true and P is true a corresponding substitution instance will hold in column II. This also will hold by beginning with column II.

If $(\exists x)Fx \cdot P$ is false, then $(\exists x)(Fx \cdot P)$ also is false and vice versa. We can show this by extending the previous cross section.

	I			II		
(2)	$(Fa \lor Fb \lor \ldots \lor Fn) \cdot P$			$(Fa \cdot P) \lor (Fb \cdot P) \lor \ldots \lor (Fn \cdot P)$		
(6)		F		F	F	F
(7)	F F	F		F	F	F

If P is false [line (6)], then the truth value for any expression symbolized by line (2) is false. If every substitution instance of $(\exists x)Fx$ is false [line (7)], then any expression symbolized by line (2) is false. In all cases where one of the complete forms in line (2) is false the other also must be false. Thus, the two forms $(\exists x)Fx \cdot P$ and $(\exists x)(Fx \cdot P)$ have identical truth values. And they are equivalent.

Comparable illustrations for the other equivalences can be given and the student can work these out for himself.

Similar analyses show that other argument forms can be used in quantificational logic. These valid argument forms can be called *quantifier manipulation and principles of inference in special cases of disjunction, conjunction, and implication (QMI)*. They are logical truths based on such forms as $[(x)Fx \lor (x)Gx] \supset (x)(Fx \lor Gx)$ and $[(\exists x)Fx \supset P] \supset (x)(Fx \supset P)$. These inferences can be justified by an analysis of a cross section of a truth table. (The student can do this for himself.)[8] Truth values cannot be assigned to substitution instances of these forms so that the consequent (the conclusion in the following cases) is false and the antecedent (the initial form) is true.[9]

These principles of inference of QMI are expressed as follows:

(1) $(x)Fx \lor (x)Gx$ (2) $(\exists x)(Fx \cdot Gx)$
    $\therefore (x)(Fx \lor Gx)$ $\therefore (\exists x)Fx \cdot (\exists x)Gx$

---

[8] A quantifier such as (x) is written as a quantifier of a complete statement using as major connectives expressions such as "if . . . then . . . ," "either . . . or . . . ," "and," "not both . . . and . . ." only if the quantifier has a substitution instance in each principal part of the expression. For example, the expression "If all teachers are scholars, then all teachers are researchers" can be written "$(x)[(Tx \supset Sx) \supset (Tx \supset Rx)]$." The expression "If all teachers are scholars, then all (graduate) students are researchers" is written "$(x)(Tx \supset Sx) \supset (y)(Gy \supset Ry)$."

[9] The forms, $(x)(Fx \lor Gx), /\therefore (x)Fx \lor (x)Gx$ and $(\exists x)Fx \cdot (\exists x)Gx, /\therefore (\exists x)(Fx \cdot Gx)$ are not accepted as holding. Rejection of these forms has an intuitive basis. If it is true that "everything is either organic or inorganic," it can be false that "everything is organic or everything is inorganic." The former permits some things to be organic and other things to be inorganic. The latter requires that everything be only one of these. If it is true that "some things are organic and some things are inorganic," it can be false that "some organic things are inorganic." Thus, the forms $(x)(Fx \lor Gx) \supset [(x)Fx \lor (x)Gx]$ and $[(\exists x)Fx \cdot (\exists x)Gx] \supset (\exists x)(Fx \cdot Gx)$ are *not* accepted for justifying QMI steps in proofs.

(3) $(x)(Fx \supset Gx)$
$\overline{\therefore (x)Fx \supset (x)Gx}$

(4) $(\exists x)Fx \supset (\exists x)Gx$
$\overline{\therefore (\exists x)(Fx \supset Gx)}$

(5) $(\exists x)Fx \supset P$
$\overline{\therefore (x)(Fx \supset P)}$

(6) $(\exists x)(Fx \supset P)$
$\overline{\therefore (x)Fx \supset P}$

They can be used in proofs like basic argument forms in quantificational logic, and their use is accompanied by the notation QMI. They are not to be confused with the use of QE in the forms discussed earlier in this section:

$$[(\exists x)Fx \vee (\exists x)Gx] \equiv (\exists x)(Fx \vee Gx)$$
$$[(x)Fx \cdot (x)Gx] \equiv (x)(Fx \cdot Gx)$$

The examples that follow illustrate the use of some of the equivalences and argument forms discussed in this section. Alternative ways of writing these proofs can be followed.

EXAMPLE 1

(1)	$(x)Mx \cdot (x)Nx$	
(2)	$(x)(Mx \cdot Nx) \supset (y)(Oy \supset Py)$	
	$\overline{\therefore (y)(Oy \supset Py)}$	
(3)	$(x)(Mx \cdot Nx)$	(1) QE
(4)	$(y)(Oy \supset Py)$	(2), (3) MP

EXAMPLE 2

(1)	$(\exists x)Lx \vee (\exists x)Mx$	
(2)	$(\exists x)(Lx \vee Mx) \supset (y)(Ny \supset Oy)$	
(3)	$(y)(Ny \supset Oy) \supset [(z)Pz \cdot (z)Qz]$	
	$\overline{\therefore (z)(Pz \cdot Qz)}$	
(4)	$(\exists x)(Lx \vee Mx)$	(1) QE
(5)	$(y)(Ny \supset Oy)$	(2), (4) MP
(6)	$(z)Pz \cdot (z)Qz$	(3), (5) MP
(7)	$(z)(Pz \cdot Qz)$	(6) QE

EXAMPLE 3

(1)	$(x)Kx \vee (x)Lx$	
(2)	$(x)(Kx \vee Lx) \supset (\exists y)(My \cdot Ny)$	
	$\overline{\therefore (\exists y)My \cdot (\exists y)Ny}$	
(3)	$(x)(Kx \vee Lx)$	(1) QMI
(4)	$(\exists y)(My \cdot Ny)$	(2), (3) MP
(5)	$(\exists y)My \cdot (\exists y)Ny$	(4) QMI

EXAMPLE 4

(1)	$(x)(Hx \supset Ix)$	
(2)	$(x)(Ix \supset Kx)$	
(3)	$(x)(Hx \supset Kx) \supset [(\exists y)Ly \vee (z)(Mz \supset Nz)]$	
	$\overline{\therefore (\exists y)Ly \vee (z)(Mz \supset Nz)}$	
(4)	$Ha \supset Ia$	(1) UI
(5)	$Ia \supset Ka$	(2) UI
(6)	$Ha \supset Ka$	(4), (5) HS

(7) $(x)(Hx \supset Kx)$	(6) UG
(8) $(\exists y)Ly \vee (z)(Mx \supset Nx)$	(3), (7) MP

EXAMPLE 5

If some pass receiver fumbles, then all the opposition players are motivated.

If all the opposition players are motivated, then the opposition players are difficult to beat.

Therefore, if some pass receiver fumbles, then the opposition players are difficult to beat.

(1)	$(\exists x)(Px \cdot Fx) \supset (y)(Oy \supset My)$	
(2)	$(y)[(Oy \supset My) \supset (Oy \supset By)]$	
	$\therefore (\exists x)(Px \cdot Fx) \supset (y)(Oy \supset By)$	
(3)	$(y)[(\exists x)(Px \cdot Fx) \supset (Oy \supset My)]$	(1) QM
(4)	$(\exists x)(Px \cdot Fx) \supset (Oa \supset Ma)$	(3) UI
(5)	$(Oa \supset Ma) \supset (Oa \supset Ba)$	(2) UI
(6)	$(\exists x)(Px \cdot Fx) \supset (Oa \supset Ba)$	(4), (5) HS
(7)	$(y)[(\exists x)(Px \cdot Fx) \supset (Oy \supset By)]$	(6) UG
(8)	$(\exists x)(Px \cdot Fx) \supset (y)(Oy \supset By)$	(7) QM

EXAMPLE 6

Every diplomat is trained and cautious.

If every diplomat is trained and cautious, then all negotiations are difficult.

If all negotiations are difficult, then some progress is slow.

Therefore, it is false that no progress is slow.

(1)	$(x)[Dx \supset (Tx \cdot Cx)]$	
(2)	$(x)[Dx \supset (Tx \cdot Cx)] \supset (y)(Ny \supset Fy)$	
(3)	$(y)(Ny \supset Fy) \supset (\exists z)(Pz \cdot Sz)$	
	$\therefore \sim(z)(Pz \supset \sim Sz)$	
(4)	$(y)(Ny \supset Fy)$	(2), (1) MP
(5)	$(\exists z)(Pz \cdot Sz)$	(3), (4) MP
(6)	$\sim(z)\sim(Pz \cdot Sz)$	(5) QE
(7)	$\sim(z)(Pz \supset \sim Sz)$	(6) DeM & MI

EXAMPLE 7

It is not the case both that some drugs are dangerous and that some prescriptions are not risks.[10]

If all prescriptions are risks, then some regulations are needed.

---

[10] Expressions such as "it is not the case both that . . . and that . . . ," "it is false both that . . . and that . . . ," and "not both . . . and . . ." require the negation of the complete expression as in the symbolization above if no quantifier governs the complete expression. If a quantifier governs the complete expression, then a sign of negation can be placed immediately before the quantifier. The expression "It is false both that all students are wealthy and that no students are secure" can be written "$\sim(x)[(Sx \supset Wx) \cdot (Sx \supset \sim Cx)]$." The expression "It is false both that all students are wealthy and that all teachers are underpaid" can be written "$\sim[(x)(Sx \supset Wx) \cdot (y)(Ty \supset Uy)]$."

Therefore, if some drugs are dangerous, some regulations are needed.

(1) $\sim[(\exists x)(Dx \cdot Gx) \cdot (\exists y)(Py \cdot \sim Ry)]$
(2) $(y)(Py \supset Ry) \supset (\exists z)(Rz \cdot Nz)$
$\therefore (\exists x)(Dx \cdot Gx) \supset (\exists z)(Rz \cdot Nz)$

(3) $(\exists x)(Dx \cdot Gx) \supset \sim(\exists y)(Py \cdot \sim Ry)$ (1) DeM & MI
(4) $(\exists x)(Dx \cdot Gx) \supset (y)\sim(Py \cdot \sim Ry)$ (3) QE
(5) $(\exists x)(Dx \cdot Gx) \supset (y)(Py \supset Ry)$ (4) DeM & MI
(6) $(\exists x)(Dx \cdot Gx) \supset (\exists z)(Rz \cdot Nz)$ (5), (2) HS

EXAMPLE 8

If some workers are unemployed, then any new industry is helpful in strengthening the economy.

Therefore, if some new industries are not helpful in strengthening the economy, no workers are unemployed.

(1) $(\exists x)(Wx \cdot Ux) \supset (y)(Iy \supset Hy)$
$\therefore (\exists y)(Iy \cdot \sim Hy) \supset (x)(Wx \supset \sim Ux)$

(2) $\sim(y)(Iy \supset Hy) \supset \sim(\exists x)(Wx \cdot Ux)$ (1) Contrap.
(3) $(\exists y)\sim(Iy \supset Hy) \supset \sim(\exists x)(Wx \cdot Ux)$ (2) QM
(4) $(\exists y)(Iy \cdot \sim Hy) \supset \sim(\exists x)(Wx \cdot Ux)$ (3) DeM & MI
(5) $(\exists y)(Iy \cdot \sim Hy) \supset (x)\sim(Wx \cdot Ux)$ (4) QM
(6) $(\exists y)(Iy \cdot \sim Hy) \supset (x)(Wx \supset \sim Ux)$ (5) DeM & MI

15.11 EXERCISES

Prove the validity or invalidity of the following arguments.

1. (1) $(x)(Kx) \cdot (x)Lx$
   (2) $(x)(Kx \cdot Lx) \supset (\exists y)(My \cdot Ny)$
   $\therefore (\exists y)(My \cdot Ny)$

2. (1) $(\exists x)(Mx \cdot Nx) \supset (\exists y)(Ry \cdot Sy)$
   (2) $(x)(Ox \supset Px) \supset (Mx \cdot Nx)$
   (3) $(x)(Ox \supset Px)$
   $\therefore (\exists y)Ry \cdot \exists y(Sy)$

3. (1) $(\exists y)(Ny \supset Ry) \supset [(x)Lx \vee (x)Mx]$
   (2) $(\exists y)(Ny \supset Ry)$
   $\therefore (x)(Lx \vee Mx)$

4. (1) $(x)[(Ax \supset Bx) \cdot (Cx \supset Dx)]$
   (2) $(x)(Ax \vee Cx)$
   (3) $(\exists x)(Bx \vee Dx) \supset (\exists y)(Hy \cdot Iy)$
   $\therefore (\exists y)(Hy \cdot Iy)$

5. (1) $(x)[(Bx \vee Dx) \cdot (Ex \vee Fx)]$
   (2) $(x)(Gx \supset Hx) \supset [(x)\sim Bx \cdot (x)\sim Ex]$
   (3) $(x)(\sim Gx \vee Hx)$
   $\therefore (x)(Dx \vee Fx)$

6. (1) $(x)(Lx \supset Mx) \lor (y)(Ny \supset Oy)$
 (2) $\sim(y)(Ny \supset Oy) \lor (z)(Pz \supset Qz)$
 (3) $(\exists z)(Pz \cdot \sim Qz)$
 _____
 $\therefore (x)(Lx \supset Mx)$

7. Either some student is late or some student is absent. If all the students are well, then no student is absent. Therefore, if all the students are well, then some student is late. (S, L, A, W)

8. Either some operations are risks or some reports are exaggerated. (O, R, P, E) If some reports are exaggerated, then every (news) release is questionable. (N, Q) Therefore, if no operations are risks, then every (news) release is questionable.

9. If every bird watcher is a conservationist, then some forests are protected. (W, C, F, P) If it is false that no forests are protected, then some game laws are respected. $(L. R)$ Therefore, if every bird watcher is a conservationist, then it is false that no game laws are respected.

10. Either some bird watchers are not conservationists or some forests are protected. (W, C, F, P) Not both are some forests protected and no game laws are respected. (L, R) Therefore, if every bird watcher is a conservationist, then some game laws are respected.

11. If some guest is guilty of theft, then every guest is suspected. $(G, \text{guest}; T, \text{guilty of theft}; S)$ If every guest is suspected, then no guest is pleased. (P) Either some guest is pleased or some guest is concealing the stolen goods. (C) Therefore, if no guest is concealing the stolen goods, then no guest is guilty of theft.

12. If some conflicts are in support of self-determination, then some conflicts are justifiable. (C, S, J) If some conflicts are in support of self-determination, then some conflicts are not successful deterrents. (D) Therefore, if all conflicts are successful deterrents, then some conflicts are justifiable.

13. If all participants are supporting self-determination, then all conflicts are justifiable. (P, S, C, J) If some conflicts are in support of colonialism, then some conflicts are not justifiable. (L) Therefore, if some conflicts are in support of colonialism, then some participants are not supporting self-determination.

14. If any scholars are politicians, then some scholars are not bookish. (S, P, B) Either all scholars are bookish or some scholars are participants in public life. (L) Not both are no scholars participants in public life and some scholars are not writers. (W) Therefore, if all scholars are writers, then no scholars are politicians.

15. If some participants are supporters of self-determination, then some justifications are credible. (P, S, J, C) If every conflict is imperialistic, then no justifications are credible. (N, I) Either every conflict is imperialistic or some aggressions are threats to peace. (A, T) Therefore, if no aggressions are threats to peace, then no participants are supporters of self-determination.

16. If some television sets are radioactive, some X-rays are damaging. (S, R, X, D) Either no X-rays are damaging or some precautions are recommended. (P, M) Not both are some precautions recommended and no supervision is essential. (V, E) Therefore, if no supervision is essential, then no television set is radioactive.

17. Either it is false that all students are anxious or all psychotherapists are correct. (S, A, P, C) If psychotherapists are correct, then some children are more hostile than some adults. (O, H, D) If some children are more hostile than some

adults, then some precautions are desirable. (T, R) Therefore, if no precautions are desirable, then no students are anxious.

18. If Smith wins, Jones loses some money. (W, L, M) Either Jones does not lose some money, or someone complains. (C) If someone complains, then Smith is a stronger candidate than Rogers. (D) Not both is Smith a stronger candidate than Rogers and Smith is not popular. (P) Smith is not popular. If Smith does not win the election, Jones buys a color television. (B, T) If Jones buys a color television, some replays are watched. (R, W) Hence, it is false that no replays are watched.

19. If any opposition is alert, then someone does not surprise them. (O, A, S) If any opposition is prepared, then someone does not attack them. (P, T) If any opposition is warned, then either any opposition is alert or any opposition is prepared. (W) It is false that some opposition is not warned. Therefore, either someone does not surprise them or someone does not attack them.

20. If anyone is successful, he is ambitious. (S, A) If he is ambitious, he is a hard worker. (H) If he is a hard worker, then he is motivated. (M) Not both is he motivated and not lazy. (L) Therefore, if someone is not successful, he is lazy.

21. Everyone wants peace and no one desires conflict. (W, D) If no one desires conflict, then some solution is attainable. (S, A) If everyone wants peace, then some new procedures are essential. (O, E) If some solution is attainable and if some new procedures are essential, some new initiatives are recommended. (I, R) Therefore, it is false that no new initiatives are recommended.

22. If anyone is in favor of lower taxes, then he is opposed to increased spending. (F, I) If he is opposed to increased spending, then he is against strengthening the war on poverty. (W) If he is against strengthening the war on poverty, he does not support increasing foreign aid. (S) Someone supports increasing foreign aid. Therefore, someone is not in favor of lower taxes.

23. It is not the case both that some communities are resourceful and that some slum areas are not eradicated. (C, R, S, E) Either it is false that some slum areas are not eradicated, or some educational opportunities are improved. (O, I) If no incentive is provided, then no educational opportunities are improved. (N, P) Some communities are resourceful. Therefore, some incentive is provided.

24. Either some objection is significant or some accident is serious. (O, S, A, E) If some objection is significant, then some plans are subject to review. (P, R) If some accident is serious, then some additional precautions are recommended. (C, M) If either some plans are subject to review or some additional precautions are recommended, then some delays are expected. (D, X) No delays are expected. Therefore, no objection is significant, and no accident is serious.

PART III
Logic and
Scientific
Inquiry

Chapter 16
Generalizations and Analogies in Scientific Inquiry

16.1 The Hypothetico-Deductive Method and the Experimental Sciences

Deductive logic establishes valid argument forms whose proper use assures true conclusions in all cases in which the premises are true, but it does not provide a basis for determining the material truth of premises offered as evidence. A sound argument requires not only a valid form but also true premises. Deductive arguments involve the notion of a logically necessary conclusion; statements about matters of fact are probable rather than necessary, and they are confirmed by evidence based upon experience.

The basis of any science is the development of a rigorous method by which competent investigators engage in critical inquiry and research and establish conclusions acknowledged by their peers as worthy of confidence. The sciences are distinguished by the kinds of methods used in their investigations. *Formal* sciences—of which mathematics and symbolic logic are prime examples—are concerned with the development of systems derived from an initial set of definitions of primitive terms, a set of operational procedures, and a set of postulates. Formal sciences develop the implications of these notions, postulates, and operations into an elaborate deductive system whose validity is determined by its internal consistency.

The basic method of the *empirical* sciences has been called by Karl Popper and others the *hypothetico-deductive method*. This method is other than pure induction but includes some of the procedures traditionally associated with induction. It includes rigorous methods for making reliable analyses and trustworthy generalizations based upon experience. Inquiry is guided and controlled by hypotheses yielding corrigible conclusions which, at best, are highly probable. Experimental scientists tend to regard with extreme caution any conclusions about matters of fact or their relations that are established merely by deductive procedures. Crucial in the acceptance or the rejection of any hypothesis is the degree to which its anticipated consequences hold in rigorous inquiry and experimentation.

The method of the empirical sciences develops generalizations through the formulation of hypotheses and laws, and it supports such generalizations by confirmation based on data that can be quantified by measuring instruments and classified by rational procedures. This method includes formulation of hypotheses, determination of the entailments of hypotheses, testing of the entailments of hypotheses through experimentation and verification, and application of the hypotheses. A practical concern of the empirical sciences is reliable anticipation and, in some cases, control of on-coming experience. Examples of empirical sciences are physics, chemistry, biology, geology, psychology, sociology, and political science.

Some classifications distinguish between empirical and experimental sciences. This distinction usually turns on whether experimentation is added to techniques of observation, description, and classification used to support hypotheses. For example, a sociological description of a political election may support a hypothesis by reference to observation, description, classification, and generalization, whereas a typical experiment in a physics laboratory is based upon hypotheses and experimentation. Some writers whose procedures are based upon hypotheses and rigorous experimental controls use "empirical" as a derogatory term.

Observation and description are an essential part of scientific inquiry. Facts obtained by observation provide the hard core for the development of hypotheses. But mere observation and description do not satisfy the usual standards expected of scientific inquiry, but they do provide a basis for confirming or invalidating hypotheses.

Observation and description in science need to meet expected standards of objectivity, completeness, and accuracy. Such standards are to be interpreted in the context of the nature of scientific inquiry. *Objectivity* means the observation and description are of the kind other qualified observers in similar circumstances can experience and describe. *Completeness* involves thoroughness in observing, reporting, and relating relevant data. *Accuracy* requires that observations and descriptions be sufficiently precise and exact, given the conditions under which they are conducted and the requirements set for the confirmation of the hypothesis.

Observations and descriptions are not carried out in an intellectual vacuum. A qualified observer approaches an observation with a background of knowledge and experience and a sense of the relevance of facts to hypotheses. He seeks to check the accuracy of measurements by using the best practical instruments available and by repetition of his own observations and measurements. Some interpretation is unavoidable in description, since the observer attempts to select what is relevant; yet good descriptions distinguish between the recording of the basic facts observed and the offering of interpretations to interrelate a set of facts or to indicate the significance of a particular fact in a larger context. The scientist focuses on a problem with the aim of determining facts that will be clues in formulating hypotheses or in testing hypotheses already formulated. His observations are selective rather than general and are directed toward determining the acceptability of a hypothesis.

16.2 Some Common Features of the Methods of the Experimental Sciences

The methods of the experimental sciences, such as physics, chemistry, and biology, can be analyzed to determine their common features. These common features are a part of the *scientific method*. Although some persons regard speaking of the "scientific method" as unwarranted, we may, if we allow for some variations in their application to differing subject matter, list six general conditions that tend to characterize the methodology of any experimental science.

1. *The methods and the manner of obtaining the evidence and conclusions of science are public.* Other trained and qualified observers can perform similar experiments and reach similar conclusions—or at least they can examine the evidence and appraise the conclusions drawn from such evidence on its merits. Claims to secret cures or to evidence not available for examination by other qualified persons are indications of a pseudo-scientific approach. The language of science can always be understood and appraised by others with critical knowledge in the subject area.

2. *The experimental sciences are concerned with quantifiable or measurable data.* Precise instruments are perfected to increase the accuracy of such measurements. Atoms are differentiated from each other in quantitative terms. Atoms have particles whose effects are measurable. Molecules are distinguishable in quantitative terms. Bodies fall at a rate specifiable in quantitative terms. The speed of light is measured in quantitative terms. Quantitative distinctions are made about genes. Laws of heredity are expressed in a quantitative manner.

3. *The hypotheses used to establish conclusions in the experimental sciences are confirmable.* Experiments are devised to test hypotheses under at least two sets of conditions: The occurrence of one set supports the hypothesis and the occurrence of the other discredits the hypothesis. If the *Anopheles* female mosquito is the sole carrier of the causal agent of malaria, then under specifiable conditions the insertion of the proboscis of a carrier *Anopheles* mosquito will be accompanied by malaria and in the absence of such an insertion (or an experimental substitute) the malaria will not occur. If the light from a distant star travels on a curved line in the presence of a mass rather than on a straight line, then when the star is in a specifiable position behind the sun, its light will still be observable during an eclipse. (This was

one of the confirming instances in Einstein's theory of relativity.) Other qualified investigators also can set up comparable conditions for obtaining the data and for repeating similar experiments or tests.

4. *The conclusions of scientific investigations as well as the data and the methods used to establish them are corrigible in the light of further inquiry and experience.* Claims to absolutely certain knowledge about experience are regarded as unwarranted. Rather, the experimental scientist seeks warranted knowledge claims more worthy of acceptance than any alternative set of consistent conclusions. Such claims to knowledge may be highly probable but still correctable on the basis of new experience. The experimental scientist regards a closed system or a dogmatic position or a fixed *a priori* approach as opposed to scientific inquiry and progress. An established hypothesis in science is subject to refutation by further experimentation. This is regarded not as a limitation of the method of science but rather as a prerequisite for its continued growth. Incorrigible knowledge in experimental sciences would signify the end of further experimentation, testing, and the growth of knowledge in the concerned area.

5. *The experimental sciences provide explanations of events by formulating general laws.* Experimental scientists are not content with procedures limited to descriptions and classifications; rather, they insist on hypotheses that establish why events occur as they do. Not satisfied merely to describe the electrical circuit of a television set or the physical features of a lever, they seek to explain through well-founded hypotheses why television sets or levers function as they do. The experimental scientist is particularly interested in determining causal connections through the use of explanatory hypotheses, which are either uniform or statistical in character. Within a given range of temperature and pressure two parts of hydrogen combined with one part of oxygen will form water. In dry air at 70°F, sound will travel 1,130 feet per second. One-half of the radioactive carbon atoms (C^{14}) will decay by beta emission in 5,760 years.

6. *The method of the experimental sciences establishes interrelated general hypotheses and laws.* Particularized knowledge in science has significance in suggesting and confirming hypotheses. The predictive value of a hypothesis has relevance to the occurrence of a specified series of events. The discrete fact or event has significance for the scientist as an instance of a more general law. A particular case of typhoid fever for a medical scientist has technical significance as an expression of a general law related to typhoid fever and including such factors as the causal agent, the transmission of this agent, the condition of the host subject, the incubation period, and the identifying symptoms and course of the disease. Laws related to typhoid fever in turn are related to a more general law of comparable diseases such as cholera. This also is related to a more general law concerning a germ theory of disease and this in turn to other theories about microorganisms.

The experimental scientist uses generalizations expressed as laws as a basis for laying hold of particular facts and events. Such particularizations have significance for the scientist as instances of occurrence of a class of facts or events rather than as unrelated or isolated bits of experience.

16.3 Types of Generalizations in the Methods of Science

We have emphasized the interest of the scientist in the formulation of generalizations expressed as hypotheses and laws. These can be differentiated and classified as (1) generalization by enumeration, (2) generalization by analogy, (3) uniform hypothetico-generalizations, and (4) statistical hypothetico-generalizations.

Generalization by *enumeration* bases a general principle on the characteristics or properties observed in enumerated instances of a particular class. "The crow in the yard is black. The crow on the fence is black. The crow in the tree is black. The crow flying in the air is black. . . . Therefore, all crows are black." If all the members of a class are examined for a particular property and every member is found to have it, the enumeration of instances is exhaustive. In such a case no direct inference is made about the property. Although Aristotle called such a procedure perfect induction, many logicians would hold that such complete enumeration is not an example of induction. Inferences are made only if a leap is made in such cases from the statement "some objects have this property" to the statement "all objects have this property."

The pervading notion of induction prior to Hume and particularly in the approach of Francis Bacon and Aristotle was generalization by enumeration. Induction in this traditional sense refers to a process of reasoning in which evidence based upon a common property noted in selected members of a class of objects is used to justify a generalization that all members of such a class have this property. Induction involves an inferential leap from evidence based upon a restricted or representative number of cases to a claim that the unobserved members of the class will also have the same property. This type of generalization presents two particularly troublesome problems. One is the assumption that all members of the specified class will exemplify the properties established by the instances that are enumerated. The second is the tendency to form generalizations on the basis of too few enumerated instances.

Generalization by enumeration, although a useful procedure in many scientific inquiries, is not the basic approach of modern science in arriving at generalizations. Aristotle and Francis Bacon sought to make such generalizations a fundamental procedure of the sciences, but their views are no longer generally accepted. Generalizations by enumeration are focused on descriptive summaries of experience rather than on the formulation of hypotheses confirmable through appeal to their consequences. They do not lend themselves to the formulation of interrelated hypotheses and laws, a basic feature of modern science.

A second form of generalization makes use of *analogy*. Two or more objects are known to share one or more specified properties in common. It is then inferred that a property that is held by one object or class of objects and that is not known to characterize a second object also must be held by the latter. Consider, for example, the following argument by analogy: "Since a father desires the welfare of his child, his discipline is designed to assist the child in making beneficial decisions for his future. A ruler as the father of his country desires the welfare of his subjects. Therefore, his discipline of his subjects by decrees is designed for their best interests." Generalization by analogy is hazardous at best, but it may be highly useful in suggesting hypotheses that can be tested by more rigorous procedures. (Analogical arguments are appraised later in this chapter.)

A third form of generalization is a *uniform* generalization based upon hypotheses and testing. This procedure is adaptable to many laboratory experiments. A hypothesis is formulated, conditions for its confirmation are set forth, and these conditions are tested. The confirmed hypothesis is accepted as applicable to every member of a given class. Thus, Newton's "law of gravity" was applicable to any falling body.

A fourth form of generalization is a hypothesis based upon *statistical* generalizations. In this case a set of specifiable statistical ratios are said to characterize a given set of variables. It is postulated that 95 percent of the students in a freshman class with a certain level of scores on their college entrance examinations and a certain rank in their graduating high school class will have a passing average at a given university after their freshman year. It is postulated that 75 percent of another group of freshmen with lower scores on their college entrance examinations and poorer averages in their high school work will fail to have a passing average at the end of their freshman year.

A major strength of the methods of science is the use of rigorous procedures based upon the confirmation of hypotheses by testing of their consequences. However, science also uses many deductive procedures. The experimental sciences require confirming experiments that test the entailments deduced from hypotheses and other deductive procedures, including the interrelating of hypotheses and of laws.

16.4 The Difference Between Descriptive and Argumentative Analogies

We have pointed out that an analogy is a form of comparison of entities or processes on the basis of properties that they share or are alleged to share in common. For example, it has been claimed that "An atom is like a solar system in that both the atom and the solar system have fast-moving parts orbiting around a central nucleus."

Some analogies are merely illustrative or descriptive and do not advance an argument. The statement just quoted about atoms and solar systems is a descriptive analogy. It was designed to develop an insight or understanding about the material being discussed. Descriptive analogies are to be appraised as useful or unserviceable, as guiding or misleading. They are not intended to be taken literally in every detail. If they are interpreted literally, they usually are misrepresentative. In an illustrative or descriptive analogy, evidence is presented to strengthen insight into a problem.

A second kind of analogy presents an argument with a conclusion supported by analogical evidence. An analogical argument states that since two or more entities or processes have an identifiable set of properties in common and since an additional property is known to characterize one object or class of objects, then the second object also must have this stated property by virtue of properties it is known to share with the original object. For example, two ancient coins are found having (1) the same kind of metal, and (2) similar kinds of inscriptive work. The first coin bears additional inscriptions that enable its date to be placed at approximately 75–50 B.C. By analogy one could propose that since the second coin had all the characteristics of the first coin except the more detailed inscription, the second coin must have been made at about the same date as the first coin.

An argument by analogy differs from an argument by enumeration in several respects. In an argument by enumeration the entities or processes being compared are usually in a more limited or restricted class, and the properties held in common by them are much more numerous than in an analogical argument. If it is proposed in an argument by enumeration that all ducks have webbed feet, on the basis that all ducks observed have webbed feet, then the objects being compared here (ducks) share many other properties in common. There is also a much higher probability of the use of equivocal terms in an argument based upon analogy than in one based upon enumeration. If the term "webbed feet" is applicable to the observed ducks in an enumerative generalization, this term maintains its meaning when applied to unobserved ducks. In an argument based upon analogy, however, if the term "father" is applied to the parent of a child and to the ruler of a totalitarian state, its meaning shifts.

The conclusion of an argument by analogy may be suggestive or helpful in the formulation of uniform or statistical hypotheses. The persuasiveness of an argument by analogy is usually stronger in a subjective or psychological sense than in a rational and critical sense. However, in the final analysis a hypothesis suggested by analogy needs to be developed as a uniform or statistical hypothetico-generalization with testable consequences to be accepted in the experimental sciences.

16.5 Criteria for Appraising Analogical Arguments

Although analogical arguments do not reach the level of confidence required in the rigorous methodology of the sciences, they can be appraised in terms of being more satisfactory or less satisfactory, more suggestive or less suggestive, more worthy of confidence or unworthy of confidence. Consider a traditional illustration in the argument by analogy: the question of the probability of life on the planet Mars. Mars and Earth share various properties in common: (1) each planet revolves around the sun; (2) each planet derives its source of energy from the sun; (3) each rotates on its axis; (4) each is subject to the law of gravitation. Since Earth also has forms of life, an argument by analogy might propose that Mars also has forms of life.

Several criteria are applicable in appraising such analogical arguments.

One criterion is the *likeness or identity of the allegedly common properties.* In many analogies the key concepts are materially different in character and do not apply to the identical thing; the term "brother" can be used of a male sibling, or it can refer to a fellow member in a fraternity. If the identical obligations and privileges were held applicable to the sibling brother and to the fraternity brother in an argument by analogy, then we could point out that this argument has certain weaknesses because of the different meanings of the term "brother." In the example above related to the possibility of life on Mars, the terms do appear to be used essentially with the same meaning, provided it is recognized that the simplest forms of life may be referred to.

A second criterion is the *number of relevant properties the objects hold in common.* An analogy is strengthened if the relevant properties shared by the entities or processes being compared are numerous, and its strength diminishes if they are relatively few. Consider the following argument by analogy: "Broad rivers and broad minds share in common the property of their broadness. Broad rivers also have the tendency to be shallow. Therefore, broad minds have the tendency to be shallow." This analogy does not meet the first test, since the terms "broad" and "shallow" are both being used in different senses. Even if these different meanings are overlooked, it is still held that the objects being discussed hold only one property in common: "broadness." In the example about Mars and Earth the number of relevant properties they share in common could be extended, and the analogy could come nearer to satisfying the second criterion.

A third criterion is the *extent to which objects having the known properties in common also have in common the added property.* The analogy relative to life on Mars is weakened by application of this criterion. Of the other objects known to share in the properties specified, only Earth is known to have life on it. The listing of the original set of properties does not provide a basis for expectancy of life wherever such properties are found.

A fourth criterion is the *relevance of the known properties held in common by the compared objects to the additional property being attributed to the second object.* Consider again the analogy relative to life on Mars. If it were expected that any planet revolving around the sun has life, or that any planet whose source of energy is the sun has life, or that any celestial object rotating on its axis has life, or that any celestial object with some combination of these factors has life, then the analogy would be strengthened. Although each of these factors appears to be related to the presence of life on Earth, any one or any possible combination of them appears to be quite possible in other celestial bodies without the presence of life.

A fifth criterion is the *degree of restraint exercised in the formulation of the conclusion*. Conclusions with broader and more sweeping claims have less probability of reliability in analogical arguments than those with more limited scope. A conclusion proposing the simplest forms of life on Mars would be a stronger claim than one proposing advanced forms of life there. Greater restraint in the claims made in the conclusion strengthen the argument.

A sixth criterion is the *lack of significant disanalogies to the argument*. Significant differences between the two compared objects weaken the conclusion. If the object to which a property is being attributed does not have the conditions believed to be essential for the inferred property, then the analogy has a significant disanalogy. If it were found that Mars rotates on its axis in such a way that one side of the planet always faces the sun and is excessively hot and the other side is excessively cold, or that the amount of carbon necessary to support life is lacking on Mars, then these factors would constitute a significant disanalogy, tending to discredit the conclusion.

Not only can some arguments by analogy help us formulate hypotheses that lend themselves to further investigation by experimental techniques, but some descriptive or illustrative analogies also can be useful in furthering inquiry. If the orbit of a comet is like the orbit of a planet, and if the orbit of a planet can be calculated in a precise way, is it not also possible to calculate the orbit of a comet? Halley's prediction of the appearance of a comet in 1758 was based on the prior occurrence of a large comet at regular intervals in 1305, 1380, 1456, 1531, 1607, and 1682 and upon the analogy drawn from the movement of planets.

16.6 EXERCISES

Which of the following analogies are descriptive and which are argumentative? Appraise the argumentative analogies on the basis of the criteria set forth in this chapter.

1. "Let me cite another case, one in which an experimenter produces an observation and voluntarily brings it to birth. The case is, so to speak, included in the preceding case; but it differs from it in this, that, instead of waiting for an observation to present itself by chance in fortuitous circumstance, we produce it by experiment. Returning to Bacon's comparison, we might say that an experimenter, in this instance, is like a hunter who, instead of waiting quietly for game, tries to make it rise, by beating up the locality where he assumes it is."[1]

2. If it is permissible to deceive to prevent the enemy from knowing the position

---

[1] Claude Bernard, *An Introduction to the Study of Experimental Medicine*, trans. H. C. Greene (New York: Dover Publications, Inc., 1957), p. 157.

of our troops, if it is accepted that a physician may deceive a patient in order to keep alive his will to live as a means of increasing the probability of his recovery, if it is accepted that a lawyer may deceive a jury by concealing evidence that might be prejudicial to his client being tried for first-degree murder, it is permissible for a college student to deceive his teacher about his ability in a subject by paying a superior student to write his term essay for a course.

3. Computers are like brains. Both confront problems to be solved, both have procedures for dealing with problems, and both propose solutions to problems in the manner in which they have been conditioned.

4. The proton is like an onion in having layers with radii of different magnitude.

5. This western movie is like the last one I saw. In both cases, the hero was being framed by the leader of an unscrupulous gang that was trying to run the town, in both cases the hero was in love with a girl who was victimized by the leader of the gang, and in both cases the hero was accused of a crime committed by the leader of the gang. In the former case the hero killed the leader of the gang in a street gun fight. Therefore, the hero will kill the leader of the gang in a street gun fight in the present movie.

6. The person who robbed the store was about six feet tall, with blond hair, blue eyes, and a limp. He was neatly dressed in a dark suit. The defendant also is about six feet tall with blond hair, blue eyes, and a limp. He was in the neighborhood, neatly dressed in a dark suit, immediately prior to the robbery. Therefore, the defendant is the person who robbed the store.

7. A good ruler is like a good captain. He steers his ship-of-state safely through troubled waters.

8. "I wonder at the attitude of some advertisers. Their expertise enables them to recognize unlawful practices of competitors immediately. But they choose to fight their own battles—for to report the matter to FTC would be like running to mother to snitch on a brother. The FTC is a law enforcement agency and it is your responsibility to report unlawful advertising to the Commission—just as you report crimes to the police."[2]

9. "In the question period later, he was asked if lawyers are more concerned in fair trial or in getting their clients freed. Mr. Belli fielded that with an analogy to the man who obtains a lawyer to defend and free his son. Which lawyer are you going to get to get your son off? he asked adding: 'Behind every so-called crooked lawyer there is a crooked layman.' "[3]

10. "There is little doubt left that the floors of the oceans behave like gigantic conveyor belts, transporting the continents on their backs slowly but inexorably from place to place."[4]

11. "The massive technological onslaught on the Moon is at last beginning to give conclusive answers to the vexed questions surrounding the origin of our natural satellite's surface features. Photographs from the three *Ranger* probes, although very revealing on a small scale, are still open to varied interpretations.

---

[2] Paul Rand Dixon, Chairman, Federal Trade Commission, quoted in *Editor & Publisher,* March 12, 1966, p. 18.

[3] Robert U. Brown, "Shop Talk at Thirty," *Editor & Publisher,* September 23, 1967, p. 60.

[4] Peter Stubbs, "The Mechanism of Continental Drift," *New Scientist,* December 15, 1966, p. 616.

In 1965, R. B. Baldwin (with the meteorite impact theory in mind) deduced rather rashly from *Ranger's* results that: '. . . the 136-year-old argument is over.' And the official Experimenter's Reports, compiled almost exclusively by impact supporters, did little to dispel this idea.

"One of the few volumes ever entirely devoted to development of a new theory of the Moon's surface was published in 1965 by Dr. Gilbert Fielder, now heading the Lunar Group at the University of London Observatory, Mill Hill. The book was called *Lunar Geology*. In this, based on geological considerations, he explained why 'ghost rings'—the imperfect formations of low-relief classically attributed to melting of former grand ring structures by the lavas of the maria surrounding them—should instead be reclassified as among the youngest formations on the Moon. They are, he suggested, embryo craters, probably still in the process of formation today.

"His theory postulates that the large rings on the Moon were formed in identical fashion to similar structures on Earth. That is by gentle volcanic extrusion around, and subsidence within, ring-fractures originating at depth inside the planet. The most youthful formations would be expected to show just the earliest stages of this development. With its close analogy to familiar terrestrial geological processes, the theory attracted the wide attention of selenologists. Now, in *Nature* (Vol. 213, p. 333), Dr. Fielder presents evidence from the latest American Moon-probes to substantiate his conclusions.

"In August of last year, *Lunar Orbiter I* flew over the *Surveyor I* landing site and photographed sections of the 112-km ring called Flamsteed P—a typical 'ghost' formation which *Surveyor* had already hinted was a still-active area. Two of the photographs are shown right. Examining these in America, J. A. O'Keefe, R. G. Strom and E. A. Whitaker were independently struck by some interesting features of the ringwall, indicating that it is of relatively recent origin; and it is this possibility which Dr. Fielder examines in his paper.

"Shown for the first time in detail, the hills of Flamsteed P bear a remarkable resemblance to features known in volcanic regions on Earth. Although the individual eminences tend to assume a bulbous dome shape, typical of once-viscous lava, each block follows a linear form, suggesting control by fractures. The mountains end with steep terminal slopes of 20° or so, which cannot be due to erosion as a result of melting by subsequent lavas from the mare region (the dark luna-base). These lavas, being highly viscous, would immediately 'freeze' on contact with the eminences, forming a gentle 'constructional' slope rather than causing undercutting.

"The mountain sides exhibit wrinkles like those characteristic of terrestrial lava fields. In particular, the hills in the north of the ring define lobate shapes in a manner highly reminiscent of viscous lava flows on Earth. Examination of the original photographs with a magnifier can be very instructive, for it may be seen that the arcs enclosing Flamsteed P show compelling characteristics of lava. The detail resolved in these pictures is several times smaller than the grain size on the Russian *Luna 12* shots.

"At least four of the largest craters in the bright (lunarite) mountain flows are conical or 'dimple' craters, which suggests collapse following withdrawal of lava. It is also possible, says Fielder, to identify some fissures or vents from which the later lavas issued. But perhaps the strongest argument for the recent origin of

Flamsteed P concerns the rows of small craters which cluster at the foot of the mountains and wrinkle-ridge lava fronts associated with the ring-fracture. Over the area covered by the photographs, there are 16 probable cases of craters which have been overlapped by the lava flows, one certain case of a 1-km ghost ring which has been overlapped, and two cases of craters which have apparently been distorted by the flow of lava.

"From a general consideration, it appears that perhaps twice as many craters and rings were formed before the peripheral lava flows of Flamsteed P as were formed later. In a few places, the lunarite flows seem to dip under the lunabase of the surrounding plain, indicating that the lunarite and lunabase flows may at an early time have been contemporaneous. From this difference in appearance, it is apparent that much of the Flamsteed P lunarite was extruded after solidification of the lunabase. The conclusion that the ringwall of Flamsteed P is a youthful volcanic feature is inescapable."[5]

———————
[5] Ian Ridpath, "Are the Moon's Craters Volcanic?," *New Scientist*, February 2, 1967.

Chapter 17
The Hypothetico-
Deductive Method

17.1 Hypotheses and the Method of Science

Among the general features of experimental science, the function of hypotheses in guiding research is basic. A hypothesis as a proposed solution to a problematic situation entails a set of consequences testable in experience. Scientists are not content to formulate isolated hypotheses to explain sets of facts in an *ad hoc* manner; rather, as Mario Bunge and others point out,[1] they seek to interrelate a set of hypotheses into a system, which becomes a more general hypothesis or theory.

Hypotheses refer to all or to a given part of a class of objects. The former are general hypotheses and the latter are statistical. A *general hypothesis* is applicable in a uniform manner to all members of a class under a specifiable set of conditions. For example, if under given conditions light travels at the rate of 186,000 miles a second, then this condition is said to have prevailed 10,000 years ago and to hold 10,000 years hence. It is said to hold not only between Earth and the sun, but also between the sun and other bodies in the solar system.

Hypotheses may vary in their degree of generality. Frequently the development of the sciences has consisted in building up a series of confirmed hypotheses of lesser generality to hypotheses of wider generality.

Statistical hypotheses are used throughout the physical and social sciences and in many other areas of investigation. A *statistical hypothesis* asserts that within a given class of events a specifiable percentage will also

---

[1] Mario Bunge, *Metascientific Queries* (Springfield, Ill.: Charles C Thomas, Publisher, 1959), p. 109.

be of a second class of event. "In any given year the percentage of male births in relation to the total number of births in the United States will be 51 per cent." Statistical hypotheses are supported by verifiable evidence. In many cases the manner in which the evidence is collected and analyzed is highly complex.

It is customary to distinguish between hypotheses that are testable directly and those that are testable only indirectly. Claude Bernard's revised hypothesis regarding the control exercised by sympathetic nerves over the circulation of blood is testable directly by observation and experimentation. Some hypotheses testable only indirectly do not provide for direct observation and experimentation under controlled conditions at a given level of scientific development—for example, Newton's corpuscular theory of light, Bohr's construction of the atom, and Einstein's original theory of relativity. Hypotheses that can be tested directly are sometimes called experimental or empirical hypotheses, and those that can be tested only indirectly are sometimes called theoretical hypotheses; however, such a classification can be misleading.

17.2 Analysis of Basic Procedures in the Hypothetico-Deductive Method of the Experimental Sciences

The hypothetico-deductive method of the experimental sciences can be analyzed to include such basic steps as the formulation of a hypothesis, the determination of its consequences, the testing of its consequences, and the evaluation of its acceptability. An experiment discussed by Claude Bernard is suggestive of fundamental procedures characteristic of the hypothetico-deductive method.[2]

About the year 1852, my studies led me to make experiments on the influence of the nervous system on the phenomena of nutrition and temperature regulation. It had been observed in many cases that complex paralyses with their seat in the mixed nerves are followed, now by a rise and again by a fall of temperature in the paralyzed parts. Now this is how I reasoned, in order to explain this fact, basing myself first on known observations and then on prevailing theories of the phenomena of nutrition and temperature regulation. Paralysis of the nerves, said I, should lead to cooling of the parts by slowing down the phenomena of combustion in the blood, since these phenomena are considered as the cause of animal heat. On the other hand, anatomists long ago noticed that the sympathetic nerves especially follow the arteries. So, thought I inductively, in a lesion of a mixed trunk of nerves, it must be the sympathetic nerves that produce the slowing down of chemical phenomena in capillary vessels, and their paralysis that then leads to cooling the parts. If my hypothesis is true, I went on, it can be verified by severing only the sympathetic, vascular nerves leading to a special part, and sparing the

---

2 Claude Bernard, *An Introduction to the Study of Experimental Medicine*, trans. H. C. Greene (New York: Dover Publications, Inc., 1957), pp. 168–170.

others. I should then find the part cooled by paralysis of the vascular nerves, without loss of either motion or sensation, since the ordinary motor and sensory nerves would still be intact. To carry out my experiment, I therefore sought a suitable experimental method that would allow me to sever only the vascular nerves and to spare the others. Here the choice of animals was important in solving the problem . . .; for in certain animals, such as rabbits and horses, I found that the anatomical arrangement isolating the cervical sympathetic nerve made this solution possible.

Accordingly, I severed the cervical sympathetic nerve in the neck of a rabbit, to control my hypothesis and see what would happen in the way of change of temperature on the side of the head where this nerve branches out. On the basis of a prevailing theory and of earlier observation, I had been led, as we have just seen, to make the hypothesis that the temperature should be reduced. Now what happened was exactly the reverse. After severing the cervical sympathetic nerve about the middle of the neck, I immediately saw in the whole of the corresponding side of the rabbit's head a striking hyperactivity in the circulation, accompanied by increase of warmth. The result was therefore precisely the reverse of what my hypothesis, deduced from theory, had led me to expect; thereupon I did as I always do, that is to say, I at once abandoned theories and hypothesis, to observe and study the fact itself, so as to define the experimental conditions as precisely as possible. Today my experiments on the vascular and thermo-regulatory nerves have opened a new path for investigation and are the subject of numerous studies which, I hope, may some day yield really important results in physiology and pathology. This example, like the preceding ones, proves that in experiments we may meet with results different from what theories and hypotheses lead us to expect. But I wish to call more special attention to this third example, because it gives us an important lesson, to wit: without the original guiding hypothesis, the experimental fact which contradicted it would never have been perceived. Indeed, I was not the first experimenter to cut this part of the cervical sympathetic nerve in living animals. Pourfour du Petit performed the experiment at the beginning of the last century and discovered the nerve's action on the pupil, by starting from an anatomical hypothesis according to which this nerve was supposed to carry animal spirits to the eye. Many physiologists have since repeated the same operation, with the purpose of verifying or explaining the changes in the eye which Pourfour du Petit first described. But none of them noticed the local temperature phenomenon, of which I speak, or connected it with the severing of the cervical sympathetic nerve, though this phenomenon must necessarily have occurred under the very eyes of all who, before me, had cut this part of the sympathetic nerve. The hypothesis, as we see, had prepared my mind for seeing things in a certain direction, given by the hypothesis itself; and this is proved by the fact that, like the other experimenters, I myself had often divided the cervical sympathetic nerve to repeat Pourfour du Petit's experiment, without perceiving the fact of heat production which I later discovered when a hypothesis led me to make investigations in this direction. Here, therefore, the influence of the hypothesis could hardly be more evident; we had the fact under our eyes and did not see it because it conveyed nothing to our mind. However, it could hardly be simpler to perceive, and since I described it, every physiologist without exception has noted and verified it with the greatest ease.

Claude Bernard's experiment in severing the cervical sympathetic nerve of rabbits contributed to his discovery of the function of nerves in regulating the flow of blood in the arteries. This discovery is recognized as one of the most important advances in knowledge relative to the flow of blood since Harvey's initial discovery of its circulation. Although the procedures in the experimental sciences vary to some degree with different problems and subject areas, if we analyze such procedures, using Bernard's experiment as a model, we find a general methodological tendency in scientific inquiry.

The formulation of a hypothesis. As a provisional generalization with testable consequences a hypothesis related to a concrete set of facts guides inquiry. It helps the researcher focus his observation, classify his data, and find relevant tests for its validation or rejection. On an elementary level hypotheses are formed to provide a generalization for a set of facts. Claude Bernard proposed an initial hypothesis that "paralysis of the nerves . . . should lead to cooling of the parts by slowing down the phenomena of combustion in the blood" and that particularly it was the "sympathetic nerves that produce the slowing down of chemical phenomena in capillary vessels, and their paralysis that then leads to cooling the parts."

In the formulation of a hypothesis the insights, information, and techniques gained in previous experience are focused on an immediate situation. The hypothesis needs to be stated in a form conducive to the determination of conditions that would count as instances of its confirmation or its invalidation. Bernard stated his hypothesis in such a way that he would know what to look for as evidence confirming it in the experiment. Such evidence would include the lowering of the temperature in the part affected by the severing of the sympathetic nerve.

Both formulation and testing of hypotheses are controlled by factual considerations. Imaginative thought by experienced investigators aware of a set of factual conditions becomes a source of many sound hypotheses. In such cases leaps of the imagination may seize upon a new concept, a novel manner of organizing data, or a new technique of analysis. These insights may suggest hypotheses beyond the surmise of less imaginative investigators. Although many original proposals may lead only to invalidation and blind alleys, this trial-and-error procedure characterizes much endeavor of qualified investigators who may eventually formulate highly significant hypotheses. The application of the imagination to the facts at hand was stressed by Whitehead: "The true method of discovery is like the flight of an aeroplane. It starts from the ground of a particular observation; it makes a flight in the thin air of imaginative generalization; and it lands for renewed observation rendered acute by rational interpretation."[3]

The discovery of a set of factual conditions leading to the formulation

[3] Alfred North Whitehead, *Process and Reality* (New York: The Macmillan Company, 1929), p. 7.

of important hypotheses can come about during the testing of other hypotheses. In September of 1928 Alexander Fleming returned to his laboratory in Paddington, England, after a week's vacation. He had left germs in a culture to test the hypothesis that different colonies would breed true to type. He observed what he interpreted as a contamination in one of the cultures. An unusual ring around a mold, which was identified later as *Penicillium notatum,* had separated the mold from the colony of staphylococci. Although he did not develop penicillin as it was produced subsequently, Fleming demonstrated that penicillin also killed off anthrax bacilli and other varieties of bacteria. By using his trained mind with imagination he saw the possible significance of an unexpected set of facts, and he proceeded to formulate and test a hypothesis not related immediately to the one under investigation.[4]

Sometimes in the investigation of a problem alternative hypotheses may be formulated, either initially or successively. If several different hypotheses continue to offer relevant solutions to problems, the most promising are selected for further testing. Trial and error often are required in the elimination of unsatisfactory hypotheses and the refinement of others.

Newborn hypotheses in science can range from closely reasoned projections to wild guesses. Sharp insight, adequate information, seasoned intelligence, and keen imagination contribute to the formulation of fruitful hypotheses. There does not appear to be a formula that assures creative scientific work. The experience and sensitivity of the investigator may be more important in specific cases than any formal criteria for selecting the more promising proposals. Some hypotheses may require months and years of testing, as they approach satisfactory verification and refinement.

The determination of the consequences of the hypothesis. Any proposed scientific hypothesis has certain anticipated consequences. Identification of these consequences is an essential step in efforts to establish the trustworthiness of the hypothesis. The statement of the proposed consequences is offered as a deduction from the hypothesis. If the hypothesis holds, then the deduced consequences confirm its soundness. Bernard reasoned that if his hypothesis was sound, then a severing of only the sympathetic vascular nerves in a properly selected experimental animal would be accompanied in the affected part by paralysis, a lowering of temperature, and a decrease of blood circulation. He also inferred from his hypothesis that the experimental animal would remain without loss of sensation and motion, since the ordinary sensory and motor nerves were not to be disturbed in the experiment. Bernard also believed it preferable to use an animal whose anatomical structure made simpler the severing of the cervical sympathetic nerve. Thus, he proposed a series of conditions he would expect to find as a basis for confirming his hypothesis.

---

[4] R. Taton, *Science in the Twentieth Century* (New York: Basic Books, Inc., 1966), p. 549.

The deduction of the entailments of a hypothesis is also illustrated by the discovery of X-rays. In 1895 Röntgen was experimenting with electrical discharges. Noticing that photographic plates left near a vacuum tube through which electrical discharges were passing were fogged, even though they were covered by black paper, he proposed the hypothesis that rays from the tube penetrated the covering of the plates. He developed the implication of his hypothesis and tested them. If such rays were present, then a phosphorescent substance such as potassium platinocyanide would show detectable effects if left near the tube through which the electrical discharges were passing. He found this substance became luminous. He reasoned that if a thick slab of metal and a light substance such as aluminum were placed between the phosphorescent screen and the tube, a difference in shadows would be evident. He found the heavier and denser metals were casting heavy shadows and the light substances lighter shadows, although both substances were opaque to light. He further reasoned that if the rate of exhaustion of gases in the tube were accelerated, the shadows would become lighter. He also found this to be the case. Röntgen also reasoned that the shadow of bones would be greater on a photographic plate under these conditions than the shadow of living flesh. This was confirmed. This discovery of X-rays and the perfecting of techniques in its use led to advances not only in medicine but in other areas of science as well.[5]

Inductive inferences, in the form either of simple enumeration or of analogy, may suggest clues for the formulation of hypotheses and for the elaboration of their implications. The same clues also may be used later or in other situations as the expected consequences of a hypothesis to be tested. For example, the appearance of muddy water and of chunks of wood and brush in a river may suggest the hypothesis of a rise in the water level. If the hypothesis of a rise in the water level is made, the implications of the hypothesis would include a muddying of the water and the appearance in it of chunks of wood and brush.

Testing the hypothesis to determine whether its anticipated consequences hold. Testing a hypothesis requires that anticipated consequences of the hypothesis hold. In the experimental sciences such testing includes purposeful observation, careful measurement, and effort at producing a set of consequences or events that confirm or disconfirm the hypothesis. Röntgen's testing of the proposed consequences of his hypothesis exemplifies such a procedure. Likewise, after selecting a rabbit as an experimental animal whose cervical sympathetic nerves were suited anatomically for the carrying out of his experiment, Bernard severed this nerve to test the consequences of his hypothesis. He expected to find a lowering of temperature and a decreased cir-

---

5 Sir William Cecil Dampier, *A History of Science,* 4th ed. (New York: The Macmillan Company, 1949), pp. 369–370.

culation of blood; what he found, however, was an increase in temperature and increased blood circulation. He immediately set about "to observe the facts at hand" in order to have some basis for a new hypothesis.

Bernard emphasized the significance of the original hypothesis even though it proved to be faulty. It served to guide an experiment and to focus observation on a given set of data. Many other experimenters had cut the cervical sympathetic nerve in experimental animals without noting the resulting higher temperature in the animal. They had not formulated the consequences of their hypotheses to include an examination of this phenomenon. "The hypothesis had prepared my mind," Bernard stated, "for seeing things in a certain direction, given by the hypothesis itself." Bernard previously had cut the cervical sympathetic nerve in experiments but "without perceiving the fact of heat production which I later discovered when a hypothesis led me to make investigations in this direction." He further adds, "Here, therefore, the influence of the hypothesis could hardly be more evident; we had the fact under our eyes and did not see it because it conveyed nothing to our mind." Such experiments help to support the view that the hypothetico-deductive method proceeds by confirmation and by trial and error. When a hypothesis is set forth, the decisive factor is its confirmation by testing to determine whether its anticipated consequences hold.

Some hypotheses become fruitful in producing anticipated consequences although they are later rejected. Near the end of the nineteenth century a Danish veterinarian named Schmidt developed a hypothesis that milk fever in cows was due to autointoxication by absorption of "colostrum corpuscles and degenerated old epithelial cells" from the cow's udder. He believed that injection into the udder of a solution of potassium iodide together with small amounts of air would provide a cure for the disease. The treatment was effective. It was found subsequently that the injection of the air without the use of the iodine was equally effective in treating the disease. In this case the hypothesis worked even though it was formulated on an erroneous basis, and what was thought to be a secondary factor was established as the basic difference in effecting a cure.[6]

Evaluation of the acceptability of the hypothesis. The acceptability of the hypothesis must be determined by the investigator by examination of a number of factors. Basic considerations include the degree of confirmation provided by testing of the anticipated consequences, the significance of additional independent evidence, and the success of the hypothesis in solving the problem for which it was designed. On the basis of such considerations the investigator may accept the hypothesis, reject it, modify it, recommend further testing, or formulate alternative ones. In the experiment by Bernard the

[6] W. I. B. Beveridge, *The Art of Scientific Investigation* (New York: Vintage Books, 1957), p. 59.

initial hypothesis was rejected and another was formulated. The new hypothesis had importance in the study of the role of the sympathetic nerves in the control of the circulation of blood.

A reliable hypothesis should be supported by evidence not immediately related to the experiment designed to test its acceptability. Such evidence includes other prevailing and accepted theories in science as well as data collected in other scientific experiments. In his initial experiment on the severed cervical sympathetic nerve, Bernard believed his original hypothesis was supported by the existing body of scientific theory at that time. Other experiments believed to support this proposed hypothesis had been performed. However, his subsequent experiment led not only to the rejection of his initial hypothesis and the formulation of an alternative but to the modification of prevailing hypotheses and theories related to his investigation. The original views were accepted as guiding principles but they were not regarded as infallible and incorrigible. The growth of experimental research makes possible not merely modification but the rejection of older hypotheses unable to stand up under further testing.

A basic reason for corroborating a hypothesis by data and theories other than those derived from the immediate experiment is to avoid prejudicial *ad hoc* hypotheses. In general, *ad hoc* hypotheses account for events or conditions retrospectively; a *prejudicial ad hoc* hypothesis either has no explanatory power or is limited to the particular set of cases for which it was invented. A classical example of an *ad hoc* hypothesis was the view that ether provides the medium for light waves to traverse interplanetary space, somewhat as air serves as a medium for sound waves and water as a medium for other waves. The hypothesis that ether had such a function sought to describe how light might travel through space. It did not provide any explanation for other kinds of facts. Experiments designed to test the view did not show any effects attributable to ether. The theory came to be regarded as unfruitful and worthless.

Another *ad hoc* hypothesis, developed in the effort to support the view that the medium through which light waves traveled was ether, was the Lorentz-Fitzgerald position that bodies contracted as they traveled through space or ether at high velocities. This hypothesis was supported by experimental findings but it was not generally accepted in the scientific community until it came to be incorporated into another system of explanation related to Einstein's general theory of relativity.

A hypothesis is not to be rejected merely because it is *ad hoc,* but in such cases further analysis and testing are required; the aim is to find definite reasons either for its rejection (in cases of definite negative results in experimental testing) or for its acceptance (through continued positive results in testing and through search for corroboration and support by other well-founded hypotheses and theories). We can avoid prejudicial *ad hoc* hypotheses by providing experimental means for testing the explanatory power of a hypothesis, by finding a basis for its incorporation into a structure of other scientific theories and hypotheses, and by relating it to more than one set of facts or events to which it has predictive relevance.

If a hypothesis is reliable, then it should be able to solve the problem that gave rise to its formulation. But it is possible for a hypothesis both to have confirming instances of its proposed consequences and to solve the problem that gave rise to its formulation without being finally acceptable. Its usefulness in solving a particular problem is not a sufficient condition for accepting it as reliable. Let us now consider the criteria for evaluating hypotheses.

17.3 Criteria for the Evaluation of Sound Hypotheses

Criteria developed for the appraisal of hypotheses are not to be regarded as absolute, and no set of criteria can assure either that a hypothesis is ultimately accepted or that creative work in scientific inquiry occurs. The use of such criteria may assist in the elimination of poorer hypotheses and in the choice of those offering greater promise. The application of standards testing the soundness of hypotheses usually requires training in the particular subject area to which they are relevant.

A sound hypothesis serves as a useful instrument in guiding research. "In science, the primary duty of ideas is to be useful and interesting, even more than to be 'true.' "[7] Claude Bernard said of the hypothesis that he sub- sequently rejected: ". . . without the original guiding hypothesis, the experi- mental fact which contracted it would never have been perceived. . . . The hypothesis, as we see, had prepared my mind for seeing things in a certain direction, given by the hypothesis itself. . . . They [physiologists, contem- poraries of Claude Bernard] should consequently have very little confidence in the ultimate value of theories, but should still make use of them as intellectual tools necessary to the evolution of science and suitable for the discovery of new facts."[8] The hypothesis should both further inquiry and focus attention on the direction that the inquiry takes.

A sound hypothesis is confirmable. It should be possible both to state what consequences can be expected from a reliable hypothesis and to test these consequences in experiments. Equally important, one should be able to state a set of conditions that, if they hold, would constitute sufficient evi- dence for the rejection of the hypothesis. On some occasions the theory of psychological hedonism has been advanced as a basis for interpreting human behavior. This theory states that human behavior is determined by the response that a person believes will provide him with the greatest pleasure and the least pain. For this to count as a sound scientific hypothesis, those

---

[7] Wilfred Trotter, quoted in Beveridge, *The Art of Scientific Investigation*, p. 56.
[8] Bernard, *An Introduction to the Study of the History of Experimental Medicine*, pp. 169–170.

proposing it must state the conditions that, if fulfilled, would justify the rejection of the theory. In practice those who have advanced the theory of psychological hedonism have not set forth such conditions. Unless they are able to do so, the hypothesis cannot be regarded as sound within the accepted scientific meaning of the term.

When Newton first developed his hypothesis of attraction between masses in his "law of gravitation," he sought to confirm the hypothesis by showing that the implications of the hypothesis were true. After developing differential calculus as a basis for determining these implications, he proceeded to test the hypothesis by observing the monthly revolutions of the moon. However, these revolutions did not conform to his calculations of the predicted consequences of his theory. Newton set aside his theory for twenty years, after which time a French expedition provided new and corrected information about the circumference of the Earth. On the basis of this revised information, Newton also revised his calculations with regard to the movement of the moon. The movement of the moon was found to be in accord with these calculations, and he interpreted this as a confirming instance of his hypothesis of attraction between masses. The original instance, in which the implication of the hypothesis was found not to hold, was discovered to be an error in calculation; new measurements made possible the confirmation of his original hypothesis.

Another criterion for developing sound hypotheses is *the simplicity of the hypothesis itself*. Simplicity is a relative term. It includes not only the language of the statement of the hypothesis but also the number of other assumptions it may entail. Other things being equal, the fewer the assumptions involved the stronger the hypothesis. Simplicity of the hypothesis includes the technical problems related to its confirmation and its applicability in resolving the problematic situation that gave rise to it. The hypothesis that ether provided the medium through which light traversed interplanetary space was abandoned after it was found that the same phenomenon could be accounted for without the use of any notion of ether.

A sound hypothesis provides an explanation for a given set of events at least as efficient or satisfactory as any alternative hypothesis. It is preferable for such a hypothesis to provide an even more satisfactory explanation. Kepler's hypothesis establishing that the orbits of the planets are ellipses rather than circles or epicycles was not only simpler but explained the behavior of planets such as Mars in a more satisfactory manner.

A sound hypothesis needs to be inclusive. It should account for all relevant cases that are instances of its application and for any apparently negative instances. Kepler originally proposed to establish that there were many mathematical harmonies exemplified in the orbits of heavenly bodies. He used the traditional hypothesis with regard to epicycles and their deviations to account for the order of the heavenly bodies. He compared his calculations based upon his developing theories with the observations made by Tycho

Brahe. He found that if he accepted an error of up to eight minutes in Brahe's data, his theory of the celestial harmony based upon epicycles could be "confirmed." Eight minutes of longitude, however, was not something that he could ignore, and so he set aside his original theory (designed to establish the notion of celestial mathematical harmony) and proceeded to develop his much more fruitful hypothesis with regard to the elliptical orbits of planets.

A sound hypothesis needs to be corroborated or supported by data other than those found in the immediate experiment and by other theories that have been repeatedly tested in the area. Kepler's hypothesis about the elliptical orbit of planets provided a foundation for Newton's later theory of gravitation. Newton's theory of gravitation in turn was consistent with Kepler's law relative to the elliptical orbits of planets. Bernard's revised hypothesis about the control of blood circulation exercised by the sympathetic nerves provided the foundation for many other subsequent theories in this area.

Occasionally, some previously tested hypotheses are found to be unsound, as was the original hypothesis in Bernard's experiment. However, if a well-established hypothesis is challenged, the burden of proof rests upon the person seeking to challenge it. It is not sufficient to point out that a particularly well-tested hypothesis is not consistent with the kind of results supported by a new hypothesis.

17.4 Problems in Testing Consequences of Hypotheses

A troublesome logical problem in testing the consequences of a proposed hypothesis takes the following form. If the hypothesis, *H,* is true, then consequences *A, B,* and *C* are true. Consequences *A, B,* and *C* are true; therefore, the hypothesis, *H* is true. This logical form affirms the consequent of a hypothetical proposition and then proceeds to affirm the antecedent. This is a formal fallacy. Although recognition of this formal fallacy does not justify a rejection of the procedure, it suggests caution in its use and reveals the difference between confirmation of a hypothesis and a formal demonstration of its truth. The revision and even the rejection of hypotheses regarded as highly confirmed in the past are explicable on this basis.

Another logical oddity occurs in laboratory experiments in relation to the principle of formal logic. Consider the hypothetical proposition: if hypothesis, *H,* is true, then the consequence, *A,* will follow under proper experimental conditions. In subsequent experiments, *A* does not occur. Formally, this would constitute the strongest of reasons for the rejection of the hypothesis as false. However, in an experimental situation a hypothesis is not rejected this readily. It could be, for example, that *A* is not an appropriate consequence to expect if the hypothesis is true. Some error may have occurred in the experiment; an unobserved factor may have intervened to account for the nonoccurrence of *A.* Human error may have entered in. Newton's first efforts to confirm his "theory of gravitation" by a study of the elliptical orbit of the moon were not successful. Only after correction of an error in estimating the circumference of the earth did the data corroborate his theory. However, if A is a consequence of the hypothesis, $H,$ and if A does not occur in testing the hypothesis under suitable conditions and "human error" does not affect the experiment, then the nonoccurrence of A justifies the rejection of the hypothesis.

Carl G. Hempel proposes a troublesome paradox regarding confirmation of hypotheses. He argues that any evidence can provide confirmation of a hypothesis such as "All ravens are black." An equivalent form of this statement is "All nonblack things are nonravens." He holds that any evidence confirming an equivalent statement also confirms the original statement. Thus, to find an object that is not a raven and is not black provides confirming evidence to the hypothesis "All nonblack things are nonravens" and to its equivalent hypothesis "All ravens are black." His emphasis here is that in a classificatory or qualitative concept of confirmation this paradox holds on syntactical grounds. He does not claim that different kinds of positive confirmation confirm to the same degree or carry the same weight in the testing of a generalization.[9]

Hempel's paradox points to the importance of determining the different kinds of consequences of a hypothesis that are relevant for its confirmation and of indicating the kinds of conditions that, if they hold, would count against its confirmation. It also is significant that the kind of generalization chosen by Hempel to illustrate his argument is based upon simple enumeration. It is less adaptable to hypotheses having a variety of consequences testable through experimentation.

17.5 EXERCISES

1. In the following examples state the hypotheses, determine what consequences might be reasonably expected from these hypotheses, and indicate how these consequences might be tested.

(a) Pasteur developed chicken cholera microbacilli in chicken broth heated at 37°C. Inoculation of chickens with the microbacilli resulted in their death. He left on a vacation and on his return he found that chickens were not seriously affected when inoculated with the microbacilli from the broth that had been left standing. He also found that by passing the attenuated bacilli successively through several chickens within a brief period he could restore its virulence.[10]

(b) In the confirmation of Einstein's theory of relativity, a basic problem was that within the customary accuracy of observation most of its anticipated consequences were similar to those of Newton's theory of gravitation. However, three consequences were proposed to distinguish the predictive ability of the two

---

[9] *Aspects of Scientific Explanation* (New York: The Free Press, a division of The Macmillan Company, 1965), pp. 3–5, 48.
[10] René Taton, ed., *Science in the Nineteenth Century,* trans. A. J. Pomerons (New York: Basic Books, Inc., 1965), pp. 394–395.

views. One consequence was that the deflection of a ray of light by the sun would be twice as great as would be anticipated by Newton's theory. The second was that it would be possible to account for the precession (in seconds of arc per century) in the orbit of the planet Mercury in a more accurate manner. The third was that an atom would vibrate less rapidly in a gravitational field. To test the first consequence the image of a star barely on the outside of the sun was photographed in 1919 in Brazil and in the Gulf of Guiana. It was found that the apparent displacement of the star was in accord with the anticipation of Einstein's theory. In the case of the discrepancy of 42 seconds of arc per century in the orbit of the planet Mercury, the Einstein view improved on the Newtonian view by calculating a change of 43 seconds of arc. The confirmation of the third consequence was more difficult, but barely perceptible differences were found in studies of the spectrum of the sun.[11]

(c) "When a ferromagnetic material is viewed by electron microscopy, the magnetic domain structure is revealed in sharp contrast. This effect can be explained simply as a result of the bending of the electron beam by local magnetic fields. Alternatively, the beam can be thought of as a wave phenomenon: in this case, the explanation is that the waves suffer a phase-delay on passing through a magnetic field, resulting in a form of diffraction. Two Cambridge physicists have taken this idea further, and considered the general case of an electron beam— regarded as a beam of waves—passing through a magnetic field which is non-uniform, varying from point to point in a regular fashion.

"The beam is taken to be coherent (that is, the waves are in step with one another at different points in it). The situation is therefore very like that of any regular wave-phenomenon striking a diffraction grating—in this case, a grating consisting of variations in a magnetic field. M. J. Goringe and J. P. Jakubovics, of the Cavendish Laboratory, Cambridge, derive a general set of equations, and then apply them to the diffraction of electrons by ferromagnetic materials, antiferromagnetic materials, and superconductors in the 'mixed' state (partially superconducting and partially normal).

"Their prediction for a ferromagnetic material includes the effect already observed: there are certain angles through which the beam is very strongly diffracted. But within each of these diffraction peaks there should be a number of smaller peaks. This proves to be the case, as the researchers discovered when they bombarded a thin cobalt foil with a coherent electron beam at a low angle. Antiferromagnetic materials, on the other hand, give no observable diffraction peaks.

"The case of a superconductor in the mixed state is of some interest, since the theory suggests a new technique for observing the magnetic flux lines which characterize this state (in which a magnetic field applied from outside the superconductor is concentrated into very thin filaments of normal conductivity). Goringe and Jakubovics calculate that a low-angle interaction between a coherent electron beam and a thin-film superconductor in the mixed state should give observable diffraction (*Phil. Mag.*, Vol. 15, p. 393)."[12]

(d) "Any middle-aged woman concerned with the effect of advancing years on her complexion (and that includes most), will tell you that her face and hands

---

[11] Dampier, *A History of Science,* pp. 408–409.
[12] "Diffraction by Magnetic Gratings," *New Scientist,* March 9, 1967, p. 471.

are the worst sufferers. These are of course the areas of her skin not covered by clothing, and in 1963, Professor Sam Shuster and Dr. Eva Bottoms, of the department of dermatology, Newcastle University, showed that ageing is associated with a decrease in the total collagen (a protein that is the main component of all connective tissue) in the exposed skin. They compared skin samples from the arm and thigh and found that, although the collagen content decreases in both areas with age, the decrease in skin from the arms was more marked.

"One of the features of ageing collagen is its decreased solubility, and the same workers found that when skin taken from hairless mice is exposed to ultraviolet radiation there is a decrease in soluble collagen together with an increase in intermolecular cross linkage similar to that in ageing skin. The question therefore arose as to whether ultraviolet radiation would produce the same effect in intact, living mice.

"Shuster and Bottoms explain in the current *Nature* (Vol. 214, p. 599) how they exposed 24 mice to an ultraviolet lamp for a 17-hour period. Their skin showed the typical symptoms of sunburn, with red patches and swollen areas, but otherwise the mice appeared healthy. They were killed and skinned, the pelts cut up with scissors and the soluble collagen extracted. The levels of soluble collagen were significantly lower in the exposed mice than in control animals that had not received any radiation.

"Thus, the suspicion that reduced solubility of collagen produced by ultraviolet light is caused by the formation of new intermolecular cross linkages has now been confirmed *in vivo,* and 'these findings take on greater significance in relationship to the changes which occur with age in human skin exposed to sunlight.'

"An interesting corollary, confirming Shuster and Bottoms' earlier work with humans and mice, is that females have less collagen than males. This may explain the greater propensity for wrinkles among women than among men, and they are now investigating this aspect further to discover whether this sex-difference has a genetic or glandular cause."[13]

(e) "The use of copper conductors in electrical circuits has been so universal for so long that the advantages of other materials have seldom been seriously considered—until recently only aluminium has been developed as a practical alternative. Nevertheless, other metals have occasionally been proposed. In particular, the advantages of sodium have led to a number of patents being issued for its use in conductors ever since the first proposal by J. A. Sinclair in 1901.

"The reasons for this interest in sodium are easy to understand. The metal shares with copper and aluminium the basic properties needed for any power-distribution conductor: it is flexible and easily worked, has a high current-carrying capacity, and is available at reasonable cost. Sodium is in fact considerably cheaper than copper or aluminium (about £150/ton compared to £355/ton and £195/ton respectively), but this is not the whole story as resistance is measured in ohms per unit volume and the volume of a ton of metal depends on its density. A comparison between metals to determine their current-carrying capacity ('ampacity') for a given outlay must take all these factors into consideration, and the low density of sodium gives it an even greater advantage (Table I).

---

[13] "Sunlight and the Ageing of Skin," *New Scientist,* May 11, 1967, p. 351.

"Furthermore, sodium is the sixth most abundant metal in the earth's crust and can readily be obtained in any reasonably developed country in the world. This, of course, relieves any country without indigenous sources of copper or aluminium from complete dependence on world supplies and the fluctuations in price which have recently had such deleterious effects on the U K export/import trade balance.

"The most obvious difficulty in the use of sodium in permanent cable installations stems from its high reactivity, especially towards air and water. It corrodes rapidly to oxide and hydroxide in air, and reacts so vigorously with water that the evolved hydrogen can easily ignite. The problems raised by this sensitivity defeated practical application of sodium in cables until relatively recently, when the unique properties of polyethylene as an insulant and a barrier to contamination were appreciated.

"Polyethylene has excellent electrical properties, and the rate at which water and oxygen permeate through it is so low that no short-term experiment could hope to show any significant effect. Indeed, results extrapolated from accelerated tests with 15-kV sodium-cored polyethylene cables under hot water indicate a useful life for such cables under ambient conditions of over 40 years.

"Furthermore, the melting-point of polyethylene can be sufficiently higher than that of sodium for the molten metal to be extruded directly into polyethylene tubing without melting it; and indeed the metal 'wets' the plastic surface so that good adhesion occurs between the core of the cable and its polyethylene insulating sheath.

"The mechanical properties of cables extruded in this way compare favourably with those of conventional copper or aluminium cables. Sodium as a conductor is soft and malleable but has little or no tensile strength. The mechanical strength of insulated cables must therefore be provided by the insulant, jacketing or other external components of the cable. Since sodium is so light in weight, the polyethylene insulation alone provides adequate strength for installation and handling, just as polyethylene pipe requires no additional reinforcement. For special applications requiring greater strength, or operation at higher temperature, the polyethylene can be upgraded by irradiation. Table II shows the yield strength in lbs. to be expected from No. 4 CuE (copper equivalent) 15-kV cable at various temperatures.

"The flexibility of cables is an important consideration, making for ease of manufacturing, handling and laying them, especially when they must be hauled into position through zig-zag conduits. In all but the smallest conventional cables flexibility is achieved by 'stranding,' combining a series of small wires to build up a cable with the required cross-sectional area.

"This technique needs special equipment and handling, necessarily implying increased costs. Furthermore, the unavoidable incidence of voids in a stranded cable reduces the cross-sectional area of metal available and effectively reduces the equivalent ampacity of the cable compared to that of a solid-cored one. By contrast, sodium metal is so soft and malleable that a solid sodium cable is far more flexible than even a stranded copper or aluminium one. This is illustrated in Table III in which the loads resulting in a standard (1%) deflection of similar cable sample are shown. It can be seen that the flexibility of a sodium cable is only half that of the insulation alone. Tests in which cables were pulled through irregular conduits revealed that sodium cables could be successfully threaded with only a small fraction of the tractive effort necessary for copper ones.

"A further valuable feature of polyethylene-insulated sodium cables, arising from the relative lack of rigidity of their components, is their remarkable ability to stretch as much as 25 per cent without fracture, and yet recover their original dimensions completely on removal of the load. Even stretched to one and a half times their original length, test cables retained their structural and electrical integrity, and largely recovered on release; the strong bond between the sodium core and its jacket prevents any separation of the two even under considerable mechanical abuse. Neither copper nor aluminium show any such self-recovery properties, and both fracture at much lower extensions.

"In practice any electrical conductor is subject to unpredictable abuse which could result in exposure of the conductor core, clearly an undesirable event with a sodium core. The exposure to air results only in slow corrosion; even when deliberately ignited (a surprisingly difficult task), the cables burn only slowly and do not drip molten sodium. The effects of water on insulated sodium conductors subjected to varying degrees of insulation damage were studied by drilling holes ranging from $\frac{1}{32}$ in. to $\frac{1}{4}$ in. through the insulation to the sodium and then immersing the damaged conductors in water. Even with the $\frac{1}{4}$-in. hole size the reaction subsided within a few minutes, due to formation of a salt layer and a gas cushion in the drilled hole. The $\frac{1}{4}$-in. hole represents approximately the largest size hole which will automatically seal itself in this way against reaction with free water. In another series of tests, the open ends of 0.5 in. sodium-cored cables were immersed in damp soil, mud or water. Reaction with the first two was very slow. But when such a cable was partially immersed in free water to simulate accidental fracture of a buried cable in a trench partially filled with water, the hydrogen gas evolved from the reaction of sodium and water took fire. The flame could be readily extinguished by covering the exposed end with loose sand, soil or even mud. This experiment has been repeated a number of times, and whenever a fire resulted, it was always easily controlled and safely extinguished. In tests resulting in complete accidental rupture to a loaded high voltage cable the danger from electrical effects far surpassed the danger of chemical reaction.

"The electrical properties of sodium cables compare favourably with those of normal ones. One important factor is their behaviour under high voltages, particularly with regard to the 'corona' effect. The field-gradient near a conductor depends on its radius; the smaller this is, the greater the gradient, and the greater is the risk of ionizing any gas in contact with the conductor, with consequent 'corona' discharging and possible degradation of the insulator.

"As normal cables consist of bundles of small-radius wires with inevitably much airspace between them, corona discharges represent a serious menace. They are guarded against this by wrapping a layer of a poorly-conducting plastic material round the cable, and moulding the insulation into intimate contact with this layer. The wrapping charges up to cable voltage, to give a uniform field within it; it has a larger radius than the strands and is not in contact with external gas, so that corona effects are considerably reduced. The wrapping is usually a carbon-loaded plastic; it must not be too good a conductor or it will carry an appreciable fraction of the cable current and overheat.

"By contrast, a solid sodium cable-core has a large radius, and thanks to its excellent adhesion to its polyethylene jacket there are no voids at the conductor surface in which gas-ionization can occur, and none develop even under severe mechanical stressing. Sodium cables therefore need no conductive wrapping, although it would not be difficult to extrude one round the sodium if desired. A unique characteristic of sodium cables is their behaviour under short-circuit. The normal reaction to a short-circuit is a rapid increase in conductor temperature which, if the short-circuit conditions are continued, melts the insulation. Circuits are normally fused, and fuses are designed to fail at an early stage in the overload situation; but, if they or the circuit breakers do not operate, a cable failure results. The physical characteristics of sodium give rise to certain differences when compared to copper in short-circuit conditions. Sodium has a latent heat of fusion of 27 calories per gram, and all this heat is taken up during melting at a constant temperature (the melting point of sodium), 97.8°C. This latent heat of fusion is about 90 times the heat required to raise one gram of sodium one deg. C, so that the melting of the conductor absorbs as much electrical energy as would normally be required to raise the conductor from room temperature to the melting point. Accordingly, since the polyethylene insulator can withstand 97.8°C, and the cable cannot exceed this temperature until all the sodium has melted, an extended safety-period is available with sodium cables.

"These characteristics also enable a considerable degree of self-protection to be built into sodium cable installations. In normal operation heat is continually lost through the entire length of an operating cable. During the short-circuit the cable is unable to dissipate the increased amounts of heat and failure occurs at some unpredictable location where the heat build-up is a maximum. A sodium cable can absorb heat harmlessly at such a hot-spot by melting; and if a thermally insulating cap is installed at the connectors (as is commonly done for other reasons), the confined heat at this point will cause them to fail first. Repairs can thus be simply effected at the exposed site of the connectors rather than requiring exposure of the cable at inconvenient locations.

"Sodium cable is already in production. The mechanical characteristics of insulated sodium conductors are adequate for certain direct-buried and messenger-wire supported aerial power-cable applications. They have sufficient strength for normal cable handling and installation practices, and are tough enough to resist considerable abuse, possibly more so than conventional insulated conductors.

"A considerable part of the work on sodium cables has been devoted to developing suitable connectors. The reactive metal cannot be exposed for splicing, and special junction units have been devised which screw into the soft sodium to produce a well-insulated terminal. For the moment, however, the junctions are being installed on accessible pedestals rather than being buried with the rest of the cable, and sodium conductors are not being used for service connection to houses until more experience with the new installations has been gained.

"The evidence of field trials, however, indicate an extremely promising future for these new cables in electrical distribution systems where their characteristics provide important advantages compared to older and more conventional materials."[14]

---

[14] L. E. Whitmore, "Sodium as a Conductor of the Future," *New Scientist,* May 11, 1967, p. 347.

2. What would count as the hypothesis and as consequences of the hypothesis in each of the following cases?

(a) An accident occurs at an intersection. The driver of one car accuses Smith, the driver of the other car, of having been traveling at an excessive rate of speed. What would count as confirming the view that Smith was traveling at an excessive rate of speed?

(b) During the Cuba crisis in the fall of 1962, President Kennedy's advisors were seeking to anticipate whether the Russians would pull out their larger missiles. What would have counted as evidence that these larger missiles would be pulled out?

(c) What hypothesis might Columbus have formulated prior to his voyage in 1492 and what consequences would count as confirmation of his hypothesis?

(d) In the hypothesis that a conspiracy was involved in the assassination of President Kennedy, what would constitute consequences of the hypothesis and how might these be established—if at all?

3. Discuss a hypothesis that has been or might be formulated, some consequences of such a hypothesis, and the manner of confirming this hypothesis in each of the following cases.

(a) A significant hypothesis related to some area of your interest.

(b) A hypothesis related to a current case to be tried in a court of law.

(c) A hypothesis related to the political future of a contemporary politician.

(d) A hypothesis related to the development of a particular social tension in a large city in your general geographical area.

(e) A hypothesis related to a college or university athletic team that is "most likely" to win a conference title for the coming season.

Chapter 18
Explanations
and Causal
Relations

18.1 The Meaning of an Explanation

The major function of scientific hypotheses is to provide a basis for explanations of events and of other hypotheses. Explanations account for a fact or generalization by reference to other facts or generalizations; they state *why* an event happens or a given condition holds or a specified generalization is trustworthy.

Explanations would be expected in cases such as the following: Why s the sum of the angles of a triangle equal to 180 degrees? Why does the rate of automobile insurance go up? Why do the planets follow elliptical orbits? Why does the Governor oppose the bill that was proposed by Senator Jones? Why do the lungs function as they do? Why did Congress pass the Medicare bill? Why is John absent from class? Answers to such questions seek to increase understanding of the matters under consideration. "John is absent from class because he has a severe headache and students with severe headaches are not expected to attend class." "All professional athletes are interested in televising of games in which they play because they want higher incomes and televising of games increases their income."

Scientific explanations have been classified by Nagel and others as deductive, probabilistic, functional, and genetic.[1] A *deductive* explanation contains premises (the explicans) stating a general principle or law and a reference to a particular case relevant to this principle to account for the fact or principle to be explained (the explicandum). This type of explanation, which is found

---

[1] Ernest Nagel, *The Structure of Science* (New York: Harcourt, Brace & World, Inc., 1961), pp. 20–26.

frequently in the natural sciences, has been regarded as a model. Kepler explained his law regarding the motion and orbits of planets by showing it was deducible from Newton's law of gravitation.

Probabilistic explanations contain premises that cannot be reduced to a formally valid deductive argument in which the conclusion must be true if the premises are true. They are sufficiently relevant to support a conclusion regarded as probably true. Frequently such explanations include a general statistical statement or assumption and singular statements relevant to the matter to be explained. For example: "There likely will be showers tonight because a front is moving this way and it should reach here by midnight."

A *functional* explanation accounts for a fact or principle by reference to its purpose, use, or instrumental role. An explanation of why Congress passed the Medicare bill would include reference to a growing need by elderly people for adequate medical care. An explanation of why people breathe would refer to the body's need for oxygen for the breaking down of food particles and for the proper functioning of body cells. Functional explanations are found with some frequency in biology and in social sciences.

Genetic explanations account for events or conditions by reference to the set of circumstances or context out of which they developed. Explanations of the Boston Tea Party refer to the policies of England toward the colonists and to the colonists' responses. Genetic explanations tend to be related to a wider set of assumptions, not all of which are made explicit. Genetic definitions are used in historical analysis, in biology, and in accounts of personal and social behavior.

A set of reasons offered to account for any given fact or generalization may contain elements of more than one type of explanation. If functional and genetic explanations have statistical statements or assumptions as principles, they also can be interpreted as special cases of probabilistic explanations.

Explanations based on experimental or empirical premises do not require the notion of the necessity or the necessary truth of the premises, but they are expected to have a critical basis for acceptance as warranted. The necessity in a deductive empirical explanation holds between the logical relation of the premises and the conclusion rather than with regard to the content of the premises and the conclusion. To insist that explanations require necessarily true premises would require a standard that the experimental sciences, whose statements in principle are corrigible and open, are unable to meet.

The view that explanations are necessarily causal in character, although widely accepted at one time, is no longer generally held. Such a view would make impossible explanations of generalizations by other generalizations as well as explanations by reference to noncausal or quasi-causal reasons in formal science and in common sense; one generalization does not cause another, nor does a formal rule or principle cause another. Yet the older view persists, emphasizing the significance of causal explanations in science.

18.2 Different views of causation

The major function of hypothesis in science is to develop causal explanations for events. In ordinary language the notion of cause and effect occurs often, usually in oversimplified form. "The team lost the game because they were overconfident." "The television came on owing to my turning the switch." "The accident occurred as a consequence of Jones' failure to yield the right-of-way." "The boiler exploded because the steam pressure became too high." Examining just one of these examples, we note that a series of complex circumstances are relevant. In the production of the picture and the sound in the television set the turning of the switch to close the electrical circuit is only one factor.

In the interpretation of cause-and-effect relations in scientific inquiry, several identifiable properties of causes or of causally connected events are identifiable. Several of these were emphasized by David Hume.

1. A given cause in similar circumstances always has the same effect.
2. A given cause is always prior to the effect.
3. A cause or causal connection always is related to events.
4. A given kind of effect is repeatable by the use of similar causal connections in relevantly similar circumstances.

The proper identification of causes or causal relations in this strict sense and with the use of statistical principles makes possible the prediction of events whose causes are known. Such identification also facilitates the establishment of controls over conditions connected with the occurrence or nonoccurrence of a specific event.

If the term "cause" were limited to situations meeting the conditions listed above, its application would be restricted primarily to repeatable and controlled situations such as those testable under laboratory conditions. As testing by laboratory techniques becomes less applicable, these standards for interpreting the meaning of "cause" must be applied with less rigor. Such variation in standards relevant to the use of causal notions has hindered the development of a satisfactory theory of causation. If we accept the criterion of repeatability of a given effect under similar circumstances, then social sciences concerned with events whose relevant antecedent conditions are nonrepeatable under similar conditions cannot use the notion of cause. Historical events also are nonrepeatable.

An interpretation of causation can be based on the notions of necessary conditions and of sufficient conditions. A *necessary* condition is a state of affairs that must be present for the occurrence of a given kind of event, but that may be present without the occurrence of the event. A necessary condition for a student's completing his college work is his attainment of a certain level of intellectual development and ability. However, it is possible for him to attain this level of development and ability without satisfactorily completing his college work. A *sufficient* condition is a state of affairs that, in the presence of necessary conditions, always is accompanied by the occurrence of a given kind of event. If the notion of effect is interpreted in a broad rather than a narrow sense, more than one sufficient condition may produce a given kind of effect. A given effect may occur in the absence of any given sufficient condition, but only in the presence of at least one sufficient condition. In treating a given illness a physician might use any one of several different drugs that statistically had achieved a high degree of success in the treatment of this illness. He may prescribe only one of the drugs. The taking of this drug might be called, in a loose sense, a sufficient condition for the improvement of the patient. A sufficient condition usually includes the notion of some triggering action or event that sets off the reaction known as the effect.

By combining the notions of necessary and sufficient conditions, we can define a cause as any combination of necessary and sufficient conditions that always is accompanied by the occurrence of a given kind of event and in whose absence the given event never occurs. In this case the cause should never be restricted either to the necessary condition alone or to the sufficient condition alone. Ancillary or contributing conditions strengthen the probability of attaining other conditions prerequisite for the occurrence of an event. A condition such as "being run down" may be an ancillary condition to weakened resistance, which in turn might increase the probability of catching a common cold. The common cold might come on without such "lowered resistance," and such "lowered resistance" might be present without the person's catching a common cold.

Another interpretation of causation is based upon statistical correlations supported by experimentation or other rigorous types of investigation. If a significant degree of correlation in a stated group occurs between two variables, such as income and formal education, then one of these variables is often said to be causally related to the second. If the amount of yearly income earned by a group of persons is correlated with the level attained in their formal education, the income is called a "function" of the formal education. In this statistical correlation the income represents a bound variable, functioning as an effect, and the formal education is a free variable, functioning as a cause. In such correlations, if X is a function of Y, then Y has resemblances to a cause and X has resemblances to an effect. If in a given statistical table a significant correlation between performance in high school and performance in college is found to apply to a given group, then success in college can be called a function of performance in high school for that group. The performance in high school of the group is causally related to the degree of success of the group in college.

The causal relationships discussed in such statistical data relate to the performance of a whole class of persons and not to a particular person singled out in the class. It would be highly fallacious to infer on the basis of the statistical data in the previous illustration alone that a given person with less than a high school education will necessarily have less income during his lifetime than a person who is a college graduate. Such tables function comparably to those compiled by insurance companies. They show the frequency of the occurrence of certain variables and some correlations between them. They make possible a more accurate prediction of the behavior of a group of persons, including the degree to which a given set of variables will be scattered in the group. They do not provide assurance that a particular individual in the group will conform to the statistical norm for the group. A man with a life expectancy of an additional forty years may die within a week or a year or he may live sixty years. In dealing with the group of which the individual policyholder is a member, a successful insurance company formulates policies enabling it to make a profit on the predicted life expectancy of all the members of the group rather than any specific member of the group. Likewise, in the interpretation of causal relationships in a statistical table, the variables interpreted as being causally connected provide a basis for determining probabilities in dealing with comparable groups but they provide no assurance that a specific individual will conform to the statistical norms for his group.

Interpreted on the basis of statistical correlations, the notion of cause provides a basis for manipulating conditions in a large group. If given conditions are manipulated, then certain results can be anticipated. Thus, an increase in a given group of the percentage of persons with a higher level of formal education may provide a basis for predicting an increase in the amount of annual income in this group. Social planning uses statistical correlations to provide a basis for rendering judgment in determining the variables to manipulate to secure a preferred state of affairs.

18.3 Mill's Methods for Determination of Causes

In the development of modern scientific inquiry five different methods for identifying causal relations are regarded as basic. The discussion of these methods was carried out by the nineteenth-century British philosopher, John Stuart Mill. They are referred to as "Mill's methods of experimental inquiry," although Mill did not originate any of the methods nor was he the first to identify and discuss them. The positive application of these methods is concerned with the identification of causal relationships. In some instances their negative application establishes that a given event or condition either is not causally related or cannot be the sole cause of an event. Their use in a negative way makes possible the stating of a set of conditions that, if they hold, usually discredit a hypothesis.

Let us look at Mill's methods of determining causal relation in explanatory hypotheses.

The method of agreement. The *positive method of agreement* states that in cases involving a common effect with only one common circumstance, the cause is to be found in the factor that is present in all antecedent cases. If it is found that some of the students in a dormitory have food poisoning, an effort is made to determine the food eaten by all of those who have become ill. If a tunafish salad is the only food common in each case of illness, then there are strong reasons for identifying this salad as the source of the food poisoning.

The *negative method of agreement* eliminates possible causes. In the example above, it might have been believed at first that rice pudding was related to the food poisoning. If several persons were found in this case to have food poisoning without having eaten any rice pudding, the effect occurred without this factor. Therefore, the rice pudding would not be regarded as the probable cause of the food poisoning.

In the strict use of the method of agreement a manipulation of other variables regarded as not causally related to the effect needs to be made. The demonstration of a causal relation by this method proposes to show that "All cases of A are followed by cases of B" and "All cases of B follow cases of A and only cases of A." The first form is easier to establish than the second. Consider the case of a physician seeking to determine the cause of a patient's allergy. He may inject extracts of different common sources of allergies under her skin. The patient may show a high sensitivity to face powder; all cases of the use of face powder are found to be followed by an allergy reaction. She does not have a positive reaction to any of the other factors tested. The positive method of agreement has been followed. In midwinter, however, although she has ceased to use face powder, the patient shows symptoms of an allergy reaction. Further tests show that she has a positive reaction to wool. In the latter case a plurality of causes is present, and the model that the same effect is always preceded by the same cause breaks down, unless the notion of cause is refined to a more general notion of "irritating substances of a particular class" or the notion of effect is refined to include "allergy of 'type A' and allergy of 'type B,' " where "type A" refers to reactions in which face powder is involved and "type B" refers to reactions involving wool.

In the method of agreement (as well as in other methods discussed later) the variable tested as the cause is usually more complex than the causal factor singled out. Thus, in the case of determining the cause of boiling water, if it is found under repeated testing that water boils when the temperature of the liquid reaches 212°F, the claim that the cause is the reaching of this temperature ignores the relevant factor of atmospheric pressure. An adequate statement of cause needs to specify the pressure at which water boils at 212°F. For such reasons many writers prefer to speak of *causal connections of events* rather than merely the cause of an event.

The method of difference.   The *method of difference* states that if all conditions or variables are kept constant save one and if the effect fails to occur in the absence of this latter condition or variable, but it does occur in its presence, then this condition or variable is the cause of the effect. This method is probably used more often than any of the others in the formulation of experimental designs for laboratory experiments. It was used by Pasteur in the following example.

Pasteur was requested by the Agricultural Society of Melun to demonstrate the effect of vaccination with attenuated anthrax bacilli. On May 5, 1881, Pasteur inoculated 24 sheep, 6 cows, and 1 goat with attenuated anthrax bacilli, and on May 17 he inoculated them again but with a less attenuated bacilli. On May 31 Pasteur inoculated these animals with a highly virulent anthrax culture, and the same inoculation was given to a second group of 24 sheep, 6 cows, and 1 goat. None of this second group had been given any attenuated anthrax bacilli. On June 2, 1881, the large crowd gathered to examine the results observed that all of the animals previously inoculated with the attenuated bacilli were well. In the other group the goat was dead, all the sheep were dead or dying, and four of the cows showed extensive swellings at the point of inoculation.[2]

The *negative method of difference* refers to cases where a variable is introduced with other conditions remaining constant, and this variable has no significant effect. If the introduction of a variable under stated conditions makes no difference relative to the occurrence of an effect, then this variable alone cannot be the cause of the effect. The use of the negative method of difference is the justification for introducing null hypotheses in statistical surveys in such areas as psychology and education. The null hypothesis proposes to establish that a particular variable introduced in a controlled situation makes no significant difference in the occurrence of a particular kind of event.

The use of the method of difference requires that the proposed causal factor be relevant and that the other variables remain constant without the introduction of other possible causal factors. W. I. B. Beveridge reports on his efforts to prepare a medium in which the infective agent in foot-rot in sheep would grow. On the basis of his prior experience he concluded that sheep serum would be a satisfactory medium, and after repeated failures he one day found the infective agent growing in the medium provided. Yet he could not duplicate his success by growing the infective agent in other media prepared with sheep serum. In checking his notes Beveridge found that at the time of producing the successful medium he had been out of the sheep serum and had used horse serum as a substitute. With this fact as a lead he soon isolated and identified the disease's causal agent, which would grow in the horse serum but not the sheep serum. In his experimental work an unnoticed but causally significant variable had been introduced, and this difference accounted for the possibility of satisfactorily resolving his problem at that time.[3]

---

[2] René Taton, ed., *Science in the Nineteenth Century,* trans. A. J. Pomerons (New York: Basic Books, Inc., 1965), p. 395.
[3] W. I. B. Beveridge, *The Art of Scientific Investigation* (New York: Vintage Books, 1957), p. 219.

The joint method of agreement and difference. The previous methods can be applied jointly in a given inquiry. Mill makes the following statement about this method: "If two or more instances in which the phenomenon occurs have only one circumstance in common, while two or more instances in which it does not occur have nothing in common save the absence of that circumstance, the circumstance in which alone the two sets of instances differ is the effect, or the cause, or an indispensable part of the cause, of the phenomenon."

Consider the following possible case. In a particular study it is found that persons who have malaria have one common antecedent factor: they were bitten by a female *Anopheles* mosquito. Subsequently a control group and an experimental group are placed in similar conditions save one. Female *Anopheles* mosquitoes previously exposed to malaria patients are permitted to bite members of the experimental group, but they are not permitted to bite members of the second group. The bitten persons subsequently have malaria, but no member of the second group develops malaria. Here the joint method for determining a cause has been used. In the first instance a common factor is found. In the second instance this factor is introduced in the experimental group but withheld from a control group. In this case the effect accompanies only those cases where the difference (the bite of the female *Anopheles* mosquito in recent contact with malaria patients) is present.

The joint method of agreement and difference strengthens any conclusion found by the use of only one of these methods. The joint method occurs in a successful experiment where control groups are used. The common factor in the experimental group exemplifies the method of agreement. The absence of the effect in the control group with other conditions the same (save the experimental variable) and the occurrence of the effect in the experimental group illustrates the method of difference.

The method of concomitant variations. The *method of concomitant variations* focuses on two variables that vary or fluctuate in some ratio with each other. In *A System of Logic,* Mill made the following statement about this method: "Whatever phenomenon varies in any manner whenever another phenomenon varies in some particular manner, is either a cause or an effect of that phenomenon, or is connected with it through some fact of causation." The variations may occur in direct proportion to each of the variables considered or in inverse proportion to them. For example, if it were found that within given limits the more fertilizer that was put on a field of maize, the greater the yield of the maize, the two variables (the fertilizer and the yield of the maize) vary directly with each other. The yield of the maize is said to be a function of the amount of fertilizer used. If a barometer is taken on a mountain hike, the higher it is taken the lower it reads. The pressure on the barometer declines as the altitude increases. The variation here is inverse.

In both of the cases above a concomitant variation between the concerned factors suggests a causal relationship.

The method of residues. The *method of residues* is stated by Mill in *A System of Logic* as follows: "Subduct from any phenomenon such part as is known by previous inductions to be the effect of certain antecedents, and the residue of the phenomenon is the effect of the remaining antecedents." If the value of four variables is known and these four variables are joined with a fifth variable, the value of the fifth variable is "the residue," or what is left over after the value of the four original variables have been "subducted" from the value of the five variables together.

A classic illustration of the method of residues is the discovery of the planet Neptune. In the middle of the nineteenth century, astronomers working separately noted that the orbit of the planet Uranus could not be accounted for on the basis of known celestial objects. After determination of the value of the gravitational pull on Uranus by the known celestial objects, it was proposed that another planet must be accounting for this unexplained movement of Uranus. Careful observation of the area where such a planet would likely be revealed Neptune in the expected place. In a similar way, the planet Pluto was discovered during the present century.

Another traditional illustration of the method of residues occurred in the work of the Curies with pitchblende. The radioactivity of pitchblende was found to be much higher than that of its known components. The Curies developed the hypothesis that an unknown element in the pitchblende accounted for this great variation from its predicted radioactivity. Their subsequent investigation resulted in the discovery of radium, which accounted for the otherwise unexplained radioactivity.

The method of residues has been particularly useful in some areas of scientific research, including astronomy and physics.

18.4 Evaluation of Mill's Methods

The experimental methods proposed by Mill for the determination of causal relationships are not applicable in the same manner or in the same degree to all subject matters. They can be abused. In the method of agreement the factor found to be in agreement can be trivial or unrelated to the effect. The observation of the common factor also can be too limited. Prior to the discovery of the Salk vaccine, a physician said he had never known of a case in which a person who had received the Pasteur treatment for the prevention of rabies also subsequently had polio. After more thorough research, it was found that this proposed agreement between persons taking the rabies treatment and their subsequent immunity to polio did not hold. If a given effect has many common antecedents, great difficulty may be experienced in separating causal from noncausal factors. Likewise, an unidentified factor may be the causal one. If contaminated tap water is the source of dysentery, the dysentery might be spread even though the victims did not drink tap water. Vegetables washed in the water or ice made from it might be an unidentified source. In testing by this method the use of a number of varied cases helps assure accurate results.

A difficulty of the method of difference arises if, when two factors vary with each other, the cause-and-effect relationship is not always in one direction. Higher prices may accompany increases in wages. Are higher prices due to increases in wages, or are increases in wages due to higher prices? It is also possible to emphasize differences that are trivial. In a neighborhood in which a contractor is building two houses with the same crews under similar conditions, one of the sites might be sprayed for termites before the laying of the foundation. After the houses are built, the house sprayed for termites has a poor foundation. Although the spraying constitutes a difference, any suggestion that it is the cause of the poor foundation would require further investigation and corroboration. Another difficulty in applying the method of difference can be that of keeping all variables constant save the one that is the object of the experiment, or of making certain that all relevant factors and their involvement in the causal connection are included.

A given effect may occur only if two (or more) variables occur together, and the introduction of any one variable when the other already is present may be accompanied by a given effect. If factors ABC are not followed by a given effect but the introduction of factor D is followed by the effect, a similar situation might result if factors ABD are present without an effect and the introduction of C is followed by the given effect. If an experienced fisherman is in good waters and variable A represents his observance of procedures designed not to spook the bass, variable B represents his throwing his lure in places where bass are most likely to be feeding, variable C represents his throwing a particular lure, such as a perch scale black Chugger, and D represents a slow twitching of the lure around the rocks, logs, brush, and foliage along the bank, then the introduction of either variable D or variable C in the presence of the others might result in his catching bass, but the absence of either C or D with variables A or B present might result in an absence of strikes or catches. Although this example fails to attain the exactness needed for scientific inquiry, it suggests the difficulty that may arise when the introduction of either of two variables in the presence of the other can be the difference in an occurrence of a given kind of effect.

The joint method of agreement and difference provides a stronger means of establishing a case for causally connected events than does either of these methods separately. It is questionable that it should be classified as a separate method. It has the common weakness of the methods it combines, including the difficulty of precisely determining the common relevant variable and that of adequately designing the experimental procedure to test it.

Several problems also occur in the use of the method of concomitant variations. The control of the variables may present difficulties. The range of some variables may obscure a significant degree of difference in the reaction of subclasses. If the variable "high school graduate" is correlated with the variable "superior performance in college work," the first variable would not distinguish high school graduates with good records from those with poor records. For some purposes it would be preferable to reduce the range of the variable to "high school graduates in the upper 25 percent of their class." The concomitant variations of concerned variables also tend to be relevant only to a limited range of the effect studied. If the relation of the application of commercial fertilizer to the growth or productivity of plants is being studied, the application of fertilizer beyond a certain point may be injurious to the growth or productivity of the plants. The concomitant variations in some processes may involve a combination of variables rather than the one isolated for study. An investor might note that over a considerable period of time the worth of stock in electronic companies varies directly with government contracts in electronics. He might assume that additional government contracts would be accompanied by further increases in the price of the stocks. After buying some stock in such companies, he may find the value of the stock diminishes even though the number of government contracts with these firms increases. The variable appearing to account for the variation in the price of the stock was not the only significant one. Likewise, some variation might be due to chance or to coincidence. The stock market might vary directly with the number of bananas imported into the country.

Mill regarded the method of residues as a special variation of the method of difference. He regarded it more as a method of using mathematical calculations and deduction than as a strict experimental method, since the factor left over (the residue) does not lend itself to the kind of manipulations found in the other methods. He also interpreted this method as designed to deal with cases similar to those treated by the method of difference but not adapted to that method. Both of these methods present some of the same difficulties, particularly in the identification of relevant causal factors.

If an experiment is made with the playing of quiet popular music during work hours to discover the effect on the productivity of a control group and an experimental group, and if the productive ability of both groups had been determined in advance to be relatively equal, a greater productivity on the part of the experimental group during the experiment would not in itself be sufficient to establish that the music was the cause. Another unnoticed variable might have been introduced. The members of the experimental group might have been aware that a study was being made of the difference the music made in their productivity, and this awareness might have motivated extra work efforts.

Although each of these methods of determining causal relations has its limitations and can be abused, each procedure can be useful in providing supporting evidence for explanatory hypotheses. It does not prove the explanatory hypotheses to be true, but it provides a basis for accepting the probability that they may be reliable. Its negative use provides a basis for the elimination of unsound explanatory hypotheses. Effective application of these methods usually requires knowledge of the subject matter, the use of the imagination, the identification of the relevant variables, and some technique for measuring their value.

18.5 Causal Fallacies

In the application of the notion of cause several fallacies occur with some frequency. Some of these we have already mentioned.

Temporal relationship between two variables is not an adequate basis for establishing a causal relationship. The *post hoc* fallacy attributes a cause-and-effect relationship to two variables merely because one event follows another, the prior event being accepted as the cause of the second. If wars have followed periods of relatively high armaments, it does not necessarily follow that the cause of wars is high armaments. If one loses heavily on the stock market after he has broken a mirror, the cause of his loss on the stock market need not have been the breaking of the mirror.

Some correlations do not indicate causal relations. If a connection were found between the price of potatoes in Idaho and the success of the New York Yankees baseball team in winning games, it would not follow that there was any connection between these two statistical tables. Statistical correlations may suggest a need for further inquiry about causal relationship, which might be corroborated by further research.

Common effects of a prior cause can be misinterpreted as a cause-and-effect relationship. A person may have both a rash and a high fever, but each may be the effect of another cause, such as an infection.

The reversal of cause and effect is also known as the fallacy of putting the cart before the horse. In this case the effect is identified as the cause and the cause is identified as the effect. For example, one might propose that the cause of a person's lack of motivation was his having dropped out of school, when in fact his having dropped out of school was caused by his lack of motivation.

Another causal fallacy is the confusion of a condition for an effect with the cause of the effect. For example, someone might say that the winning of the football conference title by the state university was caused by their superior job of recruiting.

The misuse of common factors in a causal explanation may derive from the neglect of common relevant factors or from emphasis upon common irrelevant factors. A traditional illustration of this fallacy refers to the inebriate who decided to determine the cause of his inebriation. He found periods of intoxication followed drinking gin and soda, vodka and soda, bourbon and soda, and scotch and soda, and he decided that the cause of the inebriation was the soda.

The confusion of reasons and causes is another type of causal fallacy. The word "because" frequently is used to refer to causal relations. For example, one might say, "The fire occurred because of a short in the wiring of the house." This use of "because" to signify a causal relationship is to be distinguished from the use of the same word to indicate a "reason" providing evidence in an argument. For example: "Professor Smith knows modern mathematics because he is a physicist and all physicists know modern mathematics." Here the word "because" offers a reason for the conclusion rather than a causal explanation for it. It would be inappropriate to say that the cause of Professor Smith's knowledge of mathematics is his being a physicist.

18.6 EXERCISES

Identify the causal fallacies in the following examples.

1. If you had not been late for work, you would not have been at the intersection at the time of the accident. Therefore, the accident was your fault, since it was caused by your leaving late for work.
2. New England and the Middle Atlantic states became major industrial centers because there were large deposits of coal and iron readily available.
3. Smith struck out after he lost his temper. Therefore, he struck out because he lost his temper.
4. Jones is paranoid because he feels persecuted.
5. The river is beginning to rise because the water is becoming muddy.
6. Japan entered upon a program of expanding its empire because it was faced with the problem of overpopulation.
7. The patient's pain was relieved on three occasions. On the first occasion he took aspirin and water; on the second he took Bufferin and water; and on the third he took Excedrin and water. Therefore, the pain was relieved because he drank water.
8. The cause of his industriousness is his working long hours.
9. The cause of the intoxicated person's stumbling was his double vision.
10. The high grade was made after Mary arrived late for the test. Therefore, the high grade was made because she was late for the test.

Discuss the methods used for establishing explanatory hypotheses in the following examples. How significant do you regard the evidence?

11. Louis Pasteur poured liquid from the same container into two flasks. He left one flask open. The second flask was constructed to minimize any possibility that air would reach the liquid. After several days he found that "microscopic beings began to develop in the first flask." In the second flask, however, microscopic beings did not develop.
12. Pasteur continued his experiment with germs in liquid by exposing flasks in the streets of Paris, in his laboratory, in the open fields, and in the Alps. His reasoning was based on the premise that the greater the dust content of the air,

the greater would be the bacterial growth in the flask. His subsequent investigations demonstrated that the growth of the bacteria in the flasks varied directly with the amount of dust in the air. He gave this to support his thesis that the bacteria occuring in the liquid had as their source the particles of dust that were deposited in the liquids.

13. "Magendie once made investigations on the uses of the cerebrospinal fluid and was led to the conclusion that removing this fluid produces a kind of titubation in animals and a characteristic disturbance in their motions. Indeed, after uncovering the occipito-atloidian membrane, if we pierce it to let the cerebrospinal fluid run out, we notice that the animal is seized with peculiar motor disturbances. Apparently nothing could be simpler or more natural than the influence on their motions of removal of the cerebrospinal fluid; yet this was an error, and Magendie told me how another experimenter chanced to find it. After cutting the neck muscles, this experimenter was interrupted in his experiment at the moment when he had just laid bare the occipito-atloidian membrane. Now when he came back, to go on with his experiment, he saw that the simple preliminary operation had produced the same titubation, though the cephalorachidian fluid had not been removed. What was merely the result of severing the neck muscles had therefore been attributed to removal of the cerebrospinal fluid. Comparative experiments would obviously have solved the difficulty. In this case, two animals, as we have said, ought to be placed in the same conditions save one, that is, the occipito-atloidian membrane should be laid bare in both animals, and it should be pierced, to let the fluid flow out, in only one of them; then it would be possible to judge by comparison and thus ascertain the precise part which the removal of the fluid plays in the disturbances."[4]

14. When he was a boy, Edward Jenner heard of a local belief in Gloucestershire that persons who had contracted cowpox appeared to be immune from smallpox. The local physicians tended to discount this theory as an old wives' tale, and Jenner did not investigate it in detail until after he had practiced medicine a number of years. After Jenner's marriage at the age of thirty-eight, he inoculated his son with swinepox and subsequently showed that his son also appeared to be immune from smallpox. Subsequently, Jenner took material from a pustule on the hand of Sarah Nelmes and placed it on James Phipps. Jenner showed subsequently that after Phipps' vaccination, he appeared to be immune to smallpox. This vaccination, which occurred in 1796, may not have been the first vaccination, but it was the first to be widely publicized. In a later discussion of his research, Jenner showed that some twenty-three persons appeared to be immune from smallpox, and each of these had had either cowpox or a vaccination.

15. An English biochemist, Frederick Gowland Hopkins (1861–1947), became interested in the relation between proteins and amino acids, particularly as these were related to health. Protein had been shown to be essential for living organisms, but in some cases some forms of protein were lacking in the feature essential to preserve life. Different kinds of amino acids had been found in protein. Hopkins discovered in 1900 a new amino acid, tryptophan, and he devised a chemical test to indicate its presence. Zein, a protein derived from corn, did not respond to

---

4 Claude Bernard, *An Introduction to the Study of Experimental Medicine*, trans. H. C. Greene (New York: Dover Publications, Inc., 1957), pp. 182–183.

this test. He concluded that it was lacking in tryptophan. Although zein was a protein, it would not sustain life if it were the only protein in the diet.[5]

16. Claude Bernard devised a test of the prevailing view that organic compounds were not synthesized but only broken down by animals—a hypothesis in accord with the view that plants rather than animals synthesized organic compounds. Bernard examined the blood leaving the liver of a dog that had been fed a diet heavy with sugar. He found what he expected: the blood had a high sugar content. However, Bernard was not content to leave the matter at this point. His experimental method required that he examine a dog fed a meal without sugar; and when he did so, he found a high concentration of sugar in the dog's hepatic blood. Bernard rejected the hypothesis that he was testing, and he formulated and later established a hypothesis concerning the glycogenic activity of the liver.[6]

17. A study is made of persons from a slum area. One group, whose members have been leaders in protests involving violence, are found to come from home situations characterized by (1) inadequate housing, (2) unemployment or underemployment, and (3) a strong sense of frustration. Another group, whose members have been recognized as the "moderates" in the community, are found to come from home situations characterized by similar factors. A group of "dropouts" in the community are found to come from comparable home situations. A fourth group of persons, who were in the upper 10 percent of their high school graduating classes, are found to come from comparable home situations. Discuss the problem of the use of such variables in seeking to explain the behavior of the groups concerned.

18. All conditions are constant for a control group and an experimental group, except that the persons in the experimental group are bit by a female *Aedes aegypti* mosquito previously exposed to yellow fever patients. All members of the experimental group become ill with yellow fever, and no members of the control group develop yellow fever.

19. "Does the wheezing and coughing of an asthmatic child usually have a psychological basis? Although there is a quite widespread belief that asthmatic children are 'nervy' or neurotic, the actual evidence on this point is conflicting. Furthermore, even if they are, the question of deciding which is cause and which is effect remains. Till now there has been no study of a whole population (as opposed to a selected group, such as these visiting a hospital) which has looked for any association between asthma and psychological factors, but this has now been rectified by four scientists, P. J. Graham, M. L. Rutter, W. Yule and I. B. Bless, from the Institutes of Psychiatry and Education in the University of London (*British Journal of Preventive and Social Medicine*, Vol. 21. No. 2, p. 78).

"They investigated all children aged between nine and 11 living on the Isle of Wight (3300 in all), and found that 66 (2.0 per cent) were definitely asthmatic and that probably another 10 were. They then compared these children with a group of control children, 147 in all, who were selected at random, with regard to such features as social class, intelligence and any psychiatric symptoms. One point to emerge was that significantly more of the children came from social

[5] Isaac Asimov, *A Short History of Biology* (Garden City, N. Y.: The National History Press, 1964), p. 109.
[6] W. I. B. Beveridge, *The Art of Scientific Investigation* (New York: Vintage Books, 1957), p. 216.

classes I (professional) and II (white-collar workers), and fewer from the lower social classes. It is not yet clear why asthma should be more common in these classes, though there are some possibilities, such as a more varied diet, with more possible allergy-producing components, or a greater chance of moving from place to place, giving more opportunity for inhaling different allergens.

"On the intelligence tests, the asthmatic children did only slightly better than the others on nonverbal, reading and arithmetic tests, so there is no evidence that they were markedly superior, as is sometimes supposed. When they were checked for behavioural disorders, the proportion of the asthmatic children who were rated high enough to be classed as having a definite psychiatric disturbance was not significantly different from that in the children as a whole. However, when assessed as a whole by their parents' reports, the asthmatics did show a significantly higher level of behavioural symptoms than the general population, but they were not any worse in this respect than another group of children with other physical handicaps.

"These workers thus suggest that the small degree of psychiatric disorder they find to be associated with asthma is not specific, or a cause of the condition, but is more likely to be a general consequence of chronic illness, with its legacy of impaired social relationships. They do, however, point this out, that once asthma has begun, psychological factors cannot be ruled out altogether, since in over a third of the asthmatic children, some attacks had been precipitated by emotions, such as fear or anxiety, this happening both among children with a family history of eczema or asthma, and those with none. The conclusion that some, if not all, of the psychiatric disorders found associated with asthma are in fact caused by it, though supported by the fact that the children with psychiatric symptoms had little in common except their asthma, cannot at the moment be established with certainty. To clarify this complex situation, we need a lengthy investigation of younger (pre-school age) children, known to be especially likely to develop asthma on the basis of family history, to see whether particular behaviour patterns or aspects of personality regularly precede its development, or whether those who develop asthma reveal, by the subsequent development of such symptoms, the occurrence of some degree of stress."[7]

20. "One of the arguments surrounding those weirdies of the botanical world, the carnivorous plants (such as the Venus flytrap), is whether in fact they digest their insect prey themselves. Digestion has seemed too 'animal-like' to some botanists, who have proposed instead that, since the dead insects (or small animals) are quickly decomposed by bacteria and small fungi in any case, the plant itself is a mere parasite feeding on the products of microbes who really do the work of digesting the hapless insects.

"The main purpose of the plant's carnivory is to obtain a source of nitrogen with which to make its protein. Such plants are usually found growing on soils that are poor in minerals, especially nitrogen, and the insects are a useful supplement to their diet. But before it can obtain nitrogen, in the useful form of amino acids all ready to build up again into the plant's own protein, the animal's protein must be broken down to amino acids by protein-digesting enzymes. To find out whether these enzymes come from the plant or from microbes, Dr. Ulich Lüttge, assistant professor in the department of botany at the Technological

[7] "Is Asthma Really Psychosomatic?" *New Scientist,* May 11, 1967, p. 323.

University at Darmstadt, West Germany, studied the carnivorous plant *Nepthenes,* or Pitcher leaf.

"As its name implies, the insect-catching apparatus of the plant is a leaf rolled up to form a pitcher-like vessel. Animals are attracted by the mottled colour of the 'urn' and by the excretion of nectar from glands on its very smooth margin. They alight on this margin, slip and fall into a sap, containing digestive enzymes, in the base of the trap. They drown and are digested.

"Dr. Lüttge took a young pitcher, still closed by a lid, and which could safely be said to be free of microbes. He removed some of the sap from within the pitcher with a syringe, introduced the sap into a protein solution and showed, by ultraviolet spectrophotometry, that the sap indeed contains protein-digesting enzymes.

"Other enzymes were found in the sap from mature and open pitchers which did come from microbes, since they only occur in pitchers containing the remains of insects and small animals infested by microbes. They are absent in a sterile secretion and on sterile feeding. So although the plant does derive some benefit from microbes which help by a form of predigestion, this is only an additional aid, and the plant can quite well digest its prey without it."[8]

21. "It is impossible to know to what extent all human behaviour has an identifiable physical cause. However, the list is growing of extreme cases of abnormality that can be coupled with specific defects like genetic aberrations. In *Science* (Vol. 155, p. 1682) three researchers at the National Institute of Arthritis and Metabolic Diseases, Bethesda, Maryland, now describe for the first time a link between compulsive aggressive behaviour in human patients and the lack of a particular enzyme from their constitutions.

"The disease from which these patients suffered is a recently recognized hereditary neurological condition producing cerebral palsy coupled with mental retardation, involuntary bodily movements, and abnormal manifestations of aggression. One of the additional symptoms is the overproduction of uric acid which may be three to six times higher than normal in the urine of such patients.

"J. E. Seegmiller, F. M. Rosenbloom and W. N. Kelley discovered that this excess of uric acid results from the absence of an enzyme (hypoxanthine guanine phosphoribosyltransferase). Biochemical tests on cells from children affected with the disease showed that the activity of this enzyme was less than ½ per cent of normal, but that this effect was not due to the presence of an enzyme inhibitor.

"Uric acid is derived from the purine base hypoxanthine, and it was supposed that the function of the absent enzyme was in making use of both this and another base, guanine, one of the 'letters' of the genetic code. When the enzyme is lacking it seems that the biosynthesis of these purines is not properly regulated, though the precise mechanism remains obscure. It is, in fact, the first time than an enzyme *deficit* has been shown in humans to result in an *increased* output of a metabolic end product.

"The disease is sex-linked, occurring only in males, so that the site of the genetic defect giving rise to it probably lies on the chromosome.

"The authors conclude: 'The association of a specific enzyme with a neurological disease, mental retardation, and a compulsive aggressive behaviour may

---

[8] "Meat-Eating Plant Digests Unaided," *New Scientist,* April 27, 1967, p. 217.

serve to reorient our fundamental approach to other behavioural disorders.' "[9]

22. "When we say that an athlete is 'fit,' we generally mean that he can perform some arbitrary feat, like 50 press-ups, without getting unduly puffed. But 'fitness' in the athletic sense actually has much the same meaning as 'fitness' in the Darwinian sense—a marathon runner, who can cover 26 miles 385 yards in a little over two hours, is metabolically different from a sprinter. Physiologists are only now beginning to understand the metabolic factors that enable some athletes to shine at particular events and cause them to fail at others. When these factors are understood, we will be able to gauge the theoretical limits of human athletic achievement.

"Recent work by Dr. L. G. C. E. Pugh, of the National Institute of Medical Research, London, and his colleagues, has shown that the good marathon runner is distinguished by being able to work hard while enduring body temperatures that would, in a sick patient, be designated 'high fever'; he can also withstand fluid loss equal in volume to that of his blood.

"Dr. Pugh and his colleagues examined most of the 77 runners in a Road Runners Club marathon held at Witney, near Oxford, last summer (*Journal of Applied Physiology*, Vol. 23, p. 347). Sixty-three runners finished the course. By the end of the race, the finishers had lost an average of 6½ lb. But the first four runners had lost an average of nine pounds—which, in the case of the winner, amounted to 6.7 per cent of his body weight. Most of the weight loss was due to fluid loss, calculated at a fraction under seven pints. 'Dehydration of this degree,' says Dr. Pugh, 'if rapid and combined with hard stress, reduces performance and is a cause of collapse in nonathletes.' Blood tests of four runners who collapsed during the race showed that their blood was not unduly concentrated, so most fluid loss probably occurred extra-vascularly.

"In 47 runners, the rectal temperature was recorded immediately after the race. Body temperature ranged from 'normal' (about 98°F) to 105.8°F. The winner had the highest temperature, and three of the first four runners had temperatures in excess of 103.8°F. Previous workers have suggested that 105.8°F is the critical temperature, so the winner probably went to the absolute limit.

"The day of the race was warm and sunny. Dr. Pugh calculated that the heat from solar radiation alone would have been enough to raise the temperature of a 10-stone runner by 1.8°F. An individual's rate of heat loss is related to his surface area/weight ratio, and in this respect the second and third runners had a 10 per cent advantage over the winner. On an even sunnier day they might well have won.

"One limiting factor not approached by the Witney runners was oxygen intake, which in cross country skiers has been calculated at 83 ml per kg body weight per minute. A marathon time of 2 hr 10 min (about two minutes outside the present world record) would require an intake of 61 ml/kg/min. The Witney race winner took in a calculated average of 54 ml/kg/min. But to approach world record times he must choose a cloudier day."[10]

23. "While it is known that the sex of toads can to some extent be determined by the environment in which they develop as tadpoles, comparable studies

---

[9] "Missing Enzyme Can Cause Aggression," *New Scientist*, April 13, 1967, p. 75.
[10] "Marathon Runners Run at Fever Pitch," *New Scientist*, December 28, 1967, p. 766.

on other vertebrates such as rats and mice have been inconclusive. Joseph Stolkowski, a biologist at the Faculté des Sciences, Paris, was therefore interested in observations by a cattle breeder in the Redon region that the sex ratio of calves fathered by the same bull over a number of years differed at different farms—that is, with the type of pasturage grazed by the mothers. Further, by the addition of magnesium-based minerals to the fodder during the breeding period, the breeder claimed to have avoided a preponderance of male calves at a farm heavily treated with potassium fertilizer, thought to give rise to an excess of males.

"The breeder's observations were, however, empirical, and he had not preserved his notes. Stolkowski and his colleagues therefore sought to verify his conclusions by means of a questionnaire addressed to farmers in various parts of France and to a breeder in Ireland. The data requested included particulars of the number of males and females calved each year, the breeding time, the soil and any lime, manure, fertilizer, or litter applied to it, the fodder, and any dietary supplements. Replies relating to less than 40 births in any one herd, or providing insufficient data for recognition of the dominant food mineral, were ignored. And the investigators who determined the dominant mineral were deliberately kept unaware of the corresponding sex-ratio data.

"The findings, on the basis of 134 valid returns relating to a total of 25,653 births, have been reported to the French Academy of Sciences (*Comptes rendus,* 1967, Vol. D265, p. 1059). The sex ratio varied around the theoretical 50:50 to the same extent as was the case with the tadpoles, that is, to maxima of 69 per cent of males and 70 per cent of females, and a statistically highly significant correlation (coefficient 0.60) between the various ratios and the dominant mineral was established.

"In brief, the results suggest that an excess of potassium in the diet of breeding cows is indeed conducive to the birth of a majority of males, an excess of alkaline earths such as calcium and magnesium on the other hand encouraging an excess of females."[11]

---

[11] "Sex Balance Tipped By Minerals," *New Scientist,* January 4, 1968, p. 38.

Chapter 19
Probability

19.1 Probability Statements, Hypotheses, and Events

The hypotheses developed in the experimental sciences and the statements used in their confirmation are regarded as probable rather than certain—a position consistent with the view of the corrigibility of knowledge claims in scientific inquiry. "Probability" here does not imply a lack of trustworthiness in such hypotheses and statements; rather, it points to critical problems related to the use of a rigorous method in the establishing of knowledge claims.

The notion of probability is applied not only to statements and hypotheses but also to events. The *probability of statements* refers to the degree of confidence that is warranted in their reliability as testable by evidence, such as first-hand experience based on observation. The *probability of hypotheses* refers to the degree of confidence that is warranted in their reliability as testable by confirmation of their relevant consequences. A rigorous and elaborate set of testing standards are usually applicable in the testing of hypotheses used in scientific inquiry. Hypotheses of a lower order of generality have consequences that can be confirmed by first-hand experience. The *probability of events* refers to the degree to which a prediction of the occurrence of a specified class of events is warranted on the basis of criticized evidence.

Probability with regard to hypotheses has been called by other names, such as confirmation, credibility, acceptability, and reasonableness. Probability related to events has been called relative frequency, statistical probability, and empirical probability. To state that a scientific hypothesis is reasonable is to assert that if it is part of a system of beliefs, there are strong reasons for keeping it within this system, and that if it is not part of such a system of beliefs, there are strong reasons for incorporating it into such a system. Probabilities with regard to events are stated in a statistical fashion; for example, the probability that a card drawn from an ordinary deck is the ace of hearts is $\frac{1}{52}$. Statistical probability for the reliability of a statement or of a general hypothesis cannot always be stated accurately in terms of a percentage.

19.2 Meanings of "Certainty"

There are many different senses of the word "certainty." Although many of these are accepted in ordinary discourse without much difficulty, in critical discourse it becomes necessary to differentiate these different senses and to determine which, if any, are to be regarded as applicable. Consider the following statements:

(1) I am certain that John is honest.

(2) I am certain that I see a book on the table.

(3) I am certain that in a component of radium 50 percent of the radium atoms will disintegrate in a period of 1,660 years.

(4) I am certain that all triangles have three angles.

In each of these statements, reasons can be given to justify the clause that follows the expression, "I am certain." Cognitive certainty, however, is not assured to be warranted in every case. The type of certainty expressed in the statement "John is honest" is *psychological*. A person making such a statement apparently is asserting that in a state of affairs in which John might be dishonest, he has confidence that John would be honest.

The second assertion, which concludes "I see a book on the table," represents a *common-sense* notion of certainty. Anyone making this statement might conceivably be mistaken. Although some philosophers hold that statements such as "I feel a sharp pain" are indubitable, many others would assert that any statement about matters of fact can be mistaken. Claims to cognitive certainty in such statements are quite difficult to justify. One can make a strong case, however, for insisting that a given statement has a much higher degree of probability than possible alternative statements relative to the specified state of affairs. Common-sense notions of certainty are special cases of psychological or subjective certainty.

The third statement, "I feel certain that in a component of radium 50 percent of the radium atoms will disintegrate in a period of 1,660 years," represents a *systematic* certainty. The statement is grounded in a particular system of beliefs; it supports other statements within the system and they support it. The statement also is supported by experimental evidence. The system may be found to contain certain errors or deficiencies; on this account it would not be desirable in a scientific context to close the system, and scientists prefer to leave a system open for correction by further observations and experiments. Even if we insist that this statement is preferable to any other relevant statement, there remains a significant gap between "strong, justifying evidence" and "absolute certainty."

The fourth statement, "I am certain that all triangles have three angles," contains an assertion that is true in any conceivable set of circumstances. A part of the meaning of the word "triangle" is "to have three angles." The truth or falsity of the statement is determined entirely by the meaning of the subject and predicate terms. The type of certainty asserted here is *analytic*. Given the meaning of its components, the assertion is necessarily true.

To summarize, statements about matters of fact are regarded as probable rather than as certain. In a rigorous and theoretical sense "certainty" signifies the impossibility of an assertion's being false. This is to be distinguished from psychological certainty, in which there may be complete confidence in the truth of an assertion or belief, but the possibility remains that the assertion or belief is in error. If statements about matters of fact are claimed to be certain, the theoretical meaning of "certainty" becomes less rigorous. If such statements are regarded as certain in a systematic sense, elements in the system can be in error and the system needs to remain corrigible. Rigorous theoretical certainty is possible only in statements that are analytic. In such cases it is impossible for the statement itself to be false, given the meaning of its subject, predicate, and relational terms. Analytic certainty is possible only if a statement's denial constitutes an internal contradiction. To deny that all triangles have three angles would involve such a contradiction. Statements about matters of fact are contingent. Their denial does not involve necessarily an internal contradiction in the statement.

19.3 Necessity, Possibility, Contingency, and Impossibility

Like the word "certain," "necessary" has a variety of meanings in ordinary language. Many statements containing "necessary" entail a condition that is left unstated. Consider the statement "It is necessary to go to the grocery store." What is asserted here is that if certain food items are to be secured, then going to the grocery store is a condition for securing them. It might be asserted, "It is necessary to pass calculus before taking an advanced course in physics." Again, a condition is implicit. If a student is to take an advanced physics course, then a condition for his enrolling in the course is his having a final passing grade in calculus. Consider the statement "It is necessary for 50 percent of the radium atoms of a component of radium to disintegrate within a period of 1,660 years." Although a claim might be made that some "necessity" was operative here, the statement contains the implicit assumptions such as, "If the present statistical laws are dependable and if they continue to hold in the future, then the most reliable predictions would indicate that 50 per cent of the radium atoms will disintegrate in 1,660 years." Consider another statement: "It is necessary that a square contain four and only four right angles." The "necessity" here is logical in character. Unless the plane figure has four and only four angles and unless each angle is a right angle, it is impossible for this figure to be a square.

The same kind of "necessity" holds in the statement "It is necessary that all bachelors are unmarried men." If an adult male is married, he is not a bachelor. Necessity here has an analytic meaning. Not both can the terms of the statement have their usual meaning and the statement be false. In a strict sense necessity, like analytic certainty, is logical or analytical in character.

Statements containing such expressions as "It is possible that," "It may be," and "It must be" are analyzed in modal logic. In the traditional notation for basic concepts in this type of logic, the symbol "□" indicates the notion "It is necessary that" and the symbol "◊" indicates the notion "It is possible that." Thus the expression "◊P" means "P is possible" and the expression "□P" means "P is necessary." Various combinations of this notation with "not," indicated by the tilde (∼), yield the following notions:

$$\Box P \qquad\qquad P \text{ is necessary}$$
$$\sim\Diamond\sim P \qquad\qquad P \text{ is necessary}$$
$$\Diamond P \qquad\qquad P \text{ is possible}$$
$$\sim\Box\sim P \qquad\qquad P \text{ is possible}$$
$$\Box\sim P \qquad\qquad P \text{ is impossible}$$
$$\sim\Diamond P \qquad\qquad P \text{ is impossible}$$
$$\sim\Box P \cdot \sim\Box\sim P \qquad\qquad P \text{ is contingent}$$
$$\Diamond P \cdot \Diamond\sim P \qquad\qquad P \text{ is contingent}$$

A statement is contingent if it is not necessary and not impossible.

A statement is logically necessary if its denial would constitute a logical contradiction. A logically necessary statement includes the form "P or not P," "Either this is a logic class or this is not a logic class." A statement is impossible if it cannot be logically meaningful. A logically contradictory statement would be "P and not P," "This plane figure is round and it is not round."

A statement is logically possible if it does not contain logical notions that are inconsistent or incompatible. A contingent statement, neither necessary nor impossible, is "The automobile has air-conditioning."

If the occurrence of an event is either necessary or impossible, the necessity or impossibility is derived from logical considerations. It is (logically) impossible for a sum greater than 12 to be cast on a pair of dice if each die has 6 as its highest number. It is (logically) necessary to cast a number between 2 and 12 with a pair of properly constructed dice.

Probability statements are concerned with values ranging from zero to one. In mathematical probability, a value of zero signifies that an event is impossible and a value of one signifies that an event is necessary. If an event has a probability greater than zero, then it is possible. If any probability is greater than zero but less than one, then it refers to a contingent event. The probability of drawing five aces from an ordinary deck of playing cards (one that is not rigged) is zero. The probability of throwing either a head or a tail on a coin, if at least one of these events must occur in any given case, is one. The probability of throwing a "7" on a pair of dice is contingent, as is the probability of throwing heads on a flip of a coin.

19.4 Probability and Hypotheses

From a traditional philosophical point of view, statements of the experimental and empirical sciences are concerned with probabilities of a contingent character. Hypotheses in these sciences are neither necessary nor impossible. Strictly speaking, an event is impossible only if the statements of the conditions necessary and sufficient for its occurrence contain logically incompatible notions. At the same time it is justifiable to hold that certain statements about matters of fact are highly unwarranted and that others are warranted.

If a statement (one that is not self-contradictory) about a given state of affairs is said to be impossible, what is being asserted, strictly speaking, is that from the standpoint of all available evidence the probability of the truth of this statement approaches zero; that is, the statement is false. There also may be every reason for confidence that the probability of the truth of a given "nonnecessary" statement about a matter of fact approaches one; that is, the statement is true. Here one might assert "a practical certainty" that such a matter of fact is the case.

19.5 Probability Applied to Events

There are two methods for determining the probability of the occurrence of a particular kind of event: (1) empirical or *a posteriori* probability and (2) mathematical or *a priori* probability. *Empirical* probability is calculated on the basis of the frequency of the specified event in relationship to all events that have occurred in a given circumstance. To determine the empirical probability that any given car will stop at a traffic stop sign, one would need to establish a probability table based upon observation of cars stopping at this sign. If 5,000 cars passed this sign and 4,763 stopped, the empirical probability that the next car approaching the sign would stop would be $4763/5000$. Likewise, if, in tosses of a particular coin, "heads" occurred on 493 occasions in 1,000 tosses, then the empirical probability for the occurrence of "heads" on the next toss would be $493/1000$.

In some cases a special circumstance may be relevant to determining the empirical probability of an event. A given baseball player may have a batting average of .303. Irrespective of other conditions, the empirical probability of his hitting safely his next time at bat is $303/1000$. If he is hitting 353 against right-handed pitching and 253 against left-handed pitching and if he is batting against a left-handed pitcher, the empirical probability of his getting a safe hit is $253/1000$ rather than $303/1000$.

The basic formula for determining empirical probability is the number of times the specified event occurs divided by the total number of occurrences of the events of this general class (including favorable and unfavorable events). In this formula, $p = s/t$, p means "the probability of occurrence of the specified event," s means "the specified event," and t means "the total number of events of that class."

We determine mathematical probability by calculating the chance for the occurrence of a specifiable event in relation to the total number of events of this class that can occur. In the flipping of a coin when the specified event is "heads," the mathematical chance of the event's occurring is $\frac{1}{2}$. Two possible events may occur, namely heads or tails. Only one of these, the occurrence of heads, is the specified event. It is assumed that either heads or tails is an equally probable event. The formula for determining this kind of probability again is $p = s/t$, with s again signifying "the specified event" and t meaning "the total number of events possible, and equally probable." The application of this formula in specific cases can be quite difficult.

The use of mathematical probability is accompanied by several trouble-some problems. In a given situation several different events may occur, but the chance of occurrence of a given event may be greater or less than the mathematical probability accorded it. A roulette wheel, for example, can have a mechanical defect or can be manipulated, so that it stops less frequently at some positions and more frequently at others than the mathematical probabilities indicate.

Mathematical probability is restricted to cases in which a formula for determining the chances of the occurrence of specific kinds of events can be applied independently of experience. If an automobile approaches a traffic sign indicating "stop," the two possible events, the driver stopping or not stopping the car, do not appear to be equally probable. A satisfactory formula for calculating the chances of the occurrence of one of these events cannot be imposed without reference to observed cases. Such probability tables, based upon observation, have to be built on the basis of past experience.

Another problem with mathematical probability is more theoretical in character and may be phrased as a question. What is the justification for believing that events will conform to a number system that is built up independently of any specific reference to the events themselves? If the proposed answer points to a tendency of a given class of events to occur with a frequency indicated by *a priori* or mathematical probability, the justification for accepting the proposed mathematical probability is based on appeal to past experience rather than on mathematical considerations alone. Such justification is not in terms of a mathematical system itself but rather in terms of practice. The assumption is made that unobserved or future events will have the same ratio in their occurrence as those that have been observed. If the basis for according confidence to mathematical probability is a probability table based upon observation, it would appear desirable to resort to the experience itself rather than to mathematical probability. Although it is frequently stated that the mathematical probability will work out "in the long run," reasons justifying this belief combine postulates about the occurrence of events with an appeal to past experience.

Mathematical probability has the advantage of providing a critical basis for calculating probabilities without the expense and delay involved in building up a satisfactory table for determining empirical probabilities. Predictions based on mathematical probabilities have had a considerably higher degree of accuracy than those based upon hunches or guesses. A mathematical table of probabilities can serve as a hypothesis to anticipate the ratio of given kinds of events in a general class of occurrences if it is not practicable to build a probability table on the basis of observation. The mathematical probability serves as a useful guide until such empirical tables are constructed. If there is a significant discrepancy between tables of probabilities constructed on mathematical considerations alone and those constructed by reference to experience for a given class of events, further investigation to find the reason for the discrepancy can be carried out. The original mathematical formulation may have been inadequate. The experiment may have been poorly designed. The mechanism related to the occurrence of a particular event may be faulty. An unanticipated variable may be operative and may account for the difference between the expected value and actual value.

In both theoretical and applied research thousands of hours of research time are often devoted to the construction of accurate probability tables.

19.6 Calculations of Mathematical Probabilities

Although the determination of the *a priori* probability of some events may involve complex mathematical procedures, the more elementary problems can be calculated by simple procedures. Consider an ordinary die with six sides, each side bearing a dot or dots representing a different number from 1 through 6. What is the probability on a given throw of casting a 6 on the die? What is the probability of throwing a 6 consecutively on any two casts? What is the probability of not casting a 6 on the die?

The general formula is that the probability of a specified event equals the number of the specified events divided by the total number of possible events, or $p = s/t$. In the case of casting a 6, the probability is determined by dividing the number of specified events that can occur, which in this case is one, by the total number of events that can occur, which in this case is six, or $\frac{1}{6}$. The probability of throwing either a 5 or a 6 on a die would be determined by adding the probability of the occurrence of the different specified events. The total number of possible events remains six. The probability of throwing a 5 is $\frac{1}{6}$, of throwing a 6 is $\frac{1}{6}$, of throwing a 5 or a 6 is $\frac{1}{6} + \frac{1}{6}$

or $\frac{2}{6}$. Notice that the word "or" appears in the expression "a 5 or a 6." In a probability statement "or" usually indicates interdependent events. The appearance of either one of the events satisfies the conditions for the specified event. Where events of this kind are interdependent, addition is proper. The probability of the 6 is $\frac{1}{6}$, the probability of the 5 is $\frac{1}{6}$, the probability of the 5 or the 6 is $\frac{1}{6}$ plus $\frac{1}{6}$ or $\frac{2}{6}$. Thus "or" customarily signifies the need of addition. The probability of throwing a 1 or a 2 or a 3 or a 4 or a 5 or a 6 on a die is

$$\tfrac{1}{6} + \tfrac{1}{6} + \tfrac{1}{6} + \tfrac{1}{6} + \tfrac{1}{6} + \tfrac{1}{6}$$

that is, the probability is 1. In this set of events any possible event occurring would be included as one of the specified events.

Consider the probability of casting a 6 on the first throw and on the second throw of the die. The probability of its occurrence as the specified event on the first throw is $\frac{1}{6}$, and the probability of its occurrence as the specified event on the second throw is $\frac{1}{6}$. The mathematical probability of these consecutive events is $\frac{1}{6}$ times $\frac{1}{6}$, or $\frac{1}{36}$. Notice that the word "and" is used. These events are independent. What happens on the first throw has no bearing whatsoever on what happens on the second throw. In the case of independent events, the probability of the first event is multiplied by the probability of the second event. In the present example that is $\frac{1}{6} \times \frac{1}{6}$ or a probability of $\frac{1}{36}$. In independent events, the "and" conventionally indicates the need to multiply to determine the probability of the occurrence of the stated event.

What is the probability of throwing the die and not casting a 6? Notice that the "not" occurs in the statement of the problem. In such cases "not" may indicate a need to subtract the probability of the unfavorable event from one. In the present example the unfavorable event is casting the number 6. The probability of the occurrence of the unfavorable event is $\frac{1}{6}$. The probability of a favorable event or of not casting a 6 is $1 - \frac{1}{6}$ or $\frac{5}{6}$. This is one way of working a problem requiring the calculation of the probability of an event's not occurring.

What is the probability of tossing three coins and throwing at least one head on any of the coins? If this problem is restated with the use of "not," its solution is more apparent. "What is the probability of tossing three coins and not having three tails?" The probability of the unfavorable event, or of three tails, is $\frac{1}{2} \times \frac{1}{2} \times \frac{1}{2}$ or $\frac{1}{8}$. By subtracting the probability of the unfavorable event from one, we obtain the probability of a favorable event. The probability of not tossing three tails, or of tossing three coins and having at least one head on any of the coins, is $1 - \frac{1}{8}$ or $\frac{7}{8}$.

What would be the probability of throwing a pair of dice and having the sum of the numbers of both dice be 2, 3, or 12? The number 2 occurs only if a 1 occurs on each die. The probability of one dot on each die is $\frac{1}{6} \times \frac{1}{6}$ or $\frac{1}{36}$. Likewise, the probability of a 12 is $\frac{1}{6} \times \frac{1}{6}$ or $\frac{1}{36}$. The sum of 3 can be cast if we get a 1 on die A and a 2 on die B or a 2 on die A and a 1 on die B. The probability of casting a 2 is $\frac{1}{6} \times \frac{1}{6}$ or $\frac{1}{36}$, and the probability of casting a 12 is $\frac{1}{6} \times \frac{1}{6}$ or $\frac{1}{36}$. The probability of casting a 3 is $\frac{1}{36} + \frac{1}{36}$ or $\frac{2}{36}$. The probability of throwing a 2, 3, or 12 is $\frac{4}{36}$.

What is the probability of casting a 7 or an 11 on a pair of dice? There are two ways of casting an 11: 6—5 or 5—6. There are six ways of casting a 7: 1—6, 6—1, 2—5, 5—2, 3—4, or 4—3. The probability of casting an 11 is $\frac{1}{36} + \frac{1}{36}$ or $\frac{2}{36}$. The probability of casting a 7 is $\frac{1}{36} + \frac{1}{36} + \frac{1}{36} + \frac{1}{36} + \frac{1}{36} + \frac{1}{36}$, or $\frac{6}{36}$. The probability of casting an 11 or a 7 is $\frac{2}{36} + \frac{6}{36}$ or $\frac{8}{36}$.

What is the probability of not casting either a 7 or an 11 or a 2 or a 3 or a 12? The probability of the unfavorable event, or of the 2, 3, 7, 11, or 12, is $\frac{1}{36} + \frac{2}{36} + \frac{6}{36} + \frac{2}{36} + \frac{1}{36}$, or $\frac{12}{36}$. The probability of the unfavorable event substracted from one, $1 - \frac{12}{36}$ or $\frac{24}{36}$, is the probability of the favorable event or of not throwing any of the indicated numbers.

19.7 EXERCISES

Determine the mathematical probability of each event described.

1. There are 100 beans in a jar; 30 are red, 25 are brown, 20 are black, 15 are green, and 10 are purple. Each bean is replaced after each draw.

(a) What is the probability of drawing a brown bean on any given draw?

(b) What is the probability of drawing a black bean on two consecutive draws?

(c) What is the probability of drawing in order a red bean, a black bean, and a purple bean?

(d) What is the probability on any one draw of not picking a black bean or a green bean?

2. There are six sides on a die with the sides numbered 1 through 6. A pair of dice are cast.

(a) What is the probability of casting a 6?

(b) What is the probability of casting an 8 or a 9?

(c) What is the probability of casting a 4, 5, 6, 8, 9, or 10?

(d) What is the probability of not casting a 7?

3. There are 52 cards in a deck, with 13 cards in each suit. The cards are not replaced in the deck after they are drawn.

(a) What is the probability of drawing five cards of the same suit?

(b) If the king, queen, jack, and ten of spades are held in a hand, what is the probability of drawing an ace or a nine of spades?

(c) If the ten, nine, eight, and six of hearts are held in a hand, what is the probability of drawing the seven of hearts?

(d) If the jack of spades and the six of hearts are held, what is the probability of not drawing a card that will make the sum of the cards held greater than 21 if each card counts according to its own number with face cards counting 10 and aces counting 1 or 11?

4. There are numbers 1 through 20 spaced at equal intervals on each of three

wheels. Each wheel stops on a different pointer, and a pointer indicates any one of the twenty numbers on each wheel. Each wheel is spun separately until a pointer indicates a number.

(a) What is the probability of having the pointers indicate the number 20 on each wheel?

(b) What is the probability of having the pointers indicate the same number on each of the three wheels?

(c) If the pointers on the first and second wheels indicate the number 10, what is the probability of having the pointer on the third wheel not indicate the number 10?

5. Four men agree to rent four cars. Each draws a key at random from a box containing only the four keys for the four cars, and each goes to a different car to determine whether he has the proper key.

(a) What is the probability that the tallest man has the right key?

(b) What is the probability that each man goes to the car that his key fits?

(c) What is the probability that at least one man draws the key fitting the car that he seeks to drive?

Chapter 20
Statistics and
Hypotheses

20.1 Statistical Hypotheses

Hypotheses in many areas of science (such as nuclear physics, biology, medicine, economics, psychology, sociology, and political science) and in many other areas (such as national defense, education, marketing, investments, and television programs) are often based on statistical considerations. With the increasing use of computers statistical hypotheses and analyses are likely to have an even greater role in research. This chapter reviews in a rudimentary way some procedures used in the analysis of statistical hypotheses and some common fallacies occurring in statistical measurements.

The misuse of statistical procedures characterizes the research reported in many advertisements, popular magazines, and other news media. Such abuses also tend to be widely prevalent in propaganda. Consider the following examples. An article claims that the nuclear capability of the Soviet Union will increase at a rate 20 percent greater than that of the United States over the next five years and that the United States is falling behind in the race for nuclear power. No means is provided for checking the accuracy of these figures. The existing nuclear capabilities of these countries are not taken into account. The proposed 20 percent increase in the nuclear capacity of Russia can refer to an increase relative either to Russia's existing capabilities or to those of the United States. Such statistical comparisons require additional information, including some basis for estimating the reliability of the statistical data before determining what significance, if any, can be accorded them.

A drug manufacturer announces that a survey of persons suffering from sinus congestion shows that 40 percent of the persons taking the company's product experience significant relief within two hours and 80 percent report significant relief within twenty-four hours. No control groups are set up for comparison with an experimental group; no information is provided regarding a professional examination to determine either the degree of sinus infection, if any, of the persons taking the remedy or the degree of reduction in symptoms of persons who claimed some relief. No information is provided on checks made for the accuracy of the data recorded or for bias in the manner of taking the samples. Such use of allegedly statistical procedures can have persuasive force in selling the advertised drug, but there are no critical reasons for confidence in the reliability of the conclusions or of the data from which they derived.

Statistics is a critical study of the theories and reliable procedures for collecting, organizing, compiling, analyzing, and interpreting quantifiable data. Any competent analysis of statistics requires extended technical training and practice. A statistical hypothesis asserts that a given percentage of A's are B's or that a given percentage of A's are not B's. Thus it can be proposed: "Fifty percent of radioactive carbon atoms decay by beta emission in 5,760 years."

20.2 Descriptive Statistics and Sampling Statistics

Statisticians differentiate between descriptive statistics and sampling statistics. These terms can be misleading, since both types seek data relevant and applicable to the total population studied. Each type proposes to describe the characteristics of the complete population. The data of descriptive statistics cover the total population. Sample statistics collects its data from a proper sample of the population. By proper analysis of the sample we can estimate the prevalence of these characteristics in the total population.

If, for example, it is proposed to make a statement about the mean grade in freshman English of all freshmen in a particular college, this can be done in one of two ways. The grade of all freshmen can be determined and the mean computed. This mean is a descriptive statistic. Or, a random selection of one hundred freshmen can be taken, and through the use of procedures of sampling statistics a mean grade can be estimated for all freshmen. If the mean or the average of the hundred freshmen selected at random is applied to the total population of freshmen, then the mean is a sampling statistic.

20.3 The Uses of Statistical Analyses

Statistical procedures are used for a variety of purposes. Statistics provide a technique for a rigorous and critical analysis of measurable data compiled and organized by recognized standards. By enlarging the area in which a critical method can attain to reliable results, it extends the boundaries of knowledge.

Statistics are used to analyze a body of raw data for additional significant information. For example, at the end of the freshman year the raw data derived from records about the freshman class can be subjected to a variety of analyses. The grading of different departments and of different teachers can be analyzed. The first-year averages of freshmen students can be compared with their predicted grade point averages and with their high school averages. The grades of students within a given predicted grade point average can be compared in terms of subgroups: students who had cars on the campus against those who did not, or those who had jobs requiring twelve hours or more of work each week against those who did not. In such analyses the raw data can yield relevant information about the performance of the group studied.

Statistics can be used to determine levels of expected values such as growth or performance, as well as the degree of significance of deviations from any established central tendency. The weight and height of children can be analyzed to determine norms of growth for different ages. Achievement tests can be indicators of comparative intellectual development based upon specified norms.

The use of statistics projects the probable behavior of large populations of groups through an intensive study of properly selected samples. Properly conducted political polls can provide a fairly accurate description of the political preferences of a given political population by developing a satisfactory sample of the whole population and subjecting preferences found in it to critical analysis.

Statistical studies can provide data for evaluating the relative dependability of different measuring techniques. The grades of graduating college seniors can be analyzed in relation both to college-board exam scores and to high school records to evaluate which of these measuring devices is a superior indicator of college performance.

Statistics may also provide information useful in making decisions whose consequences will not become immediately apparent; that is, statistics can provide a better foundation than guesswork for making predictions and initiating controls. If a school has a limited enrollment and wishes to admit students who are likely to do superior work in college, then statistical charts based upon tests and grades can enable its admission officers to select an especially promising freshman class. Such a selection better enables the achieving of a set of goals, identified by such variables as higher performance and diversity of abilities, than mere admission in the order of original application to the college.

Statistics also are used as a basis for suggesting causal relationships. Correlations can be misleading, but they can be useful in suggesting hypotheses for further experimental study. If a high correlation holds between persons with high cholesterol counts and persons with vascular cardiac problems, and a relatively low correlation holds between persons with moderate cholesterol counts and persons with vascular cardiac difficulties, then these correlations can be suggestive of causal relationships. As another example, two different classes in logic with students of comparable abilities might be studied. One class might be assigned homework on a conventional basis and the second class might be required to use logic machines in a laboratory as a part of their homework. The relative performance of the two classes could be studied to determine whether students using logic machines did better than those following more conventional homework assignments.

20.4 Procedures of Sound Classification

Proper analysis requires a breaking down of the data into groups or classes, which requires the use of a principle of classification. A number of different rules are relevant to satisfactory classification.

The principle of classification needs to be determined by reference to the purpose of the statistical analysis. If a study of the length of residence of persons living in a neighborhood is undertaken, a classification might be made on the basis of owned and rented houses or apartments. If the purpose of a survey is to determine conditions relevant to marginal housing conditions, the principle of classification can be based on the general physical condition, including sanitary facilities, of housing in a given neighborhood. If a survey is to determine factors related to integration of different racial groups in a neighborhood, a principle of classification based on ethnic differences might be used.

Only one principle of classification should be used for a given series of classes. One might propose to classify a group of professors in a given university campus. The principle of classification here can be the professors' age, their health, their scholarly attainments, their teaching efficiency, their interest in counseling with students, their political attitudes, or the areas of their specialization. The following classification of professors violates the principle: professors, associate professors, assistant professors, instructors, good lecturers, good researchers. Any data analyzed should fit into one and only one class—that is, the classes should not overlap, and irrelevant classes should be excluded. Overlapping classes are exemplified in a classification of students as excellent, good, average, poor, and hippies.

The precise limits of each class should be determined. If a project concerns the academically related personnel of a college, three categories might be used: (a) the administration, (b) the faculty, and (c) the students. A set of criteria would need to be applied consistently in the classification of each academically related person, resolving such questions as the following: Would a person taking only a correspondence course from the university be classified as a student? Would a faculty member giving half time to an administrative position in the office of the academic dean and half time to teaching be classified as a faculty member or as an administrative official? Would a graduate assistant teaching one freshman-level course and taking three graduate courses be classified as a member of the faculty or as a student?

The division of classes must be adequate to distinguish any relevant class. A miscellaneous class with a relatively high percentage of membership should be avoided. Insufficient differentiation of classes for some surveys is represented by the following examples: A student proposed three classifications for students in the junior high school: the athletes, the delinquents, and those who were neither athletes nor delinquents. The languages spoken in the Americas might be classified as follows: English, Spanish, Portuguese, and others. This final class would group together those who speak French, those who speak a native dialect, such as Navajo or Guarani, and those immigrants who speak German or Italian. For some surveys this miscellaneous class would be both too large and too heterogeneous.

An opposite kind of violation of the rule above also should be noted: the kinds of classes should not be needlessly duplicated.

In deciding on the degree of breakdown of classes, one should consider both the possible divisions of the subject area and the purpose of the classification. If a general study is to be made of the library holdings of a given university, the breaking down of the holdings into major subject areas might be entirely sufficient for some purposes. If a study is made of the works in chemistry, additional classes with additional divisions would be desirable in this area. If all of the classes used in the latter case were also used in the former case and the same procedure used in all subject areas, there would be unnecessary multiplication of classes, at least for the purpose of many surveys.

20.5 Statistical Populations

Statistics is a critical study of the methodology for achieving accurate descriptions of estimates of quantifiable populations and of the reliable inferences that can be drawn from such descriptions. The term "population," as used in statistics, is more inclusive than in ordinary language, where it usually refers to the number of people in a specific geographical area. In statistics, "population" refers to specifiable groups or aggregates of any measurable kind of entity, event, or process. The statistician specifies the particular population to which he is referring, such as soap detergents, freshman students in four-year senior colleges, eligible voters, professional athletes, white mice, or fresh-water fishing lures. The statistician also is concerned with a description of the total group or population rather than merely with a description of the properties of individual members of the population.

It is also conventional to distinguish between finite and infinite populations. A *finite* population is one whose total membership could conceivably be counted; this would include the number of freshman students enrolling in colleges and universities in this country in any given year, or the inhabitants of Washington, D.C. An *infinite* population is one whose total membership has no practical way of being determined. The number of times that a coin might be tossed is theoretically infinite, and the number of grains of sand on beaches cannot be determined in any practical manner. In many cases the population being studied by a statistician is either so indefinite in its total membership or so large that it is regarded as infinite for the purposes of his statistical calculations.

Statisticians conventionally distinguish between parameters and estimates. A *parameter* is a descriptive property applicable to a total population. An *estimate* is a descriptive property applicable to a sample taken at random from the total population. Values of parameters in a population frequently are not known in a strict sense. They are estimated on the basis of the values found in random samples. If a study of the weight of women between the ages of thirty and forty is being made, a random sample might be taken of a thousand women in this age bracket. Let it be assumed that the value of the parameter in the total population cannot be known in any strict sense; the value obtained from the random sample constitutes an estimate of this parameter.

20.6 Types of Statistical Scales for Measurement

Traditionally, statisticians have referred to four different types of scales for measuring purposes. These are the nominal scale, the ordinal scale, the interval scale, and the ratio scale. In a *nominal* scale there is a distinction of classes based on the notions of sameness or of difference. Each class used is designated by a number. The faculties in a university might be distinguished as: (1) humanities, (2) natural sciences, (3) social sciences, (4) business, (5) engineering. Any one teacher would be either in the same class with other teachers or in a different class from other teachers. The numbers used in a nominal scale to designate such classes do not indicate any type of progression, but do identify the members of any particular class. That is, nominal scales provide identification for sameness and difference.

An *ordinal* scale makes possible the assigning of an order or rank in the scales, so that besides referring to sameness or difference we can use the comparatives "greater than" or "less than." Data can be arranged with the minimal value at the bottom of the scale. For example, the male students in a fifth-grade class can be ranked according to height in an ordinal scale. The employees of a business concern can be ranked in order of years of employment.

An *interval* scale makes possible the differentiation of classes on the basis of measurable differences or intervals. An interval scale does not have a proper zero point, although sometimes one is assumed for convenience. A traditional example of an interval scale is a Fahrenheit or centigrade thermometer. Certain types of statements about comparisons on such scales are proper while others are not. If the temperature at a given place is 40 degrees on the first of April, 60 degrees on the first of May, and 80 degrees on the first of June, it would not be proper to say that the first of June is twice as hot as the first of April. It would be proper to state that the temperature the first of May was half the difference between the temperature on the first of April and the first of June. Thus, in addition to statements of sameness or difference and greater than or less than the interval scale also makes possible statements about comparisons of intervals.

A *ratio* scale has an absolute zero expressed or implied along with grada-tions involving equality of intervals. Measurements in terms of feet, pounds, and quarts are ratio scales. The numbers used in a ratio scale represent the interval from a point of origin or of zero. Statements such as "twice as much as" and "four times greater than" are applicable on a ratio scale. It would be quite appropriate to state that 80 pounds is twice as heavy as 40 pounds. On a ratio scale one also can speak about sameness or difference, about greater than or less than, and about comparison of intervals.

Statisticians do not always insist that the method of analyzing based on one type of scale be restricted rigorously to that particular scale. However, they do point out that in any variation of procedure acknowledgment of any such deviation should be made and possible unwarranted inferences about the statistical data should be identified. Any information superimposed on the data should be identified accordingly. If this less rigorous use of the scales of measurement is followed, then one must avoid the fallacy of unwarranted shifting of the appropriate analysis of a particular scale. If an interval scale followed in measuring IQ's were interpreted as a ratio scale and the proposal were made that a person with an IQ of 130 was twice as intelligent as the person with an IQ of 65, this would constitute a fallacy.

20.7 Random Sampling Procedures

In statistical analysis it frequently is unfeasible or at least impractical to study the total population of a group. In such cases a sample is taken. The re-liability of the information obtained from a study of the sample depends upon the sample's representativeness.

The kind of sample taken by statisticians is a *random sample*. The word "random" here has a technical meaning, requiring that members of the sample be chosen in such a way that any member of the population studied has the same chance of being included in the sample as any other member. A sampling procedure that does not allow every member of the total popu-lation an equal chance of inclusion in the sample is not in strict accord with the principle of random sampling, and it may introduce a serious if not fatal bias into the research design of a statistical analysis.

A traditional way of selecting a random sample is to number the total population studied and to select the individual members of the sample by drawing numbers from a container. If the opinions of students in a given university are to be determined about a national draft law, a different number can be given to each student and the number of each student can be written on a slip and placed in a lottery wheel. If 500 students are to be included in the sample, then, after a satisfactory shuffling of the slips, 500 sample numbers can be drawn. In this case the random sample consists of those 500 students whose slips were drawn. The sample can be selected in some other way, but it is a random sample only if, at the time of selection, each student has an equal chance of being chosen as a member of the random sample.

Suppose there is a student directory with the names of every student in the university listed alphabetically. It would be possible to get a sample on the basis of selecting every *n*th numbered student. Thus, every tenth student listed in the directory might be selected and included in a sample. Such a procedure is called *systematic sampling*. Although it has many of the characteristics of random sampling, it may introduce a bias. There would be an obvious bias, for example, if the student directory listed only students with telephone numbers. Those without telephone numbers could not be included in this particular sample. Whatever the reason might be for the student's not having a telephone, this factor might exclude a significant variable from the study, and the sample would be unrepresentative of the total population. As another example, if a survey is being made of the attitudes of the students in a given university toward the foreign policy of the United States in Southeast Asia, and if the sampling is limited to students who are taking a course in political science, this is not a random sample. Every student in the university does not have an equal chance of being included in the survey. A similar error would occur if only students living in a given dormitory were surveyed or if the first 500 students volunteering to express their views were interviewed. This would be the fallacy of a biased random sample.

A *proportional stratified random sample* is used frequently for large heterogeneous groups. The population of the group is broken down or stratified according to relevant differences in the total population (assuming that some basis is known for determining the proportionate membership in each group). Then from each of the different strata a sample is drawn at random, the proportion of the sample drawn from each stratum depending on the numerical proportion of that stratum to the total population. The development of relevant criteria for the stratification of samples and the determination of any subgroups within such strata can become highly complex. Experience and training are prerequisites to sound surveys in such cases.

A significant statistical problem concerns the degree to which the sample is representative of the total population. Extensive statistical procedures are designed to determine the probability that the sample provides adequate representation. If two different random samples are taken of the same total population, the extent to which one sample might deviate from the other sample has to be estimated. This again requires extended statistical analysis and the development of a technique for estimating the deviation. For the manner of determining the probability of the reliability of the sample, the student is referred to any standard work on statistics. In general the probability that a given random sample will be representative of the total population to which it refers increases with the size of the sample in relation to the population. Proportional stratified random sampling may increase the probability that a smaller sample is representative of the total relevant population.

20.8 Measures of Central Tendency, or Averages

In the analysis of a body of data a significant measure is that of a central tendency. The three most common types of such measures or averages are the arithmetic mean, the median, and the mode. The *arithmetic mean,* often called the arithmetic average, is the one most frequently encountered and is a basis for many refinements in the determination of a central tendency. It consists in adding the sum of scores and dividing by the total number of scores listed. For example, consider the following possible test scores: 40, 50, 55, 60, 65, 70, 70, 75, 80, 80, 80, 80, 85, 95, 95. The total number of students is 15. The sum of all scores is 1,080. The arithmetic mean is the sum of all the scores, 1,080, divided by the total number of scores, 15. The arithmetic mean is 72.

The *median* is determined by the value of the entry midway in a table in which the number of scores having a lesser value is equal to the number of scores having a greater value. In the above case, student number 8 stands in this relation with a score of 75. Seven scores were lower than his and seven scores were higher; thus, the median of these scores is 75.

The *mode* is determined by the selection of the case occurring with greatest frequency. The case occurring with greatest frequency in the scores above is 80. Thus, the mode is 80.

Another way of stating the last two definitions is that the median is the point occurring midway in the distribution of the indicated measures. The mode is the measure occurring with greatest frequency.

None of these ways of computing an average of central tendency can be regarded as completely satisfactory in every case. The exclusive application of any one of them to a given sample might misrepresent the significance of an average.

The arithmetic mean is used with greatest frequency and is subject to less variation than the median, but the extreme scores may make this average misleading. The arithmetic mean reflects the exact size of each individual measure. The median reflects the relative position in the distribution. The mode represents the "typical case" or the case occurring with greatest frequency. If these methods of determining "averages" are used to supplement each other, they can add to the significance of the measures of a central tendency. For example, an employer has a study made of the number of years his employees remain with the firm. He finds that a number of them have been with the firm for 30 years, but that the arithmetic mean of service is 9 years. With a large turnover in some positions many persons have remained with the company for only one or two years. The median is found to be only 4.7 years. The mode—that is, the case occurring most frequently— is 2.7 years. Each of these averages provides data relevant to an analysis of the rate of turnover of employees.

In some instances it is necessary to weight the mean. This is particularly important if there is a wide scattering of values, with some values occurring much more often than others, and if some extremes might affect the arithmetic mean sufficiently to give a distorted picture. A given business firm might employ a chief executive at $35,000, an associate executive at $18,000, and ten other employees at $7,000 each. The average salary of the persons employed at this plant determined by the arithmetic mean would be $12,025 a year. If a weighted mean is used, each item is multiplied by a certain weight. In the present case let the weight be the number of times the item appears in the list. This factor would be one for the major executive, one for the associate executive, and ten for each of the persons making $7,000. The sum of the weighted measures is taken and divided by the number of weights. This provides a basis for determining the average salary in the business firm based upon the weighted mean, as illustrated in Table 20.1. The weighted mean

Table 20.1 Sample Weighted Measure

Salary (measure)	Weight	Weighted measure
35,000	1	35,000
18,000	1	18,000
7,000	10	70,000
7,000	10	70,000
7,000	10	70,000
7,000	10	70,000
7,000	10	70,000
7,000	10	70,000
7,000	10	70,000
7,000	10	70,000
7,000	10	70,000
7,000	10	70,000
$123,000	102	753,000

in this oversimplified illustration is 753,000 divided by 102, or $7,382.35. This would be the salary corrected by the weighted mean in contrast with the average of the nonweighted mean.

20.9 The Null Hypothesis

The *null hypothesis* is used frequently in some types of statistical research. The null hypothesis states that the presence of a particular variable makes no significant difference in a specified value in a given population. More particularly, a null hypothesis tests the view that no significant differences exist between a control group and an experimental group that is basically similar except that a relevant specified variable has been applied to the experimental group.

When the null hypothesis is being tested, the relevant data about both groups are collected and analyzed. With the assumption of the reliability of the hypothesis, an analysis is made to determine the probability that a random sample taken from the population will yield different means in the two groups. If the probability is great that any differences found might be accounted for by variations in samples from identical populations, then the null hypothesis is said to hold. Since the observed differences can be accounted for by sampling error, the statistical data do not justify confidence that they can be attributed to the variable introduced in the experiment.

If the probability is small that the difference between the means of the control group and the experimental group can be accounted for in terms of a sampling error, a statistical basis is found for the rejection of the null hypothesis. The differences in the means can be attributed to the variable introduced into the experimental group, and so the alternative hypothesis is accepted; that is, the null hypothesis is rejected.

Two major types of errors can occur in analyzing null hypotheses. The null hypothesis might be "sound" but rejected on the basis of the data secured. The null hypothesis could be in error but accepted as worthy of confidence on the basis of the available statistical data. It is customary for a research analyst to apply further rigorous tests in searching for these errors. One important test relates to the "level of significance." An acceptable level of significance is usually placed at a point not greater than .05 and in some cases not greater than .01. If the level of significance is .001, a high level of significance is accorded to the experimental hypothesis.

The level of significance of .05 indicates a probability of 5 percent or 5 in 100, that the difference between the means of the experimental group and of the control group is attributable to the sampling technique rather than to the introduction of the experimental variable. The .01 level of significance indicates that the probability of a sampling error accounting for differences between such means is 1 percent, or 1 in 100. This test is applied to the experimental hypothesis to justify the acceptance or rejection of the null hypothesis. The level of significance greater than .05 customarily requires acceptance of the null hypothesis. The experimental hypothesis may be accepted with a level of significance that is not higher than .05. In some cases a level of significance of .03, .02, or .01 is sought for the acceptance of the experimental hypothesis.

20.10 Errors and Fallacies in the Use of Statistical Analyses

Abuses of reliable procedures provide some basis for the misleading cliché that anything can be proven by statistics. Many abuses are possible in the improper collection or manipulation of statistical data and in the distortion of warrantable statistical conclusions. This section reviews some of the abuses found most often in statistical procedures.

Errors in planning a statistical analysis. A number of errors can occur in the planning stage of a statistical survey. The problem in the survey may be stated improperly, or it may be too broad or too vague. The conceptualization may be inadequate. The classification may be overlapping or incomplete. The sponsoring agency may be concerned to secure a particular kind of response and may introduce a corresponding bias in the survey design. The personnel carrying out the survey might be improperly or poorly trained. Differences in their methodological approaches or in their interpretation of certain concepts or variables in the survey can introduce biases into the data gathered.

The research design needs to be tested by a dry run, in which a restricted sample is analyzed for adequacy of result. Leading questions may evoke biased responses. Variations in response to given questions may reflect the manner in which the questions are worded. Responses may be limited improperly to black-or-white answers, making no provision for intermediate responses. If, for example, a question is asked about the involvement of the United States in Southeast Asia, provision for only two responses—approve or disapprove—would be too restrictive. Rather, a range of possible responses might be included such as completely approve, approve with some reservations, disapprove more than approve, disapprove rather strongly, and completely disapprove.

Technical errors in gathering statistics. A basic error in gathering statistics is to introduce a bias in the sample. The investigator may introduce such bias by failing to secure a random sample, by failing to obtain reliable responses, or by improper use of measuring devices. If, for example, in a survey of food costs an investigator finds coffee in one store priced below cost in a special sale, his listing of this price would misrepresent the prevailing consumer cost of coffee. In some situations respondents may not be disposed to give accurate answers. If an employee feels threatened by decisions to be based upon a survey, then his response to questions may misleadingly reflect his personal interests. Some persons traditionally underestimate their ages, overestimate their income, or exaggerate the extent of their formal education.

Such questions as "What was the amount of income reported on your last income tax return?" would be more likely to get an accurate reply than "What was your salary for the last year?" Likewise, a question such as "What was the last grade in school completed?" probably would be answered more accurately than the question "What amount of formal education did you have?" Checks on accuracy frequently are built into questionnaire design. For example, each of the following questions might be asked in different sections of a questionnaire: "What is your age?" and "In what year were you born?"

Another bias can be introduced if data are collected on the basis of easy and convenient accessibility of sources. If a random sample is made for a survey to determine the attitude of women toward the involvement of the United States in Southeast Asia, and if substitutions are made in the original sample for women who are away from home when the investigator makes the original inquiries, a bias is introduced into the sample. Likewise, if no data are secured by follow-up procedures from persons failing initially to respond to a questionnaire, an error can be introduced into the sample.

Errors also can occur in statistical data through delay between the time of securing information and the time of recording it or by inaccurate recording or copying of the data. In some instances, the manner in which the data are gathered prejudices the responses. An interviewer could ask leading questions suggesting a preferred kind of answer. Questionnaires might be constructed improperly to make some answers appear to be more acceptable than others.

Technical errors in recording of data. A variety of technical errors may occur in the recording of data. There may be guessing at answers that are not clearly expressed on the original data sheet. One item could be checked and then partially erased, leaving the respondent's intention in doubt. Abbreviations made on an interview schedule can be misinterpreted. Coding of data for computers may be improper, or mechanical errors of recording can occur.

Technical errors related to measurements used in the analysis of data. A critical use of statistics requires a notion of true value and a check on the accuracy of measurements used in the analysis of data. It customarily is held that the notion of true value is a prerequisite for a meaningful theory of error. A *true value* would remain constant in an indefinitely large number of accurate measurements. A major problem is the estimation of the degree of difference prevailing between the true value and the measurements obtained in the sample. Statisticians apply rigorous tests to determine the degree of probability of such an error. For a discussion of techniques for determining such probabilities, the student may refer to standard works on statistics.

Statisticians usually distinguish between random errors and systematic errors in an effort to determine the reliability of the collected data. *Random errors* tend to cancel each other out. If the weight of a particular object is recorded, the number recorded for each weighing may vary slightly either positively or negatively from its fixed value. Although it is generally assumed that these errors cancel each other out in the long run, in some cases tests are made for determining any possible adverse consequences of random errors in the statistical analysis.

A *systematic* error relates to some defect or imperfection in the measuring instrument itself, so that it makes the same error in each measurement. If the scales weighing an object are defective and consistently measure a greater value than the measured object has, a systematic error occurs. To avoid systematic errors, the instruments used in the measuring techniques need to be checked frequently.

Traditionally, statisticians have distinguished three methods for determining the reliability coefficient or the degree of accuracy to be accorded the data gathered. These methods have been called the test-retest method, the parallel-forms method, and the split-half method.

The *test-retest method* consists in the administration of a given test twice to the same group with a time interval between the two tests. If the time interval between the two tests is brief, the individuals taking the test may remember the answers given previously, and this may affect the reliability of the method. If the time interval is too great, other conditions may have intervened so that in certain important respects the samples may not be identical, although they are constituted by the same individuals.

The *parallel-forms method* consists in giving to an identical group two tests covering essentially the identical material, with a minimum time interval between the two tests. Correlations between the two tests support the judgment of the accuracy of the data gathered.

The *split-half method* consists in the giving of a single test, with the answers being divided into two groups. One group might consist of the odd-numbered questions and the other of the even-numbered questions. The results on the two scores are compared to determine their reliability.

Sometimes reference is made to an *internal-consistency method* in checking on the reliability of statistical data. The split-half method is one means of checking on internal consistency. Other methods, such as the Kuder-Richardson Formula No. 20, require extensive training in statistical procedures.

Other kinds of checks on the accuracy of data gathered include a more detailed study of the original sample. If the analysis concerns social processes, interviews help to provide depth and insight in the interpretation of the data.

Technical errors in the analysis of data. The analysis of the data gathered needs to be checked for accuracy. This procedure includes a re-evaluation of basic statistical procedures, such as the determination of the standard error of an estimate, the standard error of the mean, the standard error of the median, the standard error of the proportion, the correlation coefficient, and the reliability coefficient. Other possible errors to be checked for include the misuse of the null hypothesis, the abuse of the practice of weighting means, and the improper use or confusion of units of measurement.

Errors in the interpretation of statistics.   Although data-gathering procedures may be reliable and the corrected data may have been subjected to proper analysis, many errors can occur in the interpretation of statistical data. An average can be misinterpreted or misused. For example, on the basis of a report that 50 percent of the people in hospitals in the United States are patients suffering from some kind of mental illness, the inference might be proposed that within a given time span the percentage of persons who have serious cases of mental illness is as high as those who are seriously ill from other causes. An inference of this kind could ignore the relatively slow rate of turnover of patients in mental hospitals as compared to general hospitals. A mental hospital with two hundred beds may have cared for eight hundred people during one year, and a general hospital with the same number of beds may have cared for seven thousand patients during the same period.

It is also possible to misinterpret the significance of data collected under a given classification heading. A survey might state that there is a 5 percent higher accident rate in male drivers between the ages of eighteen and twenty-five than in any other group. On this basis one might propose to justify the view that the male driver of this age is much more likely to have an accident than a person at another age. However, the original statement can be highly misleading. Its significance cannot be determined merely on the basis of the percentage of drivers who have accidents who are males in the given age group. One must also determine the percentages of males and females at the different age levels who are driving cars. If the number of male drivers in the given age group were 10 percent higher than the number of drivers in the other brackets, and if they drove a greater proportionate amount of mileage in comparable conditions, then the 5 percent higher accident rate could indicate that such persons are safer drivers. On the other hand, if there were fewer male drivers at this age than at other ages or if they drove relatively fewer miles, then the accident record for this age group could be greater than the original percentage suggested.

A higher degree of accuracy for statistical data can be claimed than actually is warranted by the manner of securing measurements. A group of college students might be asked how many hours they sleep each night. After 250 persons are surveyed in a random sample, it might be concluded that the nightly average amount of sleep per student is 6.379 hours. To insist that this is a highly accurate figure when the original data included only the students' estimates would be to claim an unwarrantably high degree of accuracy.

It is also possible to extend a trend line for a period longer than the statistical data warrant. If over a five-year period it is found that the shortage of physicians in relation to population increases 2 percent annually and that the present shortage is 10 percent greater than it was five years ago, it would not be reasonable to project this trend line far into the future. To claim that in fifteen years the shortage of physicians would become 40 percent would not be warranted on the basis of such data.

Correlations are often misinterpreted. Correlations may suggest but they do not necessarily demonstrate causal relationships. If a higher percentage of high school students studying Latin go to college than those without any knowledge of Latin, the studying of Latin has not been shown to be the cause of their going to college. Plans to go to college may have been a factor in the choice of Latin by these students.

One of the more frequent misuses of statistical analyses is the attempt to apply the statistical norms characteristic of a group to a given individual of that group. If it is found that high school dropouts earn only 65 percent of the income of individuals who complete their high school work, it does not necessarily follow that a given high school dropout will earn only 65 percent of the average earnings of high school graduates. If the scores of a group of high school graduates place them in a particular class of persons of which 90 per cent have been unable to do satisfactory college work, this does not signify that a given member of that group will be unable to do college work. The statistical data indicate that in the past nine students out of ten falling into this particular group on scores also fall into another group consisting of those who are unable to complete satisfactorily their college work. Although such statistical data may provide the best guide admissions officers have in determining admission policies and may suggest the most advantageous way of investing available educational resources, they do not signify that any student refused admission on this basis would have been unable to complete college work satisfactorily.

Hasty generalization constitutes another form of unwarranted inference based on improper use of statistical data. A hasty generalization infers a general principle from too few cases. For example, a person meets two or three people from France who are *bon vivants* and concludes thereby that all Frenchmen are *bon vivants*. Hasty generalization also occurs if broad or sweeping generalizations are made from a random sample too small to justify such conclusions.

Deliberate errors in the recording and interpretation of statistics. A deliberate manipulation of data can be introduced in a proposed statistical analysis to distort or misrepresent conclusions. Extremist groups frequently engage in distortion to support their propaganda. Bias can be introduced deliberately into the sample. The data collected can be falsified, either when they are gathered or when they are recorded. A competent statistical analyst is careful to keep his method of procedure public, so that his conclusions can be confirmed by other interested and competent statisticians. It is also proper for an outsider to review the analysis of data as a means of checking on its accuracy. However, such an analyst may gloss over errors that occurred in the original analysis. It is particularly desirable to examine the level of significance claimed by a statistical survey in the event a null hypothesis is rejected.

A frequent form of misrepresentation of statistics in propaganda occurs in the use of charts and graphs. Even if the other parts of the statistical analysis are accurate, the significant differences can be minimized if they are charted as cubes rather than as lines or squares. Let us suppose that the units of difference in a survey are 1, 8, and 27. If the units are represented by lines, there will appear to be a highly significant difference. If they are presented as cubes, one cube will be one unit high, the second cube two units high, and the third cube three units high. Since the cubes represent volume, they are to be calculated as $1 \times 1 \times 1$, $2 \times 2 \times 2$, and $3 \times 3 \times 3$. Figure 20.1 illustrates this kind of pictorial representation.

A linear graph can be misreperesentative if it does not begin at zero. That is, it can overemphasize minor differences. If the units of measurement are 320, 340, and 360, and the base line on a chart begins at 300, then the chart shows what appears to be a significant difference between 320, 340, and 360. If the chart began with the base line of 0, then this difference would not appear nearly as large. Competent statisticians indicate a definite break in a statistical graph by a wavy line if any units are omitted between zero and the units presented on the chart. Figure 20.2 illustrates improper and proper procedures in presenting linear charts.

The many kinds of error possible in the use of statistics increase the need for careful appraisals of statistical data and of the conclusions derived from them. Many errors in statistical analysis can be detected only by persons technically trained in this field.

20.11 EXERCISES

1. Evaluate the following classifications and determine which rule or rules of proper classification are violated.

(a) Occupations of fathers of students in a logic class: professional, business, industrial, managerial, labor.

(b) Furniture woods: maple, oak, pine, mahogany, birch, walnut, miscellaneous.

(c) Types of colleges: public, private, church-related, independent.

(d) Type of colleges: junior, senior, technological, graduate, professional, liberal arts.

(e) Fine arts: music, painting, sculpture, drawing, architecture, drama, poetry, dancing, ballet, waltz.

(f) Citrus fruits: oranges, grapefruit, lemons, tangerines, miscellaneous.

2. Determine the type of statistical scale of measurement relevant to each of the following cases.

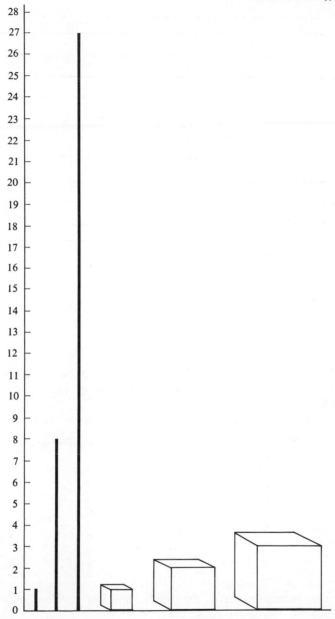

FIGURE 20.1

(a) The IQ of a group of freshmen in Jonesboro College.
(b) The scores on a logic test in this class.
(c) The years of experience in professional football of the members of team X.
(d) The age of students in a physics class.

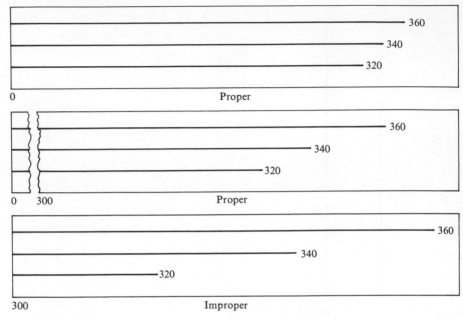

FIGURE 20.2

(e) The type of educational background of members of Congress.

(f) The full-time student equivalent enrollment of junior colleges in the United States in a given year.

3. At a given store the length of service of the employees is as shown below.

No. of years	No. of employees
26	1
23	1
19	2
16	1
14	2
10	1
7	3
3	2
2	5
1	3

Determine the arithmetic mean, the mode, and the median. How could a weighted mean for this group be secured? What would it be?

4. Evaluate the reliability of the type of statistical conclusions derived in the following examples. Give reasons for your evaluation.

(a) A teacher gave a social-attitudes test to a large introductory sociology class. He then accompanied a volunteer group consisting of one third of the class to slum areas, and he retested this group for social attitudes. He found a difference between the norms of this group and those for the larger class, and he concluded that a supervised visit to slum areas made a significant difference in the attitude of students.

(b) An "attitude survey" printed in a nationally distributed publication draws voluntary answers from readers. The readers answer either "approve" or "disapprove" to items worded as follows:

(1) Less government and more private initiative.

(2) Unfair government competition with private business.

(3) A sound dollar.

(4) Federal intervention in education.

(5) Federal domination of medical practice.

(6) Forced federal mediation of free enterprise-labor disputes.

(7) Foreign give-away programs.

(8) Honest elections.

(9) Tax-paid rent subsidies.

(10) Gag rule in Senate.

(c) A study of the effectiveness of a new approach to teaching logic is proposed. A class of 70 students is divided into two groups. The experimental group consists of volunteers who are willing to try out the new approach. A review of the results shows that the experimental group has a better knowledge of the material studied than the control group.

(d) A reporter sought to determine some of the major sources of tension in a slum area. He interviewed thirty persons in four different bars in the neighborhood, and in response to leading questions these persons claimed that unemployment, police brutality, and poor housing were major causes of the hostility. He reported that his interviews showed that all residents of the area blamed these factors for the tension. Discuss the factors involved in an evaluation of the reliability of this conclusion.

(e) A news release announces that three out of four citizens in an area are for Governor Wallace, since three out of four signs carried by persons attending a rally carry pro-Wallace slogans such as "Cleveland is Wallace Country" rather than signs such as "Wallace Must Go!"

(f) A survey is made to determine the amount of outside study done by members of a class in freshman English. The students in five classes, thirty-five students in each class, report orally to the graduate assistant a weekly average ranging from 2 to 12 hours spent in outside study. The graduate assistant averages the figures and reports that freshmen spend an average of 5.672 hours each week studying freshman English. Discuss relevant factors in evaluating the graduate assistant's statement.

5. "One of the basic tenets of Freudian analysis is that unpleasant memories are 'deliberately forgotten,' or repressed, and lurk in the subconscious until dragged out by psychoanalysis. But despite the wealth of empirical and theoretical interest in the idea that memory items which are specifically associated with unpleasant events are more readily forgotten than neutral items, no simple and effective techniques for studying 'motivated forgetting' have been reported. Sam Glucksberg and Lloyd King, Department of Psychology, Princeton University, set out to demonstrate that forgetting does occur as a function of unpleasant associations (*Science*, Vol. 158, p. 517).

"The experimental technique was adapted from an earlier method for studying retention. The subjects—sixteen male undergraduates—first learned a list of ten A-B paired associates, where A was a nonsense syllable, for instance

CEF, and B a simple word, in this case 'stem.' The nonsense syllable was projected onto a screen, and the subjects learned to respond with the associated word. When the list of ten A-B pairs was learned perfectly, the experiment moved to the next stage.

"Ten more words were presented, in random order, each of which (called a D word) was associated with one of the B words, via an inferred 'chained' word C. To make this clearer, in the above case the B word is 'stem.' The D word associated with it is 'smell,' the inferred C word being 'flower.' Another example: B word 'ocean'; inferred C word 'water,' and final D word 'drink.' Three of these ten, however, were accompanied by quite unpleasant electric shocks through the fingertips.

"It was already known that in such a limited word chain, learning an A-B pair helps the later learning of a related A-D pair. Saying the B word implicitly elicits the C, and, in turn the D word. Once such a chain has been established, simply thinking of the B word automatically brings the D word into the mind. Now, if D is associated with an unpleasant event—such as an electric shock—then the likelihood of saying, or even thinking of, the associated B response brings the fear-linked D word to mind.

"Glucksberg and King's experiment demonstrated this very neatly. Having learned which of the D words were accompanied by a shock, the subjects were again tried out on the A-B test. On being shown the nonsense syllable A, they had no difficulty at all in remembering its B partner in those instances where the associated seven D's were innocuous. However, in the three cases where the associated D words had previously been accompanied by an electric shock, some 30 per cent forgot the B response. Presumably in these cases just thinking of B would have brought the nasty D word into their minds, so they 'deliberately' forgot it—in other words, the memory of the link had been repressed."[1]

---

[1] "Deliberately Forgetting Unpleasant Memories," *New Scientist,* November 9, 1967, p. 369.

Chapter 21
Controverting
Objectionable
Arguments

21.1 Logic and the Controverting of Arguments

Sound argument requires proper use of language, adequate justification of the content of premises, and a valid structure of premises in the drawing of conclusions. Any conclusion in critical discourse is established by evidence presented in some form of an argument and is tested by its anticipated consequences and by its consistency with other critically established beliefs and knowledge claims. The person advancing an argument has the burden of proof —that is, he is required to show that his conclusion is supported by and follows from publicly available evidence presented in the form of arguments. Adequate evidence presented in a proper form is the foundation for establishing rational belief and for advancing critical inquiry.

A study of logic analyzes the forms used in establishing sound conclusions. It also can serve as an instrument for advancing inquiry, as Dewey and others have pointed out, and for the analysis of arguments to determine whether the form in which the evidence is presented justifies the conclusions. Thus, the study of logic is relevant not merely to the establishment of valid argument forms but to an analysis and appraisal of arguments in use.

This chapter reviews elementary procedures used in controverting or responding to objectionable arguments. Sometimes this is called refutation, but strict refutation of an argument establishes that a particular conclusion is false or erroneous. The controverting of an argument need not demonstrate the falsity of a proposed conclusion; rather, it questions the adequacy of evidence for the conclusion. The following suggested ways of controverting arguments are common but not exhaustive; and we should note that any given argument may be controverted by more than one kind of procedure.

21.2 Controverting an Argument by Indicating a Formal or an Informal Fallacy

Appeal to a formal fallacy.   Violation of a formal principle of reasoning constitutes a basis for rejection of an argument. Analysis of the form of the argument by the rules of traditional and modern logic is essential in controverting invalid arguments. However, in ordinary discourse the most effective manner of confronting an argument may not be to name the formal fallacy and the rule violated, but rather to show the structure of a fallacious argument to be faulty by using it to formulate an obviously absurd argument. For example, consider the following argument: "All Communists believe in the recognition of Red China. Professor Jones believes in the recognition of Red China. Therefore, Professor Jones is a Communist." A practical means of indicating the flaw in this type of reasoning is to use the same structure to construct an argument with a set of accepted premises and an unacceptable conclusion: "All Communists believe in developing natural resources and all businessmen in this community believe in developing natural resources. Therefore, all businessmen in this community are Communists."

Appeal to an informal fallacy.   An argument may be controverted if it is shown to commit an informal fallacy. In practical situations an informal fallacy can be shown to be unsound if its structure is used to propose an opposite or an absurd conclusion. For example, if it is claimed that all men are mortal since it cannot be proved that they are immortal, then it can be held that all men are immortal since it cannot be proved that they are mortal. The effectiveness of naming the fallacy (the appeal to ignorance in the present case) would depend on the circumstances.

21.3 Controverting an Argument by Claiming Grounds for Rejecting One or More Premises Offered as Evidence

Appeal to unsatisfactory evidence offered as premises.   An argument may be controverted if it is shown either that a premise used as evidence for the conclusion is false or that it is not reliably established. Consider the argument: "All drivers between the ages of eighteen and twenty-five are more inclined than older persons to be careless in driving. All persons more inclined than older persons to be careless in driving are greater insurance risks. Therefore, all drivers between the ages of eighteen and twenty-five are greater insurance risks." The reliability of the first premise can be questioned if it can be shown that some drivers between the ages of eighteen and twenty-five are not more careless than drivers of other ages.

Appeal to inconsistent premises.   An argument may be controverted if it is shown that the premises used as evidence are inconsistent. Thus, if some premises are accepted as true, others must be false, and the argument cannot be sound. A given argument might propose to establish that the government should impose further restraints on the economy in order to counteract inflationary tendencies. In a given context, a controverting of this conclusion can show that some of the premises used to support it assume a lower percentage of unemployment in the forthcoming year and other premises assume a relatively high percentage of unemployment in the forthcoming year. The inconsistency in the premises can be pointed out as a basis for rejection of the conclusion. However, if an argument is advanced in a hypothetical way to take care of several contingencies, this way of controverting it may not be proper and may not hold. Thus, the following argument does not have inconsistent premises: "If the unemployment level is low, then these curbs are needed. If the unemployment level is relatively high, then these curbs are also needed."

Appeal to inconsistency with previous positions. On some occasions the statements advanced in an argument may be challenged as being inconsistent with a speaker's previous statements. In this case, "the ghost of the past" may be used as counterevidence. Consider the following cases. A congressman makes a pre-election promise to oppose any increase in taxes. After the election, his critics claim that a program he supports requires an increase in taxes and that he is not abiding by his original promise. Some military leaders state that we should not commit ourselves to tying down large armed forces and large supplies of military equipment on the continent of Asia. Subsequently, they claim that such a procedure is in our enlightened national self-interest. These arguments can be controverted by reference to their previous statements.

The relevance of this way of controverting an argument varies significantly in different cases. Objections pointing to inconsistencies between two sets of statements made at different times under different conditions by a speaker can be psychologically persuasive. However, circumstances and events may justify a change in position or judgment. It is reasonable to expect an informed person to be consistent on any given occasion in terms of the statements he may be making. Yet, there is no reason to insist that an expressed judgment, opinion, or point of view can never be altered. A willingness to accept new evidence and to change one's views on the basis of additional inquiry and information may be necessary to avoid dogmatism and poor judgment.

Appeal to internal self-refutation. Some arguments may be controverted by a claim that its premises contain an internal self-refutation. Consider the following examples: "A Cretan says, 'All Cretans are liars.'" "All generalizations are false." Bertrand Russell has pointed out that some statements having such forms are not necessarily self-contradictory or self-refuting, since they are not necessarily self-referential. The original statement can refer to a first order of propositions from which the statement itself is excluded; the statement itself is a member of a second order of propositions. Thus, the controverting of an argument by appeal to its internal inconsistency requires considerable skill in argumentation.

The showing of internal inconsistency can be most effective against arguments in which the conclusion is inconsistent with premises used as supporting evidence. For example: "Knowledge is impossible because our senses are not known to be reliable and we know that others have been mistaken in their knowledge claims." If evidence offered to establish this conclusion is true, then the acceptance of the evidence itself is self-refuting for the conclusion. The evidence can count as evidence only if it counts as something that "is known."

21.4 Controverting an Argument by Attacking Inadequate Conceptualization

Appeal to an unsatisfactory categorical structure.   The controverting of an argument by rejection of the conceptual or categorical structure points out serious deficiencies in the manner in which the categories of the argument have been formed. This type of controverting requires more than a proposal of an alternative system of categories. It must show the categorical scheme to be sufficiently defective to prejudice seriously the reliability of the argument. If a survey of attitudes toward minority groups permits only two types of responses, one indicating complete social acceptance and a second indicating complete social rejection, arguments based on the findings of the survey could be controverted on the basis that its categories are too restricted and do not provide for views falling between these limits. The tendency of persons in extremist groups to categorize only in terms of extremes also exemplifies a defective categorical structure in their arguments.

Appeal to meaningless statements.   The controverting of an objectionable argument by appeal to meaningless statements points out that some statements in the argument have no cognitive significance or meaning. If a politician promises "to throw the rascals out" or "to establish respect abroad for our policies" or "to get the economy rolling," he uses expressions essentially emotive in character and engages primarily in redirecting attitudes and influencing voter response. In controverting such statements, one can seek to clarify the issues by insisting that specific proposals be made for preventing corruption in government, or for increasing respect for foreign policies, or for attaining economic prosperity. Although insistence on such clarification does not constitute a full controverting of the argument, it can serve either to have the issues made more explicit or to focus attention on meaningless generalities and on the lack of concrete issues in the argument. Even if elaboration is forthcoming on such issues, however, the reformulated statements may continue to be stated in glittering generalities that remain essentially meaningless.

Some advertising slogans may be highly useful persuasive techniques, but meaningless upon examination of their content. Expressions such as "Put a tiger in your tank," "There is a Ford in your future." and "Be happy—go Lucky" are designed essentially to redirect attitudes and influence buyer responses. Likewise, analysis of the statement "Dialectical analysis proves conclusively that gentlemen prefer blondes" will probably disclose that the expression "dialectical analysis" has no meaning.

Appeal to meaninglessness may have a more technical application. Rather than lacking a referent, a statement may fail to meet standards set by a particular theory of meaning and on this basis may be judged meaningless. For example, a statement whose truth or falsity cannot be determined either by appeal to the definition of its terms or (in principle) to sensory evidence is meaningless according to some theories of meaning. This kind of appeal to meaninglessness presupposes some theoretical acquaintance with semantics. In dealing with an objection of this kind, one need not accept the theory of meaning offered by the critic; however, it can become necessary to show that the proposed statement is meaningful in some sense. This way of controverting an argument requires sophisticated use and may easily be abused.

Appeal to distinctions.   The controverting of an argument by appeal to distinctions consists in demonstrating that the force of a particular argument rests upon ambiguous or vague terms. Different meanings or ranges of applicability of the term have been glossed over. The inferred conclusion is attributed to failure to make proper distinctions. A rule traditionally followed in persuasive speech may be paraphrased as follows: "If the opposition drives you into a corner in a discussion and there is no obvious way of offering a rebuttal to the argument, make some distinctions in the meanings of the terms and show that his arguments apply only to trivial or irrelevant cases."

Distinctions are highly relevant in many arguments. Courts of law have come to distinguish many different types of situations, such as homicide, with many differing degrees of gravity. If a speaker argues that with the acceptance of Medicare, socialism has been adopted, one can controvert his argument by pointing out that "socialism" is a word whose range of applicability varies widely and that Medicare does not involve socialism in any one of many accepted meanings, such as the government's owning the instruments of production or the facilities for the distribution of goods. One could claim further that the Medicare program follows a democratic policy of securing wider participation in certain social goods. Need for these social goods is recognized as a relevant claim on practices related to their distribution. This type of response does not establish the program of Medicare as the preferred national policy; rather it attacks the view identifying Medicare with the "arrival of a socialistic society."

Many statements of political views are particularly vulnerable to the appeal to distinctions. If it is argued that democratic institutions cannot be the foundation of a free society since they require the practice of "one man, one vote" whereas any effective organization requires an elite leadership in order to survive, one can controvert the argument by distinguishing different meanings of "democratic institutions." The requirement that each participant have "an equal voice" in the manner of formulating policies and of carrying them out could be distinguished and rejected as an extreme and arbitrary meaning of "democratic institutions." One could distinguish and advocate acceptance of another meaning of "democratic institutions" as "a form of participation by all citizens in determining the institutional framework for strengthening respect for human rights, in determining those privileges and restraints equally applicable to all citizens, in determining the extent and limits of such institutional power, and in providing for the selection of the persons responsible for making, executing, and adjudicating the application of any legislation or rules binding on all citizens or groups."

21.5 Controverting by Criticism of Methods Used in Formulating Arguments

Appeal to faulty sources.   Establishing that evidence used in an argument is based on faulty sources is an effective attack on an argument. Literary criticism may point out that a biographer has used a spurious passage in an attempt to show that an author held to a particular view, or it may point out that a secondary source was used that does not agree with the original source. Consider also the importance of original sources in legal proceedings. A judge may "strike from the record" testimony that is based on "hearsay" and permit the witness to testify only about what he actually saw or heard.

Appeal to methodological deficiences.   Another way to controvert an argument is to point to serious deficiencies in the methodological procedure of securing evidence. This establishes that the method followed was inappropriate or that errors introduced into the procedure justify the rejection of the proposed evidence. If a survey proposes to show that living in a desegregated housing area decreases racial prejudice, and if its evidence consists in a comparison of attitudes towards racial minorities expressed by persons living in desegregated housing areas and those living in scgrcgatcd communities, the survey is subject to attack if it does not take account of many other variables. The persons living in desegregated housing areas may have exemplified less racial prejudice when they moved there than other members of the community at large.

Appeal to a faulty model. Rejecting the model of an argument is another means of attacking it. Basic flaws or deficiencies in the model are pointed out. If it is argued that college professors should not publicly differ with the political opinions of the major representatives on the governing boards of their institutions on the grounds that management has the right to determine the political outlook taken by a corporation, it can be objected that this argument follows an inappropriate model and overlooks essential differences between a university and a business corporation. (The model also could be attacked on the basis of its leading assumption that the political position taken by a corporate management is binding on the personal political views or activities of each member of management.) One can argue that to be academically strong, a college or university must encourage freedom of inquiry and full participation by professors in their rights as citizens, including their right to take a public stand on controversial issues.

21.6 Controverting an Argument by Appeal to its Consequences

Appeal to similar consequences. In controverting an argument by appeal to its consequences, one can point out that the consequences of a view do not make a difference in practice or that they are the same as those acknowledged for another view that is being attacked. Pragmatism appeals to the principle, "If there is a difference in two positions, then this difference must be apparent in their practical consequences." Charles S. Peirce, a major formulator of pragmatism, argues that if there were a difference between the theological views of transubstantiation and consubstantiation, then there would be some difference in their practical consequences. Since he is unable to detect any practical difference in their consequences, he concludes that the two proposed theories are not essentially different. Likewise, William James uses the appeal to practical consequences in his discussion of the proposed differences between agnosticism and atheism. He concludes that no essential differences are to be found between the two beliefs on the grounds that their consequences are the same.

Appeal to disparity between proposed consequences and probable consequences. An argument can be controverted by appeal to a significant deviation between its proposed consequences and another set of consequences held to be more probable. This attack can claim that "the baby is thrown out with the bath water." If a newspaper's business manager proposes to raise the costs of advertising to increase earnings, his argument can be controverted by the assertion that an increase in the cost of advertising would decrease the revenue from advertising. Prospective advertisers can take ads elsewhere instead, or they can advertise in the newspaper with less frequency. If a director of a city transportation company argues that the company would increase its profits by reducing the number of trips made each day by the buses, the argument can be controverted by the assertion that many bus riders would be inconvenienced and would seek out other means of transportation, the consequence being a significant loss of revenue for the company. If a city councilman proposes to raise property taxes in order to increase city revenue, one can attack this argument by pointing out that increased property taxes can spur a move to the suburbs by many persons in a position to pay the taxes. As a consequence, the area would be occupied by underprivileged groups who would not have the resources to pay the higher taxes or who would permit the property to deteriorate and lose much of its tax value.

21.7 Controverting an Argument by Establishing an Alternative Conclusion

Appeal to a counterargument. An argument can be controverted by a counterargument, which uses the evidence for the original argument either to oppose its conclusion or to restrict its range of applicability and render it "less objectionable." If a student claims he plans to drop out of school because he is getting tired of it and because his family needs his financial assistance, one can controvert his argument by pointing out, "The fact that you are getting tired of school means that you need to summon up courage to stick it out instead of running away when the going gets a little tough. You can be of greater help to your family in the long run by staying in school." The argument that the government should increase the rate of income taxes to curb inflation, since the demand for consumer goods exceeds their supply, installment debts are rapidly rising, the government has entered into a program of increased spending, and industry has announced acceleration of plant expansion, can be controverted if one asserts both that these trends are apparent and that another resolution of the difficulty is preferable. "Inflation can be avoided and the economy remain healthier if we raise the cost of interest on loans and decrease some areas of government spending rather than increase the rate of income taxes."

Appeal to a different argument. An argument can be controverted by the use of a different set of premises to establish either an opposing conclusion or one restricting the range of applicability of the original conclusion. In this case new evidence can be presented or the significance of the proposed evidence can be reinterpreted. Research in the efforts to correlate cigarette smoking with the beginning of lung cancer illustrates this kind of controverting. One set of statistics is offered to support a conclusion that there is no significant correlation between cigarette smoking and the incidence of lung cancer. A controverting argument supports another conclusion with another set of statistics that include a significant correlation between these two factors.

Another example of an attempt to controvert an argument by a different argument is the classical discussion concerning the properties of light. Isaac Newton advanced the position that light moves like particles. He argued that if light moved like waves, it would spread around a corner. After failing to find evidence for such a spread, he held that light travels in a straight line. Huygens and others supported the view that light moves more like a wave. If light were a particle, he argued, then the particle should show the effect of some kind of collision or bouncing when two light waves crossed each other. Since the crossing of two light rays showed no such effect, Huygens held that a wave theory provided a more satisfactory explanation than a particle theory. As this example shows, an argument is expected to account for the facts of a case, although what constitutes the facts may be the subject of intense controversy.

Appeal to the greater simplicity of an alternative argument. The controverting of an argument by appeal to the greater simplicity of an alternative conclusion is based on the principle of parsimony. This principle holds that if alternative conclusions are possible for a given problem or if two lines of evidence are possible in the support of conclusions, then the conclusion using the simplest procedure is preferred. This principle is also called Occam's razor after its formulator, William of Occam, and is stated as follows: "[Explanatory] entities are not to be multiplied beyond necessity."

Consider the classical example of the appeal to phlogiston as a substance consumed during a fire and accounting for the fire. The notion of such a substance was discarded after the weight of ashes had been compared with the weight of the original material. If there is any substance such as phlogiston, then an object before being burned should weigh more than its remaining ashes. Measurements indicated no such differences in weight. Since experimental bases to support the view were lacking and simpler explanations were available, the use of the notion of phlogiston was dropped.

21.8 Controverting an Argument by Appeal to Irrational Positions Found Within It

Appeal to the absurdity of an argument. An appeal to absurdity points out that if the conclusion of an argument is accepted, a contradiction develops between the conclusion and another statement well established within the system of beliefs to which the conclusion belongs. The absurdity is that acceptance of the conclusion requires the holding of two propositions, both of which cannot be true. This appeal takes the form, "That argument is to be rejected, because it is obviously absurd to accept it, since it is in opposition to other beliefs that are not reasonably doubted." However, an appeal to "beliefs that are not reasonably doubted" can be highly questionable. Many of the major advances in scientific inquiry, such as the view that the earth is round, were opposed at one time as being in opposition to a well-established system of beliefs.

A classical example of appeal to an argument's absurdities is found in responses to Zeno's denial of the possibility of motion. The belief that an arrow moved in flight, he stated, was an error. At any given time an arrow is either where it is or where it is not. To suggest that it is where it is not is ridiculous, and if an arrow is where it is, then it is not moving. He presented other arguments in his efforts to show the impossibility of motion. These paradoxes of Zeno motivated extended controversy. One proposed refutation appealed to the view that Zeno's position was so contrary to common sense that it was absurd. This appeal to absurdity did not provide a theoretical refutatation; rather it sought a practical justification for rejection.

Consider another problem frequently discussed in modern philosophy. Solipsism is the view that the self is limited to knowing nothing but its own sensations and that nothing other than the self and its sensations can be known to exist. This view is skeptical about knowledge of the existence of an external world, other bodies, and other minds. It is commonly held that if a philosophical position can be reduced to a position of solipsism, then a sufficient basis is established for its rejection on the basis of its absurdity. From a purely theoretical point of view, solipsism remains a possible answer to the question, "What can be known to exist?" Although other reasons can be advanced, the appeal to the absurdity of the view continues as a basic justifying reason for the rejection of solipsism.

The controverting of an argument by appeal to its absurdity occurs also in social and political theory. Many political theorists hold that any theory of government entailing the view of anarchism is to be rejected on this basis.

The refutation of an argument by a common-sense appeal to its absurdity has stronger psychological than theoretical weight. The opposition of a view to common sense is not, in itself, a fault. There may be excellent reasons for calling into question certain common-sense notions. The appeal to the absurdity of a view on the basis of common-sense notions may, however, be the most effective counterargument available at a given stage of knowledge.

Appeal to circularity. The controverting of an argument by appeal to its circularity establishes that it uses premises to justify a conclusion and then uses the conclusion to establish the truth of the premises. (Although this type of appeal is discussed in a previous chapter, it applies to the present context.) Consider some of the arguments used in discussing problems of responsibility and freedom. Some arguments claim that man is free because he is responsible and such responsibility has meaning only if he is free. But how can it be shown that man is responsible? If it is stated that man is responsible because he is free, the argument is circular.

Many arguments proposing to show the superiority of capitalism over socialism or of socialism over capitalism are also circular. For example: "A socialistic economy is preferable to a capitalistic one, since it is based upon sharing of economic goods according to economic needs. Why is it preferable to base an economy upon the sharing of economic goods according to economic needs? Because this is the principle of a socialistic economy, and a socialistic economy is the type that is better." Consider an argument on the opposite side: "A free enterprise system is desirable because it is a part of a capitalistic economy. But why is a capitalistic economy preferable? A capitalistic economy is preferable because it makes possible free enterprise."

Appeal to an infinite regress.   An argument may be controverted by appeal to an infinite regress found in it, on the principle of the irrationality of an infinite series of reasons. A reason is given that requires a second reason, which is supported only by an appeal to reasons that appeal to other reasons indefinitely. It becomes impossible to examine the original reason for the argument. If there is no original ground supporting a given reason, but rather a given reason is referred to a prior reason and that to a prior reason, then the logical structure of the argument is dificient. The evidential reasons offered to support the conclusion become involved in an infinite regress.

Consider the argument in the Platonic dialogue *Parmenides*. Parmenides seeks to establish that Socrates' view of forms involves the notion of an infinite regress. Socrates appears to recognize that if his view involved an infinite regress, this would be a sufficient justification for its rejection. Socrates acknowledges a form for largeness and the participation of large objects in some sense in this form for largeness. Parmenides holds that this view of forms requires a third form of largeness to relate a particular large form to the form of largeness. He further suggests that the form that related the particular form of a large object to the form of largeness would, in turn, itself need a form related both to the form of largeness itself and to the form that related the form of the particular large form to the form of largeness, and so *ad infinitum*. If an argument such as Parmenides accuses Socrates of advancing has such an infinite regress, rationality is not achieved by this infinite multiplication of intermediate explanations, none of which provides for the original explanation.

Philosophers such as John Passmore[1] distinguish between a vicious and a harmless infinite regress. A *harmless infinite regress* presents merely an infinite series within which it is possible to begin an explanation anywhere without regressing to a proposed beginning of the series. The statement that in a given laboratory experiment, two parts of hydrogen and one part of oxygen mixed within certain ranges of temperature and pressure will become

---

[1] *Philosophical Reasoning* (New York: Charles Scribner's Sons, 1961).

water could be a part of an indefinite or possibly infinite series of events, but the experiment does not require that such prior causal factors be considered. This is an infinite or indefinite series that is "harmless." We can explain an event by reference to other events without explaining the causes of these additional events. The flight of a rocket to the moon can be explained, in part, by reference to the initial conditions of the thrust of the rocket, the position of the moon in relation to the earth and other bodies in the solar system, and the principle of gravitation without an explanation of each of these conditions in terms of a prior series of events. Such additional information can provide a worthy object of further inquiry, but the explanation of the event in question does not require such an elaborate and, if pressed far enough, impossible pursuit.

A *vicious infinite regress* characterizes reasons rather than facts or events. Evidence is offered in the form of a reason, which is supported by a reason supposedly of higher order, which in turn rests upon a comparable reason of still higher order without attaining to a limit beyond which such appeals need not be pushed. A vicious infinite regress is illustrated in the following attempt to justify induction. "The principle of induction can be established by appeal to a higher principle of induction. But how is this latter principle justified? It is established by an appeal to a still higher principle of induction."

Avoidance of a vicious infinite regress does not require that all reasons given in an argument be proved by other reasons, which in turn are established by other reasons indefinitely. If such an approach were pushed far enough, the result more likely would be circular reasoning rather than an infinite regress. However, we avoid an infinite regress, as well as circular reasoning, by appealing to a general set of principles that are justifiable, as Whitehead points out, on the basis of such considerations as their coherence, consistency, applicability, adequacy, and corrigibility. Such principles are justified not by appeal to an additional or higher set of principles but by their intelligibility and utility. Since they are corrigible, they can be the subject of further inquiry. Until a more satisfactory alternative has been advanced, they provide a context for the justification of beliefs. This suggestion regarding the means of avoiding a vicious infinite regress is not an appeal to a kind of metaphysical world view, such as Whitehead developed. Rather it permits a more modest kind of justification based upon rigorous inquiry and consistency within such a range of experience. Within such a range rationality, intelligibility, and usefulness remain significant considerations for the justification of a general set of principles used to determine the context of other reasons in arguments.

Sometimes in an argument an effort is made to avoid a vicious infinite regress by an appeal to a privileged assumption, such as "Man's freedom of choice is self-evident." In such cases the question can always be raised, "But is it self-evident?"

21.9 Controverting of Arguments and Persuasive Use of Language

The various ways of controverting arguments are subject to abuse. Disputations can become tedious, particularly if they stray from the central issues. Although many arguments are more than trivial quibbling, an appearance of quibbling can arouse hostility toward argumentation.

The handling of an argument in a practical situation may require a pragmatic rather than an academic approach. If the objective is to "get a job done," as it often is in business, political, and other practical activities, persuasive speech is used rather than merely rational discussion. Persons interested primarily in "getting the job done" may ignore the finer discernments of argumentation and even express scorn for those skilled in such areas. It cannot be assumed that such persons will not "get a job done" merely because the procedures they use are not sound. However, the principle that belief should be based only upon adequate and sufficient evidence, properly presented, is the foundation of progress in inquiry, knowledge, and sound judgment. The justification of conclusions by rigorous analysis both of relevant data and of possible alternatives is essential for sustained sound judgments. The abuse of rational procedures to "get a job done" appears to be self-defeating in the long run for a society seeking to strengthen its democratic foundations and individual freedoms.

21.10 EXERCISES

Using a form adapted to ordinary language, propose a controverting argument for each of the following arguments and identify the controverting argument by type.

1. We cannot accept the view of "one man, one vote," because it violates the principle of states' rights and it also helps demagogues gain greater political power.

2. Our foreign aid policy is an example of the folly of extravagance. Its principal results consist in keeping socialistic governments from going bankrupt and in making possible their bureaucratic control over the lives of their citizens.

3. Shakespeare could not have written the plays attributed to him. He lacked the educational background necessary for writing such significant works and he did not have the opportunity to acquire the kind of political and psychological insight reflected in the works attributed to him.

4. The opinion poll on the attitude of all students in this university toward the draft is reliable, since the views of over 100 students who attended the demonstration were taken as the sample.

5. You can't teach an old dog new tricks and you can't expect a man who has spent years in public office to have any new proposals for public policies.

6. The placing of Cuba in the hands of the Communists was a consequence of the deliberate planning of the federal government. Not only did they suspend in 1958 the sending of arms to the rightful government of Cuba but they used

every tactic possible to place arms in the hands of the opposition to the official government.

7. There is no question but that the economy is headed for a period of radical inflation. Workers constantly demand higher salaries without regard to increasing their own productivity. The government introduces artificial controls on the economy to prevent a lowering of prices. The only change in prices it permits is an upward change. The increased trend toward installment purchases has the net effect of a sharp increase in the availability of consumer goods in the absence of immediate resources for paying for what is used, thereby pushing prices even higher.

8. A class consciousness prevails among those who control the power structure of the American scene. Political, economic, industrial, military, and bureaucratic leaders are acutely conscious of their own status. They associate with others having comparable status and form social barriers to avoid becoming involved with persons who do not share in their status situation. The class requires that its members recognize and respect its own self-image. Those who share in this class consciousness are the leaders of government, business, industry, and the military.

9. Religion is the opiate of the people, because it takes their minds off the sources of their exploitation and the means of combating it. But how do we know that it takes their minds off the sources of their exploitation and the means of combating it? We know this simply because religion is the opiate of the people.

10. Man is not responsible for his behavior, since his actions are a result of causes that are also caused by prior events over which man exercises no control. Any efforts to control causal factors in behavior are the effects of causes over which man exercises no control.

11. If qualities like a green and a red color as splotches on a canvas require a connecting link, then what unites the connecting link with the qualities? If another connecting link unites the connecting link to the qualities, then an additional connecting link would be required to connect the connecting link connecting the connecting link to the qualities.

12. An agent is free to do an act because he can choose to do an act. He is free to choose to do an act because he is free to choose to choose to do an act.

13. If the government has followed a sound fiscal policy, then inflation is not a threat and credit is not tightened. If inflation is not a threat, then the amount of the gross national product is increased. If the amount of the gross national product is increased, then the government has followed a sound fiscal policy and credit is not tightened. The amount of the gross national product is increased. Therefore, credit is not tightened.

14. Like a biological organism the organism of the state develops through various stages. Once a state develops into a state that is wholly rational, it will be able to dominate subrational expressions of the state and to control the ends of human endeavor for the benefit of mankind.

15. Man has the power of choice because he can will to act. He can will to act because he has the power of choice.

16. We have combined a liberal political vocabulary with a conservative political behavior. More radical elements on the left and on the right engage in verbal

vitriolics, but the conservative mood under the slogan of a "middle-of-the-road policy" effectively controls the political life of the country. Changes that occur in the executive, legislative, and judicial branches of the government are justified by appeal to the action, the policies, the statements, and the decisions of predecessors in government. The past acts as a magician's hat. It provides a source for what the actors on the public scene wish to pull out of it. By having to bind the present to the past, those responsible for determining public policy are assured of the preservation of a conservative mood.

17. We can conclude that these demonstrators are in favor of our defeat in the conflict since these demonstrators, like those whom we fight, want us to stop the bombing.

18. Corporation taxes should be raised, even though the economy is sluggish, in order to prevent a greater deficit in the federal budget.

19. Expenditure of large sums of money for public works in times of high unemployment should not be practiced, since it interferes with the law of supply and demand.

20. College students should not be given an opportunity to determine those rules and regulations under which they are disciplined in college. A college is a center of learning, and if students become involved in determining policies affecting student life, they will neglect their academic work and thus miss the major purpose for which they are attending school.

21. Daylight Saving Time is opposed by most of the residents of this state. A major newspaper asked its readers to write letters to the editor indicating either preference for Daylight Saving Time or opposition to it, and the vast majority of letters received indicated opposition to this practice.

Selected Answers to Problems

<table>
<tr><td>5.3</td><td></td><td>5.</td><td>Genetic fallacy</td></tr>
<tr><td></td><td></td><td>10.</td><td>False analogy</td></tr>
<tr><td>5.5</td><td></td><td>5.</td><td>Common folks appeal</td></tr>
<tr><td></td><td></td><td>8.</td><td>Appeal to the galleries (and others)</td></tr>
<tr><td>5.7</td><td></td><td>4.</td><td>Name tagging</td></tr>
<tr><td></td><td></td><td>7.</td><td>Poisoning the wells</td></tr>
<tr><td>6.2</td><td></td><td>2.</td><td>Composition (and equivocation)</td></tr>
<tr><td></td><td></td><td>9.</td><td>Division</td></tr>
<tr><td></td><td></td><td>12.</td><td>Ambiguity of significance</td></tr>
<tr><td>6.4</td><td></td><td>3.</td><td>Ad hominem—circumstantial</td></tr>
<tr><td></td><td></td><td>7.</td><td>Argumentative leap (although a broader context is needed)</td></tr>
<tr><td></td><td></td><td>14.</td><td>Irrelevant conclusion (although a broader context is needed)</td></tr>
<tr><td></td><td></td><td>18.</td><td>Fallacy of accent</td></tr>
<tr><td></td><td></td><td>25.</td><td>Accident</td></tr>
<tr><td></td><td></td><td>33.</td><td>Ad hominem—circumstantial</td></tr>
<tr><td></td><td></td><td>40.</td><td>Argumentative leap</td></tr>
<tr><td></td><td></td><td>48.</td><td>Argumentum ad ignorantium</td></tr>
<tr><td></td><td></td><td>55.</td><td>Black and white fallacy</td></tr>
<tr><td></td><td></td><td>65.</td><td>Argumentum ad misericordiam</td></tr>
<tr><td></td><td></td><td>74.</td><td>Argumentum ad baculum</td></tr>
<tr><td></td><td></td><td>83.</td><td>Arguing in a circle</td></tr>
<tr><td>7.5</td><td></td><td>6.</td><td>A proposition, universal affirmative, $Sd < Pu$, $S\bar{P} = O$</td></tr>
<tr><td></td><td></td><td>8.</td><td>I proposition, particular affirmative, $Su < Pu$, $SP \neq O$</td></tr>
<tr><td>7.8</td><td>2.</td><td>(f)</td><td>E proposition, universal (singular) negative, $Sd \not< Pd$, $SP = O$</td></tr>
</table>

$$S \;\text{⬤}\; P$$

<table>
<tr><td>7.11</td><td>4.</td><td>Major term: risks</td></tr>
<tr><td></td><td></td><td>Minor term: creative programs</td></tr>
<tr><td></td><td></td><td>Middle term: quixotic programs</td></tr>
<tr><td></td><td></td><td>Valid categorical syllogism</td></tr>
</table>

7.14

2. Major term: (things) in movement
   Minor term: things subject to experimental control
   Middle term: atoms
   Figure III, Mood **AOI**

$Md < Pu$ $M\overline{P} = O$

$Mu \nless Sd$ $M\overline{S} \neq O$

$Su \ < Pu$ $SP \neq O$

Invalid. A valid categorical syllogism must have the middle conclusion if either premise is negative

15. Major term: chess player
    Minor term: Mr. Smith
    Middle term: engineer
    Figure II, Mood **IAA**

$Pu < Mu$ $PM \neq O$

$Sd < Mu$ $S\overline{M} = O$

$Sd < Pu$ $S\overline{P} = O$

Invalid. A valid categorical syllogism must have the middle term distributed at least once.

7.17

5. Missing (minor) premise: "This song is folk orientated."
   Invalid. A valid categorical syllogism must have the middle term distributed at least once.

7. Missing (minor) premise: "All persons who have died are persons sleeping."
   Invalid. A valid categorical syllogism must have the middle only three terms, each of which occur twice with the same meaning in the syllogism. ("Persons sleeping" does not have identical meaning in the premises.)

8.6   2.

(c) Original syllogism is in proper logical order: Figure III, **AAI**
    Valid (provided terms of minor premise are accepted as indicating class membership).

$Md < Pu$ $M\overline{P} = O$

$Md < Su$ $M\overline{S} = O$

$\quad\quad\quad$ $MS \neq O$

$Su \ < Pu$ $SP \neq O$

(h) Original syllogism has proper logical order with major premise first, minor premise second, and conclusion last.
    Figure I, **IAI**

$$Mu < Pu \quad MP \neq O$$

$$Sd \ < Mu \quad S\overline{M} = O$$

$$Su \ < Pu \quad SP \neq O$$

Invalid: Undistributed middle term

8.6   (j) Syllogism in proper order
Figure III, Mood **AAI**

$$Md < Pu \quad M\overline{P} = O$$

$$Md < Su \quad M\overline{S} = O$$

$$Su \ < Pu \quad SP \neq O$$

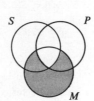

Invalid: Illicit existential assumption

9.7   1.   (c) Some catchers are not non-slow players.
      2.   (b) No particles are waves.
      3.   (d) Some nonmutations are not nonplants.

9.9   5. All cabinet members are persons of ability.
               No person of ability is incompetent.
               ∴ No incompetent person is a cabinet member.
               Figure IV, Mood **AEE**

$$Pd \ < Mu \quad P\overline{M} = O$$

$$Md \not< Sd \quad MS = O$$

$$Sd \ \not< Pd \quad SP = O$$

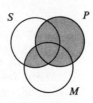

Valid

11. All creative architects are controversial.
    Mr. Able is a creative architect.
    Mr. Able is a controversial architect.
    Figure I, Mood **AAA**

$$Md < Pu \quad M\overline{P} = O$$

$$Sd \ < Mu \quad S\overline{M} = O$$

$$Sd \ < Pu \quad S\overline{P} = O$$

Valid

9.11 1.   (d) No old dogs are creatures who learn new tricks.
           (s) No members who are not on the executive committee are
                 persons leaving the room. (Required)
                 All members on the executive committee are persons leaving
                 the room. (Possible)
           (x) No person who is not a fool is a person who would take
                 that risk.

9.11   2.   (d) Some particles are extremely short-lived (things).

Some particles are things which repay the energy balance in nature.

Therefore, some things which repay the energy balance in nature are extremely short-lived (things).

Figure III, Mood **III**

$Mu < Pu \quad MP \neq O$

$Mu < Su \quad MS \neq O$

$Su \ < Pu \quad SP \neq O$

Invalid: Undistributed middle term

(j) All communities with racial troubles are situations having bad conditions for business.

Community Smithville is a situation having bad conditions for business.

Therefore, Community Smithville is a community with racial troubles.

Figure II, Mood **AAA**

$Pd \ < Mu \quad P\overline{M} = O$

$Sd \ < Mu \quad S\overline{M} = O$

$Sd \ < Pu \quad S\overline{P} \ = O$

Invalid: Undistributed middle term

3.   (m) All things helping to develop strong bones are things having nutritional value.

All vitamins are things having nutritional value.

Therefore, all vitamins are things helping to develop strong bones.

Figure II, Mood **AAA**

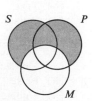

$Pd \ < Mu \quad P\overline{M} = O$

$Sd \ < Mu \quad S\overline{M} = O$

$Sd \ < Pu \quad S\overline{P} \ = O$

Invalid: Undistributed middle term

(w) All cases of growth in cooperation are cases of compromise.

All cases of strength in interdependence are cases of growth in cooperation.

Therefore, all cases of strength in interdependence are cases of compromise.

Figure I, Mood **AAA**

$Md < Pu \quad M\overline{P} = O$

$Sd \ < Mu \quad S\overline{M} = O$

$Sd \ < Pu \quad S\overline{P} \ = O$

Valid

10.5   1.   (c) Aristotelian form:
All cynics are disillusioned idealists.
All disillusioned idealists are dissatisfied.
All dissatisfied persons are frustrated.
No frustrated persons are enthusiastic about the future.
Therefore, no cynics are enthusiastic about the future.

$Ad < Bu$
$Bd < Cu$
$Cd < Du$
$Dd \not< Eu$
$\overline{\therefore Ad \not< Ed}$

Valid

2.   (b) Goclinian sorites
All non-complex problems are problems that can be worked immediately.
All problems easy to solve are non-complex (simple).
All chain arguments are problems easy to solve.
All sorites are chain arguments.
Therefore, all sorites are problems that can be worked immediately.

$Bd < Au$
$Cd < Bu$
$Dd < Cu$
$Ed < Du$
$\overline{\therefore Ed < Au}$

Valid

11.5   4. (a) False   (f) True
(b) True   (g) Undetermined
(c) True   (h) True
(d) True   (i) True
(e) Undetermined

7. (a) Undetermined   (f) True
(b) False   (g) False
(c) Undetermined   (h) True
(d) False   (i) False
(e) Undetermined   (j) Undetermined

11.7   2. Irreflexive, non-symmetrical, transitive.
13. Irreflexive, asymmetrical, transitive.

12.3   4. Proposition denying the conjunction of two propositions.
If first atomic proposition is true, the second is false.
If first atomic proposition is false, the second is undetermined.

If second atomic proposition is true, the first atomic proposition is false.

If second atomic proposition is false, the first is undetermined.

9. Hypothetical proposition: If antecedent is true, the consequent is true.

If antecedent is false, the consequent is undetermined.

If consequent is true, the antecedent is undetermined.

If consequent is false, the antecedent is false.

12.9

3. $p \lor q$

q

$\therefore \sim p$

The second premise (q) affirms the second disjunct (in $p \lor q$).

Invalid: Fallacy of affirming a disjunct

9. $p \supset q$ $\sim p \supset q$

  $\sim q$ or $\sim q$

$\therefore \sim p$ $\therefore p$

The second premise ($\sim q$) denies the consequent (q) and the conclusion denies the antecedent.

Valid: Argument form of *modus tollens*

12.11

2. $\sim (p \cdot q)$

p

$\therefore \sim q$

Valid denial of conjunction argument (form).

Equivalent form in *modus ponens*.

If a storm develops, the weather prediction is not reliable.

A storm develops.

Therefore, the weather prediction is not reliable.

7. "Only if A then B" has the form $B \supset A$.

$p \supset q$

$\sim q$

$\therefore \sim p$

Valid *modus tollens* argument

Equivalent form in *modus ponens*: If the actress is not cast properly, she will not be a success.

The actress is not cast properly.

Therefore, she will not be a success.

12.16

7. Valid complex dilemma.

$(p \supset q) \cdot (r \supset s)$ $(M \supset \sim R) \cdot (\sim U \supset O)$

$p \lor r$ or $M \lor \sim U$

$\therefore q \lor s$ $\therefore \sim R \lor O$

Rebuttals

(1) Through the horns

    $(p \supset q) \cdot (r \supset s)$ $(M \supset \sim R) \cdot (\sim U \supset O)$

    $p \lor r \lor u$ $M \lor \sim U \lor S$

    $\therefore p \lor r \lor t$ $\therefore \sim R \lor O \lor T$

(2) By the horns

$(p \cdot \sim q) \cdot (r \supset s)$ or $(M \cdot R) \cdot (\sim U \supset O)$
$p \lor r$ $M \lor \sim U$
∴ $q \lor s$ (invalid)   ∴ $R \lor O$ (Invalid
                                                              argument)

(3) Counter dilemma

$(p \supset \sim s) \cdot (r \supset \sim q)$ or $(M \supset \sim O) \cdot (\sim U \supset R)$
$p \lor r$ $M \lor \sim U$
∴ $\sim s \lor \sim q$ ∴ $\sim O \lor R$

Proposed key premises in a rebuttal:

(1) Through the horns: Either you know the material or you do not understand it or you can learn the material by study.

(2) By the horns: You know the material and you have to read outside material to make a good grade.

13.2   1.   (b)

I	II	III
5. C	1, 3 $p \lor q$, $\sim p$ /∴ q	1, 3 DA
6. $D \lor E$	2, 5 $p \supset q$, p, /∴ q	2, 5 MP
7. D	6, 4 $p \lor q$, $\sim q$, /∴ p	6, 4 DA

2.   (e)

	I	II	III
1. $(S \supset \sim A) \cdot (\sim P \supset F)$		
2. $S \lor \sim P$		
3. $\sim[(\sim A \lor F) \cdot G]$		
∴ $\sim G$		
4. $\sim A \lor F$	1, 2 $(p \supset q) \cdot (r \supset s)$, $p \lor r$, /∴ $q \lor s$	1, 2 CCD
5. $\sim G$	3, 4 $\sim(p \cdot q)$, p, /∴ $\sim q$	3, 4 DCA

13.5   4.

1. $D \supset E$
2. $D \supset F$
3. $E \supset \sim F$
4. D
∴ G

	I	II	III
5. E	1, 4 $p \supset q$, p, /∴ q	1, 4 MP
6. F	2, 4 $p \supset q$, p, /∴ q	2, 4 MP
7. $\sim F$	3, 5 $p \supset q$, p, /∴ q	3, 5 MP
8. $F \lor G$	6 p, /∴ $p \lor q$	6 Add.
9. G	7, 8 $p \lor q$, $\sim p$, /∴ q	8, 7 DA

11.

1. $J \equiv K$
2. $\sim K \lor L$
3. $(L \supset M) \cdot \sim M$
∴ $\sim J$

	I	II	III
4. $(J \supset K) \cdot$ $(K \supset J)$	1 $(p \equiv q) \equiv [(p \supset q) \cdot (q \supset p)]$	1 ME
5. $J \supset K$	4 $(p \cdot q)$, /∴ p	4 Simp.
6. $K \supset L$	2 $(\sim p \lor q) \equiv (p \supset q)$	2 MI

7. $L \supset M$ 3 $p \cdot q, / \therefore p$ 3 Simp.
8. $\sim M$ 3 $p \cdot q, / \therefore q$ 3 Simp.
9. $J \supset L$ 5, 6 $p \supset q, q \supset r, / \therefore p \supset r$ 5, 6 HS
10. $J \supset M$ 9, 7 $p \supset q, q \supset r, / \therefore p \supset r$ 9, 7 HS
11. $\sim J$ 10, 8 $p \supset q, \sim q, / \therefore \sim p$ 10, 8 MT

18.   1. $E \supset (C \vee O)$
      2. $\sim S \supset (\sim C \cdot \sim O)$
      3. $\sim S$
      4. $E \vee V$
        $\therefore V$
      5. $\sim C \cdot \sim O$ 2, 3 $p \supset q, p, / \therefore q$ 2, 3 MP
      6. $\sim(C \vee O)$ 5 $(p \cdot q) \equiv \sim(\sim p \vee \sim q)$ 5 DeM
      7. $\sim E$ 1, 6 $p \supset q, \sim q, / \therefore \sim p$ 1, 6 MT
      8. V 4, 7 $p \vee q, \sim p, / \therefore q$ 4, 7 DA

13.7

6.   1. $A \cdot (B \supset C)$
     2. $C \supset D$
     3. $\sim(A \cdot \sim B)$
     4. $\sim D \vee (\sim E \vee F)$
       $\therefore E \supset F$
     5. A 1 Simp
     6. $B \supset C$ 1 Simp.
     7. B 3, 5 DCA
     8. C 6, 7 MP
     ⌈9. $\sim(E \supset F)$ Add. *Reductio* Premise
    10. $\sim(\sim E \vee F)$ 9 MI
    11. $\sim D$ 4, 10 DA
    12. $\sim C$ 2, 11 MT
    ⌊13. $C \cdot \sim C$ 8, 12 Conj.
    14. $E \supset F$ 9-13 *Reductio* Premise Absurd

9.   1. $\sim S \vee R$
     2. $R \supset C$
     3. $\sim(C \cdot \sim P)$
     4. $P \supset I$
       $\therefore S \supset I$
     ⌈5. S Add. Cond. Premise
     6. R 1, 5 DA
     7. C 2, 6 MP
     8. P 3, 7 DCA
     ⌊9. I 4, 8 MP
    10. $S \supset I$ 5-9 Cond. Proof

14.8

6.   1. $E \supset [F \vee (G \cdot H)]$
     2. $I \supset (E \vee \sim G)$
     3. $I \cdot \sim(\sim G \vee F)$
       $\therefore H$
     4. I 3 Simp
     5. $\sim(\sim G \vee F) \cdot I$
               3 $p \cdot q / \therefore p$ 3 Comm.

6. $\sim(\sim G \vee F)$ 3 $(p \cdot q) \equiv (q \cdot p)$ 5 Simp.
7. $G \cdot \sim F$ 5 $p \cdot q, / \therefore p$ 6 DeM
8. G 6 $(p \vee q) \equiv \sim(\sim p \cdot \sim q)$ 7 Simp.
9. $\sim F \cdot G$ 7 $p \cdot q / \therefore p$ 7 Comm.
10. $\sim F$ 7 $(p \cdot q) \equiv (q \cdot p)$ 9 Simp.
11. $E \vee \sim G$ 9 $p \cdot q, / \therefore p$ 2, 4 MP
12. $\sim G \vee E$ 2, 4 $p \supset q, p, / \therefore q$ 11 Comm.
13. E 11 $(p \vee q) \equiv (q \vee p)$ 12, 8 DA
14. $F \vee$ 12, 8 $p \vee q, \sim p, / \therefore q$
     $(G \cdot H)$ 1, 13 $p \supset q, p, / \therefore q$ 1, 13 MP
15. $G \cdot H$ 14, 10 $p \vee q, \sim p, / \therefore q$ 14, 10 DA
16. $H \cdot G$ 15 $(p \cdot q) \equiv (q \cdot p)$ 16 Comm.
17. H 16 $p \cdot q, / \therefore p$ 16 Simp.

13.   1. $E \supset P$
     2. $\sim P \vee G$
     3. $E \cdot \sim G$
     $\overline{\qquad \therefore D}$
     4. E 3 $p \cdot q, / \therefore p$ 3 Simp.
     5. P 1, 4 $p \supset q, p, / \therefore q$ 1, 4 MP
     6. G 2, 5 $p \vee q, \sim p, / \therefore q$ 2, 5 DA
     7. $\sim G \cdot E$ 3 $(p \cdot q) \equiv (q \cdot p)$ 3 Comm.
     8. $\sim G$ 7 $p \cdot q, / \therefore p$ 7 Simp.
     9. $G \vee D$ 6 $p, / \therefore p \vee q$ 6 Add.
     10. D 9, 8 $p \vee q, \sim p, / \therefore q$ 9, 8 DA

17.   1. $\sim F \supset (L \vee I)$
     2. $(E \vee C) \supset \sim F$
     3. E
     $\overline{\qquad \therefore \sim(\sim L \cdot \sim I)}$
     4. $E \vee C$ 3 $p, / \therefore p \vee q$ 3 Add.
     5. $\sim F$ 2, 4 $p \supset q, p, / \therefore q$ 2, 4 MP
     6. $L \vee I$ 1, 5 $p \supset q, p, / \therefore q$ 1, 5 MP
     7. $\sim(\sim L \cdot \sim I)$ 6 $p \vee q \equiv \sim(\sim p \cdot \sim q)$ 6 DeM

14.10   2.

A	B	C	D	E	$B \cdot C$	$B \supset C$	$D \vee E$	$A \vee (B \cdot C)$	$(B \supset C) \supset (D \vee E)$	$\sim A$	$/ \therefore D$
F	T	T	F	T	T	T	T	T	T	T	F

14.12   (21)   1. $(W \cdot A) \supset S$
         2. $(\sim D \cdot C) \supset I$
         3. $\sim(\sim A \vee \sim C)$
         4. $\sim(S \vee I)$
         $\overline{\qquad \therefore \sim W \cdot D}$
         5. $A \cdot C$ 3 DeM
         6. $\sim S \cdot \sim I$ 4 DeM
         7. $\sim S$ 6 Simp.
         8. $\sim I \cdot \sim S$ 6 Comm.
         9. $\sim I$ 8 Simp.
         10. $\sim(W \cdot A)$ 1, 7 MT
         11. $\sim(\sim D \cdot C)$ 2, 9 MT

12. A 5 Simp.
13. $C \cdot A$ 5 Comm.
14. C 13 Simp.
15. D 11, 14 DCA
16. $\sim W$ 10, 12 DCA
17. $\sim W \cdot D$ 15, 16 Conj.

15.2   5. $(\exists x)$ (x is despised by everyone)
          $(\exists x)(y)$ (x is despised by y)
          $(\exists x)(y)(Dxy)$

     13. (x) (x is a good fisherman $\supset$ x always catches fish)
        (x) [x is a good fisherman $\supset$ $(\exists y)$ (x always catches y)]
        (x) [$Fx \supset (\exists y)$ (x always catches y)]
        (x) [$Fx \supset (\exists y) Cxy$]

     17. $Ij \supset Tjs$

15.5   1.   (d)   4. $Ra \cdot \sim Ta$ 3 EI
                5. $Ra \supset (Ta \lor Sa)$ 1 UI
                6. $Sa \supset (Ua \supset Wa)$ 2 UI
                7. Ra 4 Simp.
                8. $Ta \lor Sa$ 5, 7 MP
                9. $\sim Ta \cdot Ra$ 4 Comm.
                10. $\sim Ta$ 9 Simp.
                11. Sa 8, 10 DA
                12. $Ua \supset Wa$ 6, 11 MP
                13. $(\exists x)(Ux \supset Wx)$ 12 EG

      2.   (e)   1. $(x)(Mx \supset Ax)$
                2. $(\exists x)(Mx \cdot Cx)$
                3. $(x)(Ax \supset Ex)$
                  $\therefore (\exists x)(Cx \cdot Ex)$
                4. $Ma \cdot Ca$ 2 EI
                5. $Ma \supset Aa$ 1 UI
                6. $Aa \supset Ea$ 3 UI
                7. Ma 4 Simp.
                8. Aa 5, 7 MP
                9. Ea 6, 8 MP
                10. $Ca \cdot Ma$ 4 Comm.
                11. Ca 10 Simp.
                12. $Ca \cdot Ea$ 11, 9 Conj.
                13. $(\exists x)(Cx \cdot Ex)$ 12 EG

15.7   1.   (f)   1. $(x)(Gx \supset Hx)$
                2. $(\exists x)(Gx \cdot Ix)$
                3. $(x)[(Ix \cdot Hx) \supset (Kx \cdot Lx)]$
                  $\therefore (\exists x)(Kx \cdot Lx)$
                4. $Ga \cdot Ia$ 2 EI
                5. $Ga \supset Ha$ 1 UI
                6. $(Ia \cdot Ha) \supset (Ka \cdot La)$ 3 UI
                7. Ga 4 Simp.
                8. $Ia \cdot Ga$ 4 Comm.
                9. Ia 8 Simp.

10. Ha 5, 7 MP

11. $Ia \cdot Ha$ 9, 10 Conj.

12. $Ka \cdot La$ 6, 11 MP

13. $(\exists x)(Kx \cdot Lx)$ 12 EG

(j)

	$(x)(Ex \supset Ax)$	$(\exists x)(Mx \cdot Ex)$	$\therefore (x)(Mx \supset Ax)$
$Ea\,Eb\,Aa\,Ab\,Ma\,Mb$	$(Ea \supset Aa) \cdot (Eb \supset Ab)$	$Ma \cdot Ea \vee Mb \cdot Eb$	$(Ma \supset Aa) \cdot (Mb \supset Ab)$
T F T F T T	T	T	T T T F

TTF

F

15.9   1.   (e)   1. $(x)[Ox \supset (y)(Fxy \supset Sxy)]$

2. $(x)[Ox \cdot (y) Fxy]$

3. $(x)(y)[Sxy \supset (\exists z) Rxyz]$

$\therefore (x)(y)(\exists z) Rxyz$

4. $Oa \supset (y)(Fay \supset Say)$ 1 UI

5. $Oa \cdot (y) Fay$ 2 UI

6. $(y)[Say \supset (\exists z) Rayz$ 3 UI

7. Oa 5 Simp.

8. $(y)(Fay \supset Say)$ 4, 7 MP

9. $(y) Fay \cdot Oa$ 5 Comm.

10. $(y) Fay$ 9 Simp.

11. $Sab \supset (\exists z) Rabz$ 6 UI

12. $Fab \supset Sab$ 8 UI

13. Fab 10 UI

14. Sab 12,13 MP

15. $(\exists z) Rabz$ 11,14 MP

16. $(y)(\exists z) Rayz$ 15 UG

17. $(x)(y)(\exists z) Rxyz$ 16 UG

2.   (e)   Assumed premise: "Any chairs or tables in this room are furniture in this room."

1. $(x)(Fx \supset Cx)$

2. $(x)[(Hx \vee Tx) \supset Fx]$

$\therefore (x)[(Hx \vee Tx) \supset Cx]$

3. $Fa \supset Ca$ 1 UI

4. $(Ha \vee Ta) \supset Fa$ 2 UI

5. $(Ha \vee Ta) \supset Ca$ 4, 3 HS

6. $(x)[(Hx \vee Tx) \supset Cx]$ 5 UG

15.11   8. 1. $(\exists x)(Ox \cdot Rx) \vee (\exists y)(Py \cdot Ey)$

2. $(\exists y)(Py \cdot Ey) \supset (z)(Nz \supset Qz)$

$\therefore (x)(Ox \supset {\sim}Rx) \supset (z)(Nz \supset Qz)$

3. ${\sim}(\exists x)(Ox \cdot Rx) \supset (\exists y)(Py \cdot Ey)$ 1 MI

4. $(x){\sim}(Ox \cdot Rx) \supset (\exists y)(Py \cdot Ey)$ 3 QE

5. $(x)(Ox \supset {\sim}Rx) \supset (\exists y)(Py \cdot Ey)$ 4 DeM & MI

6. $(x)(Ox \supset {\sim}Rx) \supset (z)(Nz \supset Qz)$ 5, 2 HS

13. 1. $(x)(Px \supset Sx) \supset (y)(Cy \supset Jy)$

2. $(\exists y)(Cy \cdot Ly) \supset (\exists y)(Cy \cdot {\sim}Jy)$

$\therefore (\exists y)(Cy \cdot Ly) \supset (\exists x)(Px \cdot {\sim}Sx)$

3. ${\sim}(y)(Cy \supset Jy) \supset {\sim}(x)(Px \supset Sx)$ 1 Contrap.

4. $(\exists y){\sim}(Cy \supset Jy) \supset {\sim}(x)(Px \supset Sx)$ 3 QE

 5. $(\exists y)\,(Cy \cdot \sim Jy) \supset \sim(x)\,(Px \supset Sx)$ 4 DeM & MI
 6. $(\exists y)\,(Cy \cdot \sim Jy) \supset (\exists x) \sim(Px \supset Sx)$ 5 QE
 7. $(\exists y)\,(Cy \cdot \sim Jy) \supset (\exists x)\,(Px \cdot \sim Sx)$ 6 DeM & MI
 8. $(\exists y)\,(Cy \cdot Ly) \supset (\exists x)\,(Px \cdot \sim Sx)$ 2, 7 HS

21. 1. $(x)[Px \supset (y)\,Wyx] \cdot (z)[Cz \supset (y)\,\sim Dyz]$
     2. $(z)[Cz \supset (y)\,\sim Dyz] \supset (\exists w)\,(Sw \cdot Aw)$
     3. $(x)[Px \supset (y)Wyx] \supset (\exists u)\,(Ou \cdot Eu)$
     4. $[(\exists w)\,(Sw \cdot Aw) \cdot (\exists u)\,(Ou \cdot Eu)] \supset (\exists v)\,(Iv \cdot Rv)$
     $\therefore \sim(v)\,(Iv \supset \sim Rv)$
     5. $(x)\,[Px \supset (y)\,Wyx]$ 1 Simp.
     6. $(z)\,[Cz \supset (y)\,\sim Dyz] \cdot$
        $(x)\,[Px \supset (y)\,Wyx]$ 1 Comm.
     7. $(z)\,[Cz \supset (y)\,\sim Dyz]$ 6 Simp.
     8. $(\exists w)\,(Sw \cdot Aw)$ 2. 7 MP
     9. $(\exists u)\,(Ou \cdot Eu)$ 3, 5 MP
    10. $(\exists w)\,(Sw \cdot Aw) \cdot (\exists u)\,(Ou \cdot Eu)$ 8, 9 Conj.
    11. $(\exists v)\,(Iv \cdot Rv)$ 4, 10 MP
    12. $\sim(v) \sim(Iv \cdot Rv)$ 11 QM
    13. $\sim(v)\,(Iv \supset \sim Rv)$ 12 DeM & MI

Bibliography

1. Elementary works in paperbacks

Hubert G. Alexander, *Language and Thinking*, D. Van Nostrand, Princeton N.J., 1967.

David Hugh Freeman, *Logic: The Art of Reasoning*, David McKay Co. Inc., New York, 1967.

Ronald Jager, *Essays in Logic from Aristotle to Russell*, Prentice-Hall, Englewood Cliffs, N.J., 1963.

Arnold B. Levison, *Study Guide for Barker's Elements of Logic*, Mc-Graw-Hill Book Co., New York, 1965.

L. Susan Stebbing, *Thinking to Some Purpose*, Penguin Books, London, 1959.

D. B. Terrell and Robert Baker, *Exercises in Logic*, Holt, Rinehart and Winston, Inc., New York, 1967.

James D. Weinland, *How to Think Straight*, Littlefield, Adams and Co., Paterson, N.Y. 1963.

2. Introductory texts

Stephen F. Barker, *The Elements of Logic*, McGraw-Hill Book Company, New York, 1965.

James D. Carney and Richard K. Scheer, *Fundamentals of Logic*, The Macmillan Co., New York, 1964.

Morris R. Cohen and Ernest Nagel, *An Introduction to Logic and Scientific Method*, Harcourt Brace and Co., New York, 1934.

Irving M. Copi, *Introduction to Logic*, 3rd Edition, Macmillan Co. New York, 1968.

Herbert L. Searles, *Logic and Scientific Methods*, 2nd Edition, The Ronald Press, New York, 1956.

D. B. Terrell, *Logic: A Modern Introduction to Deductive Reasoning*, Holt, Rinehart and Winston, Inc., New York, 1967.

3. Standard works in symbolic logic

Alonzo Church, *Introduction to Mathematical Logic, I*, Princeton University Press, Princeton, N.J., 1956.
Irving Copi, *Symbolic Logic*, The Macmillan Co., 3rd Edition, New York, 1967.
Robert Niedorf, *Deductive Forms*, Harper and Row, New York, 1967.
Willard Van O. Quine, *Mathematical Logic*, 2nd Edition, Rev., Harvard University Press, 1961. (Paperback, Harper and Row, New York, 1962.)

4. Logic and scientific inquiry

W. I. B. Beveridge, *The Art of Scientific Investigation*, 3rd Edition, Random House, New York, 1957 (paperback).
R. B. Braithwaite, *Scientific Explanation*, Harper Torchbooks, New York, 1960 (paperback).
Carl G. Hempel, *Aspects of Scientific Explanation*, The Free Press, New York, 1965.
Ernest Nagel, *The Structure of Science*, Harcourt, Brace and World, Inc., New York, 1961.
Arthur Pap, *An Introduction to the Philosophy of Science*, The Free Press, New York, 1962.
Karl R. Popper, *The Logic of Scientific Discovery*, Harper and Row, New York, 1965 (paperback).
Dudley Shapere, *Philosophical Problems of Natural Science*, The Macmillan Co., New York, 1965 (paperback).

Index